Uncle John's Bathroom Reader®

Wonderful World of Odd

Expanded Edition

By the
Bathroom Readers'
Institute

Bathroom Readers' Press
Ashland, Oregon

UNCLE JOHN'S BATHROOM READER
WONDERFUL WORLD OF ODD EXPANDED EDITION®

For information, write:
The Bathroom Readers' Institute, P.O. Box 1117, Ashland, OR 97520
www.bathroomreader.com • 888-488-4642

Cover design by Michael Brunsfeld, San Rafael, CA (*Brunsfeldo@comcast.net*)

Uncle John's Bathroom Reader Wonderful World of Odd Expanded Edition®
by the Bathroom Readers' Institute

ISBN-13: 978-1-59223-896-5
ISBN-10: 1-59223-896-3

Library of Congress Catalog Card Number: 2007937173

Printed in the United States of America

First Printing

1 2 3 4 5 6 7 8 9 11 10 09 08 07

THANK YOU!

The Bathroom Readers' Institute sincerely thanks the people whose advice and assistance made this book possible.

Gordon Javna
John Dollison
Amy Miller
Brian Boone
Thom Little
Jay Newman
Julia Papps
Angela Kern
Michael Brunsfeld
Carole Quandt
Claudia Bauer
Maggie McLaughlin
Sydney Stanley
JoAnn Padgett
Scarab Media
Monica Maestas
Lisa Meyers
Karen Malchow
Lynn Christel
David Calder
Laurel Graziano
Publishers Group West
(Mr.) Mustard Press
Maggie Javna
Jeff Cheek
Bruce Carlson
Ed Polish
Eddie Deezen
Malcolm Hillgartner
Jahnna Beecham
Janet Spencer
Joyce Slayton
Taylor Clark
Stephanie Spadaccini
Joan Brandwein
Amy Briggs
Terri Schlichenmeyer
William Dylan Powell
Lea Markson
John Scalzi
Sue Steiner
Melinda Allman
Steven Style Group
Shobha Grace
Michelle Sedgwick
Joel & Ann Horowitz
Ricky Meatball
RR Donnelley
Raincoast Books
Chris Olsen
Porter the Wonder Dog
Thomas Crapper

CONTENTS

THAT'S DEATH

LIFE IS STRANGE

ODD OFF THE PRESSES

ODD OF THE PAST

CRAZY LOVE

YOU GONNA EAT THAT?

PR-ODD-UCTS

***REALLY* OUT THERE**

IT'S A WEIRD, WEIRD WORLD

PEOPLE ARE STRANGE

WEIRD SPORTS & GAMES

ODD BODIES

ODD ART, ODD MUSIC

INTRODUCTION

HURRY, HURRY, STEP RIGHT UP!

We at the Bathroom Readers' Institute have always had a hungry appetite for collecting and reporting tales of the odd: odd music, odd science, odd art, odd sports, odd history. And happily, we've found over the years that our readers love these odd stories as much as we enjoy sharing them. So, at the urging of our loyal fans—and not without a bit of devilish glee—we present for your enjoyment *Uncle John's Wonderful World of Odd*, a collection of the strangest people, the most unusual animals, and the weirdest events you'll ever witness. Stare with amazement at:

- The mysterious lake that "erupted"—and killed every living thing for miles around
- The weirdest—and worst—movies ever made
- The chess championship that was almost lost—over a bathroom break
- Mannequins and the people who love them
- The wildest and weirdest insects: bizarre mouthparts, strange behavior, and real "bug juice" (not for the squeamish!)

You'll see thrills and chills, tall tales, impossible aliens, royal weirdoes, bizarre conspiracy theories, and foods you'd probably rather read about than eat.

Many thanks to the menagerie of contributors to this odd endeavor, including the death-defying acts in the center ring: Amy "Monstrous" Miller, Barfin' Brian Boone, John "The Juggler" Dollison, Too-Tall Thom Little, Julia Papps and Her Invisible Friends, and "Gentleman" Jay Newman.

Keep on reading. And as always,

Go with the Flow!

—Uncle John, Porter the Wonder Dog, and the BRI Staff

The Internet is so odd that it has a site called *www.bathroomreader.com*.

YOU'RE MY ODD-SPIRATION

Proof that inspiration can come from anywhere.

METHOD ACTING

Australian actress Peta Wilson played a vampire in the 2003 film *The League of Extraordinary Gentlemen.* Where'd she get her inspiration for the part? From her infant son. "My three-month-old, Marlowe, was breastfeeding, and I couldn't get that corset off quick enough," she says. "He would scream and be ferocious until he got his milk, and afterwards he had this bliss come over him. I thought, 'Yeah, I could play a vampire.'"

YABBA-DABBA-JUDO

Judo star Christina Pro, one of the world's best, is an Olympic hopeful for 2008. And she owes it all to *The Flintstones*. "I was about five years old," she said. "Betty and Wilma took a self-defense class. I thought it was neat and wanted to do it too."

BANG! INTERNAL COMBUSTION!

Henry Ford completed his first self-propelled vehicle, the gas-engine powered *Quadricycle*, in 1896. That same year he met his boyhood hero, Thomas Edison, and told him about the *Quad*. Edison, who was working on an electric vehicle, banged his fist on the table and said, "Young man, you have it! Your car is self contained and carries its own power plant." Years later Ford said, "That bang on the table was worth worlds to me."

FROSTY THE TOE-MAN

American Rulon Gardner became a star when he won the gold medal in Greco-Roman wrestling in the Sydney Olympics in 2000. In 2002 he was severely frostbitten after a snowmobile accident, and one of his toes had to be amputated. Gardner, who now travels the country as a motivational speaker, still has the toe. "I keep it in my refrigerator," he says. "It reminds me of how lucky I am. It reminds me of how life is there to be lived to the fullest."

The world's most expensive spice: saffron. Pound for pound, it's more expensive than gold.

STRANGE BANDS

There are thousands of musicians out there vying for radio airplay and your CD-buying dollar, so every band has to make itself stand out somehow. Here are some that rely on elaborate gimmicks.

THE FIRST VIENNESE VEGETABLE ORCHESTRA

This nine-member Austrian group plays instruments made completely out of fresh vegetables, including carrot flutes, eggplant drums, and a "gurkaphone" (a hollow cucumber with a carrot mouthpiece and green-pepper bell). At the conclusion of live performances, the Orchestra chops up its instruments and makes a soup, which is shared with the audience.

MAX Q

It's the world's only soft-rock band made up entirely of former astronauts. All six members flew on the NASA Space Shuttle in the 1980s and 1990s. They play mostly love songs about space and alienation. "Max Q" refers to the maximum air pressure experienced in the Shuttle moments after blastoff.

HORSE THE BAND

This American group plays super-fast, super-heavy versions of the instrumental music from 1980s-era Nintendo video games, such as Super Mario Brothers and The Legend of Zelda.

GWAR

The band dresses in elaborate rubber ogre and monster costumes and takes stage names like "Oderus Urungus," "Flattus Maximus," and "Beefcake the Mighty." GWAR plays hard-driving heavy metal songs (such as "Maggots" and "Death Pod"). Their stage show includes staged deaths and buckets of fake vomit and blood that they throw at the audience.

MUSCLE FACTORY

First, the tank-top-and-spandex-shorts-clad sextet performs songs about weightlifting, such as "Pump to Failure" and "The Spotter." Then they lift weights—on stage.

In the Ukraine, it's considered good luck if you find a spider web on Christmas morning.

QNTAL

Qntal is a German trio that sings haunting, medieval-style ballads about all sorts of historical events in Latin and ancient German dialects. They're backed with a thumping drum machine. The name Qntal came to a group member in a dream.

TRACHTENBERG FAMILY SLIDESHOW PLAYERS

It's an old-fashioned family band! Dad Jason plays guitar and sings lead, teenage daughter Rachel plays drums and sings backing vocals, and mom Tina operates the slide projector. Why slides? Their songs are based on picture slides, bought at garage sales and thrift stores, which are projected along with the songs.

THE CANDY BAND

Four former Detroit rock musicians who became stay-at-home moms started this band to entertain their restless children. Their songs are punk-rock covers of nursery rhymes, classic children's songs, and kiddie TV show theme songs. (The Candy Band has actually performed on the *Today* show.)

SUPER FURRY ANIMALS

Playing psychedelic/electronic pop, with many songs sung in Welsh, SFA is a chart-topping band in England. What makes them so weird? During live shows, the band members—using secret special-effects technology—slowly morph into furry, hulking Sasquatches.

ARNOCORPS

Heavily inspired by Arnold Schwarzenegger, the "pioneers of action-adventure hardcore rock and roll" pretend to be action-adventure movie heroes from the mountains of Austria. They sing fake autobiographical songs about what it's like to be an Austrian he-man.

* * *

"Nuclear-powered vacuum cleaners will probably be a reality within ten years."

—Alex Lewyt, vacuum cleaner company executive, 1955

The largest known bacterium can grow to the size of the period at the end of this sentence.

BIN LADEN IS A WOMAN!

...and other great (and real) tabloid newspaper headlines.

MAN REINCARNATED AS HIMSELF

Cubs Boost World Series Hopes With Holy Water

Man Takes Out Restraining Order Against Imaginary Friend

Gnomes of Death Lure Divers to Drowning Horror

Prune Juice Makes You Stupid

God's Autograph Sells for $500 Million

NEBRASKA DOESN'T EXIST, SAYS AUTHOR

Blood-Sucking Dracula Squirrels Invade U.S.

New Study Says "Stitch in Time" Saves Only 8

GRIM REAPER TO RETIRE—PEOPLE WILL LIVE FOREVER!

World's Oldest Woman Thrives on Lard and Booze

Jungle Tribe Worships Jay Leno's Chin

Massive Loch Ness Monster Fart Swamps Tourist Boat

Earwax DNA Doesn't Lie—Osama Bin Laden Is a Woman!

Mr. Rogers' Ghost Terrorizing Children!

Beer Cans & Old Mattress Found on Mars

ALIENS TRAVEL TO EARTH FOR CHINESE TAKEOUT

VIKINGS WERE WIMPS!

Hair Space Alien Lives on Donald Trump's Head!

Art Collector Buys Forged Art With Counterfeit Money

Scientists Clone Jerry Springer

Pope Has Super Powers!

CREDIT CARD EXPLODES WHEN GAL GOES OVER LIMIT

A *lynchobite* is someone who works at night and sleeps during the day.

ODD, ODD WORLD OF BASEBALL INJURIES

Major-league ballplayers are big, tough manly-men who cannot be felled by any mere mortal destructive force...except for ice packs, donuts, sunflower seeds, and handshakes.

• Catcher Mickey Tettleton of the Detroit Tigers went on the disabled list for athlete's foot, which he got from habitually tying his shoes too tight.

• Wade Boggs once threw out his back while putting on a pair of cowboy boots.

• In 1993 Rickey Henderson missed several games because of frostbite—in August. He had fallen asleep on an ice pack.

• Ken Griffey Jr. missed one game in 1994 due to a groin injury. (His protective cup had pinched one of his testicles.)

• Atlanta pitcher John Smoltz once burned his chest. He'd ironed a shirt...while still wearing it.

• Sammy Sosa missed a game because he threw out his back while sneezing.

• While playing for Houston, Nolan Ryan couldn't pitch after being bitten by a coyote.

• Marty Cordova of the Baltimore Orioles went on the injured list after burning his face in a tanning bed.

• Atlanta outfielder Terry Harper once waved a teammate home, then high-fived him. The act separated Harper's shoulder.

• Pitcher Phil Niekro hurt his hand...while shaking hands.

• Milwaukee's Steve Sparks once dislocated his shoulder attempting to tear a phone book in half.

• San Francisco Giants manager Roger Craig cut his hand "undoing a bra strap."

• To look more menacing, Boston pitcher Clarence Blethen took out his false teeth during a game and put them in his back pocket. Later, while he was sliding into second base, the teeth clamped down and bit him on the butt.

In Liechtenstein, dairy farmers publish obituaries for their deceased cows.

• When the San Diego Padres won the National League West in 2005, pitcher Jake Peavy jumped on top of the celebration pileup. He fractured a rib and had to sit out the entire playoff series.

• Jose Cardenal missed a game for the Chicago Cubs because he had been kept awake all night by crickets chirping outside his hotel room.

• Kevin Mitchell of the New York Mets hurt a tooth on a donut that had gotten too hot in a microwave. On another occasion, Mitchell pulled a muscle while vomiting.

• Carlos Zambrano of the Chicago Cubs was on the disabled list after being diagnosed with carpal tunnel syndrome. Cause of condition: too many hours spent surfing the Internet.

• Minnesota's Terry Mulholland had to sit out a few games after he scratched his eye on a feather sticking out of a pillow.

• Pitcher Greg Harris was flipping sunflower seeds into his mouth in the Texas Rangers bullpen. It strained his elbow.

• San Diego pitcher Adam Eaton stabbed himself in the stomach with a knife while trying to open a DVD case.

• Florida pitcher Ricky Bones pulled his lower back getting out of a chair while watching TV in the team clubhouse.

• Outfielder Glenallen Hill has an intense fear of spiders. He went on the injured list after suffering multiple cuts all over his body. Hill had fallen out of bed onto a glass table while having a nightmare in which he was covered with spiders.

• Before the first game of the 1985 World Series, St. Louis outfielder Vince Coleman was fooling around on the field and managed to get rolled up inside the Busch Stadium automatic tarp-rolling machine. Coleman's injuries caused him to miss the entire Series.

* * *

"I'm a psychic amnesiac. I know in advance what I'm going to forget."

—Mike McShane

February 29, or leap day, is officially called Bissextile Day.

YOU STOLE WHAT, NOW?

Thieves...you just never know what they're gonna steal next.

STICKY FINGERS

Someone stole the head off a life-size wax statue of Wolfgang Amadeus Mozart from a museum in Salzburg, Austria, in 2005. "It must have happened between 8 p.m. Friday, when we closed, and today before 9 a.m.," employee Elisabeth Stoeckl told reporters. "When we opened up again, Mozart's head was gone," she said, adding that the stolen head was worth about $18,000.

HE'S A LITTLE SLOW

In 1999 a man in Los Angeles was arrested after leading police on a slow-speed chase...on a stolen steamroller. An officer stopped the runaway steamroller by climbing aboard and shutting it off. The man explained the theft by saying he was "tired of walking."

TIKI TACKY

Security cameras in a Wellington, New Zealand, library captured shots of three masked vandals as they walked up to a tiki—a wooden figurine made by the country's indigenous people, the Maori—chopped off its wooden penis with chisels, and then ran away. The artist who had carved the tiki, Kerry Strongman, called the theft an insult to the mana, or "pride," of the city, and immediately began work on a replacement penis for the statue.

IS THIS HOT?

In September 2006, *USA Today* reported that at least seven men had been electrocuted and killed since July trying to steal wire from live power lines. Three of the deaths were in Detroit, the latest being when the body of a 24-year-old man was found near a utility box. A pair of wire cutters was found next to his body. Authorities said the would-be thieves were motivated by record-high copper prices—the price of scrap copper has doubled in the last year, according to the report, to about $3 per pound.

Cost to U.S. economy when superstitious people stay home on Friday the 13th: $800 million.

IN THE NAME OF ART

The world would be a much less interesting place if it weren't for artists. Especially these ones.

ARTIST: Federico D'Orazio
TITLE: "Full Love Inn"
STORY: In September 2006, D'Orazio removed the seats from an Opel Kadett, replaced them with a double-bed mattress, and had the car hoisted up onto 13-foot-tall poles in downtown Amsterdam. He then invited people to write to him to request an overnight stay in the airborne car. "I tried to make a space for real love in a city where sex is dominant," he said. "You can have sex because it is a safe structure. It is shaking up very safely." He received enough requests to keep the car booked for six months, but the love-mobile art-piece only stayed up until mid-October.

ARTIST: Zhang Huan
TITLE: "Seeds of Hamburg"
STORY: In 2002 Chinese-born performance artist Zhang Huan constructed a wood-and-chicken-wire cage at a gallery in Hamburg, Germany. In the cage were some leafless tree branches and 28 live doves. Huan then entered the cage...naked...covered head to toe in honey and birdseed. The birds ate the seeds off of Huan's body while he posed in various positions. The performance ended with Huan cradling one of the birds, which had just pulled a red ribbon from his mouth. The doves, the ribbon, and the birdseed, Huan said, symbolized "hope, freedom, and rebirth."

ARTIST: Kittiwat Unarom, Thailand
TITLE: "Human Being Parts"
STORY: Unarom, 28, has an unusual art studio near his home south of Bangkok. It's an everyday working bakery, except that it sells bread products that look like human body parts—feet, hands, torsos, and heads. Unarom studied real corpses to get the look down perfectly. He told reporters that he hopes the human-bread-food, which he said was selling well, will leave people wondering whether they consume food—or food consumes them.

Looney law: It's illegal to tickle a girl in Norton, Virginia.

ARTIST: Lisa Newman
TITLE: "Kobe"
STORY: In July 2006, Newman took off her clothes and got down on all fours inside a small plastic bin. She was then fed beer through a tube from a container held by one of her "handlers," doused with the Japanese rice wine *sake*, and thoroughly massaged. Sounds like fun, but Newman and her collaborator, Llewyn Maire, part of the art duo *Gyrl Grip*, were hard at work on a performance art piece. Performed at a gallery in Toronto (and videotaped), the show mimicked the preparation of prized Kobe beef cattle, who are, just as in the performance, fed beer, coated with sake, and massaged daily to produce their prize-winning taste and texture. The show, they said, "deals with the fetishization of food and Japanese culture."

ARTIST: James Robert Ford
TITLE: "Bogey-ball"
STORY: Ford is a respected British installation artist, and he's got a giant ball of his own snot to prove it. He collected the mucus from his nose from 2004 to 2006 until his "Bogey-ball" was nearly the size of a golf ball. He showed it at four exhibitions and then announced he would be putting it up for sale. Price: $20,000. "It's a physical record of all the different places I've been and people I've met," he said. As for selling it, "It will be hard to let go," he said, "but at the same time, it's hard not to have any money."

* * *

ODD CELEBRITY BABY NAMES

- Actor Lance Henriksen (*Millennium*, *Aliens*) has a daughter named Alchamy.
- Rachel Griffiths (*Six Feet Under*) named her son Banjo.
- Jason Lee (*My Name is Earl*) named his son Pilot Inspektor.
- Actress Shannyn Sossaman, who used to be a deejay, named her son Audio Science.
- Ving Rhames (*Pulp Fiction*) named his daughter Reignbeau.

The skin under your fingernails is called the *whickflaw*.

WEIRD BRITAIN

Ah, merry old England. Tea time, Big Ben, and...protesting clowns?

THE CHECK'S IN THE MAIL

A £117,000 check intended for a 70-year-old Wimbledon woman was accidentally delivered to her neighbor, 19-year-old Andrew Curzon. But rather than hand the check over, Curzon wrote his own name on top of his neighbor's and then tried to deposit it in his bank account. His excuse: Curzon, a law student, said he couldn't help himself—he claimed he suffers from *dyspraxia*, a condition that, among other symptoms, doesn't allow the brain to "engage in logical thinking."

SO SLEEEEEEPY

In 2006 police in Hastings discovered 638 marijuana plants growing in a warehouse rented by David Churchward. But Churchward had an excuse: He wasn't growing them for himself...they were for his wife. He said marijuana—of which he had enough to make 280,000 cigarettes—was the only thing that could cure his wife's insomnia. (Churchward was attending the plants—naked—when arrested.)

GET A LEG UP

Adhering to strict aviation guidelines prohibiting passengers from bringing on board anything resembling a weapon, British Airways refused to allow runner Kate Horan to carry her prosthetic leg on board a flight to a world-championship track meet in Amsterdam. The $10,000 leg (in a duffel bag) was confiscated, then lost at London's Heathrow airport. The leg's manufacturer scrambled to make a new one in time for Horan's event. They did...and Horan won a bronze medal. (The leg was found a week later.)

EVER HEAR OF A MEMO PAD?

Vanda Jones, 49, of Wales has five kids. She kept forgetting their birthdays, so she had the dates tattooed on her arm. "Whenever I took my kids to the health clinic, I could never remember their birthdays off the top of my head," she said. "It's much easier now because I just have to look at my arm and I don't forget."

NEW LIFE FOR AN AGING ROCK STAR

In the United States, singer Chris de Burgh is best known for his 1986 hit song "Lady in Red." When his singing career ended, DeBurgh took up a new one: faith healing. In 2006 a woman named Marisa Mackle told reporters that her arm, paralyzed for a decade, was made completely normal again after DeBurgh laid his palms on it. DeBurgh also claims to have a helped a 57-year-old man lose his slight limp. DeBurgh touched the bum leg and said the man was walking better "within 20 minutes."

THE WAY TO A MANN'S HEART

While driving in Hampshire in 2006, 77-year-old medical researcher Ronald Mann had a heart attack. As his heart stopped beating, he slipped into unconsciousness and slumped over the steering wheel, causing his Honda Civic to careen out of control and crash into a tree. During the impact, Mann's chest hit the steering wheel so hard that it restarted his heart. "Perversely," Mann later said, "the crash saved my life."

INSULTING...WE THINK

Officials at England's Norwich Prison were fed up with prisoners' profane language, so they hired college Shakespeare professor Jane Wirgman to teach them better English. Thanks to Wirgman, prisoners at Norwich now insult each other with lines from Shakespeare plays, calling each things like "thou odiferous stench" and "thou crusty botch of nature."

CLOWNING AROUND

In 1992 a London circus hired American clown Denise "Baby D" Payne to headline its Christmas show. Homegrown clowns were outraged. "We are funny," said British clown "Mr. Jam." "American clowns are all shout and glitter." Mr. Jam and dozens of other clowns protested at Heathrow Airport upon Baby D's arrival. How do clowns protest? They threw pies and tickled police officers.

The original birth control pill contained five times as much estrogen as today's pills.

CHINDOGU

Chindogu \chin-doh-goo\ *n 1) an almost useless object; 2) an invention that actually exists, but that consumers would be too embarrassed to use; 3) an object that is not for sale, and that nobody would buy anyway.*

BACKGROUND

Since the 1990s, writer Kenji Kawakami has been collecting unusual inventions that he calls *chindogu* (Japanese for "weird tool"). These objects offer clever (and strange) solutions to everyday problems. But what makes them unusual isn't their brilliance or simplicity. In fact, chindogu inventions are complicated, inconvenient, wildly impractical, embarrassing when used in public and, ultimately, completely useless.

Through Kawakami's four books, chindogu has developed into a humorous art form, with more and more fans worldwide inventing odd contraptions. There's even an International Chindogu Society. The "rules of chindogu": The invention cannot be patented ("If the idea's worth stealing, it's not chindogu"), it cannot be for sale, it must actually exist, and it must "challenge the suffocating dominance of utility." To join the Society, a prospective member has to invent a new chindogu. But watch out—many truly useless ones have already been invented. Here are some classics:

COMMUTER'S HELMET. This red hard hat straps to the user's head, then sticks to the wall of the train with a small toilet plunger, preventing the user from toppling over if he falls asleep. A handy card attached to the forehead lists the commuter's destination, so fellow travelers can wake him when it's time to disembark.

PORTABLE CROSSWALK. Finding a safe place to cross the street can be a challenge. But now there's the Portable Crosswalk, a roll-up mat that's printed with white stripes. Simply choose a spot, unroll the crosswalk into the street, and walk out into traffic.

HAY FEVER HAT. Perfect for allergy sufferers, this headgear consists of a roll of toilet paper that sits on top of your head, secured by a halo-shaped frame and chinstrap. At the first sign of a sneeze, just reach up and pull.

SWEETHEART'S TRAINING ARM. Teach your loved one to hold hands properly with this artificial limb. Designed to dangle by your side as you walk down the street, the Training Arm lets your boyfriend or girlfriend perfect their hand-holding techniques —pressure, duration, finger position, etc.—without subjecting you to embarrassing sweaty palms.

AUTOMATED NOODLE COOLER. Who hasn't put a forkful of noodles in their mouth, only to find out that they're scalding hot? The Noodle Cooler solves all that. A small battery-operated fan attaches to your fork, spoon, or chopsticks, blowing a cooling breeze across the noodles as you bring them to your mouth. (Also works for soups or stews.)

CAT TONGUE SOOTHER. Designed for anyone who feeds their cat hot "people food," this invention does for cats what the Noodle Cooler does for humans. This little fan attaches to the rim of the cat's food bowl, cooling the meal to a safe temperature.

AUTOMATIC CHEW COUNTER. Experts agree: Most people don't chew their food enough. For a strong jaw and good digestion, adults should chew at least 2,000 times per average meal. But who keeps count? Enter the Chew Counter, a strap that runs under the jaw and records each chew on a digital readout. Also recommended for dieters, who can practice "vigorous air-chewing."

PERSONAL RAIN SAVER. With fresh water becoming such a valuable resource, it's a shame that so much of it is washed into gutters on rainy days. Now you can capture your own rainwater with this device, an inside-out umbrella that you hold over your head. A drain in the handle siphons rainwater into your own shoulder-harnessed reservoir tank. As the description says, "Every drop that falls is yours to keep."

WIDE-AWAKE OPENER

Students, workaholics, and narcoleptics can finally keep their eyes open with this simple device. Attach the gentle alligator clips to

Q: What are *jinglebobs, heel chains,* and *rowels*? A: Parts of a cowboy's spurs.

your eyelids, then set the padded ring—attached to the clips with short tethers—on top of your head. Keeps your eyes open no matter how late it is or how boring the lecture.

DADDY NURSER

For millions of years, mothers have enjoyed bonding with their babies through the experience of nursing. Now Dad can finally feel the joy of breast-feeding, too. Twin breast-shaped bottles attach to a harness that the father wears like a brassiere. Fill them with formula or breast milk, and let the bonding begin.

EARRING SAFETY NETS

These are just what they sound like: little nets, similar to the kind you catch goldfish with, attached to clamps that sit on the shoulders of your jacket or blouse. Large enough to catch any falling or flying earring, these ensure you never lose another one.

*   *   *

RANDOM (ODD) FACTS

- One of the most popular toys of the 2006 holiday season, FurReal Friends Butterscotch Pony, had this disclaimer on the package: "Pony comes unassembled in box with head detached. You may wish to not open the box around your children if they may be frightened by a box with a decapitated horse inside."
- A street musician from the Dutch town of Leiden was so inept at playing his saxophone that local shop owners called the police. After hearing the man play, the cops confiscated his instrument.
- According to a study by researchers from the University of Tennessee College of Medicine and the B'nai Zion Medical Center in Israel, there is a cure for hiccups: "Rectal massage."
- Centerville, Ohio, is commonly referred to as "the geographic center of the United States." But it's not—the real geographic center is a hog farm near Lebanon, Kansas.
- A cornfield in Queen Creek, Arizona, was planted and plowed into the likeness of Arizona Diamondbacks slugger Luis Gonzalez, who observed, "It's amazing to see your face on ten acres of corn."

ODD BOOKS

If Uncle John's Wonderful World of Odd *isn't quite odd enough for you, here are some even weirder books to look for.*

The Toothbrush: Its Use and Abuse, Isador Hirschfield (1939)

The Romance of Leprosy, E. Mackerchar (1949)

Sex After Death, B. J. Ferrell and D.E. Frey (1983)

American Bottom Archaeology, Charles John Bareis and James Warren Porter (1983)

The Resistance of Piles to Penetration, Russell V. Allin (1935)

Flashes From the Welsh Pulpit, J. Gwnoro Davies (1889)

Constipation and Our Civilization, J. C. Thomson (1943)

Making It in Leather, M. Vincent Hayes (1972)

The Foul and the Fragrant: Odor and the French Social Imagination, Alain Corbin (1986)

Queer Doings in the Navy, Asa M. Mattice (1896)

Handbook for the Limbless, Geoffrey Howsen (1922)

Eternal Wind, Sergei Zhemaeitis (1975)

Why People Move, Jorge Balan (1981)

Practical Candle Burning, Raymond Buckland (1970)

The Romance of Rayon, Arnold Henry Hard (1933)

Careers in Dope, Dan Waldorf (1973)

What To Say When You Talk to Yourself, Shad Helmstetter (1982)

Historic Bubbles, Frederic Leake (1896)

How to Fill Mental Cavities, Bill Maltz (1978)

A Do-It-Yourself Submachine Gun, Gerard Metral (1995)

Nuclear War: What's In It For You? Ground Zero War Foundation (1982)

Ach, *du lieber!* Average number of days a German goes without washing his underwear: 7.

LET'S TALK TURKEY

If you think radio talk shows get a lot of strange calls, take a look at some of the questions that the folks at the Butterball Turkey Talk-Line have fielded over the years.

DIAL "T" FOR TURKEY

If you bought a Butterball Turkey in the 1970s, it would have included a sheet of cooking instructions, just like they still do today. But people still called the company to complain when their birds didn't come out right, which made Butterball wonder if people even bothered to read and follow the instructions. Disappointing dinners make for poor repeat business, so in 1981 Butterball started printing a toll-free number on the packaging and inviting customers to call in with any cooking questions they might have.

In those days 800 numbers were fairly rare, and the idea of calling one to get free cooking advice was a novelty. The company wasn't sure that callers would get the concept or even understand that the long-distance call was free. But they hired six home economists, set them up with phones in the company's test kitchen, and waited to see if the phone would ring. They were flabbergasted when more than 11,000 people jammed the line during the holiday season, especially on Thanksgiving, when the company figured hardly anyone would bother to call. An American institution was born.

CLUELESS ON LINE 4

Today Butterball has an automated phone system (and a Web site) to handle the most frequently asked questions. Still, more than 100,000 people call in each year to talk to the 50 turkey experts who now staff the phones from November 1 through December 25. The advent of cordless and cellular phones has put the Talk-Line in even greater demand: People now call right from the dinner table to have someone talk them through the carving of the bird.

What's your favorite way to cook a turkey? Over the years, Butterball has tried to come up with cooking tips for every weird turkey fad that has come down the pike. In the early 1980s, they perfected a technique for cooking a turkey in the *microwave*—which, believe it or not, was the third-most popular question in those days. (By 1987 it had dropped all the way to #20.) Do you cook your turkey in a big brown paper bag? In a deep fryer? In a pillowcase smeared with butter? On a countertop rotisserie? The Butterball people won't always approve, but they will try to help.

DO TURKEYS HAVE BELLY BUTTONS?

Butterball has fielded some pretty bizarre questions over the past 25 years. Here are some favorites, along with the answers:

• **Should I remove the plastic wrap before I cook my turkey?** Yes.

• **I don't want to touch the giblets. Can I fish them out with a coat hanger?** Yes.

• **Can I poke holes all over the turkey and pour a can of beer over it to keep it moist?** You'll do more harm than good—the skin keeps the moisture in. Poking holes in it will dry it out.

• **Can you thaw a frozen turkey using an electric hair dryer? Or by wrapping it in an electric blanket? In the aquarium with my tropical fish? In the tub while the kids are having their bath?** No, no, no, and no. If you're in a hurry, thaw the turkey in the kitchen sink by immersing it in cold water. Allow half an hour per pound, and change the water every half hour.

• **How can I thaw 12 turkeys all at once?** The caller was cooking for a firehouse, so Butterball advised them to put them all in a clean trash can and hose them down with a firehose.

• **The family dog bit off a big piece of the turkey. Can the rest of it be saved?** Maybe. If the damage is localized, cut away the dog-eaten part of the bird and serve the rest. Disguise the maimed bird with garnishes, or carve it up out of view of your guests and serve the slices. The less your guests know, the better.

• **The family dog is *inside* the turkey and can't get out.** A few years back, Butterball really did get a call from the owner of a Chihuahua that climbed inside the raw bird while the owner's back was turned. The opening was big enough for the dog to get in, but not big enough for it to get back out. The turkey expert instructed the owner on how to enlarge the opening without injuring the dog.

For the record, turkeys do *not* have belly buttons.

(No word on whether the bird was eaten.) Butterball has also fielded calls from owners of gerbils and housecats. "I was told not to talk about that," one Talk-Line staffer told a reporter in 1997.

• **I need to drive two hours with my frozen turkey before I cook it. Will it stay frozen if I tie it to the luggage rack on the roof of my car?** The caller was from Minnesota, so the answer was yes. If you live in Florida, Hawaii, or Arizona, the answer is no.

• **I'm a truck driver. Can I cook the turkey on the engine block of my semi while I'm driving? If I drive faster, will it cook faster?** There've been cases in wartime where soldiers cooked turkeys using the heat from Jeep engines, but Butterball gives no advice on the subject.

• **I scrubbed my raw turkey with a toothbrush dipped in bleach for three hours. Is that enough to kill all the harmful bacteria?** The *heat of the oven* is what kills the bacteria; scrubbing the turkey with bleach makes it inedible. (In extreme cases like these, or anytime the Talk-Line staffers fear the bird has become unsafe to eat, they advise the cook to discard the bird, eat out, and try again next year. If the caller can't imagine Thanksgiving without turkey, they can get some turkey hot dogs.)

• **I didn't want to cook the whole turkey, so I cut it in half with a chainsaw. How do I get the chainsaw oil out of the turkey?** Toss the turkey and go get some hot dogs.

• **The turkey in my freezer is 23 years old. Is it safe to eat?** Butterball advised this caller that the bird was safe, but that it probably wouldn't taste very good. "That's what we thought," the caller told the Talk-Line. "We'll give it to the church."

MORE QUESTIONS FOR THE TALK-LINE

• How long does it take to thaw a fresh turkey?

• How long does it take to cook a turkey if I leave the oven door open the entire time? That was how my mom always did it.

• Does the turkey go in the oven feet first, or head first?

• Can I baste my turkey with suntan lotion?

• When does turkey hunting season start?

• How do I prepare a turkey for vegetarians?

FALSE TRUTHS, FALSE TEETH

Years ago, every kid "learned" two things about George Washington: He chopped down a cherry tree and confessed to doing it, and he had wooden teeth. Neither is actually true, but the wooden teeth are at least rooted in fact: Throughout his life, Washington had serious—and strange—dental problems.

SIDE EFFECTS

He eventually became an army general, but as a young man, George Washington was often too sick and weak to get out of bed. He contracted smallpox at age 19, and then dealt with bouts of dysentery, dengue fever, pleurisy, malaria, flu, and arthritis. A treatment often prescribed in those days (for many conditions) was large doses of *calomel*, a poisonous mixture of mercury and chlorine. The potent stuff certainly killed infections, but it had a nasty side effect: It rapidly rotted teeth. Trying to halt the tooth loss, Washington started to brush his teeth daily, which was unusual in the 1700s. Nevertheless, by age 22, Washington—now free of the major illnesses he'd been battling—regularly suffered from toothaches, inflamed gums, and mouth sores.

Washington sought the help of dentists. Dentistry was still in its infancy, so the dentists' solution was simple: yank out each tooth as it rotted. Washington lost about one tooth per year for nearly 30 years. It's said that over the entire period, he suffered from horrific throbbing pains in his mouth. Shortly after he became the first president of the United States in 1789 at age 57, he had just one tooth left.

A BAD FIT

Washington consulted New York City dentist Peter Greenwood, who fashioned a pair of dentures for the president. But they weren't made of wood—they were made out of a number of suitable objects, including ivory, hippopotamus teeth, a cow's tooth, and even a few human teeth (including some of Washington's rotted ones that had been cleaned up). Metal springs held the top and bottom plates

After rising each morning, Thomas Jefferson recorded the day's temperature...

together. The bottom plate had a hole in it, allowing the contraption to fit snugly over Washington's one remaining tooth.

The dentures may have looked like real teeth (sort of), but they didn't function like real teeth. He couldn't chew most food, and after just a few months, the teeth started breaking loose. He sent them back to Greenwood with an admonition to repair them quickly, as the spare pair (also made by Greenwood) "are uneasy in my mouth and bulge my lips out in such a manner as to make them appear considerably swelled."

Fun fact: it was while wearing those uncomfortable, bulbous substitute dentures that Washington sat for the portrait now used on the $1 bill. The president's mouth is notably puffy in the painting. Some historians say artist Gilbert Stuart didn't get along with Washington and played up the facial flaws on purpose. Others say Washington's terrible dentures gave him a sunken jaw, which Stuart padded with cotton so it would look more natural.

THE FINAL TOOTH

By 1796, Washington was still wearing Greenwood's often-repaired original dentures. Washington lost his last real tooth that year, so Greenwood, unable to fit it into the dentures, made a piece of jewelry out of it: He wrapped it in a piece of wire and put it on Washington's watch chain.

Until Washington's death, Greenwood's dentures never fit right, never worked properly, pursed his lips, made it hard to chew, and had to be repaired frequently. As a result, Washington was almost always in pain. Another unfortunate feature of the dentures: They turned black after Washington drank his nightly glass of port. Greenwood advised him to brush them with chalk afterward to whiten them up again.

DENTURES ON DISPLAY

The two sets of Washington's dentures still exist. The "backup" set is on display at the Baltimore College of Dental Surgery in Maryland. The main set—the ones with the hippo teeth, port stains, and big hole—reside in the museum at Mount Vernon, Washington's Virginia estate. Greenwood's descendant, Joseph R. Greenwood, carries Washington's last tooth around his neck, encased in a gold locket.

STRANGE STATISTICS

Statistics don't lie: The world's gone crazy.

• According to *Popular Science* magazine, 1,000 fans holding up cigarette lighters at a rock concert will produce about 2.6 pounds of carbon dioxide.

• The average pitch of Australian women's voices has decreased by 23 hertz since 1945.

• Harvard's library has two books bound in human flesh.

• One in four British veterinarians say they've treated a drunken dog.

• Since 1990, cheerleading injuries in the United States have increased by 110%.

• Since 1960, there have been 55 movies that feature an albino villain.

• It costs the U.S. Treasury 1.73¢ to make and distribute a penny.

• On his Web site, singer Art Garfunkel keeps a full list of the books he's read since 1968. As of October 2006, he'd read 980.

• Each year, approximately 13 people die from being crushed by falling vending machines.

• Three people die annually from using their tongue to check if a battery works.

• Parasites account for 0.01% of the average person's weight.

• 40,000 Americans participate in "fantasy fishing" leagues.

• Three sisters in Scotland have a $1.84 million insurance policy to cover the cost of raising Jesus Christ, should he be born to one of them.

• In a recent poll, 1% of Americans named Jesus "the greatest American of all time."

The blood of a honeybee never clots.

LET THERE BE LIGHT

For eight centuries their winters were clouded in darkness...until one man had a bright idea.

WINTER'S SHADOW

Nestled in the Alps, the Italian town of Viganella is a beautiful place to live...some of the time. Unfortunately, on November 11 the sun disappears behind the steep mountains and doesn't return for 84 cold, dark days. It's been like this since the town was founded, nearly 800 years ago.

How do the residents deal with it? Most of them don't stick around once they reach adulthood, leaving this dwindling town with mostly older people and fewer and fewer children to replace them. In fact, Viganella has been on the brink of extinction for centuries. Today there are less than 200 people left, and most of them aren't a happy lot, suffering from winter depression.

Modern medicine has a term for it: Seasonal Affective Disorder, or SAD. Lack of sunlight inhibits the production of melatonin, a hormone which people need in order to feel happy. Deprived of it for a prolonged time, humans begin to feel depressed. Viganella has suffered the effects of SAD for a long, *long* time. But that all changed, thanks to a strange man with a strange dream.

MAYOR MIDALI

Pierfranco Midali stayed in Viganella after most of his friends had left. A railway worker by trade, Midali wanted to help his town. So in 1999 he ran for mayor with an eye-opening campaign promise: "I will bring the sun to Viganella!"

The townspeople weren't sure if they believed Midali, but they were curious enough to elect him. But then the question became, "How do you plan to do this, Mr. Mayor?" Midali's response: "We'll build a huge mirror on the mountain to the north and reflect the sun's rays onto our village!" There were two big problems with this plan, though: 1) Midali had no idea how to do it; and 2) he had no idea how to pay for it. So he called up an architect friend of his named Giacomo Bonzani who had built a sundial on the wall of a church in Viganella. Bonzani thought the plan was feasible and went to work studying the mountain. What he came up with would have been a mammoth project for even a big city, and seemed impossible for a town of 197 people. The plan: place a 2,000-pound mirror 3,600 feet above the town on top of the mountain. Measuring in at 26 by 16 feet, the mirror would be mounted on a giant computer-activated motor that would move the lens with the sun. For up to six hours a day, the mirror would redirect sunlight onto a section of town about the size of three football fields. The plan's cost: $131,000. (Did we mention that the town only has 197 people?)

It was obvious that the town would need some outside help to pay for the mirror. First they asked the regional government to fund it. They said no. Midali then traveled across Italy and Europe, asking private citizens, banks, and corporations to pitch in. It took seven years, but Midali finally pulled it together. Meanwhile, Bonzani (the architect) had finished his plans for the mirror, and found a company to build it. By this time even the townspeople had warmed up to the idea. "I was a bit skeptical at first," said a local tavern owner named Franco. "But now I'm all for the giant mirror. It's freezing in my tavern and we have to keep the light on all the time." Yet no one was as enthusiastic as Midali. "I can already see my little old ladies coming out of the church after mass," he said, "and just standing there, enjoying a bit of sun!"

HERE COMES THE SUN

The big day finally came: December 17, 2006. Villagers gathered in the town square while Midali readied himself at the mirror control center. While the crowd waited in the shadow, their mayor slowly rotated the mirror, and for the first time in its long history, Viganella basked in the winter sun. "I have been waiting for this moment for seven years," said Midali.

* * *

Hack Job: Many other alpine towns suffer the same winter fate as Viganella, and one local mayor thinks he has a better idea: In the town of Sedrina, also in the Italian Alps, the mayor doesn't want reflected sun light; he wants the real thing. His proposal: remove 75 feet of rock from the top of the mountain overlooking Sedrina.

ACCORDING TO THE LATEST RESEARCH

Here's a look at some of the more unusual scientific (and a few not-so-scientific) studies we've been reading about lately.

VIDEO GAMERS MAKE BETTER SURGEONS

Researchers: Beth Israel Medical Center, New York City

Who They Studied: Surgeons

What They Learned: Are your kids playing video games when they should be doing their homework? They may be smarter than you think: This study of 33 surgeons found that those who "warmed up" for surgical practice drills by playing a video game called Super Monkey Ball before attempting the drills worked faster and made fewer mistakes than surgeons who did not play Super Monkey Ball. After playing the video game for 20 minutes, surgeons were tested on their ability to complete what is known as the "cobra rope" drill, which simulates inserting a tiny video camera and surgical instruments into a small incision in the skin and using them to suture an internal wound. Surgeons who played Super Monkey Ball before attempting the drill finished an average of 11 seconds faster than surgeons who didn't, which suggests that the video game improved eye-hand coordination, visual skills, and reaction times.

PROBLEM GAMBLER? IT MAY BE YOUR MEDS

Researchers: The Mayo Clinic

Who They Studied: Parkinson's disease patients

What They Learned: A 2005 article in *Archives in Neurology* reported a study which found that certain drugs used to treat symptoms of Parkinson's disease may have a rare and unusual side effect: They may cause patients to become compulsive gamblers, even if they have *never* been interested in gambling before. The article described the cases of 11 Parkinson's patients who were taking drugs known as *dopamine agonists*, which mimic the chemical dopamine. (Parkinson's disease kills the brain cells that pro-

It's a crime to punch a bull in the nose in Washington, D.C.

duce the dopamine.) Dopamine also plays a role in stimulating the pleasure centers of the brain, leading researchers to speculate that the dopamine agonists may overstimulate these areas of the brain, causing compulsive "pleasure-seeking" behavior. When the drug doses were reduced or eliminated entirely, the compulsion to gamble ended as abruptly as it had started.

YOUR DESTINY IS IN YOUR OWN HANDS

Researchers: Various

Who They Studied: Athletes

What They Learned: According to a 2006 study published in the *British Journal of Sports Medicine*, women whose ring fingers are longer than their index fingers are better at sports involving running—soccer, tennis, and track-and-field events—than women whose ring fingers are shorter than their index fingers. A similar study published in 2001 found that 304 male English professional soccer players had "a significantly larger ring-to-index-finger ratio than a control group of 533 other men," and other studies have also shown correlations between ring/index-finger length and things as diverse as sexuality, musical ability, and susceptibility to different diseases.

LET'S PRAY THAT THIS STUDY IS FLAWED

Researchers: Mind/Body Institute, Boston

Who They Studied: Heart-bypass patients

What They Learned: In a $2.4 million, 10-year study involving the cases of more than 1,800 patients, researchers found that prayers offered by strangers for the recovery of heart-bypass patients in six different hospitals had no effect on their recovery. The patients were divided into three groups: 1) those who were prayed for by strangers and were told so; 2) those who were prayed for by strangers but who were told they "may or may not" be prayed for; and 3) those who were not prayed for and were told nothing. (The praying was done by an order of monks, an order of nuns, and a nondenominational prayer ministry.) The study found no difference in outcome between those who were prayed for and those who were not. Then, when the researchers compared the two groups who received prayers, the results got more interesting: Those who were told they were prayed for actually suffered *more*

The poisonous copperhead snake smells like fresh-cut cucumbers.

complications after surgery than those who were told they may or may not be prayed for. Being told "may have made them uncertain, wondering, 'Am I so sick they had to call in their prayer team?'" says cardiologist Dr. Charles Bethea, one of the co-authors of the study. "Our conclusion from this is that the role of *awareness* of prayer should be studied further." The study's findings are similar to those of a 1997 University of New Mexico study which found that alcoholics in rehabilitation who knew they were being prayed for did worse than those who didn't.

GRAPEFRUIT MAKES WOMEN SEEM YOUNGER

Researchers: Smell and Taste Institute, Chicago

Who They Studied: Several male volunteers

What They Learned: Researchers smeared several middle-aged women with a number of substances, including grapefruit, spearmint leaves, lavender, bananas, and broccoli, and then invited male volunteers to sniff the subjects and guess their ages. None of the substances made any difference in the men's ability to guess the women's ages...except for the grapefruit, which caused the men to perceive the women as being an average of six years *younger* than they really were.

MARIJUANA: FOOD FOR THOUGHT

Researchers: Scripps Research Institute, California

Who They Studied: Alzheimer's disease patients

What They Learned: According to this study, smoking marijuana may help delay the onset of Alzheimer's disease by preventing the breakdown of the brain chemical *acetylcholine*. Reduced levels of acetylcholine, which transmits nerve impulses in the brain, is one of the symptoms of Alzheimer's disease. Amazingly, smoking pot may also help to block the formation of protein clumps in the brain, which are known to impair memory and clear thinking in Alzheimer's patients.

SHOCKING DISCOVERY: IT'S ALL IN YOUR HEAD

Researcher: Swiss doctor Olaf Blanke

Who They Studied: An epileptic patient

What They Learned: In a 2006 article in the journal *Nature*,

Blanke described a case in which he and a colleague evaluated a woman to see if she was suitable for surgery to treat her epilepsy. When he electrically stimulated an area on the left side of her brain, she became convinced that she was being watched by someone who was standing behind her. When they applied the same stimulation as she leaned forward and grabbed her knees, she became convinced that the mysterious person behind her was grabbing her. Though unrelated to her epilepsy, the creepy, unexpected discovery is potentially important to the study and treatment of mental illness: "Our findings may be a step toward understanding the psychiatric manifestations such as paranoia, persecution," Blanke writes, "and alien control."

* * *

GETTING THE STAR TREATMENT

One of the nice things about being a famous act like the Beach Boys or Prince is that you get to ask for whatever you want in your contract...and concert promoters have to give it to you. Here's what these folks asked for:

Little Richard: "Artist retains the right to distribute souvenir books to the public free of charge. The book is the summary of Little Richard's moral beliefs."

The Dixie Chicks: "Fan base is approximately 70 percent female. Therefore the possibility of overcrowded female restrooms exist. Remedy this by turning around some of the men's restroom facilities in the main concourse into women's facilities."

Prince: "All items in this dressing room must be covered by clear plastic wrap until uncovered by artist."

The Beach Boys: "No form of media advertising shall contain the word 'oldies' in conjunction with artist's name or logo."

Foo Fighters: "Any strange or lingering odors should be dealt with and covered up wherever and whenever possible."

The town of Ding Dong, Texas, is located in Bell County.

AN "E" FOR EFFORT

One of our favorite topics is dumb crooks. Here are a few people who tried extra hard to commit crimes...and still failed.

PLAY A HAPPY SONG

Clifton Lovell is the owner of a musical instrument store called Guitars and Cadillacs in DeQueen, Arkansas. One day in 2006 he saw a man leaving the store with a strange guitar-shaped shape in his pants. Lovell followed 29-year-old Morgan Conaster out of the store and asked him what he had in his pants. "Nothing," said Conaster...but he eventually confessed, opened his jacket, and pulled a solidbody electric guitar from his pantleg. He was arrested.

SAAB STORY

Joshua E. Reed of Rutland, New York, was arrested on theft charges in late 2006, and as a condition of his bail had to report to the local sheriff's office once a day. One day in November, he suddenly realized he didn't have a ride to the sheriff's office and he was going to be late for his meeting...so he *stole* a car. Rutland police spotted the green 1994 Saab, pulled Reed over, and arrested him. "He has a once-daily reporting requirement and, as ridiculous as it sounds, he was concerned about reporting on time," Reed's lawyer said. "He just wasn't thinking." Reed was thrown back in jail and now faces up to 12 years in prison.

DON'T DRINK AND EAT

Police in Kemerovo, Russia, pulled a man over in 2006 on suspicion of drunk driving when they saw his car weaving down the road. The man, who was not identified, admitted that he'd drunk half a quart of pure grain alcohol. When the police told him they were going to confiscate his car, the man decided to try to thwart them...by popping his keys in his mouth and trying to swallow them. One of the officers tried to retrieve the keys, fearing that the driver would choke, but the driver bit him. The police were finally able to get the keys out of the man's mouth (after putting gloves on), and arrested him for drunk driving...and disobeying police orders.

Among ancient Incas, a couple was considered officially wed when they exchanged sandals.

WHEN THE DUMB TURN PRO

A 20-year-old man in a Springfield, Massachusetts, courtroom was refused his request to be released without bail after the judge looked at the identification form the man had filled out. Under occupation he had written "Drug Dealer."

CLAUS, SANTA (D-NORTH POLE)

In 2004, 22-year-old Chad Staton was arrested after he attempted to register more than 100 false names into the Defiance County, Ohio, voter rolls. Some of the names he used on the forms: Mary Poppins, Jeffrey Dahmer, and Janet Jackson.

FAIL, FAIL AGAIN

In May 2001, Shawn Myers drove his pickup truck to Lynn's Market in Wellsville, Pennsylvania. Then he drove *into* Lynn's Market. Backwards. He crashed through the plate-glass window and tried to steal the store's ATM machine by dragging it out with a chain attached to the truck. It didn't work. A few days later, he went back and crashed his truck through the plywood that was covering the broken window, and again tried to steal the ATM. Again he failed. A few days after that, he drove through the front window of nearby Rutter's Farm Store. This time he actually made off down the street with the ATM bouncing along behind the truck...until it hit a parked car and broke free. Several months later, Myers returned to Lynn's Market, drove through Lynn's plate-glass window (again), chained up the ATM, and drove off. This time the ATM stayed with him; he got away and later broke into the machine...but there was no money in it. Myers was eventually arrested, ordered to pay thousands of dollars in restitution, and sentenced to six years in prison. He told the judge he only tried to steal the ATMs because he needed money for court costs from previous trials.

THAT WAS JUST PRACTICE

Two men in Benicia, California, did almost everything right: Ski masks? Check. Semiautomatic handguns? Check. Burst into the bank and order everyone to lie down on the floor? Check. Get the money? Uh, there was no money. It was a credit union that didn't use cash—at all. The two men ran away and were never caught.

The town of Waterproof, Louisiana, has been flooded numerous times.

MARRY ME!

...or I'll throw this baby in the river! (And other strange wedding proposals.)

WHO: Adam Sutton of Rome, Georgia
PROPOSED TO: Erika Brussee
HOW: By crashing a plane (with her in it). In 2006 Sutton talked Brussee into accompanying him on a "sightseeing trip" on a small chartered plane around Rome. But on the ground his family was waiting with a large tarp that read, "Will you marry me?" The pilot flew over the message. Brussee saw it. "The tarp was upside down," she said later. "But I saw the word 'marry.' I turned to look at him...and that's when we crashed." The plane's low altitude and speed caused it to go down and burst into flames at Richard B. Russell Regional Airport. The pilot needed surgery, but luckily everyone else was okay. (And she said "yes.")

WHO: Ugur San of Berlin, Germany
PROPOSED TO: Melek, his girlfriend
HOW: By subway train closed-circuit television. In December 2006, San used his position as an employee of the Berlin underground to make his unique proposal to his girlfriend Melek, whom he had met on one of the trains. He recorded the message, "Hello Melek, my angel. Since meeting you, I realize how beautiful life can be. Will you marry me?" and then had it transmitted on the trains for ten hours straight. (No word on whether she accepted.)

WHO: Col. William Fitzhugh of Virginia
PROPOSED TO: Ann Rousby of Maryland
HOW: By threatening to drown her baby. Fitzhugh was a friend of George Washington and a supporter of the American Revolution. Long before that, in 1752, the 32-year-old proposed to the widowed Ann Rousby. She refused. He proposed again. She refused again. After five rejections, he grabbed her infant daughter, ran to his boat on the Patuxent River, and had his sailors row away. Once he was far enough out, he held the baby over the water and threatened to throw her in if Ann didn't marry him. She married

How many dogs appear in Shakespeare's plays? Only one: Crab, in *Two Gentlemen of Verona.*

him. They went on to have four children and were married until Ann's death—43 years later.

WHO: "JP," of Hendersonville, Tennessee
PROPOSED TO: Undisclosed
HOW: Via the Super Bowl. In 2006 a man identified only as "JP" started "My Super Proposal," a Web site asking people to donate money so he could buy a 30-second commercial during the Super Bowl, in which he would propose to his girlfriend. How much would he need? $2.5 million. Five weeks later he had $45,000. In six weeks it was over $70,000. By the time he had $75,000, all Super Bowl ad time was sold out. Out of luck, "JP" announced plans to donate the money to a children's hospital. But so far, he hasn't—he's still hoping to find a sponsor. Will he? Stay tuned.

WHO: Phil Hodson of Manchester, England
PROPOSED TO: Katie Thornton
HOW: By human lettering. Hodson and Thornton were childhood sweethearts. In 2006 he took her on a helicopter flight to celebrate their ten years together. The flight took them over Saddleworth School, where they had met as teens. As they flew over the school, Katie looked down and saw 200 students standing in the sports field in the shape of the letters M-A-R-R-Y M-E. "I saw the words, turned around and Phil was on bended knee with a ring," Katie said. "I burst into tears." Of course, she said "yes." And then the helicopter crashed. (We're kidding.)

WHO: Godwin Kipkemoi Chepkurgor of Nakuru, Kenya
PROPOSED TO: Chelsea Clinton
HOW: By offering President Clinton farm animals. In 2000 the Clintons traveled to Kenya. In anticipation of the visit, Chepkurgor wrote them a letter, asking for Chelsea's hand in marriage. He offered 20 cows and 40 goats for a dowry. Did he get his wish? No. But he did get a visit from National Security agents, who asked a lot of questions and did background checks on him, his family, and his friends. "Had I succeeded in wooing Chelsea," said a disappointed Chepkurgor, "I would have had a grand wedding. I would have invited Archbishop Desmond Tutu to preside at the ceremony." He's still awaiting word from the Clintons.

What do Bgug, Bra, and Rayon have in common? They're all types of cheese.

OH NO! IT'S JELL-O!

Wonderful Jell-O! Versatile, beloved standby of American cooking. Now behold the dark side in these forgotten (but real) Jell-O recipes from the 1950s and '60s.

Chicken Mousse. Bouillon cubes are dissolved in lemon Jell-O (while it's still hot liquid), then added into a mixture of Cool Whip, mayonnaise, chicken, celery, and pimento. Then it coagulates.

Soufflé salad. Partially hardened Jell-O is whipped and mixed with vegetables and beef—perfect for when you don't have time to eat dinner and dessert separately.

Artichoke Salad. Throwing artichokes into lime Jell-O will *not* get kids to eat them.

Sequin Salad. It won't work with cauliflower, either.

Horseradish Relish. For those who prefer their gelatin spicy, this dish combines lemon Jell-O with green peppers, pimentos, and a half cup of horseradish.

Summer salad. Tomato, celery, cucumber, green pepper, and radishes, seasoned with a dash of oregano, floating in a mold of lemon Jell-O, flipped onto a plate of lettuce.

Florida Seacoast Salad. Grapefruit, cheese, avocado, shrimp, and lemon Jell-O, together at last.

Barbecue Jell-O. Combine a bottle of barbecue sauce (any brand) with Jell-O (any flavor). Chill, cut into cubes, and serve on salad like croutons.

Spanish Tuna Salad. It's unclear what's particularly Spanish about lemon Jell-O mixed with vinegar and tuna.

Olive Relish. Eat your greens: lime Jell-O stuffed with olives, sweet pickles, and celery, served in slices.

Shrimp Salad Surprise. Shrimp, garlic, onion, and sour cream in orange Jell-O, smothered in Italian dressing. Cut it carefully into squares to ensure everybody gets some shrimp.

Deviled Jell-O Eggs. Pour Jell-O into egg-shaped molds, then halve them and fill with deviled egg mixture.

Green Sardine Cupcakes. Chopped sardines are suspended in tiny, individual "cakes" of lime Jell-O.

A *timbromaniac* is someone obsessed with postage stamps.

SCARY MOVIES, SCARIER REVIEWS

Film critics enjoy good movies, but when a movie—especially a horror film—is really, really bad, they seem to have a lot of fun writing the review.

***Orca* (1977)**
"If it were medically possible to overdose on claptrap, *Orca* would be compelled to carry a warning from the Surgeon General."
—***New York Times***

***Kingdom of the Spiders* (1977)**
"A hammy William Shatner battles yucky spiders. Too bad the spiders don't win."
—***Journal and Courier* (Lafayette, Indiana)**

***House of Wax* (2005)**
"Midway through, the heroine falls face first into a stinking pit of animal guts. The experience of watching this movie feels a lot like that."
—***News Tribune* (Tacoma)**

***Mary Shelley's Frankenstein* (1994)**
"Although it wouldn't be fair to say that this horror is entirely absent, you could miss it if you blink."
—***Orlando Sentinel***

***I Still Know What You Did Last Summer* (1998)**
"*When Bad Things Happen to Stupid People* might have been a better title."
—***San Francisco Chronicle***

***Jaws: The Revenge* (1987)**
"Thrillseekers, this one's pretty dismal. There's more suspense in *On Golden Pond*."
—***Washington Post***

***Children of the Corn* (1987)**
"Plenty of corn, for sure, but no chills."
—***Kalamazoo Gazette***

***The Phantom of the Opera* (1989)**
"All the terror and suspense of Charlie Brown in *Macbeth*."
—***New York Times***

***Halloween III: The Season of the Witch* (1982)**
"Assembled out of familiar parts from other, better movies."
—***Chicago Sun Times***

Will Smith turned down the lead in *The Matrix*. Instead he made *Wild Wild West*, which tanked.

"THE BLAST BLASTED BLUBBER BEYOND ALL BELIEVABLE BOUNDS"

We at the BRI are always on the lookout for great urban legends. For years the tale of the Exploding Whale has floated around the Internet. But it's not an urban legend—it's 100% true. Here's the story.

A WHALE OF A PROBLEM

How do you get rid of a 45-foot-long stinking dead whale? That was the bizarre question George Thornton had to answer on the morning of November 12, 1970. A few days earlier, an eight-ton rotting sperm whale carcass had washed ashore on a Florence, Oregon, beach, and the responsibility fell on Thornton—assistant highway engineer for the Oregon State Highway Division—to remove it. His options were limited. He couldn't bury the rapidly decomposing corpse on site because the tides would soon uncover it, creating a health hazard for beachgoers. And because of the whale's overpowering stench, his workers refused to cut it up and transport it elsewhere. He also couldn't burn it. So what could he do? Thornton came up with an unbelievable solution: blow up the whale with dynamite.

WHALE WATCHING

Thornton's expectation was that the whale's body would be nearly disintegrated by the explosion, and he assumed that if any small chunks of whale landed on the beach, scavengers like seagulls and crabs would consume them. Indeed, many seagulls had been hovering around the corpse all week.

Thornton had the dynamite placed on the leeward side of the whale, so that the blast would hopefully propel the whale pieces toward the water. Thornton said, "Well, I'm confident that it'll work. The only thing is we're not sure how much explosives it'll take to disintegrate the thing." He settled on 20 cases—half a ton of dynamite.

As workers piled case upon case of explosives underneath the whale, spectators swarmed around it to have their pictures taken—upwind, of course—in front of the immense carcass, right near a massive gash where someone had hacked away the beast's lower jaw. Even after officials herded the crowds a full quarter of a mile away for safety, about 75 stubborn spectators stuck around, most of them equipped with binoculars and telephoto lenses. After almost two hours of installing explosives, Thornton and his crew were finally ready to blow up a whale. He gave the signal to push in the plunger.

THAR SHE BLOWS!

The amazing events that followed are best described through the eye of a local TV news camera that captured the episode on tape. The whale suddenly erupts into a 100-foot-tall plume of sand and blubber. "Oohs" and "aahs" are heard from the bystanders as whale fragments scatter in the air. Then, a woman's voice breaks out of the crowd's chattering: "Here come pieces of . . . WHALE!" Splattering noises of whale chunks hitting the ground grew louder, as onlookers scream and scurry out of the way. In the words of Paul Linnman, a Portland TV reporter on the scene, "The humor of the entire situation suddenly gave way to a run for survival as huge chunks of whale blubber fell everywhere."

For several minutes after the blast, it rained blubber bits. Fortunately, no one was hurt by the falling chunks, but everyone—and everything—on the scene was coated with foul-smelling, vaporized whale. The primary victim of the blubber was an Oldsmobile owned by Springfield businessman Walter Umenhofer, parked well over a quarter of a mile away from the explosion. The car's roof was completely caved in by a large slab of blubber. As he watched a highway worker remove the three-by-five foot hunk with a shovel, a stunned Umenhofer remarked, "My insurance company's never going to believe this."

THE AFTERMATH

Down at the blast site, the only thing the dynamite had gotten rid of were the seagulls. They were either scared away by the blast or repulsed by the awful stench, which didn't matter because most of the pieces of blubber lying around were far too large for them to eat. The beach was littered with huge chunks of ripe whale, including the whale's entire tail and a giant slab of mangled whale meat that never left the blast site. And, because of the explosives, the smell was actually worse than before.

Thornton had hoped his work was done, but it was just beginning—he and his workers spent the rest of the day burying their mistake. His blunder drew the attention of news stations all over the country, but amazingly, he was promoted just six months later.

Twenty-five years later, the tale of the exploding whale is documented all over the Internet. And the Oregon Highway Division still gets calls about it today—many callers hoping to get their hands on the video. The whale is still dead, but the story took on a life of its own (and you can find the video on YouTube).

* * *

ASK THE EXPERTS

The Heart Was Taken

Q: Why do people cross their fingers for good luck?

A: "The practice may have evolved from the sign of the cross, which was believed to ward off evil." (From *The Book of Answers*, by Barbara Berliner)

Yee-Haw!

Q: In movie Westerns, people fire guns straight up into the air as warning shots or just to make noise during a celebration. But those bullets have to come down somewhere. How dangerous will they be if they hit somebody?

A: "Physics tells us that when it hits the ground the bullet will have the same velocity it had when it left the muzzle of the pistol, 700 to 800 mph. But that ignores air resistance. Realistically, the bullet's landing speed can be around 100 to 150 mph. That's more than enough speed to do serious or lethal damage to a cranial landing site.

And by the way, the jerk who fires the bullet isn't very likely to be hit by it. In one experiment, out of 500 machine-gun bullets fired straight upward, only 4 landed within 10 feet (3 meters) of the gun. Wind has a great effect, since bullets can reach altitudes of 4,000 to 8,000 feet (1,200 to 2,400 meters) before falling back down." (From *What Einstein Told His Barber*, by Robert. L. Wolke)

A full bladder is about the size of a softball.

WEIRD ROMANIA

We have no idea why, but an unusually high amount of bizarre stuff seems to go down in this eastern European nation.

DOG DAYS

In 2003 officials at the Otopeni Airport in Bucharest opened the animal-transport area of a plane that had just arrived from Frankfurt, Germany. Inside, they discovered a dog that had apparently died during the journey. Certain the owner would sue, officials scoured local animal shelters until they found a dog that looked exactly like the dead one. When the dead dog's owner was given the live dog, she was stunned—her dog was *already* dead when she'd put it on the plane. She'd wanted to bury it in Romania. Happy ending: The woman adopted the new dog.

THEIR PRAYERS WERE ANSWERED

In March 2002, a fire broke out on the roof of a monastery in Parepa. The monks residing there evacuated the building while the fire burned for about 10 minutes. When the monks no longer saw flames on the roof, they went up to assess the damage…and found no trace of fire.

A ROPE OF SAND

Victor Dodoi of Botosani tried to commit suicide by hanging himself. He put a noose around his neck and tied the other end of the rope to a light fixture in his living room. Under the weight of Dodoi's body, the light broke off and sent him crashing to the floor, alive. Dodoi is reportedly suing the *rope* manufacturer for making faulty merchandise.

OH, DEER

Romanian Gheorghe Paschu, 72, estimates he's been hit by cars more than 40 times—on purpose. Despite suffering multiple concussions and countless broken bones, Paschu says he just can't help himself. "I just can't resist jumping out into the middle of the road when I see a car coming," he said. Apparently he was telling the truth—Paschu continued his "hobby" even after insurance companies refused to pay for his crash-related medical bills.

DON'T LEAVE HOME WITHOUT YOUR HOME

Gheorghe Lascarache of Roman City went to a neighboring town one day in 2003 to look for work. When he came home later that day, his house was gone. While he was out, four thieves had stolen his house, brick by brick. (Police discovered the plot when one of the thieves was caught selling a quarter of the bricks for $2,000.)

FROGS VS. HITLER

A Romanian TV station that runs Discovery Channel shows was inundated by complaints from viewers in 2004 when it ran six documentaries (including films about World War II, ancient Egypt, and submarines) that were all broadcast with the same subtitles…from a show about frogs.

THUS PROVING THE FORTUNE-TELLER CORRECT

In 2002 a fortune-teller told 51-year-old Mircea Teodarescu that either he or his son would die before the week was over. Unwilling to leave it to chance, Teodarescu went home and slit his own throat, fulfilling the prophecy and allowing his son to live.

WITCHY WOMAN

Basile Birsan, 72, of Roznov hired a witch in 2003 through a newspaper classified ad. Birsan paid her $400 to cure his sick wife and get his 40-year-old son to marry. After a few months, the witch's spells had failed to make any difference on Birsan's wife or son, so he called the police. To avoid arrest, the "witch" agreed to a full refund.

DON'T BANK ON IT

Late one night in 2006, a trio of criminals broke into the Nova Bank in Constanta by forcing the main doors open. They got away with…nothing. The robbers didn't know that the bank had been closed and moved to a new location. Angry that there was no money to steal, the criminals wanted to at least take *something* for their trouble, so they tried—unsuccessfully—to steal the heating pipes off the wall.

NO, THAT WASN'T ME

While she was really at the Mamaia Beach on the Black Sea, Lucica Dragomirescu phoned her husband Victor and told him she was sick and couldn't leave her bed. Victor told Lucica that he was stuck at his parents' house doing renovations, but he was lying, too—he was also at Mamaia Beach. The Dragomirescus both hung up, then looked up...and saw each other on the beach. The couple later divorced.

* * *

ANIMALS IN THE NEWS

• **It's a Smell World:** In an average month, trains operated by the West Japan Railway Company strike and kill 10 deer that wander onto railroad tracks. In 2003 the railroad decided to test a new kind of deer repellent on the rails—lion poop. Lions and deer are natural enemies, the thinking went, so the smell of the predator would keep the deer away. In August 2003, the railroad scrapped the experiment, not because it didn't work, but because it worked *too* well—the poop kept the deer away, but it smelled so bad that it kept everything else away too, including local residents. "The track really did stink," says railroad spokesperson Toshihiko Iwata. "We're experimenting with more environmentally friendly methods now."

• **Revenge:** A wildlife officer in Saskatchewan was attempting to shoot a moose—when he shot a fellow officer instead. The officer was trying to "mercy kill" the wounded animal when the shot from his shotgun missed, hit a tree, and ricocheted into the other officer's leg. The officer was treated at a local hospital.

• **Whale of a Vacation:** In the summer of 2003 the Johnson family of Coventry, England, took a 10-day sailing vacation in Australia. But their trip came to a sudden end when a 10-ton humpback whale leapt out of the water and onto their 40-foot sailboat, damaging the rigging and pulling down the mast. "It's amazing no one was hurt or killed," 61-year-old Trevor Johnson told reporters. Total cost of chartering the boat: $238,000. (No word on whether the Johnsons got a refund.)

Elaine Davidson of Edinburgh, Scotland, has a world-record 720 body piercings.

UH-OH, WHAT'S THAT IN THE FREEZER?

Think about this next time you're wondering how much of a tip to leave.

THIS GUINEA PIGGY WENT WHERE?

In December 2005, a health inspector was examining the contents of a freezer in the La Sabrosa restaurant in DeKalb County, Georgia. He found a dead guinea pig in it. The restaurant's owner said it was his, and insisted that the rodent wasn't intended to be a menu item...he was going to eat it himself. Even stranger, the restaurant received a score of 87 out of 100 for the inspection, up from the 79 it got the previous year (when it didn't have any guinea pigs in the freezer).

WHAT, NO PANDAS?

In 2003 mall security workers in Edmonton, Alberta, called health inspectors when they found some suspicious items in the freezer of a Panda Garden restaurant. "They took me back to the walk-in freezer and when you open the door there were four carcasses," said inspector Richard Reive. "Two were inside black garbage bags and the other two were exposed on the floor of the freezer." They were coyotes. They'd been skinned and gutted, and were definitely intended for human consumption. Amazingly, the owners were never charged with any crime, since serving dog meat is technically legal in Canada. (But the restaurant did have to close due to the bad press.)

WE PASS THE SAVINGS ON TO YOU!

In June 2002, a power outage knocked out the walk-in freezer at Ricardo's Pizza in Milwaukee, Wisconsin, and all the food in it had to be thrown out. A few hours later employees were surprised to see that many of the boxes of food—containers of pepperoni, jalapeño peppers, cheese sticks, and other snack items—they had thrown in the dumpster were gone. The owner called the health department because he knew the food was bad and he didn't want

Your voice tires more quickly from whispering than speaking in a normal tone.

anybody eating it. A few days later, inspectors were doing a routine check of Eleanor's restaurant, down the street from Ricardo's... and they found the dumpster food, which was clearly marked "Ricardo's" and still had the expired "freshness" dates on them. Eleanor's owner, Gerard Symes, denied taking the dumpster food at first, then blamed it on his employees. Then he was fined (a whopping $197).

KIDS MENU

A manager of a McDonald's restaurant in Roodepoort, South Africa, was turned in to police by her employees because of the contents of the restaurant's freezer: a six-year-old boy. The child had come to McDonald's begging for food when the angry manager grabbed him and threw him into the walk-in. She left him there, without shoes or a shirt, for about 10 minutes. As soon as the door was opened, the boy ran away—shivering, according to news accounts. The manager was suspended for two weeks.

MEMBERS ONLY

If you go to the Guolizhuang restaurant in Beijing, China, there's a good chance you'll find a variety of animal "private parts" in their freezer. The restaurant specializes in dishes made from the odd culinary choice, the BBC reported in 2006, and it's a popular place too. The male organs of sheep, horse, ox, and seal are all good for circulation, says the restaurant's "staff nutritionist," adding that donkey "privates" are good for the skin, and snake "privates" are the cure for impotence.

ON SECOND THOUGHT, LET'S EAT IN

In 1996 a crew was sent to repossess equipment from a Middle-Eastern restaurant in Brussels, Belgium, called the Baalbeck when the restaurant owners failed to make their loan payments on time. They found a human hand in a freezer. A subsequent search by police uncovered the remains of three human bodies in the restaurant's other two freezers. Their investigation found that the bodies were just being hidden—and weren't intended for consumption. (Three years later three men were convicted of the murders and imprisoned.)

Brazil produced a coffee-scented postage stamp in 2001.

THE WEIRDEST GRAVE IN THE WEST

Here's the story behind one of the most peculiar (and most popular) grave sites in the entire United States. More than 60 years after it was completed, it still attracts tens of thousands of visitors a year.

FORBIDDEN LOVE

In the mid-1870s, a college student named John Davis was forced to drop out of Urania College in Kentucky after his parents died and he was unable to pay the tuition. He became an itinerant laborer, taking work wherever he could find it, and in 1879 he signed on as a farmhand for Tom Hart, a wealthy landowner in tiny Hiawatha, Kansas. Davis was a good worker, but that didn't count for much when the penniless lad fell in love with Sarah Hart, the boss's daughter. When the two announced their plans to marry, Mr. and Mrs. Hart, furious that Sarah would marry so far beneath her station, disowned her.

MOVING UP

Ever heard the expression "living well is the best revenge"? John and Sarah got back at the Harts by becoming one of the most prosperous couples in Hiawatha, though it took them a lifetime to do it. After scraping together enough money to buy a 260-acre farm, they managed it so wisely that they were able to use the profits to buy a second farm, which also did well. Then, after 35 years of living in the country, the childless couple moved to a stately mansion on one of Hiawatha's best streets. They were still living there in 1930, after more than 50 years of marriage, when Sarah died from a stroke.

At first John commissioned a modest headstone for Sarah in Hiawatha's Mount Hope Cemetery, but soon decided it wasn't enough. He'd never forgotten how Sarah's family had spurned them when they had nothing; now that they were more prosperous than the Hart clan, he decided that he and Sarah should be laid to rest in the nicest, most expensive memorial in town.

A third of all pet owners admit to having more photos of their pet than of their spouse.

EDIFICE COMPLEX

Davis was friends with a local tombstone salesman named Horace England, and together the two men designed a memorial consisting of life-size marble statues of John and Sarah as they looked on their 50th wedding anniversary. The statues would stand at the foot of the graves and face the headstones; the cemetery plot would also be protected from the elements by a 50-ton marble canopy supported by six massive columns.

England stood to make a small fortune on such a grandiose memorial. Even so, he suggested that it might be a little much, especially considering that the country was in the depths of the Great Depression and folks in Midwestern towns like Hiawatha had been hit especially hard. Davis thanked him for his opinion and then offered to give the business to another tombstone salesman. England assured Davis that that would not be necessary and committed himself wholeheartedly to the task at hand. As far as anyone knows, he never raised another objection.

Davis approved the final design and sent his and his wife's measurements off to Carrara, Italy, where master craftsmen carved their likenesses out of the finest Italian marble. Completed in 1931, the Davis Memorial was easily the most impressive in Hiawatha, probably in the entire state. And yet when Davis got a look at it he felt something was missing. The giant stone canopy dwarfed the pair of statues beneath it. The solution? More statues. "I thought it still looked too bare, so I got me another pair," Davis explained. The second set of statues depicted John and Sarah as they would have looked on their tenth wedding anniversary, much earlier in life than the first pair of statues showed them.

NO STATUE OF LIMITATIONS

By now Davis was pretty much out of loose cash, so he signed over his two farms to Horace England for $31,000—more than enough money to pay for the second set of statues. What did he do with the money that was left? He bought a *third* set of statues, showing Sarah and himself seated in comfy chairs as they would have looked in 1898, after 18 years of marriage. (John is depicted clean-shaven —in the late 1890s, he had burned his beard off fighting a brush fire and for a time went without his flowing beard.)

Why stop at three pairs? Davis then decided he wanted a *fourth* pair of statues. Again John is shown seated, this time missing his left hand, which he lost to infection in 1908 after he injured it while trying to trim his hedges with an axe. (The axe is on display in the nearby Brown County Agricultural Museum.)

Because this fourth set of statues depict John after his wife's death, her absence is represented by a statue of an empty chair. (Just in case anyone misses the symbolism, the words "THE VACANT CHAIR" are carved into the chair.) Unlike the other statues, this pair was done in granite instead of in marble. Davis claimed it was because he thought men looked better carved in granite.

FORMING A CROWD

Who says four pairs of statues are enough? Davis commissioned a fifth and then a sixth. When the money from the sale of his farms ran out, he signed over his mansion to Horace England for $1, on the condition that he be allowed to live in it for the rest of his life. That solved Davis's money problems, which may be why the fifth and sixth pairs of statues were once again done in Italian marble. The sixth—and final—statues depict John and Sarah as angels kneeling over each others' graves.

When the odd jumble of statues started to attract visitors, some of whom were disrespectful and climbed the statues or sat in The Vacant Chair, Davis had a three-foot-high marble wall built around the entire memorial, with marble urns at the corners inscribed "KINDLY KEEP OFF THE MEMORIAL." The wall is just low enough for the seated figures to be seen peeking over the top.

ANYONE'S GUESS

Why did Davis keep adding statues? Some people speculate that with no family of his own, he was determined to blow his entire fortune to keep his wife's relatives from getting a penny of his money. Others speculate that Davis was motivated by guilt—he was apparently a very jealous man and during the more than 30 years that he and Sarah had lived on the farm, he had rarely let Sarah go into town alone or even visit the neighboring farm wives. Now, realizing too late how hard that must have been for Sarah, he was making it up to her in marble.

A third theory, simple but compelling, is that Davis was just

In the 1950s, it was against French law for a flying saucer to land in any vineyard.

plain nuts. He became a compulsive memorial builder in much the same way that some people are compulsive collectors. Even if he did realize that each new addition of statues further cluttered an already crowded memorial, he couldn't stop himself.

THE END...OR IS IT?

In 1937, the same year that he signed over his mansion to Horace England, John Davis learned from his doctors that he had less than six months to live. Davis quickly gave away the rest of his fortune—possibly as much as $55,000—and prepared to join his wife in their final resting place. Six months passed...and then a year...and then two years, until eventually Davis realized that the same doctors he blamed for losing his hand after his axe incident had also botched the diagnosis of his "terminal" illness. He didn't have six months to live, he had *ten years* to live, and now that he had given away his entire fortune he couldn't even afford to live in his mansion, even though it was rent-free. He moved into the local poorhouse and lived there for the rest of his days, though he did spend a lot of time out at the cemetery, proudly showing off the 11 life-size statues and The Vacant Chair to the throngs of people who came to see it. He died in his sleep in 1947.

In all, Davis is believed to have spent $200,000 on his memorial, the equivalent of well over $1 million today. (Many locals also credit him with giving tens of thousands of dollars to the needy during his lifetime, usually in small sums. But since this giving was done in private, it has been overshadowed by the memorial.)

A SIGHT TO BE SEEN

The Davis Memorial isn't the prettiest grave in America. It looks like a cross between a gas station and a statue-company showroom. Nevertheless, it attracts as many as 30,000 visitors a year, many of whom go straight to the cemetery without bothering to visit the town. Perhaps it's only fair, then, that Hiawatha's townspeople are as ambivalent about Davis today as they were during the Depression, when he memorialized his wife in stone instead of building a library or a hospital that would have honored her memory while contributing to the common good. But Davis wouldn't have had it any other way. "They hate me," Davis admitted late in life, "but it's my money and I spent it the way I pleased."

Forgotten First: Emilio Onra was the first human cannonball (1871).

40 ODD USES FOR WD-40

Fifty years after its invention in 1953, WD-40 can be found in four out of five American homes. (We even have a couple of cans here at the BRI.)

L IS FOR LUBRICANT

Sure, it loosens and lubricates, but what else can it do? Well, if you believe what you read on the Internet and in tabloid newspapers, a lot. It removes makeup from carpet, liberates stuck Lego blocks, kills weeds, exterminates cockroaches, and even foils squirrels from climbing into bird feeders. New uses are discovered every day; here are 40 of the best known. (WARNING: We haven't tested these and *do not* recommend trying them...so don't call us if you wreck your carpet trying to get ink stains out with WD-40.)

1. Removes grime from book covers and marker from dry erase boards.

2. Prevents mud and clay from sticking to shovels and boots.

3. Removes grease and oil stains on clothes.

4. Softens new baseball gloves.

5. Cleans chrome fixtures in bathrooms.

6. Makes the puck slide faster on an air hockey table.

7. Cleans and softens paint brushes.

8. Cleans and protects cowboy boots.

9. Removes crayon from walls, carpet, wallpaper, plastics, shoes, toys, chalkboard, television screens, screen doors, and rock walls.

10. Eases arthritis pain...just spray it on the joint that hurts.

11. Cleans piano keys.

12. Removes super strong glue from fingers.

13. Keeps wicker chairs from squeaking.

14. Removes scuff marks from ceramic floors.

15. Cleans and protects copper pots and pans.

16. Polishes and shines seashells.

17. Removes water spots from mirrors.

18. Removes tea stains from counter tops.

19. Keeps pigeons off window ledges (they hate the smell).

20. Removes ink from carpet.

21. Keeps metal wind chimes rust free.

22. Prevents mildew growth on outdoor fountains.

23. Removes gunk from plastic dish drainers.

24. Cleans dog doo from tennis shoes.

25. Removes tomato stains from clothing.

26. Gets ink stains out of leather.

27. Removes roller-skate marks from kitchen floor.

28. Unkinks gold chains.

29. Penetrates frozen mailbox doors.

30. Removes tar from shoes.

31. Cleans silver plates and trays.

32. Removes soap scum from bathtubs and showers.

33. Polishes wood.

34. Takes the squeak out of shoes.

35. Removes a stuck ring from a finger.

36. Wipes off graffiti.

37. Removes Silly Putty from carpet.

38. Loosens burrs, thistles, and stickers from dogs and horses.

39. Removes bumper stickers from cars.

40. Removes duct tape.

ODDEST USES

• When John Glenn circled the earth in 1962, his spacecraft, *Friendship VII*, was slathered in WD-40 from top to bottom. NASA engineers hoped it would reduce friction upon reentry.

• In 2001 a burglar in Medford, Oregon, broke into an apartment wielding a can of WD-40. He sprayed the occupant with the lubricant and demanded money, then escaped with the man's wallet and car keys (but was later apprehended).

• Responding to inquiries from the Pike Anglers Committee of Great Britain, the British Environment Agency states that they do *not* recommend the use of WD-40 as fish bait.

Streptomycin, an antibiotic, was discovered in fungus found in a chicken's throat.

SAY WHAT?

Occasionally we'll read a quote and have no idea what the speaker is talking about, so we'll read it again, hoping that the meaning will reveal itself. We're still hoping.

"I used to be very hands-on, but lately I've been more hands-off and I plan to become more hands-on and less hands-off and hope that hands-on will become better than hands-off, the way hands-on used to be."

—George Steinbrenner

"I would not live forever, because we should not live forever, because if were supposed to live forever, then we would live forever, but we cannot live forever, which is why I would not live forever."

—Miss Alabama in the 1994 Miss USA contest. (The question was: "If you could live forever, would you and why?")

"Most critics write critiques which are by the authors they write critiques about. That would not be so bad, but then most authors write works which are by the critics who write critiques about them."

—Karl Kraus

"Concentration-wise, we're having trouble crossing the line mentally from a toughness standpoint."

—Bill Parcels, football coach

"I would be batting the big feller if they wasn't ready with that other one, but a left hander would be the thing if they wouldn't have knowed it already because there is more things involved than could come up on the road, even after we been home for a long time."

—Casey Stengel

"I think today that a few remarks I might make, we go back to the relationship in this great nation with the people who was the foundation of America, the people they've paid such a price that we may enjoy the blessings of enjoyments that we have, has been spoken this morning."

—Evan Mecham, former Arizona governor

Who knew they were so sensitive? A snail has 2 pairs of antennae: 1 for seeing, 1 for smelling.

GENIUS SCHOOL

Imagine a school without formal classes, without curriculum or degree programs, without exams or requirements...and without tuition or fees. Want to apply? There's just one small hitch: To get in, you have to be a genius.

FLEXNER'S PARADISE

Schoolteacher Abraham Flexner had a vision: Why couldn't there be an idyllic setting where the world's greatest minds could come together to share their thoughts and conduct research? Why wasn't there a place where geniuses would be free to lose themselves in the world of ideas without the everyday demands—like earning the rent, cooking, and commuting—that ordinary people have to deal with?

Flexner knew a thing or two about genius. The son of immigrants, he found himself uninspired by the schools he attended in Louisville, Kentucky, in the 1880s. But he loved books, and through reading on his own he learned the things that he couldn't learn in school. At age 17, he entered Johns Hopkins University and graduated in just two years. Afterward he returned to Kentucky to teach at his old high school.

While he was teaching in Kentucky, Flexner found his true calling. After a boy was expelled from a prep school, his parents asked Flexner if he'd be willing to tutor their son; they still hoped he might be admitted into Princeton. Flexner agreed, and the tutoring was a success. Soon other parents were sending Flexner their children to be tutored, with similar results: All of his private students gained admission to prestigious schools.

A DIFFERENT WAY OF TEACHING

Flexner's teaching methods were highly unorthodox. There were no homework assignments or exams. Students could come to their lessons or not; they could do as little or as much work as they wished. Eventually, the students would find their own pace, and their own will to learn...and went on to achieve more than anyone would have thought possible. These early successes formed the core concept for what was to become Flexner's Institute for Advanced Study.

Bill Clinton's birth name was Bill Blythe. (He took his stepfather's name.)

By 1930, Flexner's reputation had caught the attention of Newark, New Jersey, department-store magnate Louis Bamberger and his sister Caroline Bamberger Fuld. The wealthy siblings were in an enviable position—they had pulled all of their money out of the stock market just before the crash of 1929. And now they were looking for a philanthropic investment to show gratitude to their home state of New Jersey. They wanted to found a dental school, and needed an educational expert. So they consulted Flexner.

But Flexner suggested another use for the Bambergers' generosity: a nurturing educational environment for genius to flower. And so the Institute for Advanced Study—a New Jersey mecca for scholars that still exists today—was born.

GENIUS AT WORK?

Dr. Flexner's idea was surprisingly simple. If the world's great thinkers could be freed of mundane concerns, they could devote all their time to research and the pursuit of abstract ideas. The Institute provided the academic setting—classrooms, meeting rooms, libraries, and dining halls. And better yet, it was (and still is) entirely free of charge, funded by endowments instead of tuition. The lucky scholars who were accepted into the Institute had almost all of their everyday needs met. Their housing and food was subsidized by the Institute; there was even an on-campus nursery school to look the scholars' children.

And in return, Institute scholars had to do...nothing. In keeping with Flexner's philosophy, there were no formal classes, no assigned research projects (scholars picked their own topics of study), and students didn't have to publish their findings in the journals of the day. The assumption was that students who were intelligent enough to be admitted to the Institute would make good use of their time there.

STARTING WITH MATHLETES

The Institute began with just one department—mathematics, because it required the smallest investment in facilities and equipment. Over the years, other departments were added: the School of Historical Studies, the School of Natural Sciences, and the School of Social Sciences. Today, the permanent faculty numbers 26 (plus 12 emeriti). Each year approximately 200 students (offi-

Of men and women who sleep alone, more men sleep with a Teddy bear.

cially known as "members") are accepted for periods ranging from three months to several years. All members are required to have a Ph.D. or equivalent degree.

Though the Institute for Advanced Study was first housed in Princeton University's Fine Hall, it moved to its own campus three miles away in 1939. The two institutions have always been, and remain, separate entities, but both schools benefit from the close relationship. Institute members are free to use Princeton's libraries and facilities, and they occasionally teach graduate courses there.

FAMOUS ALUMNI

A list of the Institute's alumni reads like an international who's-who in the natural and social sciences. Albert Einstein is probably the best known alumnus; he came to the Institute in 1933, when he was at the peak of his fame and the entire academic world was wooing him. Einstein spent the last two decades of his life teaching at the Institute.

Other faculty members have included the brilliant mathematician John Nash, made famous by the movie *A Beautiful Mind.* Another veteran is mathematician John von Neumann, considered the father of game theory and the developer of many early concepts of computer architecture. J. Robert Oppenheimer, director of the Manhattan Project and widely known as the father of the atomic bomb, was another. More than a dozen Nobel laureates number among the Institute's alumni, as well as winners of many other prestigious awards.

READY?

The Institute is still going strong, and accepts about 190 new members per year (out of 1,500 applicants). Think you're smart enough to apply? Just send your application to Institute for Advanced Study on Einstein Drive in Princeton, New Jersey. (Uncle John applied. They said no.)

* * *

In a recent survey, 25% of the respondents said that surveys invade their privacy.

ANIMAL BATHROOM NEWS

Birds do it, fleas do it. And according to these reports, even moose and bees do it.

STOCKHOLM, SWEDEN

After posting security guards in their parking lot, the Peab Construction Company finally figured out who—or what—was responsible for spraying a mysterious yellow substance on light-colored vehicles. The culprit: a swarm of more than 30,000 bees from a nearby beekeeper's hive. As the beekeeper explained after moving his hive a little farther away, "It is well known in the trade that bees like to defecate on light-colored objects."

QUEBEC, CANADA

An 80-year-old pet owner named Gerard Daigle lost more than a pint of blood after he was attacked by his cat Touti while giving his parrot a shower. The cat attacked after it was accidentally sprayed with water. According to news reports, "It is not known why Daigle was giving his parrot a shower."

OSLO, NORWAY

An amorous moose attempted to mate with a yellow Ford, only to defecate all over it when the car did not respond to its advances. "The front yard was simply transformed into an outdoor toilet," said owner Leif Borgersen. Still, it could have been worse: Other than being covered in "lick marks, saliva, and moose excrement," the only damage to the car was a bent side mirror. "I'm not sure whether I should risk letting the car stand alone and defenseless in the front yard anymore," Borgersen said.

SANTA FE, NEW MEXICO

The state health department has pulled an anti-smoking TV ad that compared smoking to inhaling methane gas, and illustrated the point with the sound of cows passing gas. "We had about 10 complaints," said department spokeswoman Jackie Campo.

THE WEIRD WORLD OF SPORTS

Some of the strangest sporting moments from the last 100 years.

LOST BY A NOSE

Minutes before a bout in the 1992 Golden Gloves Championships, boxer Daniel Caruso decided to psych himself up the way his hero, Marvin Hagler, often did—by punching himself in the face with his gloves on. Bad move: The self-battering broke Caruso's nose, and before the match could begin, the ring doctor declared him unfit to box. He had to forfeit the match.

JUST A SNACK

Cuban postman Feliz Carvajal realized his dream of running in the marathon at the 1904 Summer Olympics in St. Louis. Late in the race, he was in third place with a comfortable lead over the next runner, and seemed to have the bronze medal sewn up. But, concerned that hunger might slow him down, he stopped briefly to eat some peach slices offered by onlookers. Then he stepped into an orchard to munch on a few green apples. After he returned to the course, the fruit caused severe stomach cramps, forcing him to limp along at a painfully slow pace. A few minutes later, the runner behind him easily passed him. Carvajal finished fourth...and lost the bronze medal.

PAGING MR. ALVAREZ...

In the 50-kilometer cross-country ski race at the 1988 Winter Olympics, Mexican skier Roberto Alvarez lagged so far behind his fellow skiers that racing officials actually lost track of him and were forced to send out a search party. They found him, but he finished dead last—almost an hour behind the next-slowest skier.

HOLY GOALIE

Soccer goalie Isadore Irandir, who played in the Brazilian league during the 1970s, had a strict pre-match ritual: Before each game, he'd kneel near the goal net and pray for several minutes. But at the start of one match, his prayers took so long that the kick-off began before he was ready. Three seconds into the game, an opposing player more than halfway down the field kicked an improbable 60-yard shot...which sailed right past the kneeling Irandir's head and into the goal.

SHOW'S OVER, FOLKS

Marathon runner Wallace Williams of the Virgin Islands ran the 1979 Pan-American Games marathon at such a slow pace that by the time he got to the stadium that housed the finish line, all the stadium doors were locked, and the crowd and race officials had already gone home.

THE WATER GIVETH, IT TAKETH AWAY

Soviet rower Ivanov Vyacheslav was so excited after winning a gold medal in the 1956 Olympics in Melbourne, Australia, that he threw the medal into the air in triumph during the award ceremony. But the medal didn't come down into his hand as he planned—it fell into Lake Wendouree, next to the medal stand Vyachaslav and his teammates dove into the lake and searched frantically, but the medal was never found.

AT LEAST IT WAS A RECORD

Antoin Miliordos of Greece is an Olympic record holder...for the slowest speed ever achieved in a slalom race. In the 1952 Winter Olympics in Oslo, Norway, Miliordos fell 18 times during his qualifying run, averaging a pathetic 6.33 miles per hour...and crossed the finish line skiing backwards.

I MADE IT! UH-OH.

In 1986, 52-year-old soccer fan Pedro Gatica bicycled all the way from his home in Argentina to Mexico—4,500 miles—to attend the World Cup. But when he arrived at the stadium for the opening game, Gatica discovered he didn't have enough money for a ticket. Then, while he was haggling with a ticket seller, thieves made sure his adventure would continue—they stole his bike.

BOTH HANDS ON THE BIKE, DUDE

Celebrating his fourth-place finish in the 1989 U.S. Motorcycle Grand Prix, Kevin Magee of Australia waved to the crowd as he circled the track in the traditional victory lap—then fell off his motorcycle, breaking his leg.

BAD ROAD TRIP

West Africa's annual Bandama Rally, a 2,500-mile cross-country race that pits the world's most elite car manufacturers against each other, made sports headlines in 1972. The route that year was so brutal that out of the 43 cars that started the race, only three remained at the two-thirds mark—with nearly 1,000 miles still to go. The other 40 cars had been knocked out by crashes, broken axles, and mechanical failures due to the rough terrain and high grass that often made it impossible for drivers to see the other cars. Then, as the three remaining cars set off to race the last 1,000 miles, a torrential rainstorm struck, turning the countryside into a mudpit of impassible roads. No one was able to finish and, for the first time in the race's history, no winner was declared.

* * *

REALLY, REALLY, *REALLY* ODD FADS

• In medieval England, wealthy gentlemen often wore clothing that left their genitals exposed. They wore short-fitting tunics with no pants. (If the genitals didn't hang low enough, padded, flesh-coated prosthetics called *briquettes* would be used.)

• In 16th-century Europe, tooth dyeing was popular among upper-class women. In Italy, red and green were the most popular colors, while Russian women favored black.

• Another 16th-century European beauty technique was called Solomon's Water. A primitive facelift, it was a lotion that eliminated spots, freckles, and warts. The number-one ingredient in Solomon's Water: mercury (which is now known to be toxic). It burned away the outer layers of the skin, corroded the flesh underneath, and could even cause teeth to fall out.

BEING ELVIS PRESLEY

Oddness seems to run deep in the world of Elvis impersonators.

HE HAS TOUPEE FOR HIS CRIME

A Welsh Elvis impersonator named Geraint Benney is receiving death threats from some of the King's most devoted fans. Why are they so mad? It's not because Benney, who goes by the stage name "Elvis Preseli," begins his performances by climbing out of a coffin. It's not because Benney doesn't sing Elvis songs (he performs pop hits from the 1980s and '90s as Elvis Presley *might* have...if he spoke Welsh). It's not even because Benney grills hamburgers while he performs. No, they want Benney dead because of his appearance. "Some think my act is disrespectful because I'm bald," he explains. Yet Benney's act is actually a big hit in Wales, and he has plans to take it on the road in Europe. And he refuses to wear a wig. "Elvis would be over 70 now," says Benney, "so he might even be bald himself."

TENERE ME, SUAVITER

A Latin professor from Finland named Jukka Ammondt moonlights as an Elvis impersonator, but he brings a little of his day job with him when he performs. Ammondt has translated several Elvis hits into Latin, and sings them in Finnish lounge clubs. Favorites include "It's Now or Never" ("*Nunc hic aut numquam*") and "Love Me Tender" ("*Tenere me, suaviter*"). A scholar of dead languages, Ammondt has also translated Presley hits into ancient Sumerian.

BUST ME TENDER

Although technically retired from his days as an Elvis imperson ator, 62-year-old Duke Adams still occasionally wears his Elvis outfit—complete with sideburns, black pompadour, gold medallions, and gold-framed glasses. In June 2005, Adams's wife of 21 years died, leaving him emotionally destitute. A few months later however, his life took a dramatic turn. Adams (dressed as Elvis) was leaving a Las Vegas pharmacy when a man he'd never met approached him and asked him if he wanted to buy some jewelry

Groucho Marx died on August 19, 1977...three days after Elvis Presley.

that once belonged to Elvis Presley. At first Adams said no, but something seemed suspicious about the man. And then it hit him: This could be the person who stole a bunch of Presley's jewelry and clothing from the Elvis-A-Rama Museum in 2004. That robbery left Adams as well as many other Elvis fans sad and angry—made even worse by the fact that the crook got away.

So Adams played it cool and told the man to stop by his employment agency office the next day with the goods. When the man agreed, Adams went home and called the police, who instructed him to call them immediately if the man showed up. Sure enough, he did, and he brought his entire Elvis collection with him—including gold necklaces, a gold watch, sequined shirts, a gold-plated revolver, and even Elvis's high-school ring. The price he wanted for everything: $80,000. Adams quietly called the cops, and then pretended to be interested until they arrived and arrested the man. Detective Kelli Hickle, who headed the investigation, gave Adams's police work rave reviews: "I know a lot of Elvis fans who are going to be happy. I heard from a lot of them, and they were heartbroken."

Adams was happy, too, crediting that incident with rejuvenating his crushed spirit. "I just believe my wife, God, and Elvis have got their hands in this. They set me up to do the right thing."

ELVIS HAS ENTERED THE ELECTION

In the 2000 mayoral election in Phillips, Wisconsin (pop. 1,600), there were two names on the ballot: Keith Corcilius...and Elvis Aron Presley. Inspired by the political career of former pro wrestler Jesse Ventura, a 50-year-old bar owner (real name unknown) who used to perform as an Elvis impersonator had his name legally changed to Elvis Aron Presley and then decided to run for mayor. "Ventura and I have a lot in common," "Presley" said. "He's a wrestler, and I'm a performer. We're both political outsiders. If the people of Minnesota can put a wrestler in the governor's office, I don't see what's wrong with people in Wisconsin electing an Elvis impersonator as mayor." The voters didn't agree: "Presley" lost.

Jets launched from aircraft carriers go from zero to 165 mph in two seconds.

DIDN'T SEE *THAT* COMING

Sometimes when you break into someone's apartment to steal some power tools, you end up with a bunch of human heads instead. Go figure.

THROUGH RAIN, SLEET, AND GRAVEYARDS

In 2006 Aurelia Cenusa of Severin, Romania, got a large package in the mail. Was it a present from a friend? Had she won a prize? No, it was her father's remains, exhumed from the grave he had inhabited for the last 16 years. The cemetery where he had been buried was sold, and the church that owned it mailed Ms. Cenusa the remains so that she could bury them somewhere else. "You could still even see bits of his funeral suit," she said, adding that she planned to sue the church.

IT'S JUST BATWASH

A 60-year-old woman from Woodbury County, Iowa, had been drinking from a mug of tea all day, when she got to the bottom of the cup…and found a dead bat in it. The woman—who asked to remain anonymous—put the bat in a plastic bag and took it to the health office in Sioux City. They sent it to a lab to test it for rabies which, fortunately, it didn't have. "We test many bats," said lab manager Mike Pentella, "but none that have drowned in a cup of tea before." The woman was said to be "recovering from shock."

YOU'RE UN-INVITED TO MY PARTY

Twenty-nine-year-old Jerry Rose of Jackson, Michigan, was at a party with some friends in the summer of 2006 when someone started a game of "What's the stupidest thing you ever did?" The room suddenly went silent when Rose answered, "I shot a guy in the head." For several months, police in the area had been looking for the killer of a 60-year-old man, and had no leads in the case until Rose's girlfriend, who was also at the party, told the cops about the confession. Rose was arrested and charged with murder.

It would take you more than 200 years to spend a night in every hotel room in Las Vegas.

SPEEDY DELIVERY

Barbara and Johann Meyer were speeding down a street in their hometown of Wachtberg, Germany, in 2006 when police officers pulled them over: A surveillance camera had taken an image of them speeding through an intersection. The Meyers explained that they were on their way to the hospital, where Barbara was about to give birth. Not only did the officers cancel the ticket, they gave the couple a baby present—a plastic toy policeman with a speed gun in its hand. They also gave the couple the photo from the surveillance camera, suggesting they put it in the baby's first photo album.

LET'S HEAD OUT

Thieves in Vienna, Austria, got a surprise when they broke into the basement of an apartment building looking for tools to steal... and found eight severed human heads. Police said a dentist who lived in the building was using the heads for "research," but they were looking into whether or not he had broken any laws. The thieves apparently ran away without stealing anything after they saw the heads.

CRASH, LITTLE BABY...

In 2006 a 17-year-old girl from Pleasanton, California, was driving home from the store with a doll she had just bought for a parenting class at her high school. The doll suddenly let out a loud—and apparently very realistic—baby cry, which so startled the girl that she drove into a pickup truck. The girl, who was uninjured, was charged with speeding and driving without a license. The doll, according to news reports, had cried out because it had "wet itself."

HE'S IN HOT WATER

One night in April 2005, family members in a home in Nara, Japan, were awakened by some strange noises coming from the bathroom. They investigated...and discovered a young man relaxing in their bathtub. He was drunk. And he was a policeman. The 21-year-old off-duty cop had walked into the wrong house (his was 50 yards away) after a party. Arrested and charged with unlawful entry, he told reporters, "I can't believe it wasn't my bathtub."

The Loch Ness monster is protected by the 1912 Protection of Animals Acts of Scotland.

BURNING IRONY

In April 2005, firefighters in Providence, Rhode Island, were on their way to a fire when the fire truck caught on fire. The fire started in the engine compartment, made its way through the firewall, and quickly entered the cab. Firefighters tried to put the fire out with fire extinguishers, but finally had to call another fire truck to help put the fire out. By the time help arrived, Engine 11 was completely burned. "This," said Captain Peter Celini, "is unusual."

*　　*　　*

RESCUED BY...

...SUPERMEN. In July 2006, the grandmother of one-year-old Jennifer Romero was pushing her granddaughter in a stroller, returning home from a grocery store in Oakland Park, Florida, when both were hit by a Ford van. Witnesses quickly realized that the baby was in trouble: She was still in her stroller—underneath the van, which had dragged her more than 80 yards. "We stopped traffic and got every big guy we could see," said Wayne Ackerman, a bystander who stepped in to help. Six men then worked together to lift the front of the van off the ground, allowing the child to be pulled out from under it. Amazingly, the baby was uninjured; her grandmother suffered minor fractures.

...COINCIDENCE. In June 2006, Barry Glinton and three friends were about a mile off the coast of Florida near West Palm Beach when a large wave crested their powerboat and it started taking on water. Glinton called the Coast Guard on his cell phone—he didn't have a GPS system—and rescuers were able to locate him visually within an hour only because it was a clear day. On the way back to land, Coast Guard Lt. John Reed commented that he had rescued a boater in a similar situation in the very same spot a year earlier. Glinton said, "That was me." The officer didn't find the coincidence funny. "This gentleman got very lucky twice," Officer Alber said, "but it doesn't look like he learned his lesson about boating safety."

SUPER POWERS

People with unusual abilities have been reported and described throughout history. Are they real? Who knows?

• Rosa Kuleshova grew up sighted in a family of blind people in the Soviet Union in the 1960s. She wanted to know what it was like to be blind, so she started wearing a blindfold and eventually taught herself to "see" with her fingers. According to Kuleshova, she could actually "feel" colors: yellow is slippery, violet makes the fingers stop moving, and red is sticky. Because she could differentiate between white and black she also claimed she could read newspapers and sheet music while blindfolded.

• Working as a beacon keeper on the island of Mauritius in the 18th century, Etienne Bottineau claimed he could feel subtle changes in the air and atmosphere, and "sense" ships before they appeared on the horizon. Once tested in the 1760s, Bottineau accurately predicted 109 out of 111 ships before they arrived. The two he missed had changed course after he'd sensed them.

• Jacques Aymar, who lived in France in the 1600s, had a gift for divining. One time he was dowsing for water and found a human head. He took his divining rod to the home of the dead woman and it pointed at her husband, the killer. Aymar went on to find dozens of criminals. His rod would guide him to a criminal and Aymar's symptoms—sweating and passing out—told him that he had found the culprit.

• A rabbi in Lithuania in the early 20th century known only as "Rabbi Elijah" could retain and recite every word of every book that he had ever read. Elijah considered his ability to be a curse, with the complete texts of the 2,000 books he'd read in his lifetime flooding his brain and making it hard for him to concentrate.

• Benedetto Supino was 10 years old when he discovered he could set things ablaze by staring at them. In a dentist's office in Formia, Italy, in 1982, the comic book he was reading suddenly ignited. Another day, he awoke when his bed was on fire because his pajamas were burning. Soon after, an uncle tested Supino's abilities. He held a plastic toy in his hands. Supino stared at it and it ignited.

Hey, Bugs! The back end of a bunny is called its *fud*.

WEIRD HOTELS

Part of the fun of travel is enjoying the local flavor. So on your next trip, eat the local food, see the local sights...and stay in a tiny underwater motel.

HOTEL: Hotell Hackspett

LOCATION: Vasteras, Sweden

DESCRIPTION: One of the tiniest hotels in the world, the Hackspett (Swedish for "woodpecker") accommodates just one person, or a couple if they don't mind sharing a twin bed. But what really makes the Woodpecker different is that it's a tree house situated 30 feet above a city park. It's accessible only by rope ladder. Meals are delivered with a basket and pulley. Despite its size, the hotel room includes a kitchen, a veranda, and a toilet.

HOTEL: Hotel Filosoof

LOCATION: Amsterdam, The Netherlands

DESCRIPTION: Each of this 19th-century hotel's 38 rooms is dedicated to a different philosopher or philosophy. So, depending on your mood or your level of enlightenment, you can choose a Nietzsche, Marx, Aristotle, Wittgenstein, or Zen room. Each is decorated with appropriate sculptures, murals, and quotations. Breakfast is served in the morning on a place mat covered in quotations by the philosopher of your choice. Bad joke: If the hotel is full, you're out of luck—you Kant stay there.

HOTEL: The Old Jail

LOCATION: Mount Gambier, Australia

DESCRIPTION: The Old Jail offers the accommodations—and decidedly spooky atmosphere—of a huge, 19th-century rural prison. The hotel was once the South Australian State Prison, which operated from 1866 to 1995. Not much changed when it was converted into a hotel. Showers are still communal and beds are still cots, but the cell doors can now be opened from the inside. "Inmates" sleep four to a cell (either with strangers or family) or can pay double for a private, two-person suite.

If you set fire to your house in Jackson, Mississippi, by law you must first remove the roof.

HOTEL: Dog Bark Park Inn
LOCATION: Cottonwood, Idaho
DESCRIPTION: It would be odd to sleep on your back on top of a doghouse, like Snoopy, but it's odder still to sleep *inside* the dog. The Dog Bark is a two-story wooden dog. It was built and is managed by a husband and wife team of chainsaw artists who invested the money they made selling dog-shaped wood carvings on QVC into building a dog-themed hotel. (And, yes, dogs are welcome.)

HOTEL: Hemp Hotel
LOCATION: Amsterdam, The Netherlands
DESCRIPTION: Nearly everything in this five-room hotel is made out of hemp, a plant with a wide variety of commercial uses that's often confused with its controversial cousin, marijuana. Mattresses, curtains, shampoo, soap, and even breakfast in this hotel are all made from hemp. Guests can choose from five themed rooms: Afghan, Moroccan, Caribbean, Indian, and Tibetan.

HOTEL: Utter Inn
LOCATION: Lake Malaren, Sweden
DESCRIPTION: Literally "Otter Inn," the hotel was conceived as a modern art project by artist Mikael Genberg. Guests enter through a cottage floating on the surface of Lake Malaren then descend 10 feet into an underwater "reverse aquarium," where the room is dry—but surrounded by water and fish that are visible through wall-to-wall picture windows.

HOTEL: Kakslauttanen Hotel and Igloo Village
LOCATION: Nordkap, Finland
DESCRIPTION: Guests get to sleep in real igloos made of ice and snow blocks. They are completely dark and the only source of heat are the down sleeping bags. (The less adventurous can sleep in heated glass igloos.) Facilities also include an ice-cold swimming pool, the world's largest smoke sauna, and the world's largest restaurant made of snow, which has to be rebuilt every winter.

Tibetan mating ritual: A man steals a woman's hat; if she likes him, she asks for it back.

LEADING LEDES

When we're done with the comics, the obituaries, the advice columns, the horoscopes, and the puzzles, sometimes we actually read the news. Well, maybe not all of it...

BACKGROUND

A *lede* (pronounced "leed") is the first sentence of a news story that gives the "who, what, where, when, why, and how" that will be fleshed out in the article. And as these real news ledes show, sometimes you don't have to read any further.

"Bogota, Colombia's chief prosecutor hired a psychic who hypnotized his staff and performed an exorcism over a voodoo doll in exchange for a government paycheck and use of an armored car." (*Sun-Sentinel*, South Florida)

"'E' is for embarrassed—like the teacher who inadvertently used a kinky alphabet in a handout to parents." (*Times Herald-Record*, Middletown, New York)

"Mayor Don Wright has raised eyebrows in town by allowing the makers of 'Thong Girl 3' to film in his office on a Sunday." (*News Examiner*, Gallatin, Tennessee)

"A 38-year-old Winthrop, Ark. man was hospitalized after jumping out the passenger window of a vehicle traveling an estimated 55 to 60 m.p.h. to retrieve his cigarette late Saturday, an official said." (*Texarkana Gazette*)

"The Las Vegas man whose severed fingertip ended up in a cup of Wendy's chili gave his mangled digit to a co-worker to settle a $50 debt—but had no idea it would be used in an alleged scheme to swindle the fast-food chain, the man's mother said Tuesday." (*San Francisco Chronicle*)

"A U.S. court has apparently ended the television career of a talking penis." (ABC News)

The tentacles of the giant Arctic jellyfish can reach 120 feet in length.

"Fortunately for Ezekiel Rubottom, there's no law against keeping your severed foot in a bucket on the front porch." (*Lawrence Journal World*, Kansas)

"Police went to a home in Texarkana after receiving a report that a man had entered it illegally and later found their suspect running nude through a pasture." (Tampabays10.com)

"Gambling is the only thing missing from a new Indian casino in Michigan's Upper Peninsula, mistakenly built in an area where gambling is illegal." (Yahoo! News)

"A Kentucky man wearing only a thong and carrying a knife is accused of videotaping himself attempting a burglary, then leaving the tape behind, police said." (*Herald Leader*, Lexington. Kentucky)

"A dispute that began over the capture of an opossum in a residential neighborhood ended with police shooting a Rottweiler and arresting a man after stunning him with a Taser gun." (*Independent Record*, Helena, Montana)

"A high school student convicted of battery for vomiting on his Spanish teacher has been ordered to spend the next four months cleaning up after people who throw up in police cars." (MSNBC)

"The chairman of the publicly funded Canadian Broadcasting Corp. has resigned after remarks about bestiality and ruminations about defecation, Canadian Heritage Minister Bev Oda said on Tuesday." (Reuters)

"Anti-drug campaigners today attacked the makers of a soft drink who have called their product 'Cocaine.'" (*Daily Mail*, London, England)

"Police are investigating a 'bizarre' incident in which a man claiming he was performing a religious ritual kissed a woman's feet Monday afternoon at the Perry Wal-Mart." (*Macon Telegraph*, Macon, Georgia)

WEIRD INDIA

This country was once considered very exotic, but it's one of the most quickly modernizing countries in the world. That includes the silly stuff, too.

IT COSTS AN ARM AND A LEG

In July 2006, India's Medical Association started investigating three doctors who had appeared in television advertisements to promote voluntary amputation surgery to beggars. In India, street beggars can earn more money by eliciting sympathy for missing appendages. The more missing appendages, the more they earn. The doctors charged fees of about $200 for the "investment" of removing a leg below the knee.

THE NITTY GRITTY

Ram Rati, 80, of Chinar, attributes her longevity and good health to eating sand. Rati estimates she eats about four pounds every day, splitting it among breakfast, lunch, and afternoon tea. "When young, I tried it for fun once. Now, I am used to it. My relatives pestered me to quit it, but it was all in vain."

LOVE HURTS

A man needed to ask his wife to agree to a divorce—he wanted to marry his mistress. The wife consented to end the marriage, but on one condition: that she could beat him up in public. The man agreed and a few days later his wife administered the beating in the middle of town. Satisfied, she signed the divorce papers.

DOGGERCISE

Hritik, a three-year-old German Shepherd from Ranchi, gets plenty of exercise. He doesn't chase Frisbees or go for walks—he does yoga. Under the supervision of his trainer, Nanda Dulal, he has learned several different yoga positions and exercises. "He was weak when he was born," says Dulal. "But we took special care of him and he gradually became strong after his yoga lessons." (According to Dulal, Hritik has also voluntarily become a vegetarian.)

The tall wigs worn by British judges are called *perukes*.

HEY, I RECOGNIZE THAT BUTT CRACK!

Well, I do. What do you want me to say?

In November, 1997, Minneapolis native Tom Tipton, 63, got the thrill of his life when he was invited to sing the national anthem before a Minnesota Vikings football game. Across town, an off-duty sheriff was watching the pregame show—and recognized Tipton's name. Tipton, it turned out, was wanted on two warrants in Minneapolis. He was arrested during the game.

• In 2006 a man in Mill Valley, California, was arrested after he called a bomb threat into a Walgreen's pharmacy. The clerk who answered the phone recognized his voice: The man had just been at the counter to get a prescription filled, and had called in the threat because he thought it was taking too long.

• In 2001 Chicago police arrested 19-year-old Marque Love on bank robbery charges. Love had once worked at the bank, and a teller recognized him—by his distinctive blue suede shoes.

• In 2006 Robert Russel Moore of Prince Frederick, Maryland, was arrested and charged with the robbery of an Arby's restaurant where he was recently employed. At the subsequent trial, four of his former fellow employees testified that, although he was wearing a mask, they recognized Moore in surveillance tapes—especially when he bent over and they recognized his "butt crack" above the top of his pants. A former manager also testified that he had talked to Moore repeatedly about his "butt crack problem." Moore was sentenced to 10 years in prison.

• In 1999 a man wearing a long dark coat and a mask walked into the Royal Casino in Aberdeen, South Dakota, pointed a gun at the clerk, and demanded money. The next day, local man Jerold Nissen, 44, was arrested for the crime. Nissen was a regular at the casino, and the clerk had recognized the distinctively powerful odor of his cologne. He was sentenced to seven years in prison.

Brazilians commonly ask visitors if they would like to shower before a meal.

FATAL FALLOUT

Hollywood mourned when John Wayne passed away in 1979 after a 15-year battle with cancer. Most people blamed the illness on his smoking, but others now think his death may have been caused by something else: radiation exposure on the set of the 1956 movie The Conqueror.

DISASTER IN THE MAKING

From the start, *The Conqueror* was a doomed movie. Produced by financier Howard Hughes, it starred John Wayne as Mongolian ruler Genghis Khan, who lusted for an empire and the beautiful Tartar princess Bortai (Susan Hayward). Wayne hadn't been director Dick Powell's first choice to play Khan; he'd wanted Marlon Brando. But Wayne saw an advance copy of the script and told Hughes that he wanted the part. Over Powell's objections, Hughes made sure that Wayne got it.

It turned out to be a legendary casting mistake. Before production began, Wayne said, "The way the screenplay reads, it is a cowboy picture, and that is how I am going to portray Genghis Khan. I see him as a gunfighter." But when the film was released, critics hated Wayne's performance; one called it the "most improbable piece of casting unless Mickey Rooney were to play Jesus in *The King of Kings*." The film flopped at the box office.

EXPOSURE

But *The Conqueror*'s box office woes only set the stage for a more serious problem. The movie had been shot near St. George, Utah, a perfect stand-in for the Gobi Desert. But St. George had another distinction: In 1953, two years before the film was made, the U.S. government had detonated 11 atomic bombs at Yucca Flat, Nevada, 150 miles away. The prevailing winds had carried pink radioactive clouds and dust over Utah, much of it settling on St. George and other downwind communities. Today scientists estimate that in Utah alone, 40,000 citizens were exposed to high dosages of radiation from the toxic fallout.

In 1955 the cast and crew arrived to shoot *The Conqueror* just outside St. George, unaware that the 13-week shooting schedule might expose them to contaminated soil and dust. They were aware

Bill Murray was considered for the role of *Forrest Gump*.

of the radiation, but no one thought of it as a danger; the testing had taken place two years earlier, and the long-term effects of radioactive fallout weren't well understood at the time. Publicity photos even showed John Wayne whimsically holding a Geiger counter.

To make matters worse, when the crew returned to Hollywood to finish production, Hughes shipped 60 tons of the Utah soil back to the studios to use in interior shots and retakes so the dirt would match the location shots. So the stars continued to work with the radioactive soil even after they returned to California.

DEADLY NUMBERS

In 1963, eight years after filming wrapped, director Dick Powell died of lymphatic cancer. That same year, *Conqueror* actor Pedro Armendáriz developed kidney cancer and shot himself when he learned his condition was terminal. By 1964 Wayne had developed lung cancer (attributed to his heavy smoking) and had his left lung removed. Ten years later, some were beginning to see a pattern: Before her death from uterine cancer, cast member Agnes Moorehead loudly and publicly claimed that the radiation exposure on the set of *The Conqueror* had caused her illness. Susan Hayward succumbed in 1975 to brain and skin cancer. And John Wayne, after his 1964 diagnosis, had battled frequent recurrences. In January 1979, the cancer had spread to his stomach and lymph nodes. He died six months later.

By 1980, 91 of the 220 people who had worked on *The Conqueror* had developed cancer; 46 had died from it. Under normal circumstances, only about 13% of a group that size would have had cancer; of *The Conqueror's* cast and crew, 41% were afflicted.

For years, the U.S. government denied the connection between nuclear testing and cancer. But the cancer statistics for the small town of St. George were hard to ignore: More than half of its 5,000 citizens fell ill. For almost 40 years, St. George residents and those in other "downwinder" communities fought to make the U.S. government formally recognize the damage from the Yucca Flat testing. In 1990 they met with some success when the Radiation Exposure Compensation Act was passed; residents exposed to the radiation were awarded $50,000 each. But the link between the fallout and the deaths among the *Conqueror* crew was never officially proven.

Ten different horses played the title role in *Seabiscuit* (2003).

UNIQUE MUSEUMS OF TEXAS

Texas is a big state, so it only figures that there'd be some weird stuff in there somewhere. Here are some of the strangest museums in the Lone Star State.

BUCKHORN HALL OF HORNS (San Antonio)

In 1881 Albert Friedrich opened the Buckhorn Saloon in San Antonio, decorating the bar with his collection of animal horns and antlers. His customers were mostly hunters and trappers often short on cash, so Friedrich accepted horns and antlers in exchange for beer. The collection grew to include hundreds of items and was eventually acquired by the Lone Star Brewery, which moved it to a separate facility. It's recently been expanded, and now takes up three large halls: the Buckhorn Hall of Horns, the Buckhorn Hall of Fins, and the Buckhorn Hall of Feathers.

U.S. ARMY MEDICAL DEPARTMENT MUSEUM (Fort Sam Houston)

As part of a military doctor training academy, this museum is dedicated solely to one grisly aspect of history: army medicine. In addition to uniforms and photographs from the American Revolution, Civil War, and both World Wars, there are also numerous horrifying, obsolete medical contraptions used on the battlefield, including rusty old bone saws and bullets with teeth marks in them (used by soldiers to bite on when having a limb removed with the rusty old bone saw).

DUTCH WINDMILL MUSEUM (Nederland)

Nederland was founded by Dutch settlers in 1898 (who named it after their homeland), so it makes sense that the area would have a museum honoring one of the Netherlands' most enduring icons—the Dutch windmill. The museum itself is a 49-foot-tall windmill, filled with Dutch memorabilia (including an old wooden trunk and many pairs of wooden shoes) and Dutch historical exhibits. Nederland isn't that big of a city (population: 17,000), so the

Dallas/Ft. Worth Airport is larger than New York City's Manhattan Island.

museum does double duty as a museum honoring 1940s singing-cowboy movie star Tex Ritter, who was born there.

HERTZBERG CIRCUS MUSEUM (San Antonio)

Lawyer Larry Hertzberg donated his huge collection of circus memorabilia—one of the largest on Earth and dating back hundreds of years—to the San Antonio Library in 1940. Its curiosities range from posters and handbills to memorabilia from Buffalo Bill's Wild West Show. There's even a full-scale 1920s circus tent. The museum has many non-circus related exhibits as well: Strangest is a collection of 15,000 rare books, including a 1614 first edition of Sir Walter Raleigh's *History of the World.*

ARTCAR MUSEUM (Houston)

Nicknamed the "Garage Mahal," the museum opened in 1998 to show off cars from around the world that had been painted, altered, or transformed to look like other things. To satirize America's car-crazy culture, the museum's artists in residence exhibit their bizarre works, including a car that looks like a cockroach, a car that looks like a red stiletto high-heeled shoe, a car that looks like a giant, evil Easter bunny, a car that looks like an armadillo, and a car made out of wood.

NATIONAL MUSEUM OF FUNERAL HISTORY (Houston)

With all of its coffins, hearses, and pictures of dead people, the National Museum of Funeral History would be a bad choice for a first date. Nevertheless, the museum treats the subject of death (which it calls "one of our most important cultural rituals") seriously and respectfully. All aspects of Western funeral customs are covered. There are dozens of hearses, including one that's gold-plated, as well as a 1916 "funeral bus," which transported the body along with pallbearers and mourners. Other displays: a graphic demonstration of how embalming works, and replicas of the coffins Abraham Lincoln, John F. Kennedy, and King Tut were buried in. Make sure to stop by the gift shop and pick up a coffin-shaped golf putter, a chocolate bar in a tiny casket, or a charm necklace with coffin charms. And if you *really* enjoy your visit, you can enroll in the museum's Undertakers University—a funeral director training program.

The long-lost *Venus de Milo* statue was discovered by a Greek farmer in his field in 1820.

THE STRANGEST DISASTER OF THE 20TH CENTURY, PT. I

Here's the story of how scientists unlocked the secrets of the worst natural disaster in the history of the west African nation of Cameroon ...and what they're doing to try and stop it from happening again.

THE DISCOVERY

On the morning of August 22, 1986, a man hopped onto his bicycle and began riding from Wum, a village in Cameroon, toward the village of Nyos. On the way he noticed an antelope lying dead next to the road. Why let it go to waste? The man tied the antelope onto his bicycle and continued on. A short distance later he noticed two dead rats, and further on, a dead dog and other dead animals. He wondered if they'd all been killed by a lightning strike—when lightning hits the ground it's not unusual for animals nearby to be killed by the shock.

Soon the man came upon a group of huts. He decided to see if anyone there knew what had happened to the animals. But as he walked up to the huts he was stunned to see dead bodies strewn everywhere. He didn't find a single person still alive—everyone in the huts was dead. The man threw down his bicycle and ran all the way back to Wum.

SOMETHING BIG

By the time the man got back to the village, the first survivors of whatever it was that had struck Nyos and other nearby villages were already stumbling into Wum. Many told tales of hearing an explosion or a rumbling noise in the distance, then smelling strange smells and passing out for as long as 36 hours before waking up to discover that everyone around them was dead.

Wum is in a remote part of Cameroon, so it took two days for a medical team to arrive in the area after local officials called the governor to report the strange occurrence. The doctors found a catastrophe far greater than they could have imagined: Overnight, something had killed nearly 1,800 people, plus more than 3,000 cattle and countless wild animals, birds, and insects—in short, every living creature for miles around.

The official death toll was recorded as 1,746 people, but that was only an estimate, because the survivors had already begun to bury victims in mass graves, and many terrified survivors had fled corpse-filled villages and were hiding in the forest. Whatever it was that killed so many people seemed to have disappeared without a trace just as quickly as it had come.

LOOKING FOR CLUES

What could have caused so many deaths in such a short span of time? When word of the disaster reached the outside world, scientists from France (Cameroon is a former French colony), the United States, and other countries arrived to help the country's own scientists figure out what had happened. The remains of the victims offered few clues. There was no evidence of bleeding, physical trauma, or disease, and no sign of exposure to radiation, chemical weapons, or poison gas. And there was no evidence of suffering or "death agony": The victims apparently just blacked out, fell over, and died.

One of the first important clues was the distribution of the victims across the landscape: The deaths had all occurred within about 12 miles of Lake Nyos, which some local tribes called the "bad lake." Legend had that that long ago, evil spirits had risen out of the lake and killed all the people living in a village at the water's edge.

Both the number of victims and the percentage of fatalities increased as the scientists got closer to the lake: In the outlying villages many people, especially those who had remained inside their homes, had survived, while in Nyos, which at less than two miles away was the closest village to the lake, only 6 of more than 800 villagers were still alive.

But it was the lake itself that provided the biggest and strangest clue of all: its normally clear blue waters had turned a deep, murky red. The scientists began to wonder if there was more to the legend of the "bad lake" than anyone had realized.

STILL LIFE

Lake Nyos is roughly one square mile in surface area and has a

You know that little membrane under your tongue? It's your *frenulum*.

maximum depth of 690 feet. It's what's known as a "crater lake"—it formed when the crater of a long-extinct volcano filled with water. But was the volcano really extinct? Maybe an eruption was the culprit: Maybe the volcano beneath the lake had come back to life and in the process suddenly released enough poison gases to kill every living creature over a very wide area.

The theory was compelling but problematic: An eruption capable of releasing enough poison gas to kill that many people over that wide an area would have been very violent and accompanied by plenty of seismic activity. None of the eyewitnesses had mentioned earthquakes, and when the scientists checked with a seismic recording station 140 miles away, it showed no evidence of unusual activity on the evening of August 21. This was backed up by the fact that even in the hardest-hit villages, goods were still piled high on shelves in homes where every member of the household been killed. And the scientists noticed another mysterious clue: The oil lamps in these homes had all been extinguished, even the ones still filled with plenty of oil.

TESTING THE WATERS

The scientists began to test water samples taken from various depths in the lake. The red on the surface turned out to be dissolved iron—normally found on the bottom of the lake, not the top. Somehow the sediment at the bottom had been stirred up and the iron brought to the surface, where it turned the color of rust after coming into contact with oxygen.

The scientists also discovered unusually high levels of carbon dioxide (CO_2) dissolved or "in solution" in the water. Samples from as shallow as 50 feet deep contained so much CO_2 that when they were pulled to the surface, where the water pressure was lower, the dissolved CO_2 came bubbling out of solution—just as if someone had unscrewed the cap on a bottle of soda.

Plop, plop, fizz, fizz.
Oh, what an odd tale this is!
Part II of the story is on page 287.

MY PET FAT

And other people who put the "o-d-d" in diet.

PLAN: The *Warcraft* Diet
LOST: 41 pounds
STORY: *Joystiq* magazine reported in 2006 that one of its readers, identified only as "Greg," gained a lot of weight and was up to 274 pounds because he spent so much time playing the popular video game, *World of Warcraft*. So he attached a keyboard to a stationary bike, put the bike next to a small table so he could operate the mouse, and hung a 46-inch LCD screen in front of it. Over the next three months of biking and playing his favorite game he was able to lose 41 pounds. "There is no way I could have done that without *Warcraft*," he said.

PLAN: The Fake Flat-Glob Diet
LOST: 115 pounds
STORY: Jacobs's weight was up to 380 pounds in 2002 when he happened to see a plastic model of one pound of human fat. Jacobs decided right then and there that he was going to carry that fake glob of fat wherever he went to remind himself to make good choices regarding diet and exercise. Two years later he was down to 245 pounds, and he started MyPetFat.com, offering advice, motivational tools, and one-ounce, one-pound, and five-pound globs of fake fat to anyone else who was interested in losing weight. His motto: "Fat, it's all in my head."

PLAN: The Hibernation Diet
LOST: 25 pounds
STORY: This one wasn't actually planned. In October 2006, Mitsutaka Uchikoshi was hiking on Mt. Rokko in western Japan when he fell and broke his pelvis. When he was found—after 24 days—he was emaciated, his body temperature was 71 degrees, and he barely had a pulse. Doctors said his organs, including his brain, had gone into a "hibernationlike state" and, amazingly, he was fine. Uchikoshi was released from the hospital in December, and doctors said they expected a 100% recovery.

ECCENTRIC ARTISTS

There's a fine line between genius and insanity. These people walk it.

• American painter **James Whistler** believed that art should concentrate on the proper arrangement of colors, not on realism. Putting that theory to work, he once dyed a dish of rice pudding green so it would better match the green walls of his dining room.

• Nineteenth-century French poet **Gerard de Nerval** kept a pet lobster. He liked to take it on walks around Paris on a leash made out of ribbon. Nerval later defended his choice of pet, saying, "He was quiet and serious, knew the secrets of the sea, and did not bark."

• German composer **Gustav Mahler** was obsessed with death from a young age, and wrote his first funeral dirge at the age of six. Decades later and well into his career, he noticed that Schubert, Beethoven, and many other composers had only lived long enough to compose nine symphonies. Mahler concluded it was unlucky to write more than eight, so he called his ninth symphony "A Song Cycle" instead of a symphony. It didn't work. Just after completing the "cycle," Mahler died of strep throat at age 50.

• Another German composer, **Robert Schumann,** claimed he got all of his musical ideas from two imaginary musicians named Eusebius and Florestan.

• When she was a child, *Little Women* author **Louisa May Alcott** developed an intense crush on her neighbor, author Ralph Waldo Emerson. She wrote dozens of love letters to him, but never sent them. Instead, she sat in a tall walnut tree outside of his house in the middle of the night, singing.

• Animal instincts: **Robert Louis Stevenson** had a hobby of reading the Bible out loud to sheep. Irish poet **William Butler Yeats** liked to try to hypnotize hens.

• **Charles Dickens** is said to have walked 20 miles every day. He also always arranged his bed so it faced north-south, and he liked to touch objects three times for good luck.

Canadian performer with the most celebrity impersonators: Shania Twain.

• Many artists have a series of rituals they go through to get inspired. Eighteenth-century German poet **Friedrich von Schiller** could write only with his feet resting on a block of ice. He also needed to inhale the fumes given off by rotting apples.

• Poet **Gertrude Stein** could write only while seated in the driver's seat of her Ford, which she nicknamed "Godiva." And she wrote only on random scraps of paper she'd found.

• To relax after he finished *Gulliver's Travels* in 1724, **Jonathan Swift** wrote a book called *Human Ordure*. The book, a thorough exploration and appreciation of poop, was published under the pen name "Dr. Sh*t."

• French author **Alexandre Dumas** (*The Count of Monte Cristo*) started every day the same way: He ate an apple at 7 a.m. under the Arc de Triomphe.

• When American novelist **Anne Rivers Siddons** (*Peachtree Road*) is ready to start writing a new novel, she reportedly gets in the mood by surrounding herself with a nest made of papers. Then she walks into walls, as if in a trance.

• **Henry David Thoreau** claimed that he could talk to forest creatures. "I talked to the woodchuck in quasi forest lingo, baby talk, at any rate in a conciliatory tone, and thought that I had some influence on him," he once wrote.

* * *

TWO PEEBLES IN A POD

Darryl R. Peebles, a minister in Graham, North Carolina, typed his name into an Internet search engine in 2005 to see if anyone in the world shared his name. He found one: Daryl R. Peebles of Tasmania, Australia. The American Peebles wrote to the Australian Peebles and the two struck up a correspondence, uncovering many bizarre similarities. Both were born in 1949, both have three children, both have children who were born in 1975 and 1977, and both enjoy magic and ventriloquism.

Chickens can't swallow while they are upside down.

NOW THAT YOU'RE DEAD

Apparently, being dead is not the end of the world. In some cultures a dead body can have a full life even if it isn't full of life. For instance, you might be dead, but you can still be...

...MARRIED

In the rural village of Chenjiayuan, China, the local Confucian-based religion holds that a man will have an unhappy afterlife if he dies as a bachelor. Solution: *minghun*, or "afterlife marriage." The bachelor's grieving parents seek out the parents of a young dead women who died unattached. The two are then married in an official ceremony.

...A SOUP

In the Chinese province of Zhejiang in 2003, ancient skeletons were discovered in a cave that was excavated during the construction of a tourist resort. The discovery revived an ancient lost custom that locals had followed for thousands of years: "ghost soup." According to the tradition, the bones of long-dead female corpses were boiled down to a stock to make a soup, which was then taken as medicine, believed to cure a wide range of ailments.

...THE LIFE OF THE PARTY

The Malagasy ethnic group in Madagascar has a custom that requires the dead to be dug up every five to seven years, dressed in fancy clothes, and given a massive, days-long party with food, drinks, and music. The body is then reburied, where it quietly waits for its next shindig.

...DOING SHAKESPEARE

Del Close, a theater producer and comedian, died in 1999 at the age of 64. He'd once played Polonius in *Hamlet*, but the part he really wanted was Yorick—the dead man whose skull Hamlet holds up in memory. So, he stipulated in his will that his body be cremated and his skull preserved and given to the Goodman Theatre in Chicago for a future production of *Hamlet*, with a credit in the program listing Yorick "played" by Del Close.

World record: Al Gliniecki tied 39 cherry stems into knots in three minutes using his tongue.

INSECT ODDITIES

What in the hellgrammite are those things?!!

HELLGRAMMITES

Hellgrammites are aquatic insects in North and Central America that look like centipedes with beetles' heads, fronted by two scary-looking pincers. They can grow up to four inches long and are very aggressive—they attack, tear apart, and eat other insects in the water (or out; they get around fine on land, too). They feed for one specific purpose: After two to five years, they crawl into a muddy spot by a stream or lake shore and form a cocoon, in which they will spend one winter. In the spring they emerge as the equally scary-looking Dobsonfly, a stick-like creature with four long, lacy wings. But the most noticeable thing about them are their huge jaws. A male's mandibles (pincers) are about half the length of its two-inch-long body, and are not used for eating—they are used only to grasp a female in order to mate with her. After all that time as a hellgrammite, they live only a few days, mate, and die. Extra: The Dobsonfly's jaws are of no use for fighting, either, so they have a special defense system: When attacked, they release a foul-smelling spray from their rear ends to scare the predator away.

CATERPILLAGE

Insect experts in Hawaii discovered a new species of caterpillar in 2005. *Hyposmocoma molluscivora*, or "flesh-eating caterpillars," as they are unofficially known, are tiny, only about a third of an inch long, and they use their silk to capture prey and eat it alive. This species is strictly a carnivore, eating no vegetation at all, a characteristic shared by only about 200 of the 150,000 known species of caterpillar—and it's the only one that eats snails. They crawl along branches, disguised by a silk casing that they carry along with them, littered with leaves and other detritus. When they come upon a snail, they approach it very slowly; sensing danger, the snails will either attach themselves to a leaf or simply fall to the ground to thwart a predator. But if the snail is too slow, the flesh-eater weaves its silk and attaches the snail to the leaf. The

The McDonald's "golden arches" can be identified by more people on Earth than the Christian cross.

caterpillar then corners the snail as it inevitably retreats deep into its shell...and eats it alive. Then the caterpillar takes pieces of the snail's shell and attaches it to its silk casing, either as camouflage, or, who knows—maybe as souvenirs.

TERMINAL TERMITES

In 1999 researchers at Boston University discovered that Dampwood termites send "seismic signals" to their colonies when danger is present—even though sending the signals rather than fleeing the danger means they'll die. The researchers built an artificial two-part termite nest from plexiglass, with the two parts separated by mesh the bugs couldn't penetrate. Then they introduced *Metahizium anisopliae*, a fungus whose spores are lethal to the termites, to one side of the nest. The researchers watched as the termites on the infected side started doing a shaking "dance," thrusting their bodies forward and backward, up and down (the motion was proven to not be convulsions from the poisonous fungus spores). The termites in the other side of the nest, sensing the vibrations caused by the shaking, fled the nest completely within an hour. And the ones doing the shaking? "We thought the ones at risk might flee themselves," said lead researcher James Traniello. "But they didn't. They continued to communicate, which we think is another example of self-sacrificing behavior in social insects."

BIG-BUTT ANTS

Okay, we confess: We just liked the name. But they earn a spot on our odd-insect list because they're on the menu in restaurants in some parts of the world. *Hormiga culona*, the scientific name for these South American insects which means "big-bottomed ant" (honestly), can grow to an inch long, and, not surprisingly, the rear section of their bodies is oddly large. They've been eaten in Colombia for centuries, roasted in salt and eaten as a snack, and also mashed into a spread for toast. Recently they've become a global phenomenon, and are sold as an expensive delicacy in France and England. They're said to taste like buttered popcorn.

Ancient Greeks believed that onions were an aphrodisiac.

THE REAL STORY OF MURPHY'S LAW

The amazing thing about Murphy's Law is that it's true. In other words, whatever can go wrong, actually will go wrong. Scientific experiments have proven it. For example, if we weren't careful, this paragraph might get printed backward. Boy, wouldn't that be embarrassing? Well...it could happen. Here's why.

HISTORY

The sentiment expressed in Murphy's Law, "Anything that can go wrong, will go wrong," has probably been around as long as there have been things to go wrong. In 1786, for example, Scottish poet Robert Burns wrote, "The best laid schemes o' mice an men gang aft agley [are prone to go awry]."

But the "official" Murphy's Law is much more recent. In fact, it's barely 50 years old.

HOT SEAT

In 1949 the U.S. Air Force conducted a series of tests on the effect of rapid deceleration on pilots, so they could get a better understanding of how much force people's bodies can tolerate in a plane crash. The tests, part of what was known as Project MX981, consisted of strapping volunteers into a rocket-propelled sled, accelerating the sled, and then slamming on the brakes—bringing the sled to a very abrupt stop. The volunteers wore a special harness fitted with 16 sensors that measured the acceleration, or G-forces, on different parts of the body.

The harness was the invention of an Air Force captain named Edward A. Murphy...but the 16 individual sensors were installed by someone else.

BRAKE DOWN

On the day of the fateful test, a volunteer named John Paul Stapp was strapped into the sled and the rockets were fired. The test went off as expected—the sled accelerated to a high speed and

Fat increase: In 1970 Americans spent $6 billion on fast food; in 2001, they spent $110 billion.

then abruptly braked to a stop, subjecting his body to such enormous forces that, according to one account, when he stumbled off the sled, his eyes were bloodshot and his nose was bleeding. Stapp's body is believed to have endured forces equivalent to 40 Gs, or 40 times the force of gravity. But no one will ever know for sure, because all 16 of the sensors failed, each one giving a zero reading for the test.

When Murphy examined the harness to see what had gone wrong, he discovered that the technician who had installed the sensors had wired every single one of them backward. Because of a simple human error, Stapp's life had been put at risk in vain.

There are varying accounts of what Murphy said next—he may have cursed out the technician responsible for the mistake, saying, "If there is any way to do it wrong, he'll find it." Whatever he said originally, at a press conference a few days later Stapp quoted him as having said, "If there are two or more ways to do something and one of those results in a catastrophe, then someone will do it that way."

Within months, this expression became known throughout the aerospace industry and military as "Murphy's Law."

FIRST VICTIM

Murphy's Law might never have become known beyond the participants of Project MX981 had it not been a very sound design and engineering principle. The sensors in Murphy's harness failed not just because they had been installed backward, but also because they were *capable* of being installed backward. Had they been designed so they could not be installed in the incorrect way, they would never have failed in the first place.

A few days later, Murphy himself redesigned the sensors so that they could only be installed one way, and the problem never came up again. (Murphy's Law is why two-pronged electrical plugs are now designed with one prong slightly larger than the other—so they can only be plugged in the proper way.)

Murphy's Law became a popular principle throughout the aerospace industry, and from there it spread to the rest of the world. But as it spread it also evolved into the popular, more pessimistic form, "If anything can go wrong, it will go wrong."

Over 2,500 lefties die each year "using products meant for right-handed people."

THE SCIENCE OF MURPHY'S LAW

Since 1949, any number of permutations of Murphy's Law have arisen, dealing with subjects as diverse as missing socks and buttered bread falling to the floor. As the BRI's own research has shown us, some of these laws are grounded in very solid science:

• **Murphy's Law of Buttered Bread:** "A dropped piece of bread will always land butter-side down."

Scientific analysis: The behavior of a piece of bread dropped from table height is fairly predictable: As it falls to the ground it is more likely than not to rotate on its axis; and the distance to the ground is not sufficient for the bread to rotate the full 360 degrees needed for it to land faceup. So more often than not, it will land facedown.

• **Murphy's Law of Lines:** "The line next to you will move more quickly than the one you're in." (Also with a line of traffic.)

Scientific analysis: On average, all the lanes of traffic, or lines at a K-Mart, move at roughly the same rate. That means that if there's a checkout line on either side of you, there's a two in three chance that one of them will move faster than the one you're in.

• **Murphy's Law of Socks:** "If you lose a sock, it's always from a complete pair."

Scientific analysis: Start with a drawer containing 10 complete pairs of socks, for a total of 20 socks. Now lose one sock, creating one incomplete pair. The drawer now contains 19 socks, 18 of which belong to a complete pair.

Now lose a second sock. If all of the remaining socks have the same odds of being lost, there's only 1 chance out of 18 that this lost sock is the mate of the first one that was lost. That means there's a 94.4% chance that it's from one of the complete pairs.

• **Murphy's Law of Maps:** "The place you're looking for on the map will be located at the most inconvenient place on the map, such as an edge, a corner, or near a fold."

Scientific analysis: If you measure out an inch or so from each edge of the map and from each fold, and then calculate the total area of these portions of the map, they'll account for more than half the total area of the map. So if you pick a point at random, there's a better than 50 percent chance that it will be in an inconvenient-to-read part of the map.

HUMAN HAILSTONES

Hailstones are formed when ice crystals in a thunder cloud are tossed around, gathering successive coats of ice. But people can get caught in thunderheads, too.

THE PILOT

In 1959 Lt. Col. William Rankin bailed out of his single-engine plane when the engine failed at 47,000 feet above Virginia. A storm was in progress, and he fell right through the middle of it. It would normally take a man 13 minutes to fall 47,000 feet, but Rankin got caught in the updrafts and remained aloft for 45 minutes. He tumbled about in –70° temperatures, covered with ice and sleet, his body getting pelted by hailstones. Fortunately, his parachute opened at 10,000 feet and he landed intact in a tree in North Carolina, 65 miles from where he'd bailed out. He made a complete recovery.

THE GLIDERS

In 1930 a German glider society held an exhibition. Five glider pilots flew into a towering thunder cloud hoping to set new altitude records by using the updrafts. But the updrafts were more than they had counted on—the gliders were torn to pieces by the violent winds. The pilots bailed out but were carried to the upper regions of the cloud, where they were coated by ice. All but one froze to death before finally falling to the ground.

THE PARACHUTIST

In 1975 Mike Mount jumped from a plane 4,500 feet over Maryland, expecting a two-minute fall to Earth. Although thunderstorms were building, Mount had over 400 jumps under his belt and thought he could steer himself through the clouds. He couldn't. He was sucked into the storm and pulled up to 10,000 feet. The storm swept him up and dropped him again and again. He debated whether to cut himself free of his main chute, freefall through the storm, and rely on his reserve chute to save him, but he wasn't sure he'd be able to see the ground approaching. Finally the storm released its grip and he landed, cold but unharmed, nine miles from his intended drop zone. His wild ride had lasted 30 minutes.

Mars attacks: In 1911 a meteor from Mars fell to Earth in Nakhla, Egypt, killing a dog.

THE GREAT LONDON SMOG OF 1952

On page 81, we told you the story of a strange natural disaster that killed thousands of people in Africa. Here's the story of a deadly man-made *disaster that occurred in a different part of the world.*

WEATHER REPORT

If you were living in London, England, in the first week of December 1952, the weather wouldn't have seemed unusual, except perhaps that it was a little colder than normal. But on the morning of December 5 it began to change: An area of warm, still air began to form a few hundred feet above the city streets, causing what's known as a temperature "inversion." That may not sound like much, but it was about to cause atmospheric conditions in London to take a deadly turn for the worse.

Normally the air hundreds of feet off the ground is cooler than the air at ground level, and the higher you go the cooler it gets. That's a good thing in a polluted city like London of the 1950s. When hot smoke leaves the chimneys of homes and factories and the exhaust pipes of buses and automobiles, it rises quickly and climbs to an altitude high enough for it to disperse. It is only able to do that because it *is* hotter, and therefore lighter, than the surrounding air.

But what happens when the polluted air is about the same temperature as the surrounding air, such as was the case when the smoke and exhaust hit that layer of warm air over London? The polluted air stops rising. And if there's no wind to disperse it, it accumulates. That's what happened in London on December 5th—it was as if a giant lid had been placed over the city to prevent the smoke and exhaust from escaping.

KING COAL

You may have lived in a city with smoggy air, but it was probably nothing compared to London of the 1950s. Firewood was a scarce and expensive commodity in the British Isles, and for centuries people had burned coal instead. The coal in London that December was especially bad: England had accumulated enormous debts during World War II, and one of the ways it was paying them off was by exporting its clean, hard, valuable "anthracite" coal, forcing Londoners to burn the cheaper, softer, and much dirtier "bituminous" coal in fireplaces, factories, and power plants.

SEEING IS BELIEVING

Have you ever seen what coal looks like when it is burning? If you've ever seen an automobile tire on fire, it's pretty much the same thing, at least visually: When bituminous coal burns, it gives off a filthy, choking black smoke.

Now picture a tire burning in the fireplace of every home in a city of more than eight million people, and picture those fires burning 24 hours a day. Imagine hundreds more tires burning in every factory in London, and still more tires being burned in power plants to generate the city's electricity. Add to that all the automobile exhaust generated by one of the world's largest cities, and the diesel fumes given off by the thousands of London buses that had recently replaced the city's network of electric trams. Now breathe deeply...

GASP!

London's air quality was bad even on a good day, and now that the smoke and exhaust was accumulating above the city, it became positively deadly. Scientists calculated that coal fires and other sources of pollution in London of the early 1950s belched an estimated 1,000 tons of smoke, 2,000 tons of carbon dioxide, and 140 tons of hydrochloric acid into the air every day. They released an estimated 370 tons of sulfur dioxide too, which, when combined with oxygen and moisture in the air, formed 800 tons of sulfuric acid.

On the morning of December 5, the smog around London was dry and smoky, not at all unusual for a cold winter morning. Then, thanks to the temperature inversion, the air quality and visibility deteriorated markedly over the course of the day. By evening the air pollution had become so acrid that many people suffered fits of uncontrollable coughing. Who wouldn't cough? The hydrochloric and sulfuric acid in the air had a pH of about 2—about the same

In the Jonestown Massacre, Jim Jones's followers actually drank Flav-R-Aid, not Kool-Aid.

as the acid in a lemon. The mass of warm air that held the pollution in place hadn't dispersed by the following morning, or the day after that, or the day after that. As smoke, soot, exhaust, and acid continued to be released into the air, pollution climbed to the highest levels the city had ever seen.

LOST IN THE DARK

"Seen," it turns out, was just a figure of speech: By December 7, the air was so thick with smoke and soot that visibility in many parts of the city had dropped to less than one foot—people literally could not see their hands in front of their faces. Some of the first casualties of the Great Smog of 1952, as it came to be known, were drownings—people who died when they became disoriented and fell into the Thames River.

Have you ever tried to drive your car when you can't even see to the end of the hood? Transportation slowed to a crawl as passengers got out and walked in front of or alongside vehicles to help their drivers see the way. Many people gave up and abandoned their vehicles in the middle of the street—which made driving even more difficult—or blindly followed the lights of cars ahead of them, even when they turned into their own driveways. Some homeowners offered lost drivers who'd followed them home a room for the night, rather than let them risk their lives finding their own way home in the oily, choking black smog.

FROM HEAD TO TOE

Anyone who did manage to make it home arrived covered in soot, looking like a coal miner or a chimney sweep, with the stench of sulfur in their nose and a bitter, acrid taste in their mouth. When they changed out of their clothes, they saw that the soot had penetrated all the way to their underwear, which had been burned by the acid in the air. And the air inside was no better than the air outside: Offices and factories suspended operations when their workers could no longer see what they were doing, movie theaters cancelled screenings when audiences couldn't see the screen, and at least one live theater had to shut its doors because the actors couldn't see each other onstage. At the city's Smithfield livestock show, the cattle asphyxiated before they could be slaughtered, and had to be disposed of.

Ewe've got to be kidding! Breeders in Russia once claimed to have bred sheep with blue wool.

NO BIG DEAL

As crazy as it sounds, few people who hacked and wheezed their way through the smog thought much about it at the time. London had been famous for its "pea soup" smog as far back as the 1300s, and people just accepted it as a fact of life. The word "smog" itself was coined in London in 1905 to describe the combination of smoke and fog that was a common occurrence in the city. People learned to deal with it just as they would a spell of bad weather: They waited it out, and a few days later things got better. That's what they did in December 1952—and sure enough on December 9th, 4 days and 18 hours after the air first began to turn black, a fresh wind blew into London and pushed the dirty air out to sea. Life returned to normal.

But what's even harder to understand today is how no one at the time—not even the city's medical professionals—seemed to grasp the terrible toll that the smog would take on the health of Londoners. Even at the height of the crisis, the city officials issued no warnings instructing people to stay inside or to wear masks if they did go outside. Apparently the first people to realize that something unusual was afoot were the city's undertakers and florists, who ran out of caskets and flowers because so many people had died.

The first official recognition that the Great Smog of 1952 was more than just another bad air day came three weeks after the fact, when the registrar general published the mortality statistics for the first weeks of December. Only then did people understand that they had just gone through a major environmental disaster... without even realizing it.

BY THE NUMBERS

For the week ending December 6, which included the first two days of the smog, the number of deaths in Greater London came to 2,062, or 295 deaths per day—not much higher than normal. But as the amount of pollution in the air intensified in the days that followed, the death toll soared. Nine hundred people—more than three times the daily average—died on December 8th, and another 900 died on December 9th, with the death toll remaining well above average for another two weeks.

In all, more than 4,000 people died during and immediately

Peak time for suicides on the London Underground: 11:00 a.m.

after the smog; another 8,000 died in the weeks and months that followed. Many thousands more suffered permanent lung damage, making the Great Smog of 1952 one of the deadliest environmental catastrophes in recorded history. Most of the victims were the very young, the elderly, or those who suffered from pre-existing lung conditions, such as asthma, bronchitis, or pneumonia, which were themselves often the result of a lifetime spent breathing the air in one of the most polluted cities in the world.

D.O.A.

Ironically, the enormous scale of the catastrophe may have been one of the things that kept people from realizing just how bad it was. When the air turned black, the hospitals in and around London were deluged with people who were coughing and choking uncontrollably and unable to breathe, and many of these people did die in the hospital. But many others were too sick to get to the hospital on their own and had to call for ambulances, which could not find their way through the blackness. By the time the ambulance finally did arrive, in many cases the patient had already died and was taken straight to the morgue or a funeral home instead of to the hospital. The fact that these people did not even live long enough to be seen by a doctor may have prevented public health officials from realizing the full magnitude of the disaster until the death statistics were published.

CATCHING A BREATH

More than any single incident, the Great London Smog of 1952 changed the way people in the United Kingdom thought about pollution. Instead of seeing it as an inevitable consequence of industrial progress, they came to view it as something that could and should be controlled. Clean-air legislation was passed in 1954, 1956, and again in 1968. The new laws regulated chimney heights, forced businesses and homeowners to switch over to smokeless fuels, and made other reforms as well. Gradually, the skies over London began to improve. The smog of 1952 wasn't the last one the city ever saw; a similar incident in 1962 killed 750 people. But nothing on the scale of the 1952 disaster ever happened again.

MANNEQUIN MADNESS

Some tantalizing tales of unusual uses of people who aren't really people.

THE ALMA-NNEQUIN

In 1918, after a years-long tumultuous affair, Austrian artist Oscar Kokoschka was dumped by the musician, sculptor, and infamous Viennese socialite Alma Mahler. Kokoschka, already known as a wild-tempered man, was devastated. In order to deal with the loss, he commissioned Munich dollmaker Hermine Moos to craft him a life-sized doll that looked exactly like Mahler. Over the next year he sent Moos hundreds of letters with sketches of Mahler—intimate sketches—so Moos would get the dimensions of the wood and wool doll exactly right. "Please pay special attention to the dimension of the head and neck, to the rib-cage, the rump and the limbs," Kokoschka wrote. And, "Can the mouth be opened? And are there teeth and a tongue inside? I hope so." Shortly after he finally received the doll in spring 1919, Kokoschka could be seen driving through the streets of Vienna with his Alma-nnequin riding in the passenger seat. At parties it would be seated beside him; it would be with him in his studio in Dresden. They even shared a box at the opera. But Kokoschka's Mahler mannequin didn't last. The end came, so the story goes, at the close of a champagne-soaked party in Dresden. At dawn, a drunken Kokoschka took the doll out into his garden and beheaded it.

DALI-QUIN

In March 1939, New York department store Bonwit Teller commissioned Salvador Dali to create a window display. Not surprisingly, soon after having offered the commission, the store regretted it. Dali created a two-window display he titled "Day and Night." On the "day" side was a female mannequin with bright red hair dressed in green feathers. Behind her was a clawfoot bathtub lined with Persian lambskin, and filled with water and floating narcissi. Three mannequin arms reached out of the bath water, each holding a mirror. On the "night" side, a male mannequin was depicted lying on a bed of hot, glowing coals under the mounted and

10,000-year-old brine shrimp will come back to life when rehydrated.

stuffed fore-body of a bizarre beast, which Dali described as "the decapitated head and the savage hooves of a great somnambulist buffalo extenuated by a thousand years of sleep." As soon as the window was unveiled people started complaining that the display was "too extreme." Bonwit Teller's staff took it upon themselves to alter the scene…without asking the artist. Bad idea. That afternoon Dali walked by the window and flew into a rage. He went into the store, screamed at the managers, then jumped into the display area. He picked up an end of the bathtub, spilling all the water out—and threw it through the plate-glass window and out into the street. He was arrested and thrown in jail, but released that evening by a judge who gave him a suspended sentence, saying, "These are some of the privileges that an artist with temperament seems to enjoy." (And Dali's one-man show, which just happened to be opening that night, was a hit.)

COSMONAUT-EQUIN

On March 9, 1961, Ivan Ivanovich became the first person to fly into space. Well, the first person-like *thing* to fly into space. Ivan Ivanovich (the Russian equivalent of "John Smith") was a life-sized test-flight mannequin, and he and his companion, a (live) dog named Chernushka ("Blackie"), were rocketed into space weeks before Yuri Gagarin was to take his historic flight. Ivanovich's mission: to test the Vostok spacecraft and the SK-1 pressure suit. After making a single orbit of the planet in 89 minutes, Ivanovich (and the dog) returned safely to Earth. He was so lifelike, with eyes, eyelashes, eyebrows, lips and all, that the word "Maket," or "Dummy" was written on his forehead so nobody would think he was a dead cosmonaut.

Update: Ivan the Space Mannequin was sold at Sotheby's auction house in 1993. He was purchased by Texas billionaire (and one-time presidential candidate) H. Ross Perot for $189,500.

*   *   *

Odd Movie Trivia: In 2006 a remake of *Fight Club* was released in India. Made in that country, it features all the hardcore violence of the original…and it's a musical.

The scientific name for the tomato: *Lycopersicon lycopersicum,* which means "wolf peach."

THE UFOLOGISTS

How odd would this book be without a look at some scientists who believe that aliens walk among us? Not very. So here's our report on some of the people (if they really are people) surrounding the UFO phenomenon.

SCIENCE...OR SCIENCE FICTION?

Dr. Robert Trundle, a 60-year-old philosophy professor at Northern Kentucky University, is a believer in UFOs, and he's currently facing a backlash from the scientific community for his book, *Is E.T. Here? No Politically but Yes Scientifically and Theologically*. Trundle states his case: "I believe contact was made 50 years ago—and I believe beings from other planets are here now." Why? "Mainly, to study us." Trundle is so convinced that he doesn't care about the criticism he's received from the "cowardice and vanity of American professors."

The title of his book refers to claims that the government is covering up the evidence. "They are afraid of culture shock and public panic. For them to acknowledge the existence of extraterrestrials here would be to admit they can't protect us from them." Yet from a scientific point of view, Trundle claims the information he's gathered speaks for itself. "Thousands of well-regarded witness accounts cannot simply be dismissed. I'm talking about pilots who have come forward even though it's meant they've had to undergo psychiatric exams as a direct result." But so far, Trundle's work has been ignored by his peers in the scientific community.

GOODBYE ROSWELL, HELLO HONG KONG

One place where Trundle's views are taken more seriously is Communist-run China, which is experiencing a "UFO Renaissance." From the 1950s to the 1990s, the United States was the world's unofficial UFO hotspot, but in the last few decades, the aliens seem to have switched their interest to China. Today, one out of every five sightings occurs in China. A recent survey found that more than 50% of Chinese people believe that extraterrestrials now live on Earth. It has even become a fad—there are hundreds of "UFO clubs" set up across China. The most prominent of these is the China UFO Research Association, founded in the 1980s.

80% of millionaires drive second-hand cars.

The association's president, Sun Shili, 66, a retired foreign ministry official, believes that the aliens have taken a greater interest in the Chinese because they have made the most technological advances in the last 20 years and could one day overtake the United States as the world's major superpower. "Rapid development," he says, "attracts investigations by flying saucers, and here in China we're becoming more developed." Sun also has a "gut feeling" that there are aliens disguised as humans living in China.

Unlike the U.S. government, which has distanced itself from ufology, the conservative Chinese government actually finances the Association and—through the state-run media—makes its records of sightings available to the public. As Sun Shili says, "In the U.S., scholars investigating this are under pressure and have been derided. But in China, the academic discussion is quite free, so in this area American academics are quite jealous of us."

A GUARDED APPROACH

Meanwhile, in England, the relationship with UFOs falls somewhere in between China's exuberance and America's cynicism. One of England's most prominent ufologists is Jenny Randles. Since the 1980s, she's published more than 50 books on the subject, which have collectively sold 1.25 million copies worldwide. "I had my first UFO sighting in my home village of Stacksteads as a small child," she says. But while many people claim to see UFOs, Randles sets out to prove their existence. Her method: weed out all of the pseudoscience and wishful thinkers, and focus solely on the most credible reports.

> People have a very false perception of what ufology is all about. They see cover-ups, conspiracies, spaceships, and alien bodies round every corner. The truth is usually far more mundane, but no less fascinating in my opinion. Nine out of ten UFO sightings are explained in simple terms. Many others relate to new phenomena that science has yet to understand. A few might involve contact with another intelligence that has been here on earth for centuries. I do not believe or disbelieve. I listen to the evidence, wonder what it means and then try to figure it out. If that answer is a mundane one then I consider this result to be a success, not a disappointment. But I do believe that there are some surprises waiting to be uncovered, possibly even ones that will revolutionize the planet.

We call them UFOs; in China they are referred to as *feidi*.

THEN WHAT?

No matter how many credible witnesses come out of the woodwork, the UFO phenomenon will stay nothing more than a modern myth until hard evidence is gathered and shown to the world. What happens after that all depends on the nature of the evidence—and whether or not there is a threat detected. But one thing is sure, says Robert Trundle, "it would be the most astonishing human event since the resurrection of Christ."

* * *

...*NEWS FLASH!*

• **Lost City:** "Something always gets lost in translation, but usually not an entire city. 'Jerusalem. There is no such city!' said the English-language version of a sightseeing brochure the city had published originally in Hebrew. The correct translation: 'Jerusalem. There is no city like it!' Tens of thousands of flyers had been distributed before city hall realized its mistake." (Reuters)

• **Modern Living Through Chemistry:** "In a desperate bid to increase numbers of an endangered tiger species, Chinese zookeepers have called on the services of Viagra. The anti-impotence drug is being used to encourage a pair of rare South China tigers in a Beijing zoo to mate. Chinese animal-breeding specialists have also tried a number of other 'alternative' methods to boost numbers of animals close to extinction. For instance, they showed pandas 'pornographic' films of other pandas having sex to try to provoke some mating instincts among the endangered, sex-shy mammals." (CNN)

• **Ghost Riders:** "A police-led initiative of spraying water on state highways in New Zealand to release the trapped spirits of those killed in motor crashes has been declared a success. A special police convoy carrying Maori elders sprayed 10,000 liters of Waikato River water on SH1 and SH2 in a bid to free the spirits of crash victims." (*Stuff*)

THE DOG GIRL

When you were a kid, did you ever fantasize about being raised by wolves? It's not an unusual dream. Just be careful what you wish for.

LEFT TO THE DOGS

Her name is Oxana Malaya. She was born in Novaya Blagoveschenka, Ukraine, in 1983. Her parents were alcoholics who had so many children that they couldn't (or just didn't) keep track of them all. So instead of raising Oxana themselves, they let her spend all of her time between the ages of three and eight—eating, sleeping, and playing—with dogs in a kennel behind the house. There she learned to bark instead of talk, run on all fours, and fight the rest of the dogs for scraps of raw meat.

When Oxana was discovered by neighbors in 1991, the eight-year-old was more dog than girl. She sniffed her food before eating it—without the aid of her hands or utensils, the same way she lapped up water. If she had an itch behind her ear, she would scratch it with her foot. She was also found to have heightened senses of smell, sight, and hearing. Classified as a "feral child"—one of only about 100 known children in the world to have been raised in the absence of people—Oxana had no social skills to speak of. So she was placed in the Baraboy Clinic for disabled children in southern Ukraine, which mainly treats mentally challenged kids. Yet even though she, too, was challenged, Oxana quickly learned to talk, socialize with others, and eat with a fork. Now, at 23 years old, Oxana is trying to lead as normal a life as possible. But will she ever recover from her canine past?

LEADER OF THE PACK

In 2006 a British child psychologist named Lyn Fry went to Odessa to study the dog girl. "I expected someone much less human," Fry said, and then continued:

> I'd heard stories that she could fly off the handle, that she was very uncooperative, that she was socially inept, but she did everything I asked of her. Her language is odd. She speaks flatly as though it's an order. There is no cadence or rhythm or music to her speech, no inflection or tone. But she has a sense of humor. She likes to be the

> center of attention, to make people laugh. Showing off is quite a surprising skill when you consider her background. When she walks, you notice her strange stomping gait and swinging shoulders, the intermittent squint and misshapen teeth. Like a dog with a bone, her first instinct is to hide anything she is given. She is only 1.52 meters tall (5 feet) but when she fools about with her friends, pushing and shoving, there is a palpable air of menace and brute strength. The oddest thing is how little attention she pays to her own pet mongrel. She was much more orientated to people.

Further tests showed that Oxana has the mental capacity of a six-year-old; she can count but not add, and may never learn to read.

Although Oxana still lives at the Baraboy Clinic she is as much an employee as she is a patient, working on the farm where she shepherds cows. And being a strong and pretty young woman, Oxana had a boyfriend for a while, but her canine instincts proved to be too much for him. He broke it off after Oxana performed a very chilling dog demonstration at a party.

THE DOG GIRL SPEAKS

Dr. Fry took a personal interest in the case and set out to help Oxana, who told Fry through an interpreter: "My parents completely forgot about me. Mom had too many kids. We didn't have enough beds, so I crawled to the dog and started living with her. Now when I am upset, I go off by myself into the woods and I bark." Theorizing that Oxana might be able to move on with her life if she came to terms with her troubled past, Fry arranged a reunion with the girl's father, which was covered by BBC television.

When her father arrived at the farm, he just stood there and looked at his grown daughter without saying anything. Finally, Oxana said, "Hello."

"I have come," replied her father.

"I thank you that you have come," Oxana replied. "I wanted you to see me milk the cows."

The meeting turned out to be healing for both of them, another step on Oxana's long journey to fit in. Yet there is one trait that she will always display—a trait shared by human and canine alike: "I am longing for affection and kindness. I like and respect my parents very much, no matter what kind of people they were."

ODD TO THE LAST DROP

Life can be strange, but so can death. Here are some people who looked at death in decidedly odd ways. The end.

BACK TO THE FUTURE

Newspaper readers in Fox Point, Wisconsin, were probably a bit confused by the obituary photo of a man who passed away in 2006. It was a photo of the back of his head. Jim Schinneller, a retired University of Wisconsin art professor, died on September 9 at the age of 81. Always known as an eccentric and a practical joker, his family thought Schinneller would have appreciated one final joke. His partner, Gloria Bosben, told the *Milwaukee Journal Sentinel* that she felt the photo was appropriate because it showed him "heading off into the eternal sunset."

WILL THEY OR WON'T THEY?

In 1986 Greek eccentric Yiannis Katsanis died and left his fortune of two billion drachmas ($5.28 million) to fund a hospital for his home town of Aftos. But in order for the town to get the money, one last request had to be fulfilled: Town officials had to read several letters written by Katsanis. Aloud. In the town square, once every five years. What was in the letters? Graphic details of the illicit sexual activities of several of Katsanis's relatives. The relatives fought the public-reading request for 15 years before a court finally found in their favor...and the town finally got its hospital.

FINAL ERRAND

One morning in 2001, Sylvia Robinson of Maplewood, New Jersey, reported that her 80-year-old husband, Harold Saber, was missing. At about the same time, employees at a local funeral home called police to say that they'd found an elderly man in their parking lot, slumped over the wheel of his car, dead. Saber, who had been ill for some time, had told his wife that when his time came he would drive himself to the funeral home. "He said many times he would do that," she told Reuters. "He never wanted to bother anybody." Police said Saber had apparently suffered a heart attack before driving to the home and dying. "It was a heroic act of love," his wife said.

NASDAQ was totally disabled in December 1987 when a squirrel bit through a phone line.

PAIN IN THE...

Now it can be told: An embarrassing product designed for (ahem) "southern comfort" has a secret history.

BACKGROUND

Although it's designed to treat only hemorrhoids, Preparation H has long been rumored to have other uses. And celebrities and beauty experts aren't afraid to talk about them.

• In *Beauty: The New Basics*, makeup expert Rona Berg advocates using it to reduce water retention under the eyes.

• Beauty pageant contestants reportedly use Preparation H to temporarily eliminate cellulite.

• Conan O'Brien admitted on his talk show in 1999 that his makeup artist uses it to reduce the puffiness around his eyes.

• Peter Lamas, a makeup artist for the Victoria's Secret catalog, uses Preparation H to eliminate blemishes.

• Professional bodybuilders use it to remove excess water in muscles, making them appear larger.

• Actress Sandra Bullock uses it to fight wrinkles.

• Other rumored uses: relieving the pain of dry or cracked skin; healing bed sores and surgical scars; soothing chicken pox; and giving skin a healthy glow.

Sound crazy? Not really. Preparation H cures hemorrhoids, which are just swollen tissue. Applied as directed, the ointment reduces swelling and relieves pain. And that's precisely what it does in all those other rumored uses. So if all of this were true, Preparation H would be a wonder drug. (It's even inexpensive.) But don't go down to the neighborhood pharmacy to pick up a case just yet.

BACKSTORY

Part of the legend is true: the health and beauty secrets of Preparation H have been known since the 1960s. Americans discovered how it made scars and puffiness disappear, and they passed the word along to friends, who passed it along, and so on. By the early 1990s, the rumors had reached Wyeth Consumer Care—the company that manufactures Preparation H. They were delighted; all these other purported uses could be a gold mine. Wyeth recognized that if Preparation H were marketed as a cosmetic aid or pain reliever, it could eliminate the embarrassment of buying the product. And they could sell *tons* more.

But in order to sell Preparation H for anything other than its official listed use (as a hemorrhoid medication), they would need FDA approval. To prove Preparation H was effective at healing scars and eyebags would require millions of dollars of research and government red tape that could last years. Wyeth ultimately decided it just wasn't worth it.

But they were stuck. Once Wyeth knew about the rumor, legally they couldn't boast of the medication's alternate uses. Besides, they'd be opening themselves up to lawsuits from people who injured themselves while trying to use the product for other purposes. So in 1995 they reformulated Preparation H. The chemical responsible for the skin and tissue healing, *biodyne*, a yeast derivative, was replaced with *phenylephrine HCI*, a compound that restricts blood vessels, which limits its effectiveness to treating only hemorrhoids. (The newer formula is also made without shark oil, which supposedly made the old Preparation H an excellent fish bait.)

HINDSIGHT

So the golden age of Preparation H is over, right? Nope. The FDA has jurisdiction over only American drugs. Original-formula Preparation H, with biodyne and shark oil, is still available in Canada (and can be shipped to neighboring countries). The stuff you buy in the United States cures only hemorrhoids—it's completely useless to rub on your baggy eyes. So if all those movie stars and makeup experts are using Preparation H, they're probably getting it from Canada. In fact, used non-hemorrhoidally, the new formula might actually hurt you: phenylephrine has been shown to dangerously raise blood pressure.

* * *

"I don't think necessity is the mother of invention. Invention, in my opinion, arises directly from idleness, possibly also from laziness."

—Agatha Christie

In 75 years, the human heart pumps enough blood to fill an oil tanker 46 times.

WEIRD EUROPE

We cover some of the individual European countries elsewhere in this book, but here's a roundup for the rest of the Continent. No one is spared the odd-o-scope.

STRIPPING IN CZECHOSLOVAKIA

In 1989 officials from the new democratic Czechoslovakian government planned a striptease show for visiting foreign dignitaries. It soon discovered that the previous (Communist) government had authorized only two women in the country to be strippers. Only one could be located, but she was out of practice and got too tired to continue after just a few minutes of dancing.

ROBBERS IN FRANCE

In 1990 a man tried to rob a café in Montpelier, France. He almost got away with it, too...until the the café owner realized that the revolver pointed at him was a fake gun—made out of candy. The police came, but by then the burglar had destroyed most of the evidence by eating his weapon. (He was arrested anyway.)

EL NUDE-O

In 2006 a 26-year-old lawyer and swimming champion named Albert Rivera ran for president of Catalonia, an autonomous region of Spain. His main campaign strategy: plastering the area's major cities with 10,000 posters of himself naked, with the caption "We don't care where you were born. We don't care which language you speak. We don't care what kind of clothes you wear. We care about you." Rivera, an admitted longshot, said he did it to get young people talking about politics. (He did...and he lost.)

SLIPPERY SWEDE

An inmate escaped Hall Prison outside Stockholm, Sweden, without stealing a key or filing bars. He had saved all the margarine from all of his meals for over a year. When he had enough, he covered himself with it and slipped between the bars of his cell.

INVINCIBLE BULGARIANS

Elena Marinova of Bulgaria was in a severe head-on car accident in 2006 but was saved from multiple injuries—including fractured ribs, punctured organs, and collapsed lungs—by her breast implants. Doctors say the size 40DD implants acted like airbags and absorbed the impact.

SOUPED-UP ITALIAN COWS

Organized crime is still rampant in Italy, but it's not as glamorous as it's depicted in the movies. In 2006 Italian police busted a Mafia-connected ring in Naples that was feeding steroids to buffalo and cows to produce more milk for making mozzarella cheese. In 2005 police cracked a similar ring that was drugging race horses with Viagra, which apparently makes them run faster.

SMURF SNUFF FILM

In 2005 UNICEF aired a bizarre public service announcement in Belgium, birthplace of the Smurfs, in which the entire Smurf village was eradicated by warplanes. It ended with a single live Smurf, a baby, crying, and the tagline "Don't let war affect the lives of children."

DEAD DRUNK

In 2006 police in Vilnius, Lithuania, pulled over a truck driver who was driving right down the middle of a two-lane highway. They suspected the man was drunk, and they were right—a Breathalyzer test revealed the man had 7.27 grams per liter of alcohol in his blood—18 times the legal limit…and twice the level that's usually fatal.

EXPLODING ITALIAN VEGETABLES

An Italian woman was peeling an artichoke in 2003 when it suddenly gave off a spark, then gave off a small flame, and then exploded in a fiery cloud. Police rushed to the scene, assuming the explodi-choke was the work of an Italian terrorist known to plant explosives in produce in Italian supermarkets. Testing, however, showed no signs of explosives, making it a naturally occurring exploding artichoke.

SWEDES ON THE MOON

Little red country cottages are a common sight in Sweden. Now the country wants to put one on the Moon. The Swedish Space Corporation has conducted a study and determined that it is possible to put such a structure on the Moon, at an estimated cost of 500 million kronor ($73 million), by 2011. A nationwide contest is under way for children to design the cottage, which is required to be incredibly small—it can be no more than eight square meters and weigh no more than 10 pounds.

ROELEVELD'S ARK

Police in Eerbeek, The Netherlands, found more than 250,000 dead, stuffed, and preserved animals in three bomb shelters in the backyard of 72-year-old John Roeleveld. The man claimed that God had told him to take two of every species of animal and keep them for the upcoming end of the world. (God also told him He'd resurrect the animals even if they were dead.) The collection included an elephant, a camel, a bear, apes, panthers, kangaroos, ostriches, and crocodiles.

WILL THEY STAND FOR IT?

In 2006 principal Anne Lise Gjul of the Dvergsnes School in Kristiansand, Norway, instituted a new bathroom rule: Boys have to sit down to pee. It was done, she said, because the boys have "bad aim" and the same bathrooms have to be used by boys *and* girls. The rule caused political turmoil. "When boys are not allowed to pee in the natural way, the way boys have done for generations, it is meddling with God's work," Vidar Kleppe, head of the national Democratic party, said. "It's a human right not to have to sit down like a girl."

I PREDICT I WON'T BE ON THE JURY

Here's a story for anyone who's ever tried to get out of jury duty. A woman in Oslo, Norway, got out of it in 2002 by saying that she was psychic. She told the judge that she couldn't be impartial because she already knew what verdict would be reached. She also claimed she had seen the crime committed in her crystal ball.

What's a *quidnunc*? Huh? Huh? It's someone who asks too many questions.

THUMB SALAD

Real-life restaurant horror stories from the BRI's Ultra-Gross file.

MENU ITEM: Chicken wings
SURPRISE INGREDIENT: A chicken head
HORROR STORY: Katherine Ortega brought chicken wings home from a McDonald's in Newport News, Virginia, in November 2000. To her family's surprise, along with the wings they got a deep-fried chicken head, complete with beak, comb, and even some feathers. "I screamed," Ortega later said. When she got through screaming she called the manager, who offered to replace the wings (she declined) and asked her to bring the head back. She told him he could see it on TV—she was going to tell the local news about it. "I wanted consumers to know what they're eating."

MENU ITEM: Salad
SURPRISE INGREDIENT: A piece of a thumb
HORROR STORY: In March 2004, a 22-year-old woman ordered a salad at Red Robin Gourmet Burgers in Canton, Ohio. She had eaten most of it when she bit into what she thought was a piece of gristle—except it had part of a fingernail on it. The previous day an employee had severed his thumb-tip while cutting lettuce...and they had been unable to find it. The lettuce was used in the salad the next day. The woman, who remained anonymous, was described by a Red Robin spokesman as "pretty upset."

MENU ITEM: Beer
SURPRISE INGREDIENT: A diaphragm
HORROR STORY: In 1997 a man in Zimbabwe was drinking a bottle of beer when he noticed that it smelled funny. Then he noticed something odd in the bottle. It turned out to be a female contraceptive device. The man suffered "a nervous shock of very serious degree and severe gastroenteritis," his lawyer said. The man sued Zimbabwe's National Brewery for the "shock, depression, and anxiety" the diaphragm-spiked beer caused. He was awarded the equivalent of about $400 in damages.

The Baltimore Ravens have three mascots: Edgar, Allan, and Poe.

MENU ITEM: Big Mac
SURPRISE INGREDIENT: A rat head
HORROR STORY: In June 1999, nine-year-old Ayan Abdi Jama was eating with her parents at a McDonald's in Toronto, Canada. She started eating her Big Mac, then pulled the head of a rat—complete with eyes, teeth, nose and whiskers—out of the sandwich. The girl's parent's reported that "the rat and the Big Mac were partially ingested by Ayan." They also claimed that the restaurant's assistant manager tried to confiscate the sandwich. The girl's mother kept it and took it to a lab for study. Result: It was a rat's head alright, and it was raw, meaning that it had been placed in the sandwich *after* the burgers were cooked. Note: The family filed a $11.2 million lawsuit in 2001. As of 2006, the case still hadn't been settled.

MENU ITEM: Salad
SURPRISE INGREDIENT: A frog
HORROR STORY: In February 2004, a woman on a Qantas Airline flight from Melbourne, Australia, to Wellington, New Zealand, opened her in-flight salad...and found a live frog looking at her. The one-and-a-half-inch whistling tree frog was sitting on a slice of cucumber. The passenger quickly closed the lid and hailed a flight attendant, who quietly took the salad away. After landing, the frog, though a protected species in New Zealand, was taken by quarantine officials and "euthanized" in a freezer. The airline said it changed lettuce suppliers after the incident.

MENU ITEM: A hot dog
SURPRISE INGREDIENT: Bullets
HORROR STORY: In May 2004, 31-year-old Olivia Chanes bought a hotdog at a stand in Irvine, California. She took a bite, swallowed it, and then bit again—right into a 9-mm bullet. When she got home later she started having stomach pains. She went to the emergency room—where x-rays showed that she hadn't just bit into a bullet, she had also swallowed one. Police checked all the other dogs at the stand, found nothing, and said they would continue to investigate. Chanes had a good (and odd) attitude: "If a bullet's going to be in your stomach, at least it didn't pierce the skin to get there," she said. Doctors told her it would be best to let the bullet exit her body "naturally." (When it did, she gave it to the police.)

In the late 1960s, Pez tried to market flower-flavored candies.

WEIRD CRIME NEWS

Here's a look at some of the stranger people and events that have been in the news recently.

NEVER TOO LATE

In August 2003, a man later identified as J.L. "Red" Rountree walked into a branch of the First American Bank in Abilene, Texas, handed a large envelope marked "robbery" to a teller, and told her to fill it with money. Moments later Red sped off in his 1996 Buick Regal with $2,000 in small bills. He didn't get far: A witness took down his license number and called the police; 30 minutes later police arrested Rountree and recovered the money. So what makes this story so odd? Rountree is 91 years old—probably the oldest bank robber in U.S. history. The First American job was his third heist in five years. Why rob banks? Red blames it on a bad experience with his own bank. "They forced me into bankruptcy," he says. "I haven't liked banks since."

TAKE A BITE OUT OF CRIME

On Thanksgiving day 2001, police were called to the Ohio home of Nandor Santho, 46. While searching the premises they found 150 marijuana plants growing in the basement. Who called the cops? Santho's dog Willie—the pointer apparently stepped on his master's cell phone in such a way that it auto-dialed 911—*twice*. Dispatchers mistook Willie's whimpering for a female in distress; which is why they sent the police to the home.

PIG-HEADED

In August 2003, a burglar broke into Richard Morrison's apartment in Liverpool, England, and began ransacking it. But when he saw the big jar with the human head floating in it, he went straight to the police, turned himself in, and told them what he found. Police sped over to the apartment, kicked down the door and discovered...that Morrison is an *artist*, not a psycho—the object in the jar was a mask he'd made from strips of bacon. The police apologized for the mix-up and promised to fix the door. Morrison says he's not mad. "It is a pretty macabre piece of work," he admits.

In Massachusetts, it is illegal for a mourner at a funeral to eat more than three sandwiches.

WELCOME TO COLLEGE! (NOW GET UNDRESSED)

If you thought college rituals involving nudity were strictly the province of drunken fraternities and secret societies like Skull and Bones, think again...

STUDENT BODIES

If you went to college, you probably have vivid memories of those first weeks away from home: moving into the dorms or into your first apartment, registering for classes, buying books, attending your first lecture, stripping naked to pose for "posture photographs"...

Huh?

Believe it or not, posing nude for posture photographs was a common part of the college freshman experience for several generations. The practice dates back to the 19th century, when schools felt they had a responsibility to educate the body as well as the mind. Harvard University started photographing its students in the buff in the 1880s, and by the 1930s the practice was widespread, not just at Ivy League schools but in colleges and universities across the country. Many schools, especially women's colleges, made proper posture a requirement for graduation and assigned incoming students with especially poor carriage to remedial classes. They had to demonstrate marked improvement by the time they collected their diplomas.

BARE NECESSITY

College life may have been different in those days, but it wasn't *that* different: Stripping naked so that a stranger could take your picture seemed weird even then. Yet the students meekly did as they were told, encouraged along by school officials who explained that everyone had to do it, and that everyone had been doing it for as long as anyone could remember. How many nervous freshman would have been willing to be the first to say no? Apparently, none.

The discomfort of the photo-taking experience manifested itself in the form of urban legends that swirled around more than a few college campuses: Chilling tales of break-ins at the photo labs and naked pictures for sale on the bad side of town probably kept plenty of co-eds up at night over the years.

WHERE ARE THEY NOW?

As generation after generation of students graduated and moved on with their lives, many would look back 20, 30, or 40 years later and wonder, whatever happened to that nude picture they took of me in college? Where is it now? Will it ever come back to haunt me?

The fear must have been particularly acute for those alumni who went on to become famous: Bob Woodward, Meryl Streep, Diane Sawyer, George Bush, Sr., and Hillary Clinton, to name just a few, all attended colleges where freshman nude photos were taken; presumably, all of them submitted to the ritual. Even Judith Martin, better known as the newspaper columnist Miss Manners, posed in the altogether at Wellesley College. Once, when she delivered a speech to an alumni gathering at her alma mater, she brought up the subject of the photographs and offered to sell them back to her former classmates in return for hefty donations to the school. "A lot of people turned pale before they realized it was a joke," she told the *New York Times* in 1995.

NOW SHOWING

The fears of countless alumni might have continued forever, simmering but never really materializing, were it not for the fact that when television talk-show host Dick Cavett (Yale '55) spoke at the graduation of the Yale class of '84 (which did not have to pose nude), he made an off-color reference to the urban legend. When he was in school, he explained to the crowd, the photos of the Vassar women were stolen and ended up for sale in the red-light district of New Haven, Connecticut. "The photos found no buyers," Cavett joked.

One of the graduates in the audience was Naomi Wolf, who would go on to become a bestselling author in the early 1990s. She never forgot Cavett's tasteless joke, and in 1992 she attacked him in an opinion piece in the *New York Times*. Cavett responded in a letter to the editor, and that in turn prompted a Yale history professor named George Hersey to write to the paper, claiming

Buenaventura, Colombia, is the wettest inhabited place on Earth, with 267" of rain per year.

that the so-called "posture photos" weren't really taken for that purpose at all, at least not by the 1960s—that was just a cover story for a much more sinister project. Many of the photos, he revealed, were really taken by a quack scientist who wanted to prove that body measurements could be used to predict the subjects' intelligence, personality traits, and even their likely success in life. What Hersey was saying, in effect, was that colleges all over the country had allowed their most vulnerable students to be used as guinea pigs and then had lied about it. And Hersey, it turns out, was correct.

BODY OF EVIDENCE

The "quack scientist" was a Columbia University psychologist named William Sheldon. He had once been considered a leader in his field, and that was how he gained access to the students.

Sheldon was best known for his theory that there was an inborn link between body types and personality. He came up with the idea after studying and photographing hundreds of juvenile delinquents at a reform school in Boston, Massachusetts, in 1940. After analyzing the photos, Sheldon concluded that each individual's physique was a combination of three primary physical body types: *mesomorphs* (large, muscular features and little or no body fat); *ectomorphs* (long and thin with linear features), and *endomorphs* (short and fat with round features).

With some people, one of the three body types was clearly dominant—the person was either very muscular, very thin, or very fat. But many people were more subtle combinations of all three types. Sheldon had devised a three-digit numerical scale for grading a person's physique. The values ranged from 1 to 7, with each of the three digits referring to a different body type: an extreme or "pure" mesomorph measured 7-1-1 on Sheldon's scale; a pure ectomorph scored as 1-7-1, and a pure endomorph scored as 1-1-7.

TRUE TO FORM

Sheldon believed that each of the three body types had specific character traits associated with them: mesomorphs were aggressive, self confident, and drawn to physical activity (and were more likely to commit crimes); ectomorphs valued their privacy and led lives of self restraint; and endomorphs were social people who loved food and comfort. Since he presumed a link between body type and character traits, Sheldon was also convinced that by photographing and then measuring the different parts of a person's body, he could determine what kind of personality that person had and even predict the kind of life he or she would lead in the future.

PICTURE PERFECT

That was Sheldon's *theory*, anyway, and to prove it he needed to collect photographs of many thousands of people, both to refine and perfect his measuring techniques and also to have a large enough sample of people to be able to extrapolate his findings to the population at large. A *voluntary* study was out of the question, as far as Sheldon was concerned: He believed that some body types were more likely to agree to be photographed than others, and that would make the study sample unrepresentative of the general population, and therefore worthless.

As an academic, Sheldon was well acquainted with the long-standing practice of taking posture photographs of an entire freshman class, and he began approaching colleges and universities for permission to take photographs of his own. His standing in the scientific community was such that with very little effort he was able to convince the best schools in the country to let him take compulsory nude photographs of their most vulnerable charges: young men and women who had been high school students just a few months before.

ONE THING LEADS TO ANOTHER

In the 1940s, when colleges still placed great emphasis on developing proper posture, the nude photo sessions served the school's purpose (documenting each student's posture) as well as Sheldon's. But even as the years passed and the academic world gradually got out of the business of teaching students how to stand up straight, Sheldon's nude photo sessions continued unabated. Even his own friend and colleague, Ellery Lanier, conceded that in the end the "posture photo" program had become little more than pretense, "part of a facade or cover-up for what we were really doing," he told the *New York Times* in 1995.

Don't be shy. Part II of the story is on page 313.

WEIRD CANINE STOMACH NEWS

Dogs eat the darndest things. (Now pass the haggis.)

UNCHAIN MY HEART

"A puppy called Harley has survived after wolfing down a 16-inch-long metal chain. Her owner, Devina Alderson from Cambridge, said she saw 18-week-old Harley chewing on it, and then the next minute it was gone. Vets had to carry out an urgent operation to remove the chain from the dog's stomach, and she's fine now. 'I think she may have a metal fetish because she tried to eat the scissors too,' her vet said."

—BBC

RUBBER DUCKY, YOU'RE THE ONE

"A rubber duck sat in a dog's stomach for five years before being removed by Swedish vets, a local newspaper said. The owner of Apollo, a Boxer, assumed the toy had dissolved in the dog's stomach over the years as it had not come out any other way. But Apollo's owner, from Ostersund, took the dog to a vet when he began vomiting and refused to drink. The vet removed the rubber ducky, which had turned black and gone rock hard."

—Reuters

NOT TOO SHARP

"Jake, a 12-week-old Staffordshire Bull Terrier mix who swallowed a kitchen knife nearly as long as he is, is recovering after surgery to remove the implement. Owner John Mallett, 22, says he knew something was wrong when he saw the dog 'trying to keep his body in a straight line.' Vets spotted the knife, with the handle against the dog's pelvis and the point lodged against his throat, on an x-ray. 'Dogs are always swallowing strange things,' said vet Christina Symonds, 'but this was particularly unusual because it was such a large knife in a small puppy.' They operated immediately. Jake survived, and according to Mallett, 'He's totally back to his old self.'"

—Yahoo! News

Prussia's Frederick the Great tried to ban coffee, insisting people drink alcohol instead.

UNDER(WEAR) FED

"A German vet who operated on a dog to remove a suspected stomach tumor found a g-string instead. Claudia Schuermann, head of the Troisdorf animal rescue home, said bull terrier Breiti was abandoned after his previous owners complained he ate 'anything that wasn't nailed down'. The vet noticed 'a hard lump in his stomach,' and after examining 10-year-old Breiti, she concluded he had stomach cancer and operated immediately to remove the 'tumor'. But when the pet was cut open the vet found the cancer was actually an undigested g-string the dog had stolen from his last owners. 'Bull terriers tend to have fetishes,' an aide said. 'Some like shoes, but with Breiti, it's lacy lingerie.'"

—Ananova

THAT'S RICH

"A German woman thought she had been robbed when she returned to her car to find 380 euros ($470) missing and her dog vomiting, only to discover the pet had eaten the cash. 'She thought the dog had been drugged and that thieves had taken the money,' police in the western town of Aschaffenburg said. 'The woman had withdrawn the money and hidden it under bank statements on the passenger seat.' When she figured out what had happened, she took the dog to a vet, who gave the dog a laxative and within 20 minutes six of the 50 euro notes reappeared."

—Reuters

WRETCH THE STICK, MILLIE!

"In a feat that put human sword swallowers to shame, a British dog managed to gulp down a stick only two inches shorter than its own body...and escape unscathed. Millie, a two-year-old Staffordshire bull terrier, was on a walk with her owner, John Hurst, in Portsmouth, England. Hurst threw the 16-inch stick for the 18-inch Millie to retrieve, but it stuck in the ground like a javelin and the sprinting dog impaled herself on it, swallowing it whole. Hurst rushed his pet to a vet, where micro-cameras found the stick had somehow worked its way deep into her stomach without hitting any vital organs on the way. After a two-hour operation, the only injury to Millie was a small scratch inside her stomach."

—USA *Today*

Aargh! If you lost an eye, you would only lose about 1/5 of your vision.

THE CURSE OF THE HOPE DIAMOND

The Hope Diamond is probably the most famous jewel in the Western world...and it carries with it one of the most famous curses. How much of it is legend, and how much of it is fact? Even historians can't agree

BACKGROUND

In 1668 a French diamond merchant named Jean-Baptiste Tavernier returned from India with a magnificent, huge 112.5-carat blue diamond. No one knew exactly where he'd found it...but rumors spread that it was stolen from the eye of a sacred Indian idol—and people said it was cursed.

Nonetheless, King Louis XIV bought the "Great Blue" and added it to his crown jewels. Four years later, he had it recut into the shape of a heart (which reduced it to 67.5 carats).

In 1774 the diamond was inherited by Louis XVI. His wife, Marie Antoinette, apparently wore it; she was also said to have loaned it on one occasion to the Princesse de Lamballe. Author Gordon Stuart explains in *The Book of Curses*:

> When the French Revolution broke out, the Princesse de Lamballe was murdered by a mob and her head paraded under the window where Louis the XVI and his family awaited execution. Marie Antoinette herself was executed in October 1793.

THE HOPE DIAMOND

In 1792, in the midst of the French Revolution, the Great Blue diamond was stolen. It was never seen whole again. Stuart wrote:

> Thirty years later it emerged in Holland, owned now by an Amsterdam lapidary named Fals. His son stole the diamond and left Fals to die in poverty. After giving it to a Frenchman, named Beaulieu, Fals's son killed himself. Beaulieu brought it to London, where he died mysteriously.

In 1830 an oval-shaped blue diamond weighing 44.5 carats

turned up in a London auction house. Experts recognized it as a piece of the Great Blue, re-cut to conceal its identity.

A wealthy banker named Henry Philip Hope bought the jewel for about $90,000, and it became known as the Hope Diamond.

WAS IT CURSED?

Hope was warned about the gem's "sinister influence," but owning it didn't seem to have any negative effect on his life. He died peacefully.

However, in the early 1900s, terrible things began happening again. Lord Francis Hope, a distant relative who'd inherited it, went bankrupt. Then his marriage fell apart. "His wife prophesied," said Colin Wilson in *Unsolved Mysteries*, "that it would bring bad luck to all who owned it, and she died in poverty."

She seemed to know what she was talking about. Over the next few years:

- Lord Francis sold it to a French jewel dealer named Jacques Colot. He ultimately went insane and committed suicide.
- Colot sold it to a Russian prince. He lent it to his mistress, a dancer at the Folies Bergere. The first night she wore it, he shot her from his box in the theater. The prince was reportedly stabbed by Russian revolutionaries.
- A Greek jewel dealer named Simon Manthadides bought it. He later fell (or was pushed) over a precipice.
- A Turkish sultan named Abdul Hamid bought it in 1908. He was forced into exile the following year and went insane.

TEMPTING FATE?

One wonders why anyone would want the diamond at this point. But French jeweler Jacques Cartier took possession. He quickly resold it to Edward McClean (owner of the *Washington Post*) and his wife, Evalyn. A fascinated public watched to see if the "curse" would affect them. Did it? According to some accounts, McLean's mother and two servants in his household died soon after he purchased the jewel. *Vanity Fair* magazine reported:

> After her mother-in-law's death, Evalyn McLean had a priest bless the gem. In her autobiography she writes about the experience: "Just as he blessed it—without any wind or rain—this tree

right across the street was struck by lightning. My maid Maggie fainted dead away. The old fellow was scared to death and my knees were shaking. By the time we got home the sun was out, bright as anything."

Over the next 30 years, Evalyn McLean's family was decimated. Her father soon became an alcoholic and died. Her father-in-law went insane. The McLeans' beloved 10-year-old son, Vinson, was hit and killed by a car in front of their house. Their marriage broke up and Edward McLean went insane; he died in a mental institution. McLean's daughter Emily—who had worn the Hope Diamond at her wedding—committed suicide.

AFTERMATH

Through all the tragedy and even her own gradual financial ruin, Evalyn McLean scoffed at the curse. She continued to wear the Hope Diamond until her death in 1947. Two years later, her children sold it to the famous diamond dealer Harry Winston, to pay estate taxes. He kept it (with no apparent ill effect) until 1958, then decided to give it away. He put it in a box with $2.44 in postage, paid $155 for $1 million insurance, and sent it to the Smithsonian Institution via U.S. mail. "Letters of protest poured in to the museum," wrote Gary Cohen in *Vanity Fair*. "Some reasoned that the curse would be transferred to its new owners—the American people." Cohen went on to say:

> Within a year, James Todd, the mailman who had delivered the gem, had one of his legs crushed by a truck, injured his head in a car crash, and lost his wife and dog. Then his house burned down. When asked if he blamed his ill fortune on the diamond, he said, "I don't believe any of that stuff."

Today, the diamond is owned by the U.S. government. And we all know what kind of luck the United States has had since 1959.

*   *   *

WHAT ABOUT LIZ? It's widely believed that Elizabeth Taylor once owned the Hope. Not true. She owns a larger diamond, often compared to the Hope, but now known as the Burton Diamond.

THE INCREDIBLE SHRINKING HEADS

There have been many head-hunting cultures in the world—even the French had the guillotine—but only one made shrunken heads. Here's the story.

THE JIVARO

The Jivaro (pronounced "hee-var-o") tribes live deep in the jungles of Ecuador and Peru. They don't do it anymore as far as anyone knows, but as recently as 100 years ago they were ardent head shrinkers. The Jivaro tribes were constantly at war with other neighboring tribes (and with each other), and they collected the heads of their fallen enemies as war trophies. The head, once miniaturized, was called a *tsantsa* ("san-sah"). For the Jivaro, the creation of a tsantsa ensured good luck and prevented the soul of the fallen enemy from seeking revenge.

As Western explorers came in increasing contact with the Jivaro tribes in the late 19th century, shrunken heads became a popular souvenir. Traders would barter guns, ammo, and other useful items for them. This "arms-for-heads" trade caused the killing to climb rapidly, prompting the Peruvian and Ecuadorian governments to outlaw head shrinking in the early 1900s. If you buy a head today, it's certainly a fake.

THE JOY OF COOKING...HEADS

Here's the Jivaro recipe for a genuine shrunken head (Kids, don't try this at home): Peel skin and hair from skull; discard skull. Sew eye and mouth openings closed (trapping the soul inside, so that it won't haunt you). Turn inside out and scrape fat away using a sharp knife. Add jungle herbs to a pot of water and bring to a boil; add head and simmer for one to two hours. Remove head from water. Fill with hot stones, rolling constantly to prevent scorching. Repeat with successively smaller pebbles as the head shrinks. Mold facial features between each step. Hang over fire to dry. Polish with ashes. Moisturize with berries (which prevents cracking). Sew neck hole closed. Trim hair to taste.

RED ROCKER

For 20 years this American singer was the face of rock 'n' roll in the East Bloc. Was he just a stooge of the Kremlin propaganda machine?

ALL-AMERICAN BOY

In 1958, 20-year-old Dean Reed moved from his home outside Denver, Colorado, to Los Angeles. Blessed with drop-dead good looks, and hungry for success, Reed thought he could be the next Elvis. Capitol Records agreed—they signed him to a recording contract. Over the next four years he released eight singles as the record company booked him on variety shows, trying to market him as a teen idol, like a hipper Tab Hunter. All eight records flopped in the United States, but South America was another story. His record "A Summer Romance" was a monster hit in Argentina, so Reed headed south of the border to capitalize on his regional success with a follow-up tour—and thus began one of the strangest odysseys in rock history.

"RED ELVIS"

To Reed's astonishment, he wasn't just a *hit* in Argentina—he was a *superstar*. Mobbed at every stop by screaming fans, his records outsold Elvis's. But something happened on the tour that changed Reed's life forever—he became a revolutionary. Argentina was in the midst of a grass roots social upheaval. The longer Reed stayed there, the more he got caught up in the movement, especially when he was booked to play concerts at prisons, in poor neighborhoods, and at rallies protesting U.S. nuclear testing policy.

Nicknamed "the Red Elvis," Reed churned out dozens of hit records, starred in a bunch of cheap movies (like Elvis) and had his own TV variety show in Argentina. Within a few years, Reed was the #1 performer not only in that country, but in socialist-leaning South American countries including Chile, Peru, and Venezuela.

Unknown in America, Reed had become a rock 'n' roll poster boy for the extreme left...which got him on the wrong side of the right wing Argentine government. Reed was thrown out of Argentina in 1966. But that was just a bump in the road. His star was rising—and it was red.

14 people have died during Pamplona, Spain's, annual "Running of the Bulls."

PARTY BOY

Combining American rock 'n' roll with Socialism had an unexpected bonus: it made Reed a hit in the Soviet Union and the Eastern Bloc. Melodiya, the U.S.S.R.'s state-run record label, signed him to make records and tour. It was a win-win situation: Reed became the international teen idol he'd always wanted to be and the Soviet Union got an American rock star who would speak out between songs, publicly denouncing U.S. involvement in Vietnam, insisting that the Berlin Wall was a necessary and prudent security measure, and touting the glories of the Communist system.

Some historians question whether Reed was really a Marxist-minded revolutionary, or just a fame-hungry, mildly talented musician who just went along with the Communist propaganda because it made him famous *somewhere*. Reed insisted he was sincere...but he never defected to the Soviet Union, never joined the Communist Party, and kept his money in a West German bank.

MAN WITHOUT A COUNTRY

By 1981 Reed was 43; Eastern European audiences were moving on to newer, fresher music. No longer an icon in the Soviet Union, Reed began to speak openly about wanting to return to Colorado. In an effort to rehabilitate his reputation in the U.S., he attended the 1985 Denver premiere of *American Rebel*, a documentary about his life. He even wrote a song for the film, titled "Nobody Knows Me Back In My Hometown." He gave radio interviews and was profiled nationally on *60 Minutes*. The campaign backfired—Reed received hate mail and death threats, and fled back to East Berlin.

A few months later, on June 17, 1986, Dean Reed's body was found in a lake near his East German home. The police called it an accidental drowning, but rumors quickly began to circulate. Was it really suicide? Reed had been known to suffer from bouts of depression and had cut his own arm with a machete a few months earlier. Or was it murder? Had the Stasi, the notorious East German secret police, exterminated a traitor? There was even speculation that Reed was actually a CIA mole deep undercover for over 20 years; he'd been an American patriot all along. Most historians agree with the official report: Reed committed suicide, a victim of depression and loneliness...but the real story may never be known.

A pig's snout is called a *gruntle*.

GAMES PEOPLE PLAY

Other cultures' sports and games may seem weird, but keep in mind that those same people might find the idea of a warlike game where 300-pound athletes crash into each other to move an oblong ball a few inches just as absurd.

BUZKASHI

Popular in the central Asian countries of Afghanistan and Kyrgyzstan, buzkashi is similar to polo: Teams of men on horseback have to move an object past a goal line to score. But instead of a ball, buzkashi is played with a headless, limbless, sand-weighted goat carcass, which players must toss over the goal line. To steal the carcass from the other team, players are permitted to trip horses or whip their opponents.

HASHING

British colonists created this game in Malaysia in the 1930s, and it's still played by locals. Hashing involves a lot of running, but it's not really a race. Participants start the event drunk, and then run through a five-mile maze. Every quarter mile there's a checkpoint where more booze is consumed and the course branches out into three or four possible routes, with only one being correct. It doesn't even matter who wins—just who is able to finish and tell his story after the race, which traditionally takes place at a bar.

TRISKELION

A complicated version of soccer played by three teams on a triangular field. (It was invented by Green Party chairman Steve Kramer.)

CHESSBOXING

Inspired by a Serbian comic book, chessboxing is now played by small groups across Europe. It's exactly what the name implies: chess *and* boxing. Opponents box for one round, then sit at a table adjacent to the ring and play a four-minute round of chess. Then they go back to the boxing, then the chess, until a winner is determined in either one event or the other.

In 1498 Columbus declared that the Earth was pear-shaped, not round.

POOH STICK RACING

This Japanese game is not what you think. Inspired by a game played by Winnie the Pooh in A.A. Milne's classic books, pooh stick racing involves finding sticks, dropping them into a river, and seeing which stick floats across the finish line first.

BOSSABALL

An instant sensation in Spain where it was created in 2006, bossaball combines volleyball...and bouncy castles. The net is very high; the field of play is one of those inflatable castles you see at kids' parties. Players can touch the ball with their hands or feet, but to make the game harder, the castle is set on top of large, bouncy, unstable, inflatable tubes. And to make it even *harder*, a "joker" from each team bounces on a trampoline next to the castle, trying to sabotage the other team by knocking the ball away.

COLEO

This sport is popular in Venezuela. Four men on horseback chase a bull down a narrow pen, trying to pull its tail to make it fall over. Each successful tipping earns a point. After the bull falls over, the game must continue, so the men try to get the bull back on its feet by twisting or biting its tail or shocking it with an electric prod.

KURLBOLLEN

Known as "feather bowling" in English, this sport originated in Belgium. Wooden balls shaped like large wheels of cheese are rolled down a dirt alley in the direction of a feather sticking out of the ground. The goal is to get the "ball" close to the feather without running over it. Each team gets 12 attempts; the side with the most balls closest to the feather wins.

CONGER CUDDLING

Since 1974, fans have flocked to the English village of Lyme Regis to watch two nine-man teams try to knock each off of a wooden platform...by swinging five-foot dead eels at each other. (A conger is a type of eel.) In 2006 the contest was almost cancelled when animal-rights activists protested the event because "it's disgraceful to the memory of the eel." The contest was held—with rubber boat fenders instead of dead eels.

Actor Patrick Stewart was bald by the time he was 14.

WEIRD AFRICA

You know, the place Meryl Streep got out of. Where Toto blessed the rains.

POWER TO THE PEOPLE

In order to increase membership—and gain media attention—in 2003 the Gay and Lesbian Alliance of Cape Town, South Africa, voted 19–2 to change its name to "The Death Penalty Party of South Africa."

AHH! BABOONS!

In 2006 gangs of large baboons began terrorizing Cape Town suburbs. They break into houses, eat all the food in refrigerators, and defecate everywhere before leaving. Witnesses say the baboons travel in groups of 30, forming an impenetrable front line that's several baboons wide.

TRAPPED IN THE CLOSET

At the beginning of the Iraq War, Phesheya Dube, a reporter for Swaziland's state radio station, went to Baghdad to file reports. It turns out he was actually broadcasting from a closet in Mbabne, the capital city of Swaziland. He was exposed when he was spotted trying to get an interview outside of Swaziland's parliament.

METAL MOUTH

An X-ray revealed metal in the stomach of Gezahenge Debebe, a 40-year-old woman from Ethiopia. In 2001 doctors operated for over an hour to remove the contents of Debebe's stomach, which included 222 rusty nails, 26 ounces of coins, and several keys. Debebe admitted to eating the metal over the previous 20 years.

AS OLD AS YOU FEEL

In 2006 Kenyan Youth Affairs minister Muhammad Kuti proposed changing the legal definition of the word "youth" to include people aged 31 to 50. Reason: He wants to give more people access a $14 million "youth fund." If the plan goes through, 50-year-old Kenyan "youths" will have only five years until the legal retirement age, which is 55.

Q: What do you call a cross between a yak and a cow? A: A *zum*.

HISTORICALLY STRANGE

From the dustbin of history, here are the stories of some of the past's strangest people and events.

THE FLEA KILLER

Queen Christina ruled Sweden from 1632 to 1654. What did she consider the biggest threat to her kingdom? Fleas. The Queen hated them and wanted each and every one she found in her palace killed...individually. To accomplish this feat (this was long before the invention of chemical insect repellents), she commissioned the construction of a tiny, one-inch-long cannon, that was packed with tiny flea-sized cannonballs. Whenever she spotted one, she fired the tiny cannon at it and occasionally made a killshot.

THE SKULL IS IN THE MAIL

When Germany conquered Tanganyika (a region of eastern Africa) in 1898, Chief Mkwawa, the leader of the Wahehe tribe, was killed. The Germans then sent Mkwawa's head to Germany, where it was displayed in a museum in Bremen. During World War I, the British kicked the Germans out of Africa, aided by the Wahehe. H.A. Byatt, the British administrator now overseeing the former German-controlled area, lobbied the British government for the return of Mkwawa's skull in appreciation for the Wahehes' war effort. The return of the skull was even stipulated in the Treaty of Versailles, the 1919 agreement outlining terms of Germany's surrender. But Germany denied taking Mkwawa's head and the British government didn't push the issue, accepting the German explanation that the skull was lost. In 1953 Sir Edward Twining, the British governor of Tanganyika, vowed to track down the skull... and found it in the Bremen Museum among a collection of dozens of skulls taken in the 1890s. Mkwawa's skull was finally returned to the Wahehe in July 1954 and now resides in a museum there.

THE GENDER-BENDING BULLFIGHTER

In 1900 a 20-year-old bullfighter known only as "La Raverte" debuted in the Madrid bullring. What's odd about that? La Raverte was a female bullfighter. She remained a crowd favorite for seven years until 1908, when the Spanish government decided it was immoral for women to fight bulls, and La Raverte was banned from the ring. But La Raverte wasn't worried. Why? *She* was really a *he*. At the conclusion of one of her final bullfights, La Raverte took off her wig and fake breasts, revealing she wasn't a woman, but a man named Agustin Rodriguez. Did La Raverte resume a bullfighting career as a man? Nope. Bullfighting fans instantly turned on him, angered by the fraud. Within the year, Rodriguez fled Madrid and retired quietly in Majorca.

TIME TO GET THE CLOCK FIXED

In 1996 German systems analyst Heribert Illig introduced a theory he called "phantom time hypothesis." Illig believes that the Early Middle Ages—the years 614 to 911—never actually happened and that all evidence of the 300-year period is faked. He says that in 1582, when Pope Gregory XIII replaced the Julian calendar with the Gregorian calendar (which we still use) in order to correct a ten-day error, he actually added 300 years. Among the historical evidence that Illig uses to support his claim are "fraudulent" records of Holy Roman Emperor Charlemagne, whom Illig says is actually a fictional character.

...AND THE DISH RAN AWAY WITH THE SPOON

On May 9, 1962, a Guernsey cow in Iowa named Fawn was picked up by a tornado and flew through the air for a few minutes before landing softly and safely at a nearby farm a half mile away. The flight is believed to be the longest (but not the first) unassisted solo cow flight in recorded history. Fawn safely landed in the pen of a Holstein bull at a neighboring farm before she successfully wandered home. (The brief encounter resulted in a calf.) Amazingly, Fawn had a chance to beat her own record. In 1967 she was out grazing on a country road and was caught up in *another* tornado. She flew over a busload of gawking tourists and landed safely on the other side of the road. From then on, Fawn's owner locked her up whenever there was a storm warning.

* * *

Odd Job: Before his acting career blossomed, Johnny Depp supported himself by selling ballpoint pens door to door.

THE BARBADOS TOMBS

The island of Barbados is known for its tropical climate, its sandy beaches—and its restless dead. Here are two legendary, unexplained mysteries surrounding people who have been buried on the island.

THE CHASE FAMILY CRYPT

Background. Col. Thomas Chase and his family were wealthy English settlers who lived on Barbados in the early 1800s. They owned a large burial crypt in the graveyard of Christ Church. In 1807, Thomasina Goddard, a relative of the Chases, died and was interred in the crypt. A year later, Mary Chase, Thomas Chase's infant daughter, died mysteriously. (It was widely believed that Thomas Chase beat her to death; he was known as a violent man who beat his children—a number of whom showed signs of mental illness.) She, too, was placed in the crypt. But unlike Thomasina, who was placed in a wooden coffin, Mary's body was placed in a heavy lead coffin. After her casket was interred, the vault was sealed shut with a massive marble slab.

A Mysterious Happening. A few months afterward, Dorcas Chase, Thomas Chase's teenage daughter, starved herself to death. Like her infant sister, Dorcas was placed in a heavy lead casket and brought to the crypt. But when the family unsealed and opened the vault, they saw that something peculiar had happened: Mary Chase's tiny coffin had moved to the opposite side of the crypt—and it was standing on one end. Thomasina Goddard's casket had not been moved.

The family was shocked, but assumed the crypt had been broken into by grave robbers. They returned Mary's casket to its proper place, laid Dorcas's coffin next to it, and sealed the crypt even tighter than before—this time pouring a layer of molten lead over the marble capstone.

A Moving Experience. Thomas Chase committed suicide a month later. As with Mary and Dorcas, his body was placed in a heavy lead casket. This time when the crypt was opened, all the coffins were still in place. The crypt was again tightly sealed; it would not be opened again by the family for another eight years.

In 1816 another child related to the Chase family died. This time when the vault was unsealed, the hinges on the doors were so rusty, they would not open; it took two strong men to finally pry them open wide enough to get the coffin inside. But when the family peered into the dark vault, they saw that the caskets had again been strewn about the crypt...except for Thomasina Goddard's, which was left untouched a second time.

The mourners were dumbfounded: the adult-sized lead coffins weighed more than 500 pounds each, and the child-sized ones weren't much lighter. It took four strong men to return each of the caskets to their proper places, and it seemed inconceivable that any natural forces could have tossed them around the tomb.

Keep on Moving. Less than a month after this latest interment, a woman visiting another grave heard groans and "loud cracking" noises coming from the Chase family crypt. Her horse became so agitated by the noises that it began foaming at the mouth and had to be treated by a veterinarian. And a week after that, something spooked several horses tied up outside Christ Church; they broke free, ran down the hill, and jumped into the sea, where they drowned.

By now the goings-on in the vault were public knowledge and the source of wild speculation; when the next member of the Chase family died, more than 1,000 people came to the funeral—some from as far away as Cuba and Haiti. They weren't disappointed: when the crypt was unsealed, all of the coffins were out of place, each one standing on end against the walls of the crypt... except for Thomasina Goddard's.

You Move Me, Governor. After this funeral, the governor of the island decided to investigate. He attended the next Chase funeral, and once again the coffins had been strewn about. This time, he tested the crypt's walls for secret passages (there were none), had the floor of the crypt covered with sand to detect footprints and other marks, had a new lock installed in the crypt's door, and had the crypt sealed with a layer of cement to be sure the door could not be opened. To top it off, he and other officials stamped the

One reason why Fidel Castro grew a beard: The U.S. embargo cut off his razorblade supply.

wet cement with their signet rings, making sure that it couldn't be tampered with without being detected.

On April 8, 1820, the vault was reopened to inter another member of the Chase family. The cement was still in place, but when the family removed it, something heavy leaning against the door of the crypt prevented it from being opened. Several strong men tried to force the door open...and when they finally succeeded, something crashed down inside the crypt. They opened the door all the way...and saw that it had been held shut because one of the coffins had been leaning against it. This time all the coffins had been disturbed—including Thomasina Goddard's.

The governor and several others examined the crypt closely to try and find an explanation. There was none; there were no footprints in the sand and none of the jewelry on any of the bodies had been stolen. Completely mystified, the governor ordered that the bodies be removed from the crypt and interred in another crypt on the island. They were never disturbed again; they rest in peace to this day.

THE McGREGOR CRYPT

Background. The Chase crypt wasn't the only one on Barbados to have strange things happen to it. In August 1943, a group of Freemasons unsealed a crypt containing the body of Alexander Irvine, the founder of Freemasonry on Barbados. (Irvine's remains were interred in the 1830s in the same crypt as Sir Even McGregor, the owner of the crypt, who was laid to rest in 1841.)

Strange Happenings. The McGregor crypt was even more tightly sealed than the Chase crypt: the inner door was locked tight and cemented with bricks and mortar, which itself was covered with a huge stone slab. When they unsealed the crypt, the inner door of the tomb would not open. Peeking in through a hole, they saw that a heavy lead coffin was standing on its head, leaning against the inner door. The masons carefully moved it and opened the door—only to discover that Irvine's coffin was missing; McGregor's was the one up against the door. The mystery was never solved; the island's burial records confirmed that both men had been interred in the crypt nearly 100 years before, but no evidence was ever found to explain the missing coffin.

FOOD FIGHT!

This title probably conjures up visions of leftover vegetables being hurled across a school cafeteria. But in at least two instances, people actually used food as a weapon in real wars. Here are the stories.

TAKE THAT!

"The Uruguayan army once fought a sea battle using cheeses as cannonballs.

"It happened in the 1840s. The aggressive Argentine dictator Juan Manual de Rosas, in an attempt to annex Uruguay, ordered his navy to blockade Montevideo, the capital. The besieged Uruguayans held their own in battle until they ran out of conventional ammunition. In desperation, they raided the galleys of their ships and loaded their cannons with very old, hard Edam cheeses and fired them at the enemy.

"Contemporary chronicles record that the Uruguayans won the skirmish."

—from *Significa*, by Irving Wallace, David Wallechinsky, and Amy Wallace

YOU SAY POTATO...

"A World War II destroyer once defeated a submarine with the help of a seldom-used weapon of destruction: potatoes.

"The USS *O'Bannon* was on patrol off the Solomon Islands in April 1943 when it encountered a Japanese sub. The crew shot off the sub's conning tower, preventing it from diving, but the captain of the sub brought it so close to the destroyer that the *O'Bannon*'s big guns couldn't be aimed at it.... When the Japanese came topside, the gallant *O'Bannon* crewmen pelted them with potatoes. The Japanese thought they were being showered with grenades, threw their guns overboard, then panicked, submerged the sub, and sank it.

"When the O'Bannon was decommissioned in the early 1970s, a plaque was made to commemorate the event, and donated to the ship, by the Maine potato growers."

—from *Beyond Belief!*, by Ron Lyon and Jenny Pacshall

In America, anchovies always rank last on the list of favorite pizza toppings.

AMAZING COINCIDENCES

Wow! We had a page called "Amazing Coincidences" in our last book!

NOT SO "LUCKY"

In October 2006, a small plane crashed into a high-rise apartment building in Manhattan, killing pilot Tyler Stanger and his passenger, New York Yankees pitcher Cory Lidle. *Not* on the flight were Bob Cartwright and Robert Wadkins, both of whom had been invited by Lidle to attend a Yankees playoff game. But both had declined the invitation. Their "good luck" and the bad news hit both of them hard. A month later, Cartwright invited Wadkins to join him on a trip from their home in Big Bear, California, to Las Vegas. Wadkins couldn't go—and for the second time he avoided disaster as the small plane crashed shortly after takeoff. Cartwright, the pilot, and another passenger were killed.

STRONG WILLED WOMAN

In November 2006, a 65-year-old woman in Amsterdam, The Netherlands, was visiting her husband's gravesite. After his death a year earlier, the woman began to plan her own funeral very carefully, right down to selecting what music she wanted played and having her name inscribed on the family headstone. While standing at the gravesite, the woman suffered a heart attack and died. (And police found her will in her handbag.)

YES, VIRGINIA...

On June 28, 2000, the Washington newspaper *The Columbian* printed the results of Oregon Pick 4 lottery numbers—before the Oregon Lottery had announced the winning numbers. Lottery officials notified the Oregon State Police and a detective was sent to investigate. He was informed that the paper's computer had crashed that day and a page of the newspaper had been lost—the one with lottery results. As they scrambled to reconstruct the page, a staffer was told to get Oregon's Pick 4 numbers off the news wires. The staffer found the "Pick 4" results—6-8-5-5—and they were printed. The only problem was that the staffer had grabbed the numbers for the state of *Virginia's* Pick 4...and they were the exact same numbers as the ones that were later picked in Oregon. "The odds of hitting the Pick 4 are about 10,000 to 1," lottery spokesman David Hooper said. "The odds of a newspaper pulling the Virginia lottery numbers by mistake and having those numbers be the same numbers drawn in Oregon the next day? A gazillion to one."

GERMANS *DO* HAVE DOPPELGANGERS

In 1979 Walter Kellner of Munich, West Germany, entered a story into a writing competition held by the magazine *Das Besteran*. The contest called for unusual—but true—stories, and Kellner wrote about his adventure while piloting a Cessna 421 between the islands of Sicily and Sardinia. During the flight he had experienced engine trouble and was forced to make an emergency water landing near Sardinia, where he was eventually rescued in his life raft. Kellner won the competition, and his story was printed in the magazine. Not long after, the magazine got a letter from an Austrian man accusing Kellner of plagiarism. The man wrote that years earlier *he* had piloted a Cessna 421 from Sicily to Sardinia, had engine trouble, and had to make an emergency landing in Sardinia. The stories were amazingly similar, and more amazing than that was the Austrian man's name: Walter Kellner. *Das Besteran* checked both stories. Both were true.

DIDN'T SEE THAT COMING

A 70-year-old woman crashed her car through the front window of a store in Temple, Texas, in November 2006. The store: Budget Optical of America. The woman had an appointment for an eye exam. (No one was injured.)

WHITE BUFFALO BUFFALO BUFFALO

On August 20, 1994, a white buffalo was born on the Heider family farm in Janesville, Wisconsin. White buffalo births—simply white-colored; not albino—are considered sacred omens of extremely good fortune by many American Indian nations, and are very rare. The birth at the Heider farm was the first since 1933, and "Miracle," as she was named, generated thousands of visitors to the Heiders' farm. The family even converted a corn

It is illegal to carry an unwrapped ukulele down the street in Salt Lake City.

field into a parking lot for the visiting throngs (and never charged for admission). Then in 1997 *another* white calf was born on the farm. "Miracle Lady" died four days later. Then, on August 25, 2006, a *third* white buffalo was born. And this one, a male named "Chance," wasn't even related to the other two. But if the chances for Chance's birth were long, so was his death: Three months later, on the night of November 26, 2006, Chance was killed by a lightning strike.

NAME THAT COINCIDENCE

A car crashing into a car crash isn't uncommon; just ask anybody who's been in a freeway accident. But a car crashing into a *Car Crash* is pretty weird. That's what happened in July 2005, when a car careened into the Car Crash restaurant in Santiago, Chile, just days after it opened. The restaurant's owner, Nancy Araya, said she named it that because the intersection where it was located had a reputation for accidents...but she didn't expect it to work quite so literally. "It is unbelievable," she said. "The restaurant is now a joke." The Car Crash was closed for a week to repair the car crash damages.

WAIT—I CHANGED MY MIND

In October 2006, 18 employees at Arcelor Auto Processing factory in Willenhall, West Midlands, England, decided to form a lottery "syndicate." They each chipped in £1.50 a week (about $3) for the Friday lotto drawing, buying 18 tickets with different numbers to increase their chances of winning. And of course they had an agreement that any winnings would be shared equally among the group. On the week of November 24, employee Chris Tibbetts, 56, told the group that he wanted out. He thought it was a waste of his £1.50. That week his fellow workers won the equivalent of $10.3 million, with each person's cut about $570,000. "I'm OK now, but Monday was a really tough day," Tibbetts later told reporters. "It's hard, but it's not the end of the world. Nobody died."

* * *

"I've seen aliens, so I had no problem witnessing the birth of my son."

—Will Smith

Christopher Walken once worked as an assistant lion tamer in a circus.

IT'S A CONSPIRACY!

If you know anybody who believes in these wacky theories, please send them our way (we have an invisible bridge we'd like to sell them).

THEORY: The government released a video game that was really an experimental mind control device.

DETAILS: In 1981 a game called Polybius showed up in a few arcades in Portland, Oregon. Unlike the two-dimensional, graphically simple games of the era (Pac-Man and Space Invaders, for example), Polybius featured rotating 3-D images and strobe lights. Many people played this alluring game, yet no one remembers it. Why? The combination of spatial focus and strobe lights caused brain damage. Many players suffered amnesia, insomnia, and nightmares. At the peak of the game's popularity, arcade owners noticed mysterious men in black suits who came to collect data from Polybius machines. They were from the military—Polybius was being used to test mind control techniques. After a few weeks, Polybius vanished from the arcades forever.

TRUTH: In 1980 Sinnescholsen, a small German video game maker, created Polybius, a disorienting game that simulated 3-D graphics. But arcade owners weren't interested: they said it was too new and too weird to be commercially viable. So Sinnescholsen decided to test-market the game in six arcades in Portland, Oregon. The owners were right—the game bombed. But one 13-year-old boy who played the game suffered a seizure from it. Sinnescholsen employees flew to Portland and immediately removed the game from the arcades (explaining the "men in black"). Faced with possible scandal, the company dissolved. The legend probably took off because one of Polybius's designers was Ed Rottberg, also the creator of Battlezone, a video game used by the U.S. government to train army recruits.

THEORY: Astronauts have never been back to the moon since the 1969 landing because they were scared away by an alien spacecraft base.

DETAILS: Plans to inhabit, mine, and colonize the moon were thwarted once Neil Armstrong and Buzz Aldrin visited the lunar surface. There was more than rocks and dust there: there was a massive moon city and UFO base used by aliens to spy on Earth as well as travel to and from it. Ham radio operators claim to have eavesdropped on Apollo 11's communications with NASA and report that Armstrong said, "You wouldn't believe it! I'm telling you there are other spacecraft out there, lined up on the far side of the crater edge. They're on the Moon watching us!"

TRUTH: All other "evidence" aside, there's one major hole in this theory: We haven't been scared off of the Moon by aliens; in fact, we've been back...a lot. From 1969 to 1972, U.S. astronauts visited the Moon six times, all without ET encounters.

THEORY: A left-wing Food and Drug Administration conspiracy is trying to make people gay by convincing them to eat more soy, which triggers homosexuality.

DETAILS: While the FDA claims that a diet rich in soy protein reduces the risk of cancer and heart disease, the agency knows the real truth about soy: it's extremely high in estrogen. This makes soy formula-fed American babies grow up to have sexual development problems. In men, the estrogen-rich soy delays puberty and shrinks the genitals. In women, it speeds up puberty and enlarges the uterus. These malformations, along with the estrogen, "feminize" the brain, making men more likely to become homosexual.

TRUTH: The theory can be traced back to a column written by author Jim Rutz in 2006. He outlines his case against soy but doesn't cite any specific research, instead saying "research in 2000" shows soy leads to thyroid problems without saying who did the research, and that "leukemia went up 27 percent in one year," without saying what year. Hormone imbalances were proven not to have anything to do with sexual orientation in a 1984 Columbia University study. Soy does contain trace elements of estrogen, but not enough to cause sexual deformation. As for the left-wing conspiracy in the FDA, that's unlikely because the agency's leadership is appointed by the president, who, since 2000, has been a conservative Republican.

* * *

"I don't wear makeup. I use knives." —**Phyllis Diller**

FLUSHMATE

The long and storied tradition of the World Chess Championship was nearly brought to a halt by a tiny bathroom and a player who (allegedly) spent too much time in there.

BACKGROUND

Few sporting events are more intense than the FIDE World Chess Championship. (FIDE stands for "Fédération Internationale des Échecs," or the World Chess Federation.) Two chess masters face off in a series of 12 games to determine the world's best player. Because games can last for many hours, at various times breaks are allowed between moves, during which players often get up and walk around. To keep them from cheating—such as calling an outside party for assistance or secretly using a computer program to determine the next move—video cameras are placed throughout the facility...except in the players' private bathrooms. In the 2006 championship, held in the town of Elista in Kalmykia, Russia, it turned out that as many eyes were on a private bathroom as there were on the chess table.

THE ACCUSED

The match pitted Russia's Vladimir Kramnik against the reigning FIDE world champion, Bulgaria's Veselin Topalov. After four games, the two men were tied with one win and one draw apiece. That's when things got weird: Topalov's manager filed a formal protest, accusing Kramnik of taking too many bathroom breaks. The complaint described the breaks as "strange, if not suspicious." He requested that the appeals committee change the rules, eliminating the private bathrooms and setting up a single—and monitored—common toilet for both players.

The appeals committee agreed, but Kramnik was appalled and insulted by the allegations. His manager issued a statement, demanding that the original rules be adhered to: "The resting room is small and Mr. Kramnik likes to walk and therefore uses the space of the bathroom as well. It should also be mentioned that Mr. Kramnik has to drink a lot of water during the games. Mr. Kramnik will stop playing this match as long as FIDE is not ready to respect his rights," the statement threatened, "in this case to use the toilet of his own restroom whenever he wishes to do so."

Kramnik's team also insisted that the appeals committee members were unqualified and should be changed. In the meantime, they said, Kramnik would not play again until his demands were met.

THE GAME'S AFOOT

When Kramnik showed up the next day for game five, the appeals committee had not been replaced and, even worse, he found a padlock on his bathroom door. Kramnik refused to start the game, and instead sat on the floor in front of the bathroom door waiting for someone to come and remove the padlock. "My dignity does not allow me to stand this situation!" he fumed as he sat. But no one unlocked the door, and Kramnik was charged with a forfeit, giving the lead in the match to Topalov.

LET'S CALL THE WHOLE THING OFF

The situation became so dire that the FIDE president, Kirsan Ilyumzhinov, issued an ultimatum: If the teams could not come to a bathroom agreement within three days, the remainder of the tournament would be cancelled. He added that he had full confidence in the appeals committee and there were no plans to replace it. After a series of tense meetings, Kramnik and Topalov agreed to adhere to the original bathroom rules. The lock was removed. But Kramnik wouldn't back down on his demand that the committee be replaced, and, as one of the top players in the world, he had considerable clout. Result: A new committee was put in place.

So with the original private bathrooms restored, the match continued…albeit under formal protest from Kramnik's team, who believed that game five should have been replayed instead of forfeited to Topalov. Kramnik, using the jargon of the appeals committee, said, "My further participation will be subject to the condition to clarify my rights regarding game five at later stage." If things didn't go his way, he said, he would sue the FIDE and would "not recognize Mr. Topalov as World Champion under these conditions."

India is home to 50 million monkeys. 5,000 of them live in New Delhi.

"YOU'RE A CHEATER!" "NO, *YOU'RE* A CHEATER!"

Meanwhile, Topalov's team kept on questioning Kramnik's frequent pit stops, citing "coincidence statistics" that showed that Kramnik's moves following his bathroom breaks were an 87% match for what a popular chess computer program would advise. Kramnik laughed off the allegation, claiming that Topalov's "coincidence statistics" in another tournament were even higher.

Kramnik then turned the tables and accused Team Topalov of attempting to plant a device in his private bathroom that would falsely implicate him. Topalov fervently denied Kramnik's new charges, but both bathroom entrances were now being monitored. Topalov refused to shake hands with Kramnik, as per tradition, before each game.

END-GAME

As the match continued, the hostilities between the two men grew even worse, and FIDE officials found themselves talking more to the press about bathrooms than chess. "This a black eye for the game," said one. But the game continued—tense even for a chess match. After 12 games, the two players were tied. A "speed chess" tiebreaker was held the next day, and Vladimir Kramnik barely won it, making him the chess champion of the world…even though he sat out one of his games in front of a bathroom door.

Postscript: A month later, Kramnik defended his title against a computer…and lost. (It was the same computer program that he'd been accused of cheating with in his match against Topalov.)

* * *

EATING BLIND

One night a week, a banquet hall in a Los Angeles hotel becomes a unique restaurant called Opaque. A three-course gourmet meal is served in total darkness by blind waiters. Diners choose meals beforehand from a menu in a lighted lobby before being carefully led to their tables in the pitch-black hall. "You learn how much you rely on your eyesight for cutting food and making sure there's something on your fork," said customer Russ Hemmis, "but at least I can pick my nose without anyone noticing."

Now you know: The little hole in the sink that prevents overflow is called the *porcelator*.

HEY! I'M BEING ATTACKED WITH...

Okay, drop the pork chop and come out with your hands up.

...A FISH. In 2005 a woman in Saginaw, Michigan, was charged with assault after she attacked her boyfriend with a mounted swordfish. She had pulled it off the wall during an argument and stabbed him with the fish's long, sharp bill. He was treated at the scene; she was arrested.

...A CHIHUAHUA. In June 2006, a woman in St. Peters, Missouri, bought a Chihuahua puppy from a dog breeder. When the animal died a short time later, the woman went to the breeder's house, walked in, and, according to news reports, "hit the breeder over the head numerous times with the dead puppy." Then, as she fled in her car, she waved the dead Chihuahua out of the sunroof while yelling threats and obscenities at the breeder.

...A POOPER-SCOOPER. In 2006 Leisa Reed, 47, walked into a Waukesha, Wisconsin, home in the middle of the night, wildly swinging a pooper-scooper. The home owners, John and Linda Dormer, tried to tell Reed she was in the wrong house, but Reed wasn't listening. John Dormer was hit in the face with the pooper-scooper and then fought for his life as the crazed woman came at him with two pairs of scissors. Police finally arrived and, although Reed was only 5'2" and weighed a mere 105 pounds, it took five officers, three stun gun shots, leg straps, and a large bag to finally subdue her. The fact that she was high on crack cocaine made her seemingly superhuman, police said. (She got two years in prison.)

...A PORK CHOP. A 45-year-old Australian man in Roma, Queensland, was helping his son move out of an apartment he had been evicted from when an argument broke out over a refrigerator. The fridge apparently belonged to one family, and the meat inside it to another. During the melee that followed, a woman grabbed a frozen pork chop and hit the father in the head. He was taken to the hospital to get stitches. The Australian Broadcast Company reported that the woman was charged with "assault with a pork chop," adding that the "the weapon has been removed from the scene...and probably eaten."

...A PROSTHETIC LEG. A teenager with a prosthetic leg in Cape Girardeau, Missouri, was attacked by two other teens in September 2006. The two boys pulled 17-year-old Michael Williams out of his car, pulled off his prosthetic leg, and beat him with it. Alexander Harris, 17, and an unnamed 16-year-old were charged with felony assault. Williams thinks the two probably attacked him simply because he was disabled. "What motivates someone to do that, I have no idea," he said.

...A FISH (AGAIN). Alan Bennie was walking through a park in Grangemouth, Scotland, when 22-year-old David Evans approached him, holding a fish. According to prosecutor Neil MacGregor, Evans then asked Bennie, "Do you want to kiss my fish?" MacGregor continued, "Mr. Bennie made no reply, at which point the accused said: 'You answer me next time I ask you to kiss a fish,' and slapped him round the face with it." Evans pleaded guilty to "assault with a fish" and was sentenced to six months in prison.

...A TOILET. In February 2006, a father and son were in their home in Chamberlain, Texas, watching the Super Bowl when they heard a noise outside. Looking down the street, they saw a man and woman in a heated argument that looked like it might turn violent, so they rushed over to intervene. The man pulled out a knife and was able to wound both the father and son. Luckily, a discarded toilet was lying nearby, so the father grabbed a piece of the bowl and clobbered the man, who was taken to the hospital... for *head* injuries. Then he was *throne* in jail, the *loo*-ser. (He's in the *can* now.)

*   *   *

LINE CALL

While bending over to make calls at the 2006 Wimbledon tennis tournament, line judges split 60 pairs of pants.

LOST TV PILOTS

If you thought Gilligan's Island *or* Alf *were goofy ideas for TV shows (which they were), you should see the stuff that* doesn't *make it onto the air. Someone actually filmed pilot episodes of the following shows.*

Baffled! (1973)
A race-car driver (Leonard Nimoy) gets injured in a crash and suddenly begins receiving visions of murders that haven't occurred yet. He solves the crimes before they happen with the help of a female student of psychic phenomena.

Clone Master (1978)
A government scientist (Art Hindle) makes a bunch of clones of himself (all played by Hindle) then sends them out into the world to fight crime and catch evildoers. Each episode would have focused on a different clone's adventures.

The Tribe (1974)
Set 40,000 years ago at the end of the Ice Age, this series chronicled a Cro-Magnon family's struggles to survive harsh living conditions and skirmishes with a rival tribe of primitive Neanderthals.

The Mysterious Two (1979)
A man must stop two popular televangelists...because they're actually evil aliens who are brainwashing humanity in order to take over the planet.

Judge Dee (1974)
Lots of shows in the 1970s were about sensitive people traveling around, generously helping others with their personal problems for free (*Kung Fu* and *The Incredible Hulk* are two examples). In *Judge Dee*, a judge wanders his rural district helping people and resolving disputes. The twist: *Judge Dee* is set in 7th-century China. It's not to be confused with *High Risk*, in which six former circus performers hit the road and help people solve their problems...for money.

Noted eating champion Mort Hurst once ate 16 double-decker Moon Pies in 10 minutes...

Microcops (1989)
Two microscopic cops from outer space come to Earth in pursuit of an equally tiny intergalactic criminal mastermind. To move around the planet, the tiny cops attach their tiny spaceship to people, dogs, and birds.

Danger Team (1991)
A ball of space goop crash-lands in a sculptor's studio. Naturally, he molds the goop into three figurines. The figurines come to life, but only the artist can see them. The artist and the goop men team up to go fight crime.

Steel Justice (1992)
A little boy idolizes his policeman father and likes to secretly tail him when he goes out on drug busts and stakeouts at night. One night, the kid gets killed. Dad is distraught...until he meets his new crime-fighting partner—a fire-breathing, 100-foot-tall robot dinosaur that's possessed by the spirit of his dead son.

Shangri-La Plaza (1990)
A widow and her teenage daughter inherit a donut shop in a Los Angeles strip mall and flirt with the mechanic brothers who work next door. Sounds like normal TV fare...except that all of the dialogue was sung.

Tag Team (1991)
Trying to cash in on the popularity of professional wrestling, this pilot starred 1980s WWF stars "Rowdy" Roddy Piper and Jesse "The Body" Ventura as the Lizard Brothers, professional wrestlers who quit the ring to become undercover cops.

Wurlitzer (1985)
A man inherits a decaying diner and its antique Wurlitzer jukebox. The plot: In each episode, the man selects a song on the jukebox and is then transported back in time to the year that song came out. Why? To help people with their problems. In the pilot episode, he listens to a Jefferson Airplane song, goes to 1968 San Francisco, and helps a hippie quit drugs.

...and 38 eggs in 29 seconds (which resulted in a stroke, in 1991).

America 2100 (1979)

Two stand-up comedians are accidentally put into suspended animation. They awake at the dawn of the 22nd century to find the world run by a supercomputer with the voice and old jokes of fellow comedian Sid Caesar.

K-9000 (1991)

A Los Angeles cop volunteers for a futuristic experiment: His new partner is half robot, half dog. The two are able to communicate via the microchip implanted in the cop's brain.

Danny and the Mermaid (1978)

Danny is an oceanography student failing all of his classes. Then he meets a mermaid who, along with her talking dolphin friend, helps Danny get better grades by escorting him all over the ocean and tutoring him on sea life.

Ethel Is an Elephant (1980)

A New York photographer fights with his landlord to keep his unusual pet in his apartment—an elephant (named Ethel) that was abandoned by the circus. Most of the comedy revolves around unsuccessful attempts to hide Ethel behind furniture.

Mixed Nuts (1977)

This pilot was one of the first shows to depict mentally ill people living in an insane asylum. A sensitive portrayal of forgotten people living on society's fringe? No, *Mixed Nuts* was actually a comedy.

Dad's a Dog (1989)

To the embarrassment of his children, the only work a former TV star can get is on a sitcom (also called *Dad's a Dog*), where he performs the voice of a man who is magically transformed into a dog.

Heil Honey I'm Home! (1990)

A parody of 1950s sitcoms like *Leave it to Beaver*, this British show was about Adolph Hitler and Eva Braun living peacefully in a suburban neighborhood until their lives are turned upside down by their new Jewish neighbors.

SMITHSONIAN FUN

In his spare time, Scott Williams of Newport, Rhode Island, digs up things from his backyard and submits them to the Smithsonian Institution in Washington, D.C. as authentic "paleological finds." Here is the actual (we think) response from the Smithsonian, proving that some scientists do indeed have a sense of humor.

Smithsonian Institution
207 Pennsylvania Avenue
Washington, D.C. 20078

Dear Mr. Williams,

Thank you for your latest submission to the Institute, labeled "93211-D, layer seven, next to the clothesline post... Hominid skull." We have given this specimen a careful and detailed examination, and regret to inform you that we disagree with your theory that it represents conclusive proof of the presence of Early Man in Charleston County two million years ago. Rather, it appears that what you have found is the head of a Barbie doll, of the variety that one of our staff, who has small children, believes to be "Malibu Barbie." It is evident that you have given a great deal of thought to the analysis of this specimen, and you may be quite certain that those of us who are familiar with your prior findings were loathe to contradict your analysis. However, we do feel that there are a number of physical attributes of the specimen which might have tipped you off to its modern origin:

1. The material is molded plastic. Ancient hominid remains are typically fossilized bone.

2. The cranial capacity of the specimen is approximately 9 cubic centimeters, well below the threshold of even the earliest identified proto-hominids.

3. The dentition pattern evident on the skull is more consistent with the common domesticated dog than it is with the ravenous man-eating Pliocene clams you speculate roamed the wetlands during that time.

This latter finding is certainly one of the most intriguing hypotheses you have submitted in your history with this institution, but the evi-

Cranberries are sorted for ripeness by bouncing them (a ripe one can be dribbled like a basketball).

dence seems to weigh rather heavily against it. Without going into too much detail, let us say that:

A. The specimen looks like the head of a Barbie doll that has been chewed on by a dog.

B. Clams don't have teeth.

It is with feelings tinged with melancholy that we must deny your request to have the specimen carbon-dated. This is partially due to the heavy load our lab must bear in its normal operation, and partly due to carbon-dating's notorious inaccuracy in fossils of recent geologic record. To the best of our knowledge, no Barbie dolls were produced prior to 1956 A.D.

Sadly, we must also deny your request that we approach the National Science Foundation Phylogeny Department with the concept of assigning your specimen the scientific name *Australopithecus spiff-arino*. Speaking personally, I, for one, fought tenaciously for the acceptance of your proposed taxonomy, but was ultimately voted down because the name you selected was hyphenated, and didn't really sound like it might be Latin.

However, we gladly accept your generous donation of this fascinating specimen to the museum. While it is undoubtedly not a Hominid fossil, it is, nonetheless, yet another riveting example of the great body of work you seem to accumulate here so effortlessly. You should know that our Director has reserved a special shelf in his own office for the display of the specimens you have previously submitted to the Institution, and the entire staff speculates daily on what you will happen upon next in your digs at the site you have discovered in your Newport backyard.

We eagerly anticipate your trip to our nation's capital that you proposed in your last letter, and several of us are pressing the Director to pay for it. We are particularly interested in hearing you expand on your theories surrounding the trans-positating fillifitation of ferrous metal in a structural matrix that makes the excellent juvenile Tyrannosaurus rex femur you recently discovered take on the deceptive appearance of a rusty 9-mm Sears Craftsman automotive crescent wrench.

Yours in Science,

Harvey Rowe
Chief Curator–Antiquities

Blond hair is the finest; black hair is the coarsest.

OOPS!

Everyone's amused by tales of outrageous blunders—probably because it's comforting to know that someone's screwing up worse than we are. So go ahead and feel superior for a few minutes.

BATTERY'S DONE

In Perth, Australia, in 2003 a man tried to charge his cell phone battery by putting it in his microwave. It didn't work, but it caused an explosion and set his house on fire.

BROWN ALERT

An Edmonton, Alberta, woman frantically called police in October 2003 to report that a letter she'd just opened had changed in color from white to pale yellow, to brown. A terrorist alert went out. Hazardous chemical officers in HAZMAT suits arrived and soon cracked the case. The letter had quickly changed color because it had been placed on an unseen puddle of coffee.

HAPPY OOPS

For almost 50 years, the official number of American troops killed in the Korean War stood at 54,246. In June 2000, the U.S. government announced that after the war a bureaucratic error had been made, miscounting the toll. Actual deaths: 36,940.

HE CAN'T DRIVE 712

In 2002 Lim Ang Hing of Malaysia was given a speeding ticket ...for driving 712 mph, nearly the speed of sound. While Lim admitted he was exceeding the 56 mph limit, he protested the number cited by police, claiming he was only going about 65. Police apologized for the "technical glitch."

SIGNED, SEALED, DELIVERED

Poster seen on buses in Manhattan in 2002: "Are you an adult that cannot read? If so, we can help." In related news, crossing guards who worked for schools in Glasgow, Scotland, in 2003 were sent a letter telling them that their paychecks could be provided in Braille if they were blind (which would have made it difficult to be a crossing guard).

BUY THIS BOOK...BUY THIS BOOK

In 2002 Scott Boyes sat in a Bedfordshire, England, park and dozed off while reading a book called *Helping Yourself With Self-Hypnosis*. An hour later, Boyes woke to find that a thief had apparently helped *him*self...to Boyes's cell phone and several shopping bags full of merchandise he'd just bought.

PAY NO ATTENTION TO THE CLICKING SOUND

German intelligence officers were secretly bugging the phones of 50 suspected criminals in 2002. The operation fell apart when bills for the phone-tapping service were sent to the 50 people who were being monitored.

WHAT? HUH?

In 2006 an irate Lewes, England, man called police to complain of a ringing alarm that had been blaring incessantly for over a week. After a brief investigation, it was discovered the sound was coming from an old smoke alarm in the man's garden shed.

OOPS.COM

Sometimes companies don't think about unintended results when they register Web site addresses. Some unluckily named business Web sites include ones for pen seller Pen Island (penisland.com), celebrity agent directory Who Represents (whorepresents.com), Italian electric company Italian Power Generator (powergenitalia.com), and the design firm Speed of Art (speedofart.com).

PICASSOOPS

Steve Wynn, a Las Vegas casino owner and real estate agent, owns the Pablo Picasso painting *The Dream*. He had arranged to sell the painting in 2006 for $139 million, but before parting with it he had some friends over to his office to show it off. At the party, Wynn was waving his hands around as he told a friend a story. He lost his balance and fell backward into the painting, puncturing it with what one guest later called "a $40 million elbow." Wynn had to cancel the sale.

Crash course: Florida law forbids housewives from breaking more than three dishes per day.

SILENCE IS GOLDEN

The old adage may be true, but would you buy a "recording" with absolutely nothing on it? Apparently, some people would. Here are a few examples of silent "music"...proof that you can sell anything.

UN-CAGED. "The highly eccentric American composer John Cage is responsible for composing the sheet music for his extremely quiet opus '4 minutes 33 seconds,' which is exactly that much silence. The sheet music is blank and just tells you how long not to play."

—*The Worst Entertainment*

YOURS AND MIME. "In the 1970s, a record company in Los Angeles issued a record entitled, 'The Best of Marcel Marceau.' It contained forty minutes of silence followed by a burst of applause. Strangely enough, it sold very well. The company also issued a recording especially for children—it was exactly the same pressing, but had a redesigned cover."

—*The Mammoth Book of Oddities*

SILENCE THERAPY. "In the 1960s, a Staten Island, New York, speech pathologist named Jerry Cammarata did a brisk business with a 52-minute LP designed to 'conjure up previously learned musical experiences, and provide a welcome relief from noise pollution....' It had no sound on it."

—*Oops*

STOP THE MUSIC! "In 1953 jukeboxes were so popular that there was no way to get a moment of quiet in some places...until Columbia Records issued a disc called 'Three Minutes of Silence.' According to jukebox operators, it was a big hit."

—*The Worst Entertainment*

SOUND FREE EUROPE. "The Netherlands' Foundation of the Museum of Silence opened an exhibition featuring 75 years of great silences from Dutch radio and television. The silent moments, on loan from the Museum of Broadcasting in Hiversum, are played to visitors over loudspeakers in the museum. Curator Bob Vrakking said he started the foundation in 1990 to promote silence 'because it is so scarce.'"

—*Dumb, Dumber, Dumbest*

The single most ordered item in American restaurants: French fries.

WHERE ARE THEY NOW?

Not every dead movie star rests in California. Here's the final resting place of a few of our favorite celebrities.

PAUL LYNDE (1927–1982)
The original center square on *Hollywood Squares*, Paul Lynde was also known for his comic roles in *Bewitched* and *Bye Bye Birdie*. He's buried in Amity Cemetery in Mount Vernon, Ohio.

KATHARINE HEPBURN (1907–2003)
Four-time Oscar winner for Best Actress and one of Hollywood's biggest stars, Hepburn rests in a family plot at Cedar Hill Cemetery in Hartford, Connecticut.

JACKIE GLEASON (1916–1987)
"The Great One," whose roles ranged from Minnesota Fats in *The Hustler* to Ralph Kramden in *The Honeymooners*, is buried at Our Lady of Mercy Catholic Cemetery in Miami, Florida. A white marble gazebo stands over his grave.

BURL IVES (1909–1995)
The actor and folk singer, known to kids everywhere as the narrator of *Rudolph the Red-Nosed Reindeer*, is buried in Mound Cemetery in Jasper County, Illinois. His lengthy epitaph includes a quote from Carl Sandburg, who called Ives "the mightiest ballad singer of this or any other century."

DANNY KAYE (1913–1987)
The song-and-dance man rose to fame in the 1940s and '50s in films like *The Inspector General* and *White Christmas*. His ashes are buried with his wife's under a memorial bench decorated with scenes from their lives in Kensico Cemetery in Valhalla, New York.

DIVINE (1945–1988)
The drag queen made famous by John Waters films like *Pink Flamingos* and *Hairspray*, Divine is buried at Prospect Hill Ceme-

Q: Marilyn Monroe stars in what film in which she's listed in credits only as "The Girl"?...

tery in Towson, Maryland. (His tombstone also bears his real name, Harris Glenn Milstead.)

SIR LAWRENCE OLIVIER (1907–1989)
One of the greatest Shakespearean actors of his generation, Olivier is one of the few actors interred at Westminster Abbey in London, England.

INGRID BERGMAN (1915–1982)
Bergman starred in countless classic films including *Casablanca*, *Gaslight*, and *Notorious*. Her ashes are interred next to her parents in Northern Cemetery in Stockholm, Sweden.

GORDON MACRAE (1921–1986)
Star of *Oklahoma* (1955) and *Carousel* (1956), Gordon MacRae lies in Wyuka Cemetery in Lincoln, Nebraska. President Ronald Reagan is quoted on his tombstone: "Gordon will always be remembered wherever beautiful music is heard."

MYRNA LOY (1905–1993)
The versatile star of *The Thin Man*, *The Best Years of Our Lives*, and *Cheaper by the Dozen* is buried in Forest Vale Cemetery in Helena, Montana.

DUDLEY MOORE (1935–2002)
This British comedian, piano player, and actor is interred at Hillside Cemetery in Scotch Plains, New Jersey. A picture of him at the piano is engraved on his headstone.

GRETA GARBO (1905–1990)
The famously private Garbo is buried in Woodland Cemetery in Stockholm, Sweden. A simple marker bears just her name—a reproduction of her autograph engraved in gold script.

JIM HENSON (1936–1990)
The creator of Kermit the Frog and other Muppets died suddenly following an infection. According to his wishes, his ashes were scattered at his ranch outside Santa Fe, New Mexico.

...A: *The Seven Year Itch* (1955).

GARY COOPER (1901–1961)

Though the iconic star of *High Noon* and *The Pride of the Yankees* was buried in California, Cooper's wife relocated to New York and took his body with her. He is now buried at Sacred Hearts of Jesus and Mary Cemetery on Long Island, New York. His grave is marked with a bronze plaque and a three-ton boulder.

JOAN CRAWFORD (1908–1977)

The formidable star, whose film career spanned nearly 50 years, is interred next to her fifth (and last) husband, Alfred Steele, at Ferncliffe Cemetery and Mausoleum in Hartsdale, New York.

WILL ROGERS (1879–1935)

Near the site where his plane crashed in Barrow, Alaska, the much-quoted humorist and actor is buried beneath a memorial inscribed with one of his own quotations: "If you live life right, death is a joke as far as fear is concerned."

CHARLES BRONSON (1921–2003)

The actor who made a career out of playing tough guys in films like *The Great Escape*, *Death Wish*, and *The Magnificent Seven* is buried in Brownsville Cemetery in West Windsor, Vermont. His marker features the Mary Elizabeth Frye poem "Do Not Stand at My Grave and Weep."

LEE MARVIN (1924–1987)

A venerable character actor in Westerns and war films like *Cat Ballou* and *The Dirty Dozen*, Marvin was a distant relative of Robert E. Lee and George Washington. Marvin served as a Marine during World War II, and is now buried in Arlington National Cemetery in Virginia.

SLATS THE LION (D. 1936)

Slats got more screen time than anyone else on this list—he was the original MGM lion, who roared at the start of every MGM movie between 1924 and 1928. (At least four other lions have played the part since.) Slats is buried on the grounds of his trainer's former home in Gillette, New Jersey, where a large evergreen tree has grown over the burial spot.

The word "Beatles" is never mentioned in the Beatles movie *A Hard Day's Night*.

DAVID ICKE AND THE LIZARD PEOPLE

Thirty years ago, he was a professional soccer player in England. Today, he lectures people about the shape-shifting reptilian humanoids from outer space who run the world.

RISING STAR

David Icke was born to poor parents in Leicester, England, in 1952. Raised in public housing, he left his family and school at age 17 to play professional soccer. Icke was a star goalie for two teams but had to retire at only 21: The arthritis in his knee, which had plagued him since the beginning of his career, had now become unbearable.

His lifelong ambition and career were over after just four years. Icke didn't know what to do next, so he returned to Leicester. In 1973, he got a job writing for a small local newspaper, and discovered that he actually liked reporting. He stuck with it, ascending through media jobs in radio, local television, and then to the BBC where he became a nationally known sportscaster.

In the mid-1980s, Icke became interested in politics and publicly spoke out on the importance of preserving the environment. In 1988, he left the BBC because he felt it was inappropriate for a news personality to speak out about world events. So he joined Britain's Green Party, which, banking on Icke's national recognition, made him their national spokesman. Icke had changed careers yet again. Now he was a full-time activist. In 1990 he wrote a book about environmentalism entitled *It Doesn't Have to Be Like This*.

THE CHOSEN ONE

Over 20 years' time, Icke had gone from poor kid on welfare to professional athlete to sportscaster to politician. That would qualify as a full life for anybody. But then Icke's entire world made a really bizarre shift. In March 1990, Icke claims a female "spirit" spoke to him. What did she say? She told Icke that he was "the chosen one," a man blessed with a gift to heal and was put on Earth in order to save it. The spirit further informed him that his meandering life had been predestined: soccer had taught him discipline and journalism gave him the ability to communicate with large groups of people. According to the spirit, all of it was preparation for his new role...as a prophet. One other thing Icke claims the spirit told him: within a few years, a massive earthquake would destroy the entire world, and the oceans would overtake the land as a punishment to humankind for transgressions against nature.

OUT OF LINE

Icke reported his experience to the Green Party leaders, who thought he was crazy and would make the party look bad. They immediately fired him. Now jobless and convinced he was a prophet, Icke made a "spiritual journey" to Peru in 1991. When he returned to England, he began to wear only turquoise-colored clothes and held a press conference to announce that not only was he "chosen," he was *the* chosen one—a "channel for the Christ spirit." He received the news, he said, during another encounter with a supernatural entity. "The title was given to me very recently by the Godhead," meaning Icke believed the Holy Spirit—the spiritual essence of God—told him that he was, essentially, the second coming of Jesus Christ.

Icke hadn't been a major public figure for several years, so the press conference wasn't widely attended or reported. So a few months later Icke went on Terry Wogan's popular BBC talk show to announce once again that he was Christ incarnate, as well as to warn England that planet-devastating earthquakes and tidal waves were scheduled to hit soon, with the British Isles the first to be destroyed. How did England react to this mind-blowing information? Wogan's studio audience roared with laughter. The next day, newspaper columnists and TV comedians suggested that Icke was mentally ill. Few people, if any, took him seriously.

NUTTERS

"As a television presenter, I'd been respected. And overnight, it was transformed into 'Icke's a nutter,'" he told one reporter. Icke went into seclusion and became a prolific writer. At first he wrote mainly about his "prophecies" and "special powers," but then something in Icke snapped. No longer a peaceful "nutter," he

Keanu Reeves is reportedly afraid of the dark.

turned dark and paranoid. Icke became obsessed with exposing "The Brotherhood," a massive network of secret societies that he claimed runs the world and everything in it.

Icke's main source for his theories is his "psychic link to the spirit world," (which conveniently clears him of the burden of having to actually prove any of his theories), but he also consults *The Protocols of the Elders of Zion*, a 90-year-old book that supposedly details a plan by Jewish leaders to achieve world domination through media and financial control. The book is an infamous anti-Semitic hoax, originally written as propaganda by the Tsarist secret police in Russia in 1916.

ALL HAIL THE OVERLORDS!

Yet despite being debunked, Icke trusts the book, claiming the secret society *wants* you to believe their insidious plan is a hoax. Here's how he says the world really works: At the top of the Brotherhood are the "Prison Warders," a group of Satan-worshippers with a single goal—absolute world domination. They use mind control to manipulate the world's economies, banks, military, schools, media, religion, drug companies, organized crime, and spy agencies. They also stage massive catastrophes which cause people to react emotionally, then unwittingly do the Brotherhood's bidding. For instance, according to Icke's book *Infinite Love Is the Only Truth, Everything Else is Illusion*, religions are a creation of the Brotherhood. They create conflicts which make humans easier to divide and conquer. Another example: The terrorist attacks of 9/11 were staged by the Brotherhood to encourage anti-Muslim feelings and gain support for a war in the Middle East.

Icke offers an even stranger twist: the Prison Warders aren't human—they are descended from a race of reptiles who came to conquer Earth from a planet in a distant constellation called Draco. Icke says they live in subterranean caves. Further, the most powerful members of the Brotherhood, the Prison Warders, can gain the ability to shapeshift and assume the appearance of normal human beings...by drinking human blood.

BUSH, BLAIR, AND...BOXCAR WILLIE?

But there's a bright side: the Prison Warders are not a secret, shadow government of unknown figures operating from a secret

Red scare: Most of the villains in the Bible have red hair.

location. Many are history and modern day's most well-known and powerful leaders, including the British royal family, the Bush family, Hillary (but not Bill) Clinton, British prime ministers Harold Wilson and Tony Blair, the Rockefellers, and, Icke inexplicably insists, 1970s country music singer Boxcar Willie. In a 1999 interview, Christine Fitzgerald, a friend of the late Princess Diana, reportedly told Icke that Diana had witnessed Queen Elizabeth II change from a reptile into a humanoid.

The view that all humans are under the control of hideous vampire lizards isn't even Icke's most controversial theory: He says the reptiles are Jewish. But Icke insists allegations that he's anti-Semitic are "friggin' nonsense." Icke says his qualm is with Jewish *reptiles*, not Jewish people. Yet it's hard not to think Icke has racist motives when he claims that "the white race" is most susceptible to getting their blood consumed by the lizards because they consider white people with blue eyes to be the peak of sexual desirability. (Note: David Icke is a white man with blue eyes.)

WHAT'S REAL?

In January 2003, Icke's theories took another turn during a visit to Brazil, where a shaman gave him heavy doses of *Ayahuasca*, a hallucinogenic rainforest plant with mind-altering effects similar to peyote. While one might consider Icke to be spouting the rambling nonsense of someone on drugs *before* he went to Brazil, Icke says the experience "completely transformed my view of life. What it did was take my intellectual understanding that the world is an illusion into the realms of knowing it's an illusion and there's a difference between intellectually understanding it's an illusion and this level of knowing it because you've experienced it."

In other words, no need to worry about the reptile overlords... because, according to Icke, the man who said they exist, they don't *actually* exist. They're just an illusion.

* * *

Popular new snack food in Quebec: Communion wafers. People in the traditionally Catholic area buy them by the bagful. They are reportedly low in fat and calories.

The tip of the hour-hand on a wristwatch travels at 0.0000275 miles per hour.

ODD BATHROOM NEWS

Is this series of Bathroom News stories really any odder than what we put in our regular *books? Perhaps not, but when you think about it…all bathroom news is kind of odd, isn't it?*

FLUSH BEFORE YOU FLY!

China Southern Airlines was losing money. Watching their profits dwindle while fuel prices rose, the airline needed to find new ways to save fuel. They found one, but its success was entirely dependent on their customers' cooperation. Passengers are given a simple request at the airport: "Please go to the bathroom before you board the plane." Why? Because every time an airplane toilet flushes, it uses up to a liter of fuel. "The energy used in one flush is enough for an economical car to run at least 10 kilometers," says pilot Liu Zhiyuan, who always makes sure that he does his business on the ground before doing it in the air.

SPLISH SPLASH I WAS TAKING A BATH

A Russian couple were relaxing in the living room of their apartment after dinner one evening. At the same time, in the apartment directly above, a woman was relaxing in her bathtub, soaking in the warm water, her head back, eyes closed, thoughts meandering, starting to doze offffffff.......***creeeeeeak*** ....***CRACK! (crumble crumble) CRASH!*** "EEEEE-Ahhhhggh!" ***THUD!*** After the tub and ceiling plaster landed on the floor below, the dazed woman looked up out of the tub to see the couple staring at her in bewilderment. She later told reporters, "They seemed as shocked as I was when they saw me lying there. Naked. In the bath. In the middle of their living room."

THE GREAT BATHROOM BARBIE MYSTERY

In late 2005, seemingly out of nowhere and without explanation, Barbie dolls suddenly began appearing in the ladies' bathrooms of coffee shops in the Lincoln, Nebraska, area. The first sighting occurred at The Mill, when a barista walked into the ladies' room one morning and found a Malibu Barbie standing on the paper towel holder. A few days later, another was found perched on top

Statistics show that when men are having a heart attack in a public place, they often run...

of a stall wall. Then more Barbies began showing up at other coffee shops...and it creeped out the staff. "You go to clean and there's a Barbie doll staring up at you. It's scary. I won't go in there anymore," said barista Jamie Yost. All of the Barbies were in pristine condition and came on stands (which pointed toward a collector as the culprit). Shop owners tried everything short of installing video cameras in the bathrooms to catch the woman responsible. But then, a few months after they first appeared, the Barbie visits abruptly stopped (most likely because whoever was putting them there ran out of the dolls). The mystery was never solved.

QUEEN OF POP

Michael Jackson made a pitstop in a Dubai shopping mall to touch up his make-up...in the women's bathroom. The pop star said it was a mistake (after all, the signs *are* in Arabic), but that doesn't mean it didn't enrage the Dubai citizens—especially women. For one thing, Jackson was wearing a headdress that, by Arab custom, is only be worn by females. For another, a woman who emerged from her stall was startled to see the King of Pop applying make-up to a face that has been described as "disconcerting." Recognizing the star, the woman used her cell-phone camera to take pictures of him. That's when Jackson screamed. His body guards rushed into the bathroom and forcefully confiscated the woman's cell phone and deleted the pictures. They spilled out of the bathroom, causing a melee between Jackson's bodyguards and mall cops. The ordeal culminated with the confused pop star being rushed into his heavily fortified SUV. Jackson was not charged, which further angered Muslim women. "Michael Jackson might be a big name," said one. "But it does not give him the right to go into a ladies' washroom!"

* * *

"It's better to have a relationship with someone who cheats on you than someone who doesn't flush the toilet."

—Uma Thurman

...outside. When women are having a heart attack, they're more likely to run to the bathroom.

LOONEY LORDS

Noblemen are usually dignified people who act with grace. Just as often, they're fools made insane by generations of blue-blooded inbreeding.

THE HERMIT OF NOTTINGHAMSHIRE

William John Cavendish Scott-Bentinck (1800–1879) was a member of England's parliament before he was 30, and seemed destined for a serious career in politics. Then his uncle died in 1854 and Scott-Bentinck inherited the title of fifth Duke of Portland. Almost immediately, the new duke rejected public life, preferring to be alone—*very* alone. He moved into his newly inherited estate in Nottinghamshire and quickly rid the house of everything in it, tossing most of his family's priceless treasures into a huge pile in one empty room. Scott-Bentinck then dedicated five empty rooms of the house for his living quarters, and had the rest of the empty house painted pink. But apparently that wasn't secluded enough, so the duke commissioned the construction of a series of underground rooms connected by 15 miles of tunnels. Among the subterranean rooms were a 11,000-square foot ballroom and a billiard room large enough to house 12 pool tables. But nobody ever saw them; no visitors were ever permitted. In fact, from 1854 until his death in 1879, Scott-Bentinck saw only one person—his valet.

THE AQUAMAN OF KENT

Matthew Robinson, the second Baron Rokeby (1713–1800), was from a Scottish noble family that lived in Kent, England. He inherited the title in his 40s and served in the House of Lords. Then Robinson took a vacation in the German spa-resort town of Aachen. When he returned to Kent, Robinson was suddenly and permanently obsessed with water. He started skipping work and spent most of his days swimming in the ocean at a private beach in Kent. Every day Robinson walked to and from the beach wearing tattered peasant clothes, and would then swim for so long and so strenuously that he'd faint, requiring a servant to drag him out of the sea. Robinson drank lots of water, too, and he had drinking fountains installed along the path to the beach. If commoners were caught using them, Robinson didn't punish them—he gave them a gold coin to reward "their good taste." Robinson's embarrassed family eventually talked him into installing a swimming pool at his home. He still spent most of the day swimming, but now tried to prevent fainting by eating a roast leg of veal... underwater.

THE DOG LOVER OF BRIDGEWATER

Francis Henry Egerton, the eighth earl of Bridgewater (1756–1829), wasn't a hermit, but he didn't care much for the company of people. He liked dogs. Throughout his life he always had 12 of them, and he liked to dress them in tiny, specially made leather boots to protect their paws. Every day, six of the dogs would join him on a carriage ride, then the menagerie would return home for dinner. At a long dinner table, all 12 dogs—and Egerton—would eat off of silver with white linen napkins tied around their necks. Egerton liked the dinners for the lively conversations he imagined he was having with the dogs. Egerton also liked his own shoes, wearing a new pair everyday. At night he hung the used shoes on the wall as a makeshift calendar.

THE DUKE, DUKE, DUKE, DUKE OF GIRL

Edward Hyde (1661–1723) was the third Earl of Clarendon and a cousin of Queen Anne of England. In 1701, Anne appointed Hyde to the position of governor of the American colonies of New York and New Jersey. Hyde took the task seriously and literally: He said that if he was governing the colonies on behalf of a woman, he should dress the part. So at the opening of the New York Assembly in 1702, Hyde attended wearing a blue silk gown and satin shoes, waving his face with a fan. Outside of work, he was often spotted on the streets wearing a hoop skirt. By 1708, Hyde was forced to relinquish the governorship and return to England because he was deeply in debt from spending too much money on women's clothes.

* * *

"Why doesn't Tarzan have a beard?" —**George Carlin**

A large swarm of desert locusts can consume 20,000 tons of vegetation a day.

WEIRD JAPAN

Godzilla. Mothra. Rodan. Polite gangs, sewage sausage, and stolen pants. Konichiwa!

NEVER A-SUMO YOU CAN GET AWAY WITH IT

In March 2006, Konoshin Kawabata, 48, snuck into a Buddhist temple in Osaka, planning to rob it. After gathering some antiques and other valuables, he was looking for an exit and opened an unmarked door. Behind the door was the last thing he'd expected: 20 sumo wrestlers. Kawabata tried to make a getaway, but was quickly stopped by the wrestlers.

AT LEAST IT WAS IN A BAG

In 2001 a 25-year-old woman was arrested for multiple violations of the Waste Disposal Act. Her crime: Every week for a year, the Toyoda resident, who was being treated for bulimia, went to forests, streams, and other wilderness areas and dumped plastic bags filled with her own vomit. More than 60 pounds of it was discovered. The woman said she dumped it in remote places because if she disposed of it at home, she might get caught and then she'd be embarrassed.

YOU MAKE ME SICK. REALLY.

Japanese men tend to work extremely long hours. Result: They're never home. The difficult work schedule has created a new medical condition called Retired Husband Syndrome. But it doesn't affect the men; it afflicts their wives. As men in Japan reach retirement age, more and more of them stay home and boss around their wives, who are used to being alone all day and doing things their own way. Doctors have linked the resulting stress to an increase in the occurrence of skin rashes and ulcers in women.

NICE PANTS. ARE THOSE MINE?

In 2004 Kobe police caught Kenji Hishida stealing railway employee uniform pants from a train station office. Police searched Hishida's home and discovered pants from dozens of different transportation companies. Hishida later admitted that he'd

World record bubblegum bubble: 23" in diameter, blown by Susan Montgomery Williams.

been stealing pants for 15 years and had accumulated more than 10,000 pairs.

COURTESY OF THE YAKUZA

Japanese culture places a high value on politeness and cleanliness. Even the criminals adhere. In 1992 the Yamaguchi-gumi, one of Japan's biggest organized-crime syndicates, publicly announced a new honor code. Group members were advised *not* to throw cigarette butts on the ground or hand out business cards with their gang's logo in between criminal acts so as "to not inconvenience the public."

MMMM...SH*T!

In 1993 the Environmental Assessment Center of Okayama debuted a new kind of sausage. It's made out of a mixture of soy protein, steak flavoring…and processed sewage. The soy and steak flavor are supposed to cover up the taste of human waste. And in 2006, a team of food scientists at Japan's International Medical Center announced that they had successfully developed a process to extract vanilla from cow dung. The scientists promised to use the flavoring only in nonfood items such as shampoo.

BAD DOG

At an Ogori subway station in 2005, a blind couple gave their seeing eye dog a spoken command. It's unknown what exactly they told the dog to do. The dog apparently misunderstood because after receiving the command, the dog jumped off the subway platform and onto the tracks below. The couple, still holding the leash, also plunged onto the tracks. They were all killed by an oncoming train. Sad irony: The couple was on their way to a dog-obedience course.

AND LAST BUT NOT LEAST, "FRIENDLY" PENGUINS

In 2004 a team from Rikkyo University discovered that at 16 aquariums and zoos around Japan, there were 20 same-sex penguin couples. Researchers believe it's because penguins raised in captivity have difficulty finding suitable mates of the opposite sex because of the limited population.

1 in 7 Americans say they or someone they know has had an experience involving a UFO.

THAT'S ENTERTAINMENT?

Show business wasn't always as highbrow as it is today. Before the dawn of sophisticated entertainments such as sitcoms, reality shows, and YouTube, stage performers could do almost any weird act...and people would pay to see it. Here are some well-known—and very strange—performers of yesteryear.

NAME: Clarence E. Willard

ACT: "He grows before your eyes!"

STORY: Willard was a vaudeville performer in the 1910s. Without the aid of any machinery, he would "grow" from 5'10" to 6'4" while delivering a monologue about his bizarre talent, or anecdotes about how he had horrified foreign heads of state with his act. Here's how he did it: Willard would slowly stretch every muscle in his chest, throat, knees, and hips as far as they could go to give the impression that he was growing. Then, painfully, he would hold them like that for 12 minutes and then slowly "shrink" back to his normal size.

NAME: Orville Stamm

ACT: "Musical Muscleman"

STORY: Stamm was a teenaged singer and fiddle player on the vaudeville circuit known as "The Strongest Boy in the World." As he played the violin, a huge bulldog clamped down on and hung from his bowing arm. For the finale of his act, Stamm laid down on the stage face-up while a small upright piano was lowered onto his stomach. A pianist would then jump up and down on Stamm's thighs while playing along to Stamm singing "Ireland Must Be Heaven 'Cause My Mother Came From There."

NAME: Matthew Buchinger

ACT: "The One-Man Variety Show"

STORY: This 17th-century German entertainer had a dazzling array of talents. He played 10 instruments (some of which he'd invented himself), sang, danced, read minds, was a trick-shot artist and marksman, bowled, did magic tricks, drew portraits and landscapes, and did calligraphy. Even more impressive: Buchinger had no arms or legs. He had finlike appendages instead of hands, and "stood" only 28 inches tall.

NAME: Datas
ACT: "The Memory Man"
STORY: Born W. J. M. Bottle, this early-1900s performer's talent was simply knowing lots of facts. Bottle had left school at the age of 11 to earn money for his family. But he continued to learn, repeatedly reading whatever books and newspapers he could find until he had the contents committed to memory. For his act, he would ask the audience to submit about 50 questions and then answer them in rapid-fire succession, embellishing answers with extra information or droll humor. For instance, when asked "When was beef the highest?" Datas replied, "When the cow jumped over the moon." After he died, Datas's brain was autopsied. It weighed 69 ounces, the heaviest on record at the time.

NAME: Daniel Wildman
ACT: "The Bee Wrangler"
STORY: Here's his act: He rode a bicycle around a circus ring while a swarm of bees covered his face. Then he'd tell the bees to fly to a specific location...which they did.

NAME: LaRoche
ACT: "The Human Ball"
STORY: LaRoche (born Leon Rauch in Austria in 1857) would stuff himself in a brightly colored, two-foot-wide metal ball and then roll uphill to the top of a 30-foot-high, narrow spiral track. He did it so smoothly that it appeared as if the ball had magically moved upward on its own. In fact, the audience didn't even know anyone was inside until LaRoche popped out of the ball when he'd reached the top.

NAME: Bernard Cavanagh
ACT: "The Starvationist"
STORY: In the 1830s and '40s, Cavanagh amazed large crowds

Q: What do Scottish men wear under their kilts? A: Traditionally, nothing at all.

with his claims that he had gone long periods of time—weeks on end—without eating or drinking. He had himself confined without food in a London prison cell for a week in 1841 to prove it. Cavanagh claimed he once even went five years without nourishment. But he was exposed as a fraud when a woman caught him backstage eating sausage, bread, and a quarter pound of ham.

NAME: Tommy Minnock
ACT: "The Singing Martyr"
STORY: Minnock was one of America's most popular vaudevillians in the 1890s. Every night, he'd sing a popular song of the day called "After the Ball Is Over" while he hammered nails into his own hands and feet, attaching himself to a wooden cross.

* * *

A PARTIAL LIST OF JOBS HELD BY HOMER SIMPSON

nuclear safety inspector	horse trainer	chief of police
monorail conductor	pilot	used-car salesman
food critic	artist	ambulance driver
sailor	oil rig worker	fortune cookie writer
soldier	mall Santa	sanitation commissioner
teacher	town crier	clown
talk show host	fish gutter	agent
trucker	bodyguard	informant
musician	film critic	mayor
telemarketer	bartender	personal assistant
mascot	panhandler	roadside corn salesman
marriage counselor	minister	greeter
carny	juvenile hall guard	bootlegger
chauffeur	professional arm wrestler	smuggler
missionary	voice actor	railroad engineer
candle maker	roadie	pretzel inspector
superhero	motivational speaker	attack dog trainer
snowplow driver	CEO	astronaut
car designer	baby proofer	activist
butler	mob boss	choreographer
blackjack dealer	chiropractor	plus-sized butt model

JAILHOUSE PINK

Color has long been known to affect our brain chemistry. If you don't believe us, listen to what happened when researchers painted the jail cells of violent criminals a nice, pretty pink.

PINK FREUD

Dr. Alexander Schauss became interested in the physiological effects of color in the 1960s while he was a graduate student at the University of New Mexico. He already knew that color stimulated the human pituitary and pineal glands, which in turn could alter moods. And from this fact, he arrived at an interesting theory.

In a series of experiments, Dr. Schauss concluded that the color pink—a very particular shade of pink, to be exact—had a calming effect on the nervous system: It slowed heart rate, pulse, and respiration, resulting in a feeling of well being. But to prove his theory, Schauss needed access to a large number of agitated subjects in a controlled environment. He found just what he was looking for in an unexpected place: a military prison.

JUST WHAT THE DOCTOR ORDERED

In 1979 Schauss approached the commanders of the U.S. Naval Correctional Center in Seattle. He figured he'd have trouble convincing the navy to experiment with the colors in its prison—especially if the target color was pink—but, to his surprise, the officials agreed. Not only were prison commander Mike Miller and chief warrant officer Gene Baker willing, they even helped mix the paint and applied it to the walls and ceiling of a holding cell.

The results were amazing. After 10 to 15 minutes in the pink holding cell, new arrivals who'd been tossed in there kicking, screaming, cursing—even rip-roaring drunk—were calm. And the effects lasted for 30 minutes after the prisoners were taken out of the cell. The center continued the experiment for the next 156 days, and the results were consistent. In his paper on the subject, Dr. Schauss named the color "Baker-Miller pink" in honor of the cooperative Navy officers. (Since then, it's also

The most common dream is of falling, followed by being chased or attacked.

been nicknamed "drunk tank" pink, "Pepto-Bismol" pink, and "bubblegum" pink.)

THE PEPTO-BISMOL EFFECT?

A close approximation of the color can be found at any paint store (Benjamin Moore #1328, for example), but if you're thinking that Baker-Miller pink might be just the thing for your teenager's room, think again. In later experiments, prisoners who were left in the pink room for longer than a few minutes seemed to overdose on Baker-Miller pink, becoming agitated again or severely depressed.

Other facilities duplicated the experiment, most with success. Baker-Miller pink rooms are still used to calm prisoners in various detention centers across the United States.

An added bonus (for dieters, anyway) was found during another navy experiment: Baker-Miller pink also works as an appetite suppressant. According to experts, you can get the same result—a mild decrease in the desire to eat—just by looking at a piece of paper that's the right shade of pink for a few minutes.

HUES FOR THE BLUES

If a relaxing pink isn't your thing, here's what researchers say about the effects of other colors:

- Blue is calming, lowers blood pressure, and slows respiration.
- Green is soothing, mentally and physically. It helps relieve depression, anxiety, and nervousness.
- Violet suppresses appetite, provides a peaceful environment, and supposedly relieves migraine headaches.
- Yellow energizes, relieves depression, improves memory, and stimulates appetite.
- Orange energizes and stimulates the appetite and digestive system.
- Red stimulates brainwave activity, relieves depression, and increases heart rate, respiration, and blood pressure.
- Black can increase self-confidence and even improve strength. Like pink and violet, it also suppresses the appetite.

Humans can smell over 10,000 different aromas.

JUST PLANE WEIRD

Every time Uncle John sees an airplane, he marvels that a heavier-than-air machine can fly. Here are a few more mind-bogglers from the world of human flight.

HI JACK! HOW YA' DOIN'?

Shortly after a Mongolian Airlines passenger flight landed in Ulan Bator in 2006, four men jumped out of their seats and loudly announced that the plane was being hijacked. "These hooligans went up to the pilots' cabin and tied up the pilots and threatened four passengers and kept them in the plane," a passenger later recounted. "They hit one woman and knocked her down." The standoff lasted about an hour until all of the passengers and crew were freed. Only later did the airline find out that the "hijacking" was actually a secret training exercise conducted by the Mongolian Central Intelligence Agency. The airline was incensed that they weren't alerted beforehand. The CIA argued that announcing it would have ruined the test—which, they added, the airline failed miserably. As for the passengers, many are suing the CIA (including the woman who was knocked down).

SUNDAY DRIVING

Sundays in downtown Montreal, Quebec, draw thousands of sightseers and shoppers. On one such Sunday in 2006, a single-engine Cessna interrupted the afternoon festivities when it landed on Parc Avenue, one of Montreal's busiest streets. The pilot had alerted police that the plane's engine had cut out, but there was no time to close the road. Amazingly, the pilot managed to not only land the plane safely, but he slalomed through the heavy traffic without hitting a single car or pedestrian. (The landing wasn't completely perfect, though—one of the plane's wings slightly clipped a street sign.)

I'M A LITTLE TEAPOT, SHORT AND STOUT

An RAF Nimrod, a British search-and-rescue plane, was on a flight in 2006 when a small hatch—used for dropping homing beacons from the plane—didn't close correctly. The hole let

Who are Betty Jean McBricker and Wilma Slaghoople? The *Flintstones* wives (their maiden names).

swirling winds into the plane, so the crew searched the cabin for an object to plug it with. They found something that fit almost perfectly: a teapot. Government officials called into question the safety of the Nimrod fleet (which had suffered a fatal crash a few months earlier), but the Royal Air Force calmly explained that at no time on this flight was the crew in danger; they merely plugged the gaping hole with the teapot for "comfort" reasons.

REMOTE-CONTROLLED KILLER TOY

Onlookers were enjoying an air show in Hungary when one of the planes crashed into the crowd and injured six spectators, killing two of them. What makes this tragic story so odd is that this was a *model* airplane show. When asked to comment, a government spokesman could only say that this was "the first time in the history of Hungary that a person was killed by a model airplane."

DYING TO FLY FIRST CLASS

On November 28, 2006, a British Airways flight took off from London headed to Boston. Three hours into the six-hour flight, a 75-year-old American passenger in business class suffered a massive heart attack. Calls for a doctor were made, there was a commotion among the flight attendants, but to no avail—a few minutes later, the man was dead. Now the question was: what to do with the body for the rest of the flight? Business class was full. So was coach. There were, however, a few empty rows in first class. Solution: move the body to first class.

Not surprisingly, this plan didn't go down well with the first-class passengers, who watched in horror as four flight attendants carried the body to an empty row. They put the man in a seat, reclined it, fastened the seatbelt, and put a blanket over his body...but not over his head, which flopped to one side. "It was a very strange and unsettling thing to experience," said one passenger, who had until then been enjoying the inflight movie, *Mission Impossible III*, when the corpse was placed across the aisle from him.

Another passenger told reporters, "I felt quite uneasy. But most of the passengers were being very British about it and simply not acknowledging that there was anything wrong."

In Glasgow, Scotland, it is a crime for a man to hug a store mannequin.

CLASSIFIEDS

Uncle John loves shopping through the newspaper ads—he never knows what he'll find for sale. But sometimes the ads themselves are the best part.

For sale: Antique desk suitable for lady with thick legs and large drawers.

Two wire-mesh butchering gloves, one 5-finger, one 3-finger. Pair: $15.

Dog for sale. Eats anything and is especially fond of children.

Our sofa seats the whole mob and it's made of 100% Italian leather.

Joining nudist colony, must sell washer & dryer. $300.

For sale—Eight puppies from a German Sheppard and an Alaskan Hussy.

American flag, 60 stars, pole included: $100.

Star Wars job of the hut—$15.

Wanted: Chambermaid in rectory. Love in. $200 a month. References required.

Free: Farm kittens. Ready to eat.

Wanted: 50 girls for stripping machine operators in factory.

Ecology Freak wanted for relevant work. Could be lucrative. Will be interesting. Call EARTH.

Man wanted to work in dynamite factory. Must be willing to travel.

Wanted: Preparer of food. Must be dependable, like the food business, and be willing to get hands dirty.

Wanted: Widower with school-age children requires person to assume general housekeeping duties. Must be capable of contributing to growth of family.

Long-haired freaks and weird chicks wanted. Earn $2 an hour plus food and booze for being obscene at Establishment parties. We rent beautiful people to squares.

Wanted: Man to take care of cow that does not smoke or drink.

Our experienced Mom will care for your child. Fenced yard, meals, and smacks included.

A *pentapopemptic* is someone who has been divorced five times.

POLITICS: IT'S NO LAUGHING MATTER

Sometimes politics gets so absurd that it seems the major political parties must be kidding. They're not...but these odd political parties from around the world definitely are.

PARTY: Guns and Dope Party
COUNTRY: United States
PLATFORM: Founded by conspiracy theorist Robert Anton Wilson, this party's platform is similar to the Libertarian party, which strongly supports personal freedoms, including gun ownership and legalized drugs. The difference: the Guns and Dope Party advocates that supporters vote for themselves as write-in candidates in every election and wants to replace one-third of Congress with ostriches.

PARTY: Extreme Wrestling Party
COUNTRY: Canada
PLATFORM: This party was formed in Newfoundland in 1999 after former professional wrestler Jesse Ventura's win in Minnesota's 1998 gubernatorial election. Party leader Quentin Barboni took control when he beat 11 other wrestlers in an each-man-for-himself wrestling "battle royale" match.

PARTY: McGillicuddy Serious Party
COUNTRY: New Zealand
PLATFORM: Formed by a group of comedians and street musicians, this party stood candidates in every federal election in New Zealand from 1984 to 1999. Among the group's aims were to institute a Scottish monarchy in New Zealand, replace paper money with chocolate, raise the school graduation age to 65, and lower the speed of light to 60 mph. McGillicuddy Serious also wanted to restrict voting rights among humans to women under the age of 18, but wanted to extend the rights to hedgehogs and trees.

Female sea turtles don't reach sexual maturity until they are 40 or 50 years old.

PARTY: Two-Tailed Dog Party
COUNTRY: Hungary
PLATFORM: The party is "led" by a two-tailed puppy named "Istvan Nagy," which is a common, generic Hungarian name (like "John Smith"). The idea behind running a dog for office is that something cute couldn't be dishonest. In the 2006 federal election, the party promised eternal life, world peace, two sunsets a day, one-day workweeks, free beer, less gravity, and the construction of a mountain on the Great Hungarian Plain.

PARTY: Absolutely Absurd Party
COUNTRY: Canada
PLATFORM: AAP advocates want to lower the legal voting age to 14 because "when was the last time a 14-year-old started a war?" Among the party's other ideas: the candidate coming in dead last wins the election; parliament seats should be won in a raffle, and the Department of Defense should be replaced with a team of Rock, Paper, Scissors experts.

PARTY: Church of the Militant Elvis Party
COUNTRY: England
PLATFORM: This political group, founded in 2001 by "Lord Biro," wants to overthrow capitalism. Reason: capitalism leads to a free media, which Biro blames for turning Elvis Presley into a fat, drug-addicted shadow of his former slim self.

PARTY: Official Monster Raving Loony Party
COUNTRY: England
PLATFORM: Founded in 1983 by a musician called "Screaming Lord Sutch," the party seriously calls for redistribution of wealth and food for the poor, but also advocates for a few very bizarre principles. For example, the OMRLP is against England adopting the euro—they want Europe to adopt the English pound (and also wants to introduce a 99p coin to "save on change"). Amazingly, some of the OMRLP's policies have actually been adopted as laws, including lowering the voting age to 18 and issuing passports to pets.

The "Armstrong Line" is the altitude at which blood begins to boil (65,000 ft. above sea level).

THE BODY FARM

Ahh, Tennessee—home to Dollywood, Graceland, the Grand Ole Opry… and the world's creepiest research facility.

PUTRIFIED FOREST

The Anthropological Research Facility (ARF) of the University of Tennessee lies on three landscaped acres behind the UT Medical Center parking lot. Aside from the razor-wire fence, it looks like a lovely wooded park, complete with people lying on their backs enjoying a pleasant day in the sun. That is, until you smell the foul odor. A second glance tells you these sunbathers are not all on their backs: some are face down in the leaves; some are waist deep in the dirt. Others are encased in concrete or wrapped in plastic garbage bags or locked in car trunks. None of them seem to be enjoying anything. Why? They're all cadavers, planted by scientists from the University of Tennessee for the sole purpose of studying the decomposition of the human body.

Nicknamed "the Body Farm" by the FBI, this research facility develops and provides medical expertise to law enforcement professionals and medical examiners. It helps them pinpoint the exact time of death of a body—a critical part of any criminal investigation involving a cadaver.

DR. DEATH

ARF (or "BARF," as local critics call it) was founded in 1971 by forensic anthropologist Dr. William Bass. He had been asked to guess the age of a skeleton dug up on a piece of property once owned by a Confederate Army colonel named William Shy. Bass had examined some Civil War–era remains before, but they were mostly dust. Since this skeleton still had pieces of flesh attached to it, his analysis was able to determine that the person was a white male between 24 and 28 years old, who'd been dead about a year. Bass was correct about the race, gender, and age, but way off on the time of death. The skeleton, it turned out, belonged to William Shy himself, who was buried in 1864—107 years earlier. "I realized," Bass later recalled, "there was something here about decomposition we didn't know." He started the facility to help fill in the gaps.

Isuzu means "50 bells" in Japanese.

RIGOR MORTIS 101

The first corpses Bass and his team studied were bodies that had gone unclaimed or unidentified at the local morgue. At first they had four to five cadavers a year. Today all cadavers are donated by personal request (and there's a waiting list). ARF researchers currently work with around 45 bodies a year.

"We go through the FBI reports and come up with the most common way a perpetrator will bury someone, and use these as our models," says Dr. Arpad Vass, a senior researcher at the facility. ARF scientists and graduate students then study the rate of *algor mortis*—the cooling of the body. The temperature of a corpse drops approximately 1°F per hour until it matches the temperature of the air around it—a useful clue for determining time of death. *Rigor mortis*—the stiffening of the body—generally starts a few hours after death and moves through the body, disappearing 48 hours later. If a body has been dead longer than three days, they look for other clues: What bugs have arrived to help with the decomposition? How old are the fly larvae? Are there beetles?

This process of *insect succession* (which species of insect feed on a decaying corpse, and in what order), as well as the effects of weather and climate on decomposition, are all closely monitored and measured. The scientists use this data to develop methods and instruments that accurately establish time of death. This expertise is shared with law enforcement agencies all over the world.

WHAT'S THAT SMELL?

Dr. Vass's research has shown that a body emits 450 chemicals at different stages of its decay. Each stage has a unique "bouquet," which Vass has given names such as *putrescine* and *cadaverine*. Using the same aroma scan technology used in the food and wine industry, one of his students is developing a handheld electronic "nose" for the FBI that will sniff out the time of death by identifying the presence of these different chemicals in a corpse.

Synthetic putrescine and cadaverine are now used to train "human remains dogs" (not to be confused with police dogs who search for escaped criminals). These dogs respond to the specific scent of death they've been trained to recognize, and they do it with amazing accuracy: They can tell their trainers whether a lake is concealing a corpse by sniffing the water's surface for minute bubbles of gas seeping from a rotting carcass underwater, and they can show police exactly where to dive to retrieve the body. The dogs can detect the faintest scent of a dead body on the ground, even if it was removed from the spot a year earlier.

Another researcher at ARF, Dr. Richard Jantz, has developed a computer program that can determine the gender, race, and height of a skeleton. This software has been invaluable in helping forensic teams identify the victims of ethnic cleansing in Bosnia, Rwanda, and other war crime sites.

BREAKING IT DOWN

Warning: the following may require a strong stomach.

• Rigor mortis sets in just after death. The body stiffens, first at the jaws and neck. After 48 hours, the corpse relaxes and muscles sag.

• During the first 24 hours, the body cools at a rate of about 1°F per hour until it matches the temperature of the air around it. This is called *algor mortis*. Next, blood settles in the part of the body closest to the ground, turning the rest of the body pale.

• After two to three days, *putrefaction* is underway. The skin turns green and the body's enzymes start to eat through cell walls and the liquid inside leaks out. At this stage, fly larvae, or maggots, invade and start to eat the corpse's body fat. The maggots carry with them bacteria that settle in the abdomen, lungs, and skin.

• The bacteria feed on the liquid and release sulfur gas as a waste product. With nowhere to go, the gas causes the corpse to bloat and swell (and sometimes burst). By the end of the third day, the skin changes from green to purple to black. This stage is called *autolysis*, which means "self-digestion."

• Next is *skin slip*. As cells continue to break down, liquid continues to leak. After about a week, it builds up between layers of skin and loosens it, causing skin to start to peel off in large chunks.

• After two weeks, the fluid leaks from the nose and mouth. After three weeks, teeth and nails loosen; internal organs start to rupture.

• After about a month, the bacteria and enzymes have liquified all body tissue until the corpse dissolves and sinks into the ground, leaving only the skeletal remains and what's called a *volatile fatty acid stain*. Sweet dreams...

SO YOU THINK YOU'VE SEEN A UFO

Have you ever seen strange lights in the sky that couldn't be explained? If so, you're not alone—people think *they see UFOs all the time. Here's a quick checklist of all the things they usually turn out to be.*

NOT OF THIS EARTH?

We've all seen UFO stories in movies: spaceships landing in cornfields, abductions, brainwashing, and all those probings of the human body that aliens can't seem to get enough of.

But most actual UFO sightings are much simpler—a hovering light or two on the horizon, or a strangely shaped "spacecraft" that seems to float at a distance too far for the observer to see many details. And most of the objects that are reported as UFOs turn out to be perfectly ordinary things that happen to be in an unusual spot, or just some object the "witness" isn't familiar with. So before you report a UFO, make sure it's not something on the list below.

IT MIGHT BE...

...Venus. The second planet from the Sun is the culprit in many UFO sightings because it's bright and unblinking, and can be seen while it's still light out. Venus may have even fooled former president Jimmy Carter; an examination of the UFO that he and several other witnesses reported one night strongly suggests that he was actually looking at Venus. Jupiter, which can get almost as bright as Venus, is also often mistaken for a UFO.

...a meteor. Most meteors zoom across the sky and leave only a short, momentary streak of light. But some larger ones can become fireballs and streak across the sky for a longer time, trailing smoke and sparks and even exploding in midair in a phenomenon known as a *bolis*. Fireballs and bolises are sometimes so bright that they can be seen during the day.

...falling space junk. Booster rockets, communications satellites, abandoned space stations—sooner or later, they all fall back to Earth. Even man-made satellites that are still in orbit are often mistaken for UFOs because they're relatively bright and move across the sky at a steady speed.

...a cloud. A surprising number of clouds are reported as UFOs. One of the greatest offenders is a type of altocumulus cloud that can take on the traditional "flying saucer" shape, and does such a good job that many people are fooled.

...a weather balloon. They're released every day all across the United States. They're bright and shiny, and they float up very high in the sky, well into the stratosphere. They often make course changes depending on the winds.

...a military aircraft. Most people know what a commercial airliner looks like. But lots of people were fooled in the 1960s during the early days of the sleek, black SR-71 spy plane—especially when the plane did a maneuver called the "dipsy doodle," in which the plane would dive, hover for a second, and then take off at a tremendous speed. More recently, various "stealth" planes have been mistaken for flying saucers because of their unconventional shapes.

...a flame or electrical discharge. Natural phenomena like ignited swamp gas and St. Elmo's fire can produce glowing balls of flame or electricity. Electrical discharges near high-power lines and power stations have also been reported as UFOs.

...an optical illusion. Human eyesight isn't as reliable as people would like to think it is. Involuntary eye movements can make objects that are perfectly still appear to jerk around in the night sky. And when an object is only seen briefly, our brains will sometimes embellish or "fill in" details that aren't actually there. People reporting UFOs that turn out to be falling space junk often report blinking lights, windows, and purposeful movement, when none of those things were part of the recovered debris.

Now, if what you saw wasn't any of the above, there's one other thing to do:

Get independent third-party verification. One of the problems with many UFO sightings is that no one else was there to see them. Your UFO experience will be much more believable if someone else experienced it as well, preferably someone you don't know. It won't mean that what you saw was a true UFO...but at least you'll have some backup when you tell your friends.

The elephant is the only mammal with four knees.

THAT'S CRAZY TALK

So the one cow says to the other cow, "Whaddaya think about all this mad cow disease going around?" And the other cow says, "What do I care? I'm a helicopter!"

"I don't buy temporary insanity as a murder defense. Breaking into someone's home and ironing all their clothes is temporary insanity."

—Sue Kolinsky

"We do not have to visit a madhouse to find disordered minds; our planet is the mental institution of the universe."

—Goethe

"We're all crazy and the only difference between patients and their therapists is the therapists haven't been caught yet."

—Max Walker

"When dealing with the insane, the best method is to pretend to be sane."

—Hermann Hesse

"Insane people are always sure that they are fine. It is only the sane people who are willing to admit that they are crazy."

—Nora Ephron

"Do you know what crazy is? Crazy is majority rules!"

—Jeffrey Goines

"When we remember we are all mad, the mysteries disappear and life stands explained."

—Mark Twain

"Those who can laugh without cause have either found the true meaning of happiness…or have gone stark raving mad."

—Norm Papernick

"Illusions commend themselves to us because they save us pain and allow us to enjoy pleasure instead. We must therefore accept it without complaint when they sometimes collide with a bit of reality against which they are dashed to pieces."

—Sigmund Freud

"Those who danced were thought to be quite insane by those who could not hear the music."

—Angela Monet

"Honesty is the best policy, but insanity is a better defense."

—Steve Landesberg

"Show me a sane man and I will cure him for you." —Carl Jung

WEIRD TOY ADS OF YESTERYEAR

Here are some of the peculiar playthings that toy companies pitched to kids in the 1950s and '60s. Uncle John actually remembers some of these toys and offers this observation: "Odd then; still odd today."

WITCH DOCTOR HEAD SHRINKER'S KIT

The Product: As it says—a (plastic) head shrinking kit

The Pitch: "Into the deepest jungle went Pressman Toymakers, looking for something new. The secret they brought back for you is incredible! The Pressman Witch Doctor Head Shrinker's Kit! Plastic flesh, mixing cauldron, and petrifying potion. Just pour it into the mold and in minutes you can add monster hair! Paint it with the coloring kit included, or make up your own decorations. In 24 hours, the heads shrink, shrink down. Shrunken heads for all occasions! Collect 'em, swap 'em. Give them to your witch doctor friends. You can always cook up more, with Pressman's Witch Doctor's Head Shrinker's Kit."

LIONEL BALLISTIC MISSILE RAILCAR LAUNCHER

The Product: How do you sell dull old railroad trains during the Cold War era? By adding nuclear missile cars.

The Pitch: "Hi! This is my friend the Grumman Tiger fighter plane. It's a jet, and I'm Ralph Donnell, a test pilot. It takes a lot of training to control one of these babies; my son Wayne will learn someday. Right now, though, he's getting ready by learning to control a Lionel Electric Train. With a Lionel Train, you not only get locomotives and cars, but all sorts of missile and rocket equipment, too! You can learn to operate these Lionel missile launchers. And fire this ballistic missile launcher by pressing a button. Wow! And look! You can put this boxcar target together and blow it up again and again. Remember kids, you're in control —you're the boss on the Lionel line!" (Also available: the Lionel Turbo Missile Firing Car, the Lionel Reconnaissance Copter Car, and the Lionel Aerial Target Car.)

17th-century French Cardinal Mazarin never traveled without his personal chocolate-maker.

THE DING-A-LINGS

The Product: Tiny battery-powered robots

The Pitch: "You're witnessing the creation of an entire new world. A world of unbelievable excitement and fun. The world of the Ding-a-lings! Holy smokes, what's going on? It's Ding-a-ling Fireman coming to the rescue! He's got his own built-in pumper to save the day. Ding-a-ling Shoeshine gives you the brightest shine you've ever seen! Ding-a-ling Answer Man's got all the answers in his head. Push the lever, and he'll tell your future. Ding-a-ling Chef salts your food, and Ding-a-ling gofer serves it to you!... Stand back, world—there's a whole new one on the way. The wild, wonderful, wacky world of the Ding-a-lings!"

ROY ROGERS QUICK SHOOTER HAT

The Product: A cowboy hat with a hidden derringer cap gun that pops out when you push a hidden button

The Pitch: "Hi fellas! Say, that's a pretty tricky hat, isn't it? Partners, how would you like to surprise your pals like that? Well you can with my new Roy Rogers Quick Shooter Hat. It's by Ideal. And here's how the Quick Shooter Hat works: Just press this secret button right here, and a replica of an authentic western pistol pops out and fires! It's your secret weapon, even when they think you're unarmed. So get Ideal's new Roy Rogers Quick Shooter Hat at your favorite store today. And you'll always be ready for anything!"

SUPER HELMET SEVEN

The Product: A plastic hardhat with a giant lighting apparatus on top

The Pitch: "Jet pilots wear 'em! Skydivers wear 'em! Racing drivers wear 'em! And now you can join the men of action with the most amazing speed helmet ever made, the exciting new Super Helmet Seven! Afoot! Afloat! Racing! Driving! Bike riding! It helps keep you safe, even at night! Only Super Helmet Seven does all this: One—red flasher signals automatically! Two—tinted goggles protect your eyes! Three—left and right direction lights! Four—reflector shows you're up ahead! Five—warning buzzer clears the way! Six—Super Helmet Seven absorbs the shock!

Students at Stockport College in the U.K. built an 896-lb. fully operational yo-yo...

Seven—powerful headlight flashlight: It's removable! Boys who dare will want to wear new Super Helmet Seven! Super Helmet Seven! Super Helmet Seven!"

TOMMY BURST DETECTIVE SET

The Product: There's not much here to help a young detective solve mysteries—the set doesn't contain a single crime-detecting tool—but there's plenty he can use to gun down suspects.

The Pitch: "It's some fun when Snubby Gun plays Private Eye, and you can have the same kind of fun with Mattel's Tommy Burst Detective set. The Tommy Burst tommy gun has automatic bolt action—fire off a burst of ten shots. Pull the bolt again—you're re-loaded! Or fire single shots like a rifle. The Tommy Burst alone is $3.00. In the detective set, you also get the snub-nosed .38 and snap-draw shoulder holster. The pistol fires Greenie Stickem Caps and shoots Safe Shootin' Shells. The exciting new Tommy Burst Detective Set includes wallet, badge, and ID card. $7.00, wherever toys are sold. You can tell it's Mattel—it's swell!"

MYSTERY DATE

The Product: A blind-date fantasy board game for girls

The Pitch: "Open the door for your mystery date! It's Mystery Date! The thrilling new Milton Bradley game of romance and mystery that's just for you! And you! And you! And you! Mystery Date! Will you be ready for swimming, or a dance? When you open the door, will your mystery date be a dream, or a dud? Fun and surprises! That's Mystery Date! Open the door for your mystery date!"

DICK TRACY POWER JET GUN

The Product: The two-in-one gun you never knew you always wanted—a rifle that's a squirt gun *and* a cap gun

The Pitch: "Hey Tommy, what's going on?" "I'm trying out my new Dick Tracy Power Jet Gun—it's made by Mattel! It fires caps, and that's not all, it fires water, too." "Water?" "It shoots about 30 feet—single shots and rapid fire! You can fire about 30 shots before reloading. It's the first gun EVER that shoots caps and water too! Or if you want, it shoots just caps or just water. You can tell it's Mattel—it's swell!"

...with a diameter of 10 feet, 5 inches. It was launched by crane from a height of 189 feet.

THE ZEROIDS

The Product: A set of three plastic robots

The Pitch: "The Zeroids are here—from the planet Zero. The Zeroids! Zerac, the Zeroid commander, frees himself from his own Zeroid capsule. Advance! Zobor, the Zeroid transporter. Change his Zeroid capsule into a cosmobile for hauling! Zintar, the Zeroid explorer. Change his Zeroid capsule into a lunar sled! Command the Zeroids to defend, move forward, backward, and transport! Command the Zeroids from Ideal!" Zzzzzzz.

GUNG HO COMMANDO OUTFIT

The Product: This Vietnam-era set lets a boy nation-build right in his own backyard.

The Pitch: "All the equipment you need for fun and excitement in the Gung Ho Commando Outfit, by Marx! There's a battle map and direction-finding compass. A cap-shooting automatic pistol with gun belt and holster. A helmet, a canteen, complete mess kit, and poncho! You get a cap-firing Gung Ho hand grenade! And look here—this flashing, battery-powered machine gun with moving ammo belt shoots rapid-fire bullets! There's a real-looking walkie-talkie, too, and a field pack. You get medals and battle ribbons, even dog tags! It's all for fun and excitement! Get the outfit with all the equipment you need. The Gung Ho Commando Outfit, by Marx!"

*   *   *

THEY PICKED THE WRONG BODY

In the 19th century, raiding freshly dug graves to supply medical schools with cadavers was a lucrative business. But a national outcry was raised in 1878 when someone recognized a corpse lying in the dissecting room of the Ohio Medical College as that of Congressman John Scott Harrison. Harrison, the son of one American president (William Henry Harrison) and father of another (Benjamin Harrison), had died a few days earlier, and the medical school had unwittingly purchased his body from thieves who had exhumed it during a nighttime cemetery raid. The Harrison family returned the body to its tomb, and the state of Ohio soon passed strict penalties for graverobbing.

A type of flea found in Germany lives and breeds almost exclusively in beer mats.

MMM...CHICKEN HEADS

We thought we were adventurous when we first tried sushi. But when it comes to weird food, it turns out raw fish is only the tip of the iceberg. Here are some local "delicacies" to sample the next time you're in these countries.

NANKOTSU. Normally you take the hard, bony stuff out of chicken before you eat it, but this Japanese snack *is* the bony stuff. It's bits of chicken cartilage from the leg joints and not surprisingly, it's described by one food critic as "kind of hard and chewy." You can get it fried or on a shish kabob stick, and it's a favorite with cold beer.

JELLIED EELS. Still a favorite streetside food in the east of London. The eel is boned and cooked in simmering water for about a half hour, then gelatin is added to the water and the whole thing is allowed to cool and harden. Served with meat pies, mashed potatoes, and beer, jellied eel is often doused with chili-flavored vinegar.

DUCK FEET. This is a Chinese favorite. The webbed duck feet are usually braised and then eaten as a snack with soy sauce.

COD TONGUE. Everybody's heard of cod liver oil, which is made from the fish's liver (it's an excellent source of vitamins A and D and omega-3 fatty acids). If that isn't strange enough for you, how about a cod's tongue? It's a favorite in Newfoundland, Canada. The tongues, served battered and fried, are said to be "chewy."

HELMET. This can be purchased from street vendors in the Philippines. What is it? Barbecued chicken heads. (Before they're barbecued, the beaks are removed.)

SURSTROMMING. In May and June, Swedish fishermen catch huge numbers of Baltic herring. To make this dish, the herring are soaked in a brine solution for a day, then cleaned, then packed into wooden barrels, and put in the sun for 24 hours to induce

In France, parents may not legally name their daughters Prune, Vanilla, or Cherry.

fermentation. The next day, the barrels are placed in a cool room...where they remain for several months. Then the fish is canned. The raw fish continues to ferment in the can, so the cans in the store actually bulge out. You have to cover them with a cloth before opening, because they *will* spurt out juice. (Most people open them outside.) The smell is described as exceedingly powerful and exceedingly offensive. Comparisons range from extremely rotten fish to horribly rotten eggs to dirty feet to garbage that's been left out in the sun. Surstromming is eaten—by many people in Sweden—with thin, hard bread and boiled potatoes, and accompanied with milk and distilled alcohol.

DUCK TONGUE. Pink, fleshy, and six to eight inches long, they're considered a delicacy in parts of China, and reportedly have a soft, chewy bonelike center.

FRIED PIG BLOOD. A common food in rural Hungary. After slaughter, the pig's blood is collected and usually fried with scrambled eggs.

BETAMAX. No, no one eats video cassette tapes. But in the Philippines they eat blocks of cooked chicken blood that *look like* video cassette tapes. Really. And that's really what they're called on the street.

CHICKEN SASHIMI. It's raw chicken, served like sushi with rice, soy sauce, and wasabi. Scary—but it's supposedly very good.

* * *

ALL HAIL THE GIANT CABBAGE

Officials in the Bosnian town of Banja Luka announced plans in 2006 to build an enormous monument to the town's most important product: cabbage. "Our region is famous for cabbage," said tourism director Goran Peric. "We very much appreciate this vegetable." Local artists were called on to help design the giant cabbage; Peric said construction should start sometime in 2007.

The average bout of sleepwalking lasts six minutes.

STRANGE OBSESSIONS

Here's to the people who live life on their own unusual *terms.*

TRY TO WORM YOUR WAY OUT OF THIS!

William Lyttle, a 71-year-old retiree in Hackney, East London, has an odd hobby: He likes to dig tunnels in his yard. In 2001 he made news around the world when a huge crater formed in the street in front of his home because of one of his tunnels. That was just a small part of a vast underground network that "The Mole Man," as neighbors called him, had been digging for more than 40 years. The tunnels are more than 25 feet deep and spread out in every direction from his basement. In 2006 Lyttle made the news again when he was evicted from his home and officially barred from any more digging. Engineers said they feared the entire street and several nearby homes, as well as Lyttle's own 20-room house, were in danger of disappearing into the ground. Lyttle was put up in a hotel room while city engineers began filling the holes with cement. The Mole Man has never said much about his life's work, once telling the *Guardian*, "I just have a big basement."

OBSESSION: THE FRAGRANCE (OF SOCKS)

A 41-year-old Toronto engineer who goes only by his internet alias, "Witesock," has been secretly collecting professional athletic socks for 20 years, most of them used. He says that he bought his first pair at the age of 10. "Nothing else about the uniforms impressed me," he told Toronto's *National Post*. "Just the socks." He now has more than 800 pairs from pro sports teams from around the world, ranging from football to rugby, hockey, and soccer (but not baseball—he doesn't like baseball socks). Most of them come through dealings on the internet, and that, Witesock says, makes it weird sometimes. "One of the most interesting requests I've had came from a guy in Australia. He offered to send me five pairs of Australian rugby socks if I would take pictures of myself wearing the socks, while at the same time throwing a pie in my own face." If that wasn't weird enough, he did it. "It was kind of fun," he said. He added that his wife (yes, he's married) doesn't know about his sock obsession.

A baby oyster is called a *spat*.

FART FACTS

You won't find trivia like this in any ordinary book.

THE NAME

The word *fart* comes from the Old English term *foertan*, to explode. *Foertan* is also the origin of the word *petard*, an early type of bomb. *Petard*, in turn, is the origin of a more obscure term for fart—*ped*, or *pet*, which was once used by military men. (In Shakespeare's *Henry IV*, there's a character whose name means fart—Peto.)

WHY DO YOU FART?

Flatulence has many causes—for example, swallowing air as you eat and lactose intolerance. (Lactose is a sugar molecule in milk, and many people lack the enzyme needed to digest it.) But the most common cause is food that ferments in the gastrointestinal tract.

• A simple explanation: The fats, proteins, and carbohydrates you eat become a "gastric soup" in your stomach. This soup then passes into the small intestine, where much of it is absorbed through the intestinal walls into the bloodstream to feed the body.

• But the small intestine can't absorb everything, especially complex carbohydrates. Some complex carbohydrates—the ones made up of several sugar molecules (beans, some milk products, fiber) can't be broken down. So they're simply passed along to the colon, where bacteria living in your intestine feed off the fermenting brew. If that sounds gross, try this: the bacteria then excrete gases into your colon. Farting is how your colon rids itself of the pressure the gas creates.

FRUIT OF THE VINE

So why not just quit eating complex carbohydrates?

• First, complex carbohydrates—which include fruit, vegetables, and whole grains—are crucial for a healthy diet. "Put it this way," explains Jeff Rank, an associate professor of gastroenterology at the University of Minnesota. "Cabbage and beans are bad for gas, but they are good for you."

• Second, they're not the culprits when it comes to the least desirable aspect of farting: smell.

• Farts are about 99% odorless gases—hydrogen, nitrogen, carbon dioxide, oxygen, and methane (it's the methane that makes farts flammable). So why the odor? Blame it on those millions of bacteria living in your colon. Their waste gases usually contain sulfur molecules—which smell like rotten eggs. This is the remaining 1% that clears rooms in a hurry.

AM I NORMAL?

• Johnson & Johnson, which produces drugs for gas and indigestion, once conducted a survey and found that almost one-third of Americans believe they have a flatulence problem.

• However, according to Terry Bolin and Rosemary Stanton, authors of *Wind Breaks: Coming to Terms with Flatulence*, doctors say most flatulence is healthy. What's unhealthy is worrying about it so much.

NOTABLE FARTERS

• Le Petomane, a 19th-century music hall performer, had the singular ability to control his farts. He could play tunes, as well as imitate animal and machinery sounds rectally. Le Petomane's popularity briefly rivaled that of Sarah Bernhardt.

• A computer factory in England, built on the site of a 19th-century chapel, is reportedly inhabited by a farting ghost. Workers think it might be the embarrassed spirit of a girl who farted while singing in church. "On several occasions," said an employee, "there has been a faint girlish voice singing faint hymns, followed by a loud raspberry sound and then a deathly hush."

• Josef Stalin was afraid of farting in public. He kept glasses and a water pitcher on his desk so that if he felt a wind coming on, he could mask the sound by clinking the glasses while pouring water.

• Martin Luther believed, "on the basis of personal experience, that farts could scare off Satan himself."

Panama, Ecuador, and El Salvador have all adopted the U.S. dollar as their official currency.

THE BETTER TO BITE YOU WITH

What are the oddest creatures on the planet? (Besides Uncle John's cousins in Pittsburgh, that is.) Insects. There are far more of them than there are of us, and we thought you should know something about their very weird mouths.

MAN!-DIBLE

Chewers, Spongers, and Suckers isn't the name of Uncle John's latest rock band—they're different types of insect *mouthparts*. There are more, but to become familiar with them, it helps to know that all of the eating, chewing, grabbing, and biting devices on all the millions of insect species in the world fall into two main categories: *mandibulate*, or chewing, mouthparts, which are the most primitive; and *haustellate* mouthparts, like *piercing-sucking blood feeders* and *siphoners*. (Yum!)

THE CHEWERS

Mandibulate mouths are found on ants, caterpillars, beetles, grasshoppers, and cockroaches. These mouths all consist of four main features:

- **Labrum:** a single, plate-like "upper lip" that is usually moveable and helps put food in the mouth.
- **Mandibles:** the first pair of mouthparts, "jaws" that are used to cut, tear, grasp, fight, and chew, among other things.
- **Maxillae:** the second pair of mouthparts, which sit below the mandibles and are used to sense, taste, and handle food.
- **Labium:** a third pair of mouthparts that basically make up the "lower lip." They're used to close the insect's mouth.

These parts can vary slightly or greatly depending on the type of insect, their diet, and other needs. Example: ants' *labrums* are hard plates that are extensions of the head and move up and down to help manipulate the food. The *mandibles* are like a pair of horizontal left and right pincers that meet in a vertical line at the front of the head; they have teeth or serrated ends where they meet, and are used for carrying food, digging, nest building, cutting, and fighting, and biting you, among many other things. The *maxillae* are an adapted pair of limbs, used as lower jaws; located between the mandibles and labium (the lower lip), they help handle and taste the food, and extract liquids from it. Ants also have a *hypopharynx*—a tongue—for sucking up liquid.

HAUSTELLATE

Nearly all the insects in this category have the same four parts that the chewers do, but they have evolved over eons into very different devices like *stylets* and *proboscises*. The haustellate insects are broken down into seven main groups:

Piercing-sucking plant feeders: This includes bugs like aphids, leafhoppers, lacebugs, aphids, and spider mites. Their mouths have changed into a hypodermic needlelike structure, used to pierce plant membranes and suck fluids out of them. Example: On the cicada, the labium has become a tubular beak called a *proboscis;* the mandibles are sharp *stylets* inside the tube that cut into the plant tissue; the maxillae are now two tubes—one to send in salivary secretions that keep the other tube flowing—and one that sucks the liquid out of the plant. The labrum serves basically to stabilize the whole tube structure.

Siphoners: Butterflies and some moths fall in this category. They don't need stylets because they don't have to pierce anything; they drink from puddles of water or plant nectar. If you look closely at a moth or butterfly you'll see a long, curled-up tube. That's the proboscis, which they can extend straight into a flower or drinking water.

Sponger: Houseflies have this configuration. These bugs have basically lost their mandibles and maxillae. The labium is modified into a bendable proboscis that is lowered onto a food source. On the bottom are spongelike organs called *labella.* They basically vomit salivary secretions onto the food source, be it feces or steak, that causes the food to liquefy. The labella then soak up the liquid. (Yum! Yum!)

Piercing-sucking blood feeders: You know these—fleas and mosquitoes. When a mosquito bites you, a pair of pointed, barbed maxillary stylets emerge from the sheathlike labium and stick into your skin. These are used to anchor the bug and provide leverage for the insertion of the remaining parts. Once anchored, the labium slides back and the two mandibular stylets pierce through your skin into a vein. The mosquito then injects anticoagulant saliva into your tissue, and the labrum is used like a tongue to lap up your blood.

ODDITIES

Rasping-sucking mouthparts: Of the more than one million species of insects known on Earth today, only thrips have these *asymmetrical* mouthparts, and they are weird. The left mandible and the two maxillae have been modified into a piercing stylet, and the right one is nonexistent. Thrips are tiny—only 1.5 to 3 millimeters long—and they use their stylets to scrape or rasp at the surface of plants, fungi, and sometimes animals, then drink the fluids within.

Chewing-lapping: Only honeybees use this system, which is basically a combination of chewing and sucking. They have the same flaplike mandibles that ants and other chewers do, but they also have specialized mouthparts adapted perfectly to their diet. They need to chew—they use the mandibles for things like gnawing holes in your porch for nests, manipulating wax, and biting—and they need to be able to consume fluids such as water, nectar, and honey. For that, the labium has evolved into a long tonguelike proboscis that can reach into flowers.

* * *

YOU SAY TOMATO, I TASTE BANANAS

Do you taste words? Some people do—people with *Lexical-gustatory synesthesia*, which was first recorded in 1907. When hearing certain words, people with this rare disorder get an acute sense of tasting something that goes along with the word. Neuropsychologist Julia Simner of the University of Edinburgh, in a study called "The Taste of Words on the Tip of the Tongue," said that only 10 people in all of Europe and the U.S. have the condition. One of the subjects she studied, upon hearing the word "castanets," suddenly tasted tuna fish. Another only experienced tastes when hearing people's names: "John" tasted like cornbread; "William" like potatoes. The cause of the condition is still unknown.

In China, American football is known as "olive ball."

WRINKLES IN TIME

Time travel has fascinated scientists and writers for centuries. While the mainstream scientific community continues to research it, some already claim to have done it. Are they brilliant visionaries, or just lunatics?

TIME TRAVELER: Father Pellegrino Ernetti

BACKGROUND: In 2002 Francois Brune, a French priest, wrote *The Vatican's New Mystery*, a book about how his friend, Ernetti, an Italian priest, invented a machine he called the *chronovisor* in 1952. Housed in a small cabinet (like a TV set) it displayed events from anytime in history on a screen (like a TV set). The user selected where and to what year they wanted to "travel" with a series of dials (like a TV set). Ernetti said it worked by picking up, decoding, and displaying "radiation" left behind by the passage of time. He claims he was helped on the project by Nobel Prize-winning physicist Enrico Fermi and Nazi rocket scientist Wernher Von Braun. Ernetti said he used the chronovisor to visit ancient Rome to view and produce an English translation of *Thyestes*, a Latin play thought to be lost. He also heard Napoleon give a speech in Italy in 1804 and saw Christ dying on the cross. So what happened to the chronovisor? Brune says the Catholic Church forced Ernetti to disassemble the machine because of its potential for espionage.

WHAT HAPPENED: Scientists have never found any evidence that the passage of time leaves a trail of radiation. And the existence of the chronovisor has never been confirmed.

TIME TRAVELER: John Titor

BACKGROUND: In 2000 Titor posted messages on Internet paranormal discussion boards claiming he was a soldier from the year 2036 sent back in time to retrieve a computer to fix software bugs on machines of the future. He made more posts, offered pictures of his time machine and its instructional manual, and gave incredibly detailed accounts of world events between 2000 and 2036. For instance, Titor claimed an escalating global war ends in 2015 when Russia drops nuclear bombs on the United States, China, and Europe, instantly dismantling all governments and

In Los Angeles, it's illegal for infants to dance in public halls.

killing three billion people. (Millions more die of mad cow disease.) Survivors group into agricultural communes. Despite the bleak post-apocalyptic landscape, technology is well advanced, with wireless Internet providing all phone service, television, and music. Titor achieved a huge following on paranormal websites and talk radio. Many thought he really could be a bona fide time traveler. But a few months later (in March 2001), Titor announced that he had found the computer he needed and he "returned" to the future. He was never heard from again.

WHAT HAPPENED: "Titor" contradicted himself all over the place, claiming that World War III had destroyed all governments, but also that the U.S. government sent him back in time. Other "predictions" just didn't pan out. He said a second American civil war would take place from 2004 to 2008, and that the 2004 Olympics were the last ones ever held. Also, when asked how his time machine (a modified 1967 Chevrolet, which somehow survived nuclear annihilation) worked, Titor claimed ignorance, calling himself a hired hand, not an engineer. So who was Titor? Some speculate it was a hoax concocted by author Michael Crichton.

TIME TRAVELER: Darren Daulton

BACKGROUND: Daulton was an all-star catcher for the Philadelphia Phillies and Florida Marlins during the 1980s and '90s. But he's also an amateur metaphysicist. He claims that a little-known dimension causes all objects on Earth to vibrate slightly, and that only a handful of people, Daulton included, can detect it, and use this ability to manipulate objects, the weather...and time. Daulton says that instead of dreaming, he leaves his body every night and travels into the future (but not the past). One event he's witnessed: the end of the world, which he says will occur on December 21, 2012. However, Daulton has also been arrested several times for drunk driving, charges he says he's innocent of. "I've been thrown in jail five or six times," he says. "My wife blames everything on drinking. But I'm not a drunk. Nicole just doesn't understand metaphysics."

WHAT HAPPENED: Daulton was a career .245 hitter. If he could manipulate time and objects, one would think he'd be able to give himself a better batting average.

The left drumstick of a chicken is more tender than the right one.

ALLICRACKER

The BRI's crack team of researchers has uncovered the hidden—and dangerous—link between drugs and alligators. Who knew? Nobody...until now.

ALLIGATOR CASE

Border agents in Yuma, Arizona, arrested a California man in December 2006 when their drug-sniffing dog went on alert near his vehicle. A search of the car turned up 13 grams of marijuana. And an alligator. The four-foot-long cayman was inside a suitcase. The alligator was taken to an animal refuge in Phoenix; the man was taken to jail.

THAT BITES

In 2006 a man walked into a home in Frederic, Michigan, with a sawed-off shotgun and demanded the thousands of dollars the homeowner owed a crack-cocaine dealer. When the homeowner said he didn't have the money, the man confiscated his 18-inch alligator instead. "I think he was planning to hold it for ransom, or something," Sheriff Kirk Wakefield said. "It's really weird."

AMPHETIGATOR

Sheriffs in Aransas County, Texas, received an anonymous tip in December, 2006, that someone had illegally shot a white tailed deer. They went to check it out...and found a dead alligator instead. And 15 grams of methamphetamines. Corey Flowers was arrested for drug and alligator possession. (Really.)

BAD COP

Los Angeles police were trying for months to find out who released a seven-foot-long alligator in the Harbor City community's Lake Machado when they finally got a reliable tip in December, 2005. Based on that information, they searched the home of former police officer Todd Natow, 42, and discovered three alligators, four piranhas, three desert tortoises, a scorpion...and 10 pounds of marijuana. Natow was the one who'd released the alligator, nick-named "Reggie," into the lake because it had gotten too big for

Defined scientifically, one second is "9,129,631,770 periods of radiation."

him to take care of. (As of December, 2006, the city had spent hundreds of thousands of dollars in attempts to catch Reggie the gator. He's still free.)

CRACK TEAM

In November 2006, four police officers in Lakeland, Florida, risked their lives when they jumped into a lake in the middle of the night to pull a man from the jaws of an 11-foot-long alligator. The man lost part of his left arm—but survived. He later told police he was at the lake—naked—smoking crack when he was attacked. The incident led to several odd news headlines, including: "CROCODILE BITES NAKED MAN ON CRACK."

* * *

MORE ANIMALS IN THE NEWS

MOOVY, BABY: In 2006 a woman in Lobez, Poland, was charged with "cultivating a narcotic" when police found marijuana plants on her property. The 55-year-old farmer defended herself by saying that it wasn't for humans—she was feeding the plants to her cow, which had been "skittish and unruly." She said that ever since she started feeding the cow the marijuana, it had been "calm as a lamb." She faces up to three years in jail.

CAT-ASTROPHE: Bill Jenness got in trouble with the city of Whitman, Massachusetts, because of his cat—its poop was radioactive. The 11-year-old cat, Mitzi, was being treated for hyperthyroidism with radioiodine, which can make cats radioactive for weeks. The vet had warned Jenness that he had to limit his snuggling time with Mitzi, had to keep the cat away from children, and had to use gloves when flushing the cat's litter. But Jenness was afraid the litter would clog his septic system, so he put it in the garbage instead. After alarms at the local incinerator detected the radioactivity, workers found Mr. Jenness' mail nearby, and the city fined him $2,800 to clean up the radioactive scat.

If you're average, your left lung is smaller than your right lung.

KOOKY STARS

In addition to fame and fortune, many celebrities also have some really bizarre personality quirks.

PAST LIVES

• **Sean Connery** believes that in a previous life he was a polygamist alcoholic railroad builder.

• **Sylvester Stallone** says he was a French nobleman who was executed during the French Revolution.

• **John Travolta** believes he was silent film actor Rudolph Valentino.

• In her autobiography, **Anne Heche** declared herself both "the reincarnation of God" as well as an alien named "Celestia."

QUIRKY BEHAVIOR

• **Nick Nolte** has tanks of ozone in every room of his house because he thinks ozone kills "bad things."

• Lots of people think crystals have special powers, but British actor **Michael York** says that a pocketful of crystals caused six thugs who attacked him in Brazil to suddenly run away.

• For reasons unknown, **Bruce Willis** wears his watch upside down.

• **W. C. Fields** had chronic insomnia. When he couldn't fall asleep, he'd wrap his face in hot towels and lie in a barber's chair. If that didn't work, he'd try to sleep on his pool table. If *that* didn't work, he'd lie in his yard under a beach umbrella while being sprinkled with a garden hose.

• Since he's so reclusive, author **J. D. Salinger** (*The Catcher in the Rye*) probably has a lot of quirks no one knows about. What is known: he has three cats named Kitty 1, Kitty 2, and Kitty 3.

• Actor **Andy Dick** (*NewsRadio*) and his wife divorced in 1990 but still lived together to raise their son. Then Dick and his wife both found new live-in partners…but continued to live together. Dick even had children with his new love, with everybody living in the same house for a decade.

Real Headline: SHOOTING REPORTED AT FIRING RANGE

• Comedian and author **Amy Sedaris** runs a cheese-ball and cupcake business out of her New York apartment. She also likes to pick up waitressing jobs occasionally because she enjoys the work.

PHOBIAS

• **Christina Ricci** can't stand houseplants, and will not swim in a pool because she has an irrational fear that a shark might enter through a hatch.

• **Orlando Bloom** (*The Lord of the Rings*) is terrified of pigs.

• **Roger Moore** starts twitching whenever he picks up a gun. His case of *hoplophobia* was difficult for him to control while he was playing James Bond, a role that required lots of gunplay.

• **Billy Bob Thornton** has intense fears of antique furniture, stage plays, silver cutlery, and bright colors. He also reportedly doesn't say his children's names out loud because he fears it will curse them.

• **David Gest**, the record producer briefly married to Liza Minnelli, tries not to use the phone. Reason: he has *phonophobia*, or the fear of his own voice.

• **Nicole Kidman** hates acting. Whenever she starts a movie, she becomes convinced she's a terrible actress and presents the director with a list of actresses who would be better suited for her role.

COLLECTORS

• Rush bassist and lead singer **Geddy Lee** owns the world's largest collection of monocles.

• With over 6,000, actor **Corbin Bernsen** (*L.A. Law*) has the world's largest collection of snowglobes.

• Actor **Matt Dillon** (*Crash*) collects baseball cards...but only those of 1980s New York Mets star Mookie Wilson.

• Country singer **Faith Hill** isn't into art or photography, but she does collect picture frames.

* * *

"Being Vice President means you get all the French fries the president can't get to."

—**Al Gore**

IN THE NAME OF ART

Ever been in a gallery or museum and seen something that made you wonder, "Is this really art?" Answer: If an artist says it's art, then it's art. That doesn't mean it's normal or makes any sense.

ARTIST: Mark McGowan
TITLE: "Monkey Nut"
THE WORK: In 2003, McGowan, a British performance artist, rolled a nut with his nose to the prime minister's office to protest high college-tuition costs. This was a follow up to several other "works." These include "Sausage Chips and Beans," in which he sat in a bathtub full of baked beans with two chips (French fries) stuck in his nose and sausages draped around his head to protest the decline of the traditional English breakfast; "Big Toe Bus Pull," in which McGowan pulled a bus with his big toe to protest London's department of transportation; and "Artist Eats Fox," wherein he cooked and ate a fox to call attention to the plight of crack addicts.

ARTISTS: Toronto theater company Mammalian Diving Reflex
TITLE: "Haircuts By Children"
THE WORK: In May 2006, MDR recruited a bunch of elementary school kids, gave each one a pair of scissors and a barber chair at the Milk International Children's Festival of the Arts, and told them to cut people's hair. The artist's intent, according to MDR: "Letting a child who doesn't know how cut somebody's hair is an exercise in exploring human trust."

ARTIST: Carsten Holler
TITLE: "Test Site"
THE WORK: In 2006, Holler erected five five-story-tall twisty slides inside London's Tate Modern art gallery. Holler says the slides are "a playground for the body and the brain." Not only are the slides a fun form of art, Holler says they also have practical implications: Sliding relieves stress, so the adult-sized slides should be used more in society and could possibly be used as a new form of transportation.

In Asia and England, a black cat is considered lucky.

ARTIST: Kira O'Reilly

TITLE: "Inthewrongplaceness"

THE WORK: O'Reilly staged this performance-art piece in Penzance, England. It consisted of a naked woman (not O'Reilly) holding a dead pig in her arms for four hours. People for the Ethical Treatment of Animals (PETA) denounced the show as "sick." O'Reilly said the piece was about the intimate relationship between humans and animals. She claimed it gave her "an undercurrent of pigginess," and that "unexpected fantasies of mergence and interspecies metamorphoses began to flicker into my consciousness."

ARTIST: "Banksy"

TITLE: Untitled

THE WORK: In 2006 a British "guerrilla artist" known as Banksy snuck a dummy dressed as a Guantanamo Bay terrorism prisoner into Disneyland. It was dressed in an orange jumpsuit and black hood and was first noticed by park patrons on the Rocky Mountain Railroad ride. Banksy claims he did it to highlight the plight of prisoners in the military prison. Earlier in the year, Banksy had replaced 500 copies of Paris Hilton's CD in British record stores with his own "alternate version," which criticized the socialite with song titles such as "Why Am I Famous?" and the artwork altered to show Hilton topless, with her head replaced by a dog's.

ARTIST: Ye Fu

TITLE: Untitled

THE WORK: In 2006 Ye, a 28-year-old Chinese poet and artist, locked himself inside a cage in a lion enclosure for 10 days at the Qingdao Forest Wildlife World in an attempt to call attention to the plight of caged animals. Ye ate only raw meat during his captivity. He was joined by Luo Xianhui, 26, who quit her job to participate in Ye's "art piece." As part of the performance, they also used plastic bags to go to the bathroom.

ARTIST: Rebecca Warren

TITLE: Untitled

THE WORK: In a London gallery in 2006, Warren displayed five cases filled with various things she found on the floor of her studio

Russians make a *mockba* pizza—topped with sardines, tuna, mackerel, salmon, & onions.

and the road outside. Included were bits of dust, hair, twigs, and a cherry pit. The point of the piece, according to Warren: exploring the power of perception. "I'm interested in what a bit of fluff and a bit of twig can mean. For somebody it could mean one thing, and for somebody else, it could mean something else." Amazingly, Warren's collage of garbage was the runner-up for the 2006 Turner Prize, England's highest honor for visual artists.

ARTIST: Zhang Huan
TITLE: Untitled
THE WORK: In 1998 the San Francisco-based artist took off his clothes, covered himself with liquefied hot dogs and flour, and then had eight dogs lick him. Zhang wanted to "explore the physical and psychological effects of human violence in modern society." He ended up exploring the effects of *canine* violence when one of the dogs bit his rear end, ending the exhibition at the San Francisco Asian Art Museum permanently.

* * *

THE DEADLY YEAR OF THE WAYNE

For some unknown reason, there were a lot of violent criminals with the middle name "Wayne" in the news during 1996.

- **Conan Wayne Hale:** confessed to his priest that he killed three people.
- **Michael Wayne Thompson:** murderer who escaped from prison and was the subject of a multi-state manhunt. (He was captured in Indiana.)
- **Danny Wayne Owens:** murdered his neighbor in Alabama.
- **Ellis Wayne Felker:** executed for the 1981 murder of a college student.
- **Larry Wayne Cole:** died while running from the law on rape charges.

A newborn expels its own body weight in waste every 60 hours.

MEDIEVAL MEDICINE

A lot of medicine is trial and error: Try something—it might cure you. Here are a bunch of real folk cures we found in a book about medical practices in medieval England. (We don't advocate trying them...but let us know if any of them work.)

• **For deafness,** a mixture of a rabbit's gallstone and fox grease was warmed and then poured into the ear.

• **To treat baldness,** dog urine was rubbed into the scalp. If dog urine wasn't available, horse urine could be used instead.

• **To treat a child's case of whooping cough,** milk was fed to a ferret. Whatever milk the ferret didn't drink was given to the sick child.

• **To eliminate jaundice,** nine head lice were drowned in a pint of beer. The mixture had to be drunk every morning for a week.

• **For arthritis,** the skin of a donkey was worn.

• **Gout could be cured** by boiling a red-haired dog in oil, adding worms and pig's bone marrow, and then applying the mixture to the affected area.

• **To stop an asthma attack,** baby frogs or live spiders were coated in butter and swallowed.

• **Venereal disease was prevented** by rubbing one's genitals with vinegar. By the 18th century, a more modern method was favored: The genitals were wrapped in a freshly killed chicken.

• **To cure leprosy,** a sufferer bathed in the blood of a dog.

• **Fractures, abscesses, paralysis, epilepsy, nausea, sore throats, and ulcers could be cured** by eating ancient Egyptian mummies—a medical fad of the time. Wealthy Europeans acquired them via a trade route from Egypt. The fad ended when it was discovered the corpses weren't ancient mummies, but recently murdered slaves.

When cryptography is outlawed, bayl bhgynjf jvyy unir cevinpl.

OOPS!

Have a laugh over some truly weird mistakes.

WATCH YOUR STEP

"A Yorkshire Terrier named Minty fled in terror from his owner's house as a thief broke down the door. (Owner Pauline Webb was out at the time.) Wearing gloves to avoid leaving fingerprints, the thief escaped with over $10,000 worth of loot—but stepped in Minty's excitement-induced mess and left a perfect shoeprint. A week later, when John Conroy was arrested in another break-in, police noticed that his shoes matched the poop-print perfectly. Conroy was jailed for two years."

—Fortean Times

DEAL OR NO DEAL

"Andres-Francois Raffray, 47, a lawyer from Arles, France, thought he'd made the deal of a lifetime. In 1965 he signed a contract with 90-year-old Jeanne Calment, giving her $500 a month for the rest of her life on the condition that she leave him her condominium when she died. But it didn't work out as he'd planned: 30 years later, Calment became the world's oldest known living person. "We all make bad deals in life," Raffray said on Calment's 120th birthday, by which time he'd paid $180,000 for the property, which was only worth about $60,000. To make matters worse, Raffray died two years before Calment, and was never able to live in the condo."

—Parade

WHERE'S THE INTELLIGENCE?

"The Canadian Security Intelligence Service is in hot water after a female agent left top-secret files in her car when she went to a hockey game. They were stolen by drug addicts, who then dumped them into the trash. But she didn't report the theft in time for the plans to be recovered—they're now believed to be deep in some trash pile. Worse, the head of the CSIS's oversight board heard about the security debacle from the newspaper."

—This Is True

"Seizure Alert" dogs can warn their owners up to an hour before an epileptic seizure begins.

FIRE WHEN READY

"An employee of Builders Square in the Cross County Mall poured mineral spirits on the floor and used a cigarette lighter to prove to a fellow employee that mineral spirits don't burn. The ensuing fire caused $1 million in damages to Builders Square and $2 million to the KMart store next door."

—West Palm Beach, Florida

OH, BABY

"London paramedics thought they were saving a life when they rushed a fetus to the hospital after finding it on a subway platform. ...Until they learned that the fetus wasn't human at all—it was a toy. 'They had found an alien egg, the latest toy craze to hit the area,' Reuters reported. 'It contains what looks like an unborn child curled in a fetal position and suspended in a gooey placenta-like substance.' According to the London Underground, the mistake was only discovered when the 'fetus' was examined in the hospital."

—In These Times

LETTER PERFECT

"Oh, the difference a consonant makes. In the first seconds of a TV ad for Allegheny County (Pennsylvania) Commissioner Mike Dawida, a Democratic candidate for county executive, a woman's voice says, 'The public record doesn't lie.' But when that slogan appeared on the screen in front of a picture of Dawida's primary opponent, a critical 'l' was missing from the word 'public,' leaving a much different word—'pubic.'

"'Well, we better get that fixed immediately,' said Dawida's campaign manager, Karen Hochberg."

—*Medford* (Oregon) *Mail Tribune*

CAUGHT CHEATING

"John Issa was ordered by a Painesville, Ohio, judge to submit a urine sample for a drug test before his sentencing on a theft conviction. The sample showed no evidence of drugs, but it tested positive for something else: pregnancy. The judge, who had the option of giving him probation on the original conviction, sentenced him to a year in jail instead."

—Skeptic

WEIRD CHINA

Continuing our weird world tour, we stop in China, home to over a billion people...and a lot of odd news.

MAN BITES PANDA

After guzzling a six-pack of beer, Beijing resident Zhang Xinyan decided to visit the zoo. Thoroughly drunk, Zhang jumped over a waist-high railing and stumbled into the pen holding Gu Gu, a sleeping male panda. Startled awake, the panda instinctively thought it was being attacked and bit Zhang on the leg. Equally startled by the bite, Zhang bit Gu Gu back. Zhang admitted after the ordeal that he had initially climbed into the pen because he wanted to "cuddle" with Gu Gu.

WHERE ARE MY PANTS?

In 2006 a man stole a pair of pants from a department store in the city of Sanya. Employees noticed the pants were gone, but realized the next day that the pants had reappeared on a rack—and that the same pair of pants in a different size was now missing. Police arrested the shoplifter, who admitted that he had stolen a pair of pants from the store, tried them on at home, and, when they didn't fit, "exchanged" them for a pair that did.

DEAD SEXY

In the rural area of Jiangsu, there's an ancient and widely held belief that if a person's funeral is well attended, the deceased is guaranteed a happy afterlife. Result: Family members will increase attendance at any cost. Police have recently begun to crack down on mourners hiring strippers to get funeral numbers up.

LEAD FOOT

In 2006 a 47-year-old man known as "Nai" walked three feet in a pair of 570-pound shoes. Nai made the shoes himself, out of iron. The former security guard quit his job to focus on his long-term goal: compete for China's kung fu team in the 2008 Olympics while wearing the shoes.

A person who removes armpit hair professionally is called an *alipile*.

D-I-V-O-R-C-E

In the autumn of 2006, the Tongxing Centre Primary School suspended all classes. Local officials had planned to cut the number of teaching jobs, leaving them open only to teachers who were divorced or widowed and had no other means of support. Result: All 40 of the school's teachers—all married women—filed for divorce...and got to keep their jobs.

LET IT RAIN

During the 1980s, an old tree in the village of Xinfu attracted thousands of visitors a year. Water seemed to magically poured out of the tree's leaves, and many people were convinced that the liquid had healing powers. Visits to the tree abruptly stopped, however, when it was discovered that the "water" was actually the urine of the millions of insects that lived in the tree.

KEEP OFF THE GRASS

In 2005, two Chinese men approached the China-Russia border at Slavyanka and attempted to cross into Russia on a lawnmower. Border guards refused to let them pass because they didn't have the proper documentation. So the men changed their story. Now they said they weren't trying to sneak into Russia—they claimed they had been "mowing the lawn and got lost."

CATCHING A FEW RAYS

A team of scientists in the eastern city of Hefei announced plans in 2006 to build a nuclear fusion device that could produce unlimited clean energy. Free, environmentally safe energy would revolutionize both the world of science and the world economy. How does the team plan to do it? They claim to be building a full-size artificial sun. (Exactly where they're building it remains a mystery, especially given the fact that the Sun's diameter is 100 times larger than the Earth's.)

* * *

"Anyone who stares long enough into the distance is bound to be mistaken for a philosopher or mystic in the end." —**Patrick White**

When Nicole Richie was nabbed for DUI in 2006, the arrest report listed her as 85 lbs.

TITANIC COINCIDENCES

There's something almost mystical about the Titanic. *There are so many bizarre coincidences associated with it, you'd think it was an episode of* The Twilight Zone.

THE TITAN/TITANIC

In 1898 a short novel called *The Wreck of the Titan, or Futility*, by Morgan Robertson, was published in the United States. It told the story of the maiden voyage of an "unsinkable" luxury liner called the *Titan*.

Robertson described the boat in great detail. The *Titan*, he wrote, was 800 feet long, weighed 75,000 tons, had three propellers and 24 lifeboats, and was packed with rich passengers. Cruising at 25 knots, the *Titan*'s hull was ripped apart when it hit an iceberg in April. Most of the passengers were lost because there weren't enough lifeboats. Robertson apparently claimed he'd written his book with the help of a psychic "astral writing partner."

Eerie Coincidence: Fourteen years later, the real-life *Titanic* took off on its maiden voyage. Like the fictional *Titan*, it was considered the largest and safest ship afloat. It was 882.5 feet long, weighed 66,000 tons, had three propellers and 22 lifeboats, and carried a full load of rich passengers. Late at night on April 14, 1912, sailing at 23 knots, the *Titanic* ran into an iceberg which tore a hole in its hull and upended the ship. More than 1,500 people drowned because there weren't enough lifeboats.

THE TITANIAN/TITANIC

In 1935 a "tramp steamer" was heading from England to Canada. On watch was a 23-year-old seaman named William Reeves. It was April, the month when the Titanic hit an iceberg and went down. As the *Reader's Digest Book of Amazing Facts* tells it:

> Young Reeves brooded deeply on this. His watch was due to end at midnight. This, he knew, was the time the *Titanic* had hit the ice-

berg. Then, as now, the sea had been calm. These thoughts swelled and took shape as omens...as he stood his lonely watch....He was scared to shout an alarm, fearing his shipmates' ridicule. But he was also scared not to.

Eerie Coincidence: All of a sudden, Reeves recalled the exact date of the *Titanic* accident—April 14, 1912—the day he had been born. That was enough to get him to act.

He shouted out a danger warning, and the helmsman rang the signal: engines full astern. The ship churned to a halt—just yards from a huge iceberg that towered menacingly out of the night.

More deadly icebergs crowded in around the tramp steamer, and it took nine days for icebreakers from Newfoundland to smash a way clear.

The name of the ship Reeves saved from a similar fate to the *Titanic*'s? The *Titanian*.

THE LUCKLESS TOWERS

Talk about coincidences! BRI member Andrew M. Borrok (hope we got that right—the fax is hard to read) submitted the following excerpt just as Uncle John was writing this piece. Obviously we had to include it. Thanks!

The stoker on the *Titanic* was named Frank Lucks Towers. Charles Pelegrino writes in his book, *Her Name, Titanic*:

Though he would survive this night (*Titanic*) without injury, his troubles were just beginning. In two years he'd be aboard the *Empress of Ireland* when it collided with another ship, opening up a hole in the *Empress*' side. (Note: it was the worst peacetime maritime disaster—over 2,000 lost.) It would be an usually hot night, and all the portholes would be open as she rolled onto her side in the St. Lawrence River. In minutes she would be gone—yet miraculously, Frank Towers was going to survive—virtually alone. He'd take his next job aboard the *Lusitania*, (sunk by German U-boats in 1915) and would be heard to shout "Now what!" when the torpedo struck. He'd swim to a lifeboat, vowing every stroke of the way to take up farming.

His story was destined to inspire a young writer to script a teleplay entitled *Lone Survivor*. The teleplay was so well received that it paved the way for a series. The writer's name was Rod Serling and the series became *The Twilight Zone*.

SIGNS OF GENIUS?

Some people are odd in a good *way—their oddness changed the world. How did they do it? Scientists think they may have the answer.*

THE SYNDROME

It's called Asperger's Disorder, or "Little Professor Syndrome." People who have Asperger's have many of the same traits as autistic people—social withdrawal, prodigious memory, interest in collecting and naming things, prone to outbursts, and an obsession with order. They also display some symptoms that are unique to Asperger's: higher IQs, and unusual ability in science, complex calculations, and computer programming. They often learn to speak very early, and usually function much better socially than autistic individuals. But it's the high incidence of *savant* skills—prodigy-like skill in music, art, or computation—among people with Asperger's that has interested the scientific community.

In 2001, an article in *Wired* magazine noted the unusual coincidence of autism and Asperger's Disorder in children born in Silicon Valley, California—an area with one of the highest concentrations of smart people in the world. That has led some scientists to wonder if the genetic traits that lead to disorders like Asperger's, savant syndrome, and autism also contribute to genius. Dr. Hans Asperger, who gave the disorder its name in 1944, states it unequivocally: "For success in science and art—a dash of autism is essential." Here are a few noted geniuses who fit that model.

GLENN GOULD (1932–1982)

Gould was known by friends and family as a control freak. Like many savants, he had perfect pitch and a steel-trap memory. He also tended to sing along with his playing, which drove recording engineers crazy. But his gifted interpretations of Bach are considered some of the finest ever recorded.

SAMUEL JOHNSON (1704–1784)

The author of the first English dictionary had a tendency to burst out with startling barnyard noises, or bits of the Lord's Prayer. He

During his lifetime, the average man removes 28 feet of hair through shaving.

was obsessive about doing things the same way, and would have a tantrum if there were any changes in his daily habits.

HENRY CAVENDISH (1731–1810)

The man who discovered hydrogen was one of the first people to accurately calculate the mass of the Earth, as well as the chemical composition of the atmosphere. He rarely left his house and went out of his way to avoid seeing anyone. Many discoveries credited to other scientists were found to have been made by him years earlier when his papers, which he never published, were examined after his death.

ISAAC NEWTON (1642–1727)

Another strange scientist who changed the world with his genius, Newton gave us his Laws of Motion, the binomial theorem, and calculus. Reclusive, quirky, mindless of his personal cleanliness, he seldom spoke and was so obsessed with his work that he would forget to eat. At Cambridge, Newton was known for giving lectures… even if no one showed up to hear them.

THELONIUS MONK (1917–1982)

Known as the high priest of bebop, this pianist and composer revolutionized jazz with his original compositions. He also had a unique performance style—personal tics that included unusual syncopations in his rhythms, as well as a tendency to dance around his piano. He spoke in a bizarre medley of grunts and random philosophical mutterings.

Here are some more famous brains who were never diagnosed with Asperger's but displayed the symptoms during their lifetimes.

- **Jane Austen**
- **Albert Einstein**
- **Vincent Van Gogh**
- **Wolfgang Amadeus Mozart**
- **Franz Kafka**
- **Thomas Jefferson**
- **Ludwig van Beethoven**
- **Nikola Tesla**
- **Alexander Graham Bell**
- **Emily Dickinson**
- **Charles Schulz**
- **Thomas Edison**
- **Henry Ford**
- **Jim Henson**

Insects shiver when they're cold.

JOIN THE BAD FILM SOCIETY

How does Uncle John keep busy when he's not writing great books? He watches bad movies! So many, in fact, that he's one of the founders of southern Oregon's Bad Film Society. How bad? Read on...

SILVER SCREEN

Here's a question no one has probably ever asked you: If you had to choose between watching *Citizen Kane* and *Killer Klowns from Outer Space*, which movie would you pick? How about *Gone With the Wind* vs. *Santa Claus Conquers the Martians*? Or *Casablanca* vs. *The Brain from Planet Arous*? If you picked *Killer Klowns*, *Santa the Conquerer*, and *The Brain*, then you and Uncle John have something in common. He's had a strange passion for odd and awful films ever since he was a kid.

Several years ago, Uncle John mentioned his peculiar hobby to a friend, who admitted having the same addiction to celluloid crap. How many other lovers of the lame are out there? Apparently a lot. In 2000 they created an organization called the Bad Film Society and scheduled a screening of *Frankenstein's Daughter* (1958). That showing drew quite a crowd, so two months later they ran *Bela Lugosi Meets a Brooklyn Gorilla* (1952) to even wider acclaim. And they've been showing bad movies about every other month ever since.

ANYTHING GOES

The Society keeps the definition of "bad film" as broad as possible. "That includes weird sequels like *Airport 75*, the worst of Drew Barrymore and Christina Ricci, the later films of Joan Crawford and Bette Davis, and the classic *Shakes the Clown*, starring Bobcat Goldthwait," says BFS co-founder Ed Polish. TV shows and made-for-TV movies count, too. The Society recently viewed "Soul Club," an episode of *The Partridge Family* in which the Partridges help Richard Pryor and Louis Gossett, Jr. save a community club from being shut down by a loan shark by filling in for the Motown act The Temptations at a charity concert. (Who says David Cassidy and Danny Bonaduce don't have soul?)

TWO THUMBS WAY DOWN

If you're interested in sharing your love of *Cobra Woman*, *Viva Knievel!* and *The Catskill Chainsaw Redemption* with others, consider starting a chapter of the Bad Film Society in your town. Here are some society-tested films for you consider for your screenings:

• ***The Horror of Party Beach*** (1964). Remember those 1960s "Beach Party" films starring Frankie Avalon and Annette Funicello? Now imagine a ship dumping nuclear waste offshore, and radioactive monsters emerging from the depths to eat the beach bunnies and surfer boys. And then imagine all of the carnage set to surf music...and you get *The Horror of Party Beach*, also billed as "The First Horror Musical!"

• ***The Tingler*** (1959). A coroner (Vincent Price) discovers a creature that lives in people's spines and grows by—literally—feeding on their fears. This film's claim to fame is the sneaky technique the producers used to goose the audience during the scary parts in the film—they hid electric buzzers under a few seats in theaters where the film was being shown, and set them off whenever they wanted the audience to scream.

• ***Eegah!*** (1963) Richard Kiel, best known for his portrayal of the giant "Jaws" in James Bond movies of the 1970s, plays Eegah, a stone-age caveman who somehow survives into the 1960s and falls in love with a teenage girl.

• ***Turist Ömer Uzay Yolunda*** (1973). Better known as the "Turkish *Star Trek*," this film is a low-budget Turkish rip-off of the classic TV series. Plot of the story: "The *Enterprise* picks up a Turkish hobo." If you can't find it under its original title, sometimes it's sold under the name "Ömer the Tourist in *Star Trek*."

• ***Rock 'n' Roll Wrestling Women vs. the Aztec Ape*** (1963). Another foreign classic, this time from Mexico: A mad scientist with an ape-brained human sidekick named Gomar kidnaps women for use as guinea pigs in brain-transplant experiments. Everything goes swimmingly until he kidnaps the sister of Golden Venus, a famous female wrestling star. When the sister dies on his operating table, Golden Venus and her friend Golden Ruby swear

For more awful films, be sure to review page 341.

revenge on the mad scientist. He fights back by creating Vendetta, a monster who poses as a wrestler to battle Venus and Ruby in the ring.

• ***For Your Height Only*** (1979). A Philippine James Bond-style film starring a midget named Weng-Weng as Agent 00. Standing only 2'9" inches tall, Weng-Weng is believed to be the shortest person ever to star in a feature film. (Verne Troyer, who plays Mini-Me in the *Austin Powers* films, is an inch shorter, but has played only co-starring roles.)

• ***Horror of the Blood Monsters*** (1970). Footage from three unrelated films was slapped together to make this dud, which was released under several different titles, including *Creatures of the Prehistoric Planet*, *Horror Creatures of the Lost Planet*, and *Space Mission of the Lost Planet*. The plot—to the extent that there actually is one—involves a trip to a faraway planet to trace the origins of an intergalactic vampire plague that has spread to the Earth. Hollywood legend John Carradine stars in the film. How did he justify accepting a role in this and many other terrible films over the years? "I made some of the greatest films ever made," he once explained, "and a lot of crap, too."

* * *

YOU CAN DO MAGIC

We found these spells in books on witchcraft in the Paranormal Wing of the BRI library. (Really.) Proceed at your own risk.

• **To keep the "spice" alive in a marriage:** Take some of your own nail clippings and mix them with your spouse's. Burn them together at midnight.

• **To cure infertility:** Borrow a (clean) diaper from a friend who has a baby. Tie the diaper onto the infertile woman like a bikini bottom, and drop a gemstone into the front of it.

• **To give someone the mind of a frog:** Point to the person and say, "Higady, pigady, pong! I give you the mind of a frog."

Gerber once tried to market a baby food for adults.

WEIGHT LOSS QUACKERY

The only things known to really help you lose weight are diet and exercise. But they're so hard. And so boring. Magic pants are better.

MAGIC TIGHTS WEIGHT LOSS

Embedded into the fabric of the "Slim Fit 20 Caffeine Tights" are tiny capsules of caffeine. When the caffeine comes into contact with the skin, the body absorbs it, where it supposedly stimulates metabolism, burns fat, and tightens leg muscles. The manufacturer, a British company called Palmers, promises that if the tights (which cost $50 for a pack of three pair) are worn for a whole month, about an inch in diameter can be lost from each leg.

SPRAY-ON WEIGHT LOSS

CLAmor is sprayed onto food. It contains a chemical called "clarinol" that's thought to shrink fat cells. When the clarinol-sprayed food is eaten, it reduces fat on the food *and* fat that's already inside the body. It comes in four flavors: butter, olive oil, garlic, and plain. So what is clarinol? CLAmor, the name of the product and the company, says that it's a naturally occurring bacteria found in the stomach of cows. It's "harvested" from fried ground beef.

ALCHEMY WEIGHT LOSS

A magic pill called Phena-Frene/MD sold in the mid-1990s claimed to turn fat into water, which was then flushed from the body forever by simply peeing it out. Packaging claimed users could lose up to 10 inches off their waist in just two weeks. One problem: It's physically impossible to turn fat into water. The product bombed, despite "medical school proof" from non-existent institutions such as the California Medical School and the U.S. Obesity Research Center. Phena-Frene was part of the diet-pill fad that came to an end in 1997, when the Food and Drug Administration banned all "fen-phen" products after studies showed they caused heart attacks.

MAGIC PANTS WEIGHT LOSS

Sold via late-night TV commercials in the 1980s, "Slim Jeans" weren't actually jeans, and they probably didn't make anybody slim. Slim Jeans were silver, futuristic-looking sweatpants made of "an amazing polymer material" that was actually a cheap rayon knockoff. They were supposed to cause weight loss by trapping in body heat, making the wearer lose water weight by sweating. The makers of Slim Jeans said weight loss could occur if the pants were worn exercising, sleeping, or even while watching TV. For a while, Slim Jeans were sold with a matching shiny sweatshirt to allow for even more good-looking weight loss.

CLIP-ON WEIGHT LOSS

According to Ninzu, the manufacturer of a 1990s device called the B-Trim, weight loss could be attained by clamping this little object onto the ear. Here's how it "worked": The clip put pressure on a nerve ending, which supposedly stopped stomach muscles from moving, signaling to the brain that the stomach was full. This controlled appetite and resulted in weight loss. Ads for the B-Trim said these claims could be proven by "scientific evidence." One problem: they didn't actually *list* any of that evidence. Result: The Federal Trade Commission made Ninzu stop selling the B-Trim in 1995.

* * *

ROBOTS: NOW WITH A TASTE FOR FLESH

Scientists at NEC System Technologies in Japan have invented a robot that can taste and identify dozens of wines, as well as some types of food. The green-and-white tabletop robot has a swiveling head, eyes, and a mouth that speaks in a child's voice. To identify a wine, the unopened bottle is placed in front of the robot's left arm. An infrared beam scans the wine—through the glass bottle—and determines its chemical composition. The robot then names the variety of wine, describes its taste, and recommends foods to pair it with. Scientists are still working out the kinks: At a 2006 press conference, a reporter and a cameraman put their hands in front of the robot's infrared beam. According to the robot, the reporter tasted like ham, and the cameraman tasted like bacon.

St. Paul, Minnesota, was originally called Pig's Eye.

WHEN PIGS...

We've all heard the expression, "When pigs fly," meaning "never." Turns out that even if they can't fly, they can do other things that are just as strange.

WHEN PIGS FISH

Pigs on the island of Tongatapu in the South Pacific nation of Tonga have learned to fish. Domestic razorbacks there, descendants of pigs left by European explorers centuries ago, have learned to wade into the ocean to eat seaweed, mussels, crabs, and even fish. The pigs have become a must-see for tourists to the island—and a must-eat for locals, since their seafood diet has given them a unique flavor. "It's saltier than normal," local tour guide Joe Naeata said.

WHEN PIGS ATTACK

A town in the German state of Bavaria was attacked by a drove of crazed pigs in November 2006. The wild boars knocked over bicyclists, caused traffic accidents, wrecked a store, and bit several pedestrians in Veitshöchheim, police said. The melee went on for almost two hours before police officers killed three of the boars and scared the rest away. Said local police chief Karl-Heinz Schmitt, "It wasn't your everyday kind of incident."

WHEN PIGS MILK COWS

Ermelino Rojas, from Calixto Garcia, Cuba, had a piglet picked out for Christmas dinner in 2004, but spared its life when he saw what he called a "moving scene": The piglet was suckling from one of his cows. And the cow didn't seemed to mind. Rojas spared the pig's life, unable to kill it after seeing it with its "new mother."

WHEN PIGS, YES, FLY

In 1974 flights at London's Heathrow Airport had to be cancelled when a 40-foot-long flying pig was spotted in the area. The pig was seen by pilots at nearly 40,000 feet before it finally landed in the countryside southeast of London. What was it? An inflatable pig, a prop in a photo shoot for the Pink Floyd album *Animals*, that had broken its tether.

Indiana University's main library sinks 1" per year—because of the weight of the books.

"PAGING MR. POST"

The funeral business (known as "the dismal trade" in the 18th century) necessarily deals with concepts that many people find distasteful. That led to the evolution of a unique set of euphemisms in the death biz.

Passed into the arms of God. Dead. Other euphemisms: *passed away, gone to meet his/her Maker, expired, deceased.*

Temporary preservation. Embalming—the common treatment of dead bodies in which bodily fluids are replaced with preservative fluid. Other euphemisms: *sanitary treatment, hygienic treatment*.

Grief therapy. The "therapeutic" effect of having an expensive funeral "viewing."

Burn and scatter. Slang for services that scatter cremated remains at sea. Also known as *bake and shake*.

Casket coach. Hearse.

Consigned to earth. Buried.

Pre-need sales. Funeral services sold to someone who hasn't died yet.

Corpse cooler. A specialized coffin with a window, once used to preserve the body for viewing. An ice compartment kept the corpse cool.

Interment space. A grave. Used in phrases such as *opening the interment space* (digging the grave) and *closing the interment space* (filling the grave).

Cremains. Cremated remains; ashes.

Babyland. The part of a cemetery reserved for small children and infants.

Slumber room. The room in which the loved one's body is displayed.

Memorial park. Cemetery.

Lawn-type cemetery. A cemetery that bans headstones in favor of ground markers, allowing caretakers to simply mow the lawn rather than trim each grave by hand.

Funeral director. Undertaker.

O-sign. A dead body sometimes displays what hospital workers call the "O-sign," meaning the mouth is hanging open, forming an "O." The "Q-sign" is the same—but with the tongue hanging out.

Gotta hand it to her: Queen Elizabeth I owned 2,000 pairs of gloves.

Protective caskets. Coffin sealed with rubber gaskets to keep out bugs and other invaders. But methane gas from the decomposing body has been known to build up inside such caskets, causing them to explode and spew out their contents. This prompted the introduction of *burping caskets* that allow gas to escape.

Grief counselor. Mortuary salesperson.

Mr. Post. Morgue attendant. Used by many hospitals to page the morgue when a body has to be removed from a room.

Nose squeezer. Flat-topped coffin.

Beautiful memory picture. An embalmed body displayed in an expensive casket.

Body. This term for a dead person is generally discouraged, along with *corpse*. Preferred: the dead person's name, or *remains*.

Plantings. Graves.

Selection room. Room in which buyers look at displayed caskets. This term replaces *back room*, *showroom*, *casket room*.

Companion space. An over/under grave set for husband-and-wife couples; one body is placed deep in the ground and the second buried above it.

* * *

LET'S DO A STUDY

• Colorado State University scientists concluded that Western Civilization causes acne.

• A 2003 study carried out by scientists at Edinburgh University found that fish feel pain.

• In 1994 the Japanese Meteorological Agency concluded a seven-year study into whether or not earthquakes are caused by catfish wiggling their tails. (They're not.)

• Physicists at the University of Nijmegen in the Netherlands released a report in 2000 on their study of diamagnetics, during which they claimed to have "levitated" a frog, a grasshopper, a pizza…and a sumo wrestler.

Elephants have only four teeth, which they can lose and replace up to six times.

PAC-MANHATTAN

Are you old enough to remember odd but simple college stunts like swallowing live goldfish, or cramming people into Volkswagen Beetles? Here's a new college fad that's just as nutty...but a lot more complicated.

THINKING BIG

In 2004 graduate students at New York University's Interactive Telecommunications Program set out to create a real-life version of the 1980s video game Pac-Man—one that could be played on the streets of Manhattan, with people in costumes assuming the roles of the five characters: Pac-Man and the four ghosts, Inky, Pinky, Blinky, and Clyde. They called their game "Pac-Manhattan." Been a while since you played a game of Pac-Man? Here's a refresher:

• The playing field consists of a maze that's filled with a trail of tiny white dots. Pac-Man must travel around the entire maze and eat all the dots while avoiding Inky, Pinky, Blinky, and Clyde. If they catch him, he dies.

• There are four "power pellets" on the playing field, one in each of the four corners of the maze. When Pac-Man eats one of the pellets, he becomes energized, all the ghosts turn blue, and for a short time he can eat the ghosts—so *they* have to run from *him*.

GET REAL

So if one person can play Pac-Man, how many does it take to play Pac-Manhattan? Ten—five play Pac-Man and the four ghosts, and each of the other five serves as one of the character's "generals." While the characters run around on city streets, the generals remain in a special Pac-Manhattan "control room" and keep their characters updated on the game's progress by cell phone.

• The area of play is a 6 x 4 city-block area surrounding Washington Square Park in New York's Greenwich Village, which simulates the Pac Man video game board. The city streets serve as the maze; each time a character moves to a new intersection, they are required to report their position to their general. The information is then displayed on a computer screen in the control room that looks just like the screen on the original Pac-Man arcade game.

• There are no white dots on the city streets, but they are displayed on the computer screen. As Pac-Man moves from one intersection to another, the dots disappear from the screen. His general is responsible for keeping him up to date on which streets he still has to cover.

• The intersections at the four corners of the maze serve as power pellets. When Pac-Man reaches the intersection and tags the street sign, he "eats the pellet" and becomes invincible for two minutes. If he can tag any of the ghosts before the two minutes are up, they are "eaten" and have to return to their starting point before they can continue chasing Pac-Man. Of course, after the two minutes, the ghosts can chase and eat Pac-Man again.

• Pac-Man is the only character who knows everything that is happening in the game—his general is allowed to tell him where the ghosts are, but the ghosts' generals are not allowed to tell them where Pac-Man is. Each ghost is allowed to know where the other ghosts are and whether or not Pac-Man has eaten a power pellet and become invincible, but they have to find Pac-Man on their own without help from their generals.

• The game continues until Pac-Man eats all of the dots or is eaten by one of the ghosts. Games can last anywhere from under 10 minutes to over an hour, depending on luck and how well the characters and their controllers work together.

DO TRY THIS AT HOME

Pac-Manhattan is a work in progress; the inventors say they'll open their game to the public once it's perfected. But you don't have to wait until then—if you've got 10 people with 10 cell phones and a map of the streets where you live, you can set up your own game. The rules are posted on www.pacmanhattan.com.

* * *

Famous people who have been homeless: Charlie Chaplin, Shania Twain, Jim Carrey, Ella Fitzgerald, Don Imus, David Letterman, George Orwell, Eartha Kitt, Colonel Sanders, and William Shatner.

Nutty: The first week in October is Squirrel Awareness Week.

WELCOME TO THE MÜTTER MUSEUM

Warning! This unusual museum in Philadelphia is not for the faint of heart, but it's worth a visit if you think you have the stomach. And if you don't, don't worry—they've got plenty of stomachs in the collection.

TOOLS OF THE TRADE

In the 1830s a Philadelphia surgeon named Thomas Dent Mütter made a trip to Paris to round out his medical education. At the time Paris was one of the most medically advanced cities in the world and far ahead of anything the United States had to offer. Mütter came away very impressed by the systematic, scientific approach the Parisian doctors took toward treating human illness—patients suffering from the same malady, for example, were clustered together in special dedicated hospital wards, so that the doctors could compare their cases and gain insight from the experience.

Equally impressive were the enormous collections of medical specimens and models that the doctors had amassed—healthy (as well as diseased) skulls, skeletons, tumors, hernias, blood clots, appendages, bony growths, you name it—that were used to teach physicians the art and science of their craft. Mütter learned so much studying the specimens that when he returned to the United States he began assembling his own collection of specimens and using them in the lectures he gave as a professor at the Jefferson Medical College in Philadelphia.

PASSING THE TORCH

By the mid-1850s Mütter's own health had deteriorated to the point that he had to give up his teaching post. By then his collection had grown to more than 1,700 items, and he didn't want it to sit in storage when it could still be put to good use. So in 1856 he donated the entire collection to the College of Physicians of Philadelphia, along with an endowment of $30,000 to maintain and expand it. In those days Philadelphia was one of the leading centers of

Three towns in Oklahoma: Greasy, Bushyhead, and Bowlegs.

American medicine, and the Mütter Museum naturally became a popular destination for medical oddities, thanks not only to the acquisitions made possible by Mütter's endowment, but also to the fact that physicians all over the country began sending the strange items they encountered during the course of their work—giant hairballs swallowed by patients in mental institutions, shrunken heads collected from natives in Peru, skeletons of people suffering from countless crippling and bone-twisting diseases, brains of several prominent surgeons and at least one executed murderer, deformed fetuses floating in formaldehyde-filled jars, plus any number of syphilitic skulls, gangrenous lungs, cirrhotic livers, and other diseased organs, appendages, growths, and limbs.

A WHO'S WHO OF EWWWWW!

More than a few historically significant items found their way into the Mütter Museum as well: Supreme Court Chief Justice John Marshall's bladder stones were donated to the museum; so was a piece of the "thorax" (chest) of John Wilkes Booth, and a brain sample from Charles Guiteau, the man who assassinated President James A. Garfield in 1881.

Have you ever heard of Chang and Eng, the original "Siamese" twins? When they died on the same day in 1874 at the age of 63 (Chang died first, leaving Eng to spend the last hours of his life helplessly attached to a corpse as he awaited his own imminent death), the autopsy was performed right there in the Mütter Museum. Most of their conjoined bodies were returned to the family for burial, but the museum got to keep their shared liver and a plaster cast of their bodies (complete with a visible autopsy scar and a few armpit hairs that got stuck in the plaster).

ONE THING LEADS TO ANOTHER

A lot of things have changed in the nearly 150 years since the Mütter museum collection first went on display; medical school education has progressed far beyond the point where the skeletons of midgets and two-headed babies have any real educational value. By the early 1980s the museum was virtually forgotten, and the number of visitors had dwindled to well under a thousand people a year. Was it even worth keeping the museum open? The College of Physicians decided that it was—if nothing else the museum was

A fork used for pitching dung is a *yeevil.*

certainly a fascinating artifact of 19th century medicine, and one of the few still in existence. In 1982 the museum's newly appointed curator, 35-year-old Gretchen Worden, decided that the best way to ensure its future was to raise its public profile in any way she could. She became a sort of roving ambassador of medical oddities, granting countless radio interviews over the years and appearing on TV shows as diverse as *The Late Show With David Letterman* and science documentaries broadcast on the BBC. She also wrote a coffee table book about the collection and began selling an annual calendar. These publications brought in needed funds and also did the job of putting the Mütter Museum back on the map—today more than 60,000 people visit the museum each year and pay $8–12 apiece for the privilege.

STILL GOING STRONG

One of the strangest things about the Mütter Museum is the fact that it is still adding to its collection. Two examples: In 1973 a man named Harry Raymond Eastlack died from a disease called *fibrodysplasia ossificans progressiva*, which caused bone to form in the muscles and connective tissue of his body. By the end of his life he was little more than a living statue, able to move only his lips. After he died at the age of 39, per his request his body was donated to science and his fused skeleton became a part of the collection.

In 1992, the parents of a baby born without a cranium (the part of the skull that holds the brain) donated her remains to the museum and she is currently on display in a formaldehyde-filled jar. In return for the donation, the parents asked only that they be allowed to visit the infant from time to time.

FEATURED ATTRACTIONS

Think you're ready to visit the Mütter Museum? Here are some things to watch for:

• **President Grover Cleveland's "Secret Tumor."** Early in his second term as president (1893–97), Cleveland learned that he had cancer of the mouth. At the time the country was mired in one of the worst economic depressions in American history, and Cleveland feared the situation would get even worse if the public learned of his life-threatening illness. So on July 1, 1893, he slipped aboard a friend's yacht and surgeons cut out a large part of his upper jaw as the boat steamed up New York's East River.

The secret surgery was a success—Cleveland was fitted with a rubber partial jaw that gave him a normal appearance and did not impair his speech, and he was able to serve out the remainder of his term without the public realizing what had happened. The full story did not emerge until 1917, when one of the attending surgeons, Dr. William W. Keen, donated the tumor and some of the surgical equipment used in the procedure to the Mütter Museum.

• **The Soap Lady.** Early in the 19th century (no one is sure quite when), a morbidly obese Philadelphia woman was buried in a downtown cemetery. Many years later when the cemetery was being relocated as part of an urban renewal project, it was discovered that the environment in which the woman had been buried—damp soil with just the right chemical makeup—had turned her remains into *adipocere*, a substance similar to soap. The womans' body was never claimed by relatives; the museum later acquired her for the princely sum of $7.50. A "Soap Man," who was buried near the Soap Lady, ended up in the Smithsonian Institute (no word on how much he cost).

• **The Collection of Obsolete Medical Devices.** Why stop at physical specimens? In 1871 the museum expanded into devices that are no longer put to use. Keep an eye out for the tonsil guillotines and the lobotomy picks; also watch for the brain slicing knife that, thankfully, was only put to use after the patient had died. "Two people are needed," the display reads, "one to hold the brain in place, and the other to slice."

• **The Dr. Chevalier Jackson Collection of Foreign Bodies.** Dr. Jackson was one of the leading throat doctors at the turn of the twentieth century, and part of his job was removing objects that people had swallowed. He apparently kept every object he ever fished out of a gullet and plenty that others had, too; today more than 2,000 of them are lovingly categorized and displayed in drawers with labels like "Buttons," "Pins," "Nuts, Seeds Shells or Other Vegetal Substances," "Toys," "Dental materials" (dentures), and "Meat."

FREAKY FOODS FROM AROUND THE WORLD

We gave you a heads-up on assorted international delicacies on page 187. Here are a few more tasty treats from around the world.

MONGOLIA: *Boodog*—the flesh of a goat broiled inside a bag made of the goat's cut and tied skin. The goat is then barbecued or cooked with a blowtorch.

BELIZE: *Cena Molida*, a popular mixture that includes roasted, mashed cockroaches.

JAPAN: *Odori ebi*, which are baby prawns, served live.

YUKON TERRITORY, CANADA: In 1973, a Mountie found a frozen, unidentified human toe in an abandoned log cabin. A local tavern got a hold of the digit and invented the Sour Toe Cocktail, which consists of a shot of hard alcohol (drinker's choice) sipped from a glass with the toe plopped in it. "You can drink it fast, you can drink it slow," the drinker is told, "but the lips have got to touch the toe."

ECUADOR: Fried guinea pig.

THE NETHERLANDS: Salted horsemeat sandwiches.

PORTUGAL: You've heard the word "tripe," but do you know what it is? It's three of the four stomachs of a cow. It's incredibly tough, so it's boiled until it's tender enough to chew.

THE PHILIPPINES: Rat sausage.

CHINA: A century egg is prepared by preserving a duck or quail egg in a "soup" made of clay, ash, salt, lime, and straw for several months. The white of the egg turns a translucent dark brown and the yolk turns several shades of green. Westerners who have tried

Swedish confectionery salesman Roland Ohisson was buried in a coffin made of chocolate.

it likened the taste to a combination of a hardboiled egg and Jell-O. Need something to wash it down? Try some "three-penis wine," an aphrodisiac made of one part boiled seal penis, one part boiled dog penis, and four parts boiled deer penis.

INDONESIA: Monkey toes.

CAMBODIA: *Balut*, a popular snack sold by street vendors, is a boiled duck egg with a fertilized, almost fully developed baby duck inside. Street stands in Cambodia also sell cobra blood and fried tarantulas seasoned with sugar, salt, and garlic.

MEXICO: *Escamoles*, or fried ant larvae.

ENGLAND: Black pudding is a sausage made by cooking pig, cow, or sheep blood along with the meat of the animal (and extra, added fat) until it's thick and gelatinous. It congeals as it cools and then it's served in slices.

FRANCE: In the southern part of the country, donkey meat is commonly sold in butcher shops.

VIETNAM: Whole baby mice, each about an inch long, are grilled and served with a spicy dipping sauce.

BURMA: Grilled bat.

THAILAND: Creamed slug on toast.

U.S.A.: An American specialty, *Burgoo* is found mostly in Kentucky. It's a meat and vegetable stew...where the "meat" is often squirrel brains. Some people just scoop the brains out of several squirrel skulls and scramble them with eggs.

* * *

"Hope is the feeling you feel when you feel that the feeling you feel isn't going to be permanent."

—Jean Kerr

DOCTOR STRANGE, LOVE

We thought you'd love some stories about the wild world of medicine.

CAN'T SAY HE'S HEARTLESS

In August 2006, 55-year-old Louis Selo of London died while on vacation in Ireland. His body was examined at Beaumont Hospital in Dublin, where it was determined that Selo had died of a massive heart attack. The corpse was sent home to England, where another autopsy was performed (a second autopsy is customarily done when English citizens die out of the country). That operation went a bit differently: When the English doctors opened up Selo's chest, they discovered an extra heart and two extra lungs in a plastic bag inside him. An inquiry revealed that they were from an organ donor at the Irish hospital. Those organs were returned to the family of the donor, and an investigation to find out how they ended up in Mr. Selo was begun immediately.

URINE GOOD HANDS

Dr. Savely Yurkovsky of Chappaqua, New York, says he knows a cure for the deadly disease SARS. Victims must collect some of their own infected saliva, mucus, and urine, mix it with a little water, and drink it. The potion, Yurkovsky says in his book, *Biological, Chemical and Nuclear Warfare: Protecting Yourself And Your Loved Ones*, will trigger the immune system to go after the disease. Other revelations in Yurkovsky's book: "Poison can be your best friend," "Carcinogens can protect you against cancer," and "Toxic chemicals can extend lifespan and enhance immunity."

HEART TO HEART

In 1996 renowned English heart surgeon Sir Magdi Yacoub operated on two-year-old Hannah Clark of Mountain Ash, Wales. She had cardiomyopathy, which had caused her heart to become badly inflamed, so Yacoub put in a new one. Hannah and her new heart were doing well...until the heart started showing signs of rejection 10 years later. In 2006 Yacoub came out of retirement and operated on Hannah, now 12, again. He reconnected her original heart... which had been left inside her body (surprisingly, not an unusual

The opening to a cave in which a bear hibernates is always on a north slope.

practice). It had apparently healed itself while it wasn't being used and began working immediately when it was reattached. Hannah was back home within five days. It was the first time that such an operation had ever been performed.

BUSTED

A German plastic surgeon cheated out of payments from four women upon whom he had performed breast enhancement surgery took his complaint to police…along with photos of the women's enhanced breasts. "They registered under fake names," Dr. Michael Koenig told reporters. "And then after the operations, they just ran away." Each surgery cost nearly $14,000. Police made posters of the enhanced-breast photos and distributed them to the public; the German newspaper *Bild* even printed one of the shots. "It's probably the most unusual wanted poster ever," *Bild* wrote.

GOTTA HAND IT TO HER

A doctor in New Brunswick, New Jersey, was arrested in September 2006 after stealing a hand from a cadaver and giving it to an exotic dancer as a gift. She kept it in a jar of formaldehyde. It was discovered when police were called to the woman's apartment because of a suicidal roommate. Friends said she had named the hand "Freddy."

AHHHHHHHH! I SEE!

In 2005 Joyce Urch had a heart attack. The 74-year-old was rushed to Walgrave Hospital near her home in Coventry, England, where she underwent surgery and spent the next three days unconscious and near death. She finally woke up—and started shouting "I can see! I can see!" Urch had been blind for 25 years. "Then she leaned forward," said her husband, Eric, "and she just looked at me and said, 'Haven't you got old?' And I said, 'Wait 'til you have a look in the mirror.'" Just as doctors were unable to explain why she lost her sight so many years before (they thought it might be a genetic condition), they could give no explanation for its return. But the Urches didn't care. "When Joyce first went blind," Eric said, "everything seemed to fall away from us. This has given us both our lives back."

A Louisiana law states that you may grow to be as tall as you want.

WEIRD MEXICO

The odd, the weird, the strange, and the crazy—south of the border.

WORMING AROUND

One of the most lucrative products (and exports) in Mexico is mescal, a liquor similar to tequila, and most commonly packaged with a worm in every bottle. Legend says that eating the worm triggers powerful hallucinations. In 2005 the Mexican government considered banning worms from mescal. Because of the hallucinations? Nope. The worm is too high in fat, they claim. (The proposal failed; the worm remains.)

El LOCO

In 1993 Gerardo Palomero went on an animal-rights crusade, invading Mexico City slaughterhouses and yelling at meat cutters to treat animals more humanely. While workers respected his message, they found Palomero hard to take seriously because he was dressed in the brightly colored spandex costume of his professional wrestling character, "Super Animal."

THE OLDEST PROFESSION

In 2005 women's groups in Mexico City raised funds to build a home for elderly prostitutes. The city government even donated a building. But it's not a retirement home—it's a brothel. Hopeful "resident" Gloria Maria, 74, says she "can't charge what the young ones do, but I still have two or three clients a day."

SHE KNOWS WHAT SHE'S TALKING ABOUT

In December 1998, newly elected Mexico City mayor Rosario Robles Berlanga was preparing to give an inauguration speech in which she planned to announce a crackdown on crime. Just hours before Berlanga was to speak, her top aide was mugged in a taxi. The thief stole the briefcase containing the mayor's tough-on-crime speech.

WEIRD FINDS

If you're the person who lost the bag of human skulls, write to us and get a free Uncle John's Bathroom Reader Skull Bag. Congratulations!

HE ALMOST CROAKED

In 2004 postman Jason O'Rourke was making his rounds in Stirling, Scotland, when he opened a public mailbox and encountered a strange sight. "I opened the box and 32 eyes were staring back at me,' he said. "I got the fright of my life, and just slammed the door back shut so they couldn't escape, whatever they were." What were they? Frogs. Someone had put 16 of them in the box. O'Rourke immediately contacted the Scottish Society for the Prevention of Cruelty to Animals, who were able to transfer the frogs to a nearby pond.

SOMETHING TO THINK ABOUT

Workers at a sewage treatment facility in Bethlehem, Pennsylvania, called police one day in 2001 to tell them they had found half of a human brain. The half-brain, investigators later said, was "fresh" and had apparently been flushed down a toilet. A DNA search never determined who the organ belonged to. Local coroner Zachary Lysek called the matter "very perplexing."

D.T.

In May 2006, workers at the International Bird Rescue Research Center in Fairfield, California, found an "alien" inside a duck. An injured mallard had been sent to the facility with a broken wing, and an X-ray of its abdomen showed what looked like the stereotypical portrayal of an extraterrestrial—with an oval head and big eyes. "It clearly stood out," said IBRRC director Jay Holcomb. "We were trying to look at its broken wing, but all we could see was the face." They figured the duck had eaten a doll or something similar, but when it died a short time later and they performed an autopsy, they found...nothing. The group put the X-ray up for auction on eBay to help fund the center. It sold for $9,600.

BARBARA AND JENNA IN BAGHDAD

In April 2003, American and British troops entering Baghdad discovered the palatial house of Uday Hussein, son of Saddam Hussein. Inside they found more than $1 million worth of liquor, drugs, Cuban cigars—and a gym with all the walls covered with photographs of naked women taken from the Internet. It was "the biggest collection of naked women I'd ever seen," said Army captain Ed Ballanco. Bonus: There were also several photos of President Bush's twin 21-year-old daughters, Barbara and Jenna. (No, they weren't naked.)

ARMCHAIR SPIES

In September 2006, a man in Germany was looking at images of China on the satellite-imaging Web site Google Earth when he saw something strange. It was an obviously fake model landscape set in the middle of a desert in the country's northwest region. It had fake snow-capped mountains, fake lakes, and fake river valleys. And it was huge—about 2,000 feet by 3,000 feet—and had straight, walled borders. The man posted news of his find on a Google Earth bulletin board, and someone suggested he look around China's border regions for any similar terrain. He did, and found something. The terrain in the model almost perfectly matched an area 1,500 miles southeast, on a disputed border area with India. Same mountains, same lakes, same valleys. A reporter for McClatchy Newspapers went to the region... and found it was surrounded by an armored tank base. When asked what the replica was for, a soldier said, "You wouldn't understand it."

HEAD FOR THE BUS

In 2001 police in Siliguri, West Bengal, India, were called to a bus stop after people reported a strange bag left there—and the bag smelled funny. The officers opened it and found 86 human skulls inside. "All the skulls were neatly sawn off," police superintendent Sanjay Chander said. "And some had some brain tissues sticking to them." No explanation for the bag of heads was ever found.

...because he believed the appearance of Dobby the house-elf was based on him.

PROJECT ACOUSTIC KITTY

Why did the cat cross the road? To spy on the USSR! If you didn't laugh, don't feel bad—the joke doesn't make any sense. It made even less sense during the Cold War, when the CIA tried to develop a way to get cats to spy on the Soviets. (Ahhhh, our hard-earned tax dollars at work.)

MISSION IMPLAUSIBLE

In the 1960s the CIA was looking for a way to spy on Russian diplomats strolling through the park across the street from the Soviet compound in Washington, D.C. With today's electronics and eavesdropping equipment that might not be too big a challenge, but 40 years ago things were different: Microphones weren't nearly as sophisticated as they are today, and the ones that were small enough to be hidden in a park bench or drilled into the trunk of a tree were especially bad. Unless the diplomats sat or stood right next to the microphone and happened to talk directly into it, the tiny mikes couldn't filter out nearby noises—children playing, leaves rustling, park benches squeaking—so that their conversations could be clearly understood. And since the diplomats moved all around the park, even if the microphones had been effective there would have had to have been multiple units installed all over the park. How could that be done without attracting the attention of the Soviet compound right across the street? Another way had to be found.

THINKING OUTSIDE THE (LITTER) BOX

At some point in the 1960s some clever scientist—we'll probably never know who, since the details of the program are still a closely guarded secret—decided to see if they could wire up common house cats to become mobile electronic listening devices. The project was code-named "Acoustic Kitty." (No, we're not kidding.)

CIA veterinarians selected a single test cat and performed extensive surgery on it, inserting a microphone, a transmitter, and batteries underneath its skin, and running a wire antenna down the length of the cat's tail. Have you ever been able to teach a cat to do a trick? Neither has Uncle John, but somehow the CIA fig-

Over the course of his life, Mormon leader Brigham Young had 55 wives.

ured out how to do that, too. They trained Acoustic Kitty to approach selected individuals on command and to listen for and seek out human conversation. The idea was that if the cat got close enough to the diplomats that *it* could hear their conversation clearly, the microphone would pick it up, too. If the suspects moved around the park, the cat could follow without attracting suspicion. Who would guess that the cat was working for the CIA?

The possibilities must have seemed endless. Why stop with one cat in a Washington, D.C. park? It might be just a matter of time before dozens of Acoustic Kitties were perched on windowsills all over Washington—perhaps even in the Kremlin.

SECRET AGENT CAT

The training and testing went well, except for one hitch: When Acoustic Kitty got hungry, it wandered off in search of something to eat. The CIA fixed that problem by implanting a device to suppress the cat's appetite.

Finally, everything was ready for a trial run: Acoustic Kitty was bundled into a spy van and driven to the park across the street from the Soviet compound. When some Soviet diplomats were spotted heading into the park, the CIA agents let the cat out of the van and...*SPLAT!* Before it could even cross the street, Acoustic Kitty was run over by a taxi and killed.

BACK TO THE DRAWING BOARD

Five years of research and development had gone into the program; so had $14 million of taxpayers' money. All we have to show for it is the world's most expensive roadkill—when Acoustic Kitty died, the project died with it, written off by the the CIA as a total loss. (You'd never know it from reading the handful of documents about it that have been declassified, though: One document released in 1983 praised the design team, claiming their "energy and imagination could be models for scientific pioneers.")

To this day, very little is known about Project Acoustic Kitty; most of the details are still classified, and the CIA won't say why—their reasons are under wraps, too. Is it because cat-related espionage programs are still under way? Probably not. The most likely reason for all the secrecy, say intelligence experts: "To avoid further embarrassment."

Cats can donate blood to other cats.

OTHER BEASTS OF BURDEN

• **Operation Boiler Rat.** In 1941 England's wartime spy agency, the Special Operations Executive (SOE), came up with a unique way to cripple German shipping during World War II: They cut open a bunch of dead rats and stuffed them with plastic explosives and heat-sensitive detonators, then sewed them shut. The plan was to smuggle the rat bombs into Nazi-occupied Europe, where saboteurs would sneak them onto German ships and toss them onto the coal piles next to the boilers. The expectation was that the fire stoker would see the dead rat and get rid of it by shoveling it into the boiler. The resulting explosion would destroy the boiler and cripple the ship.

The dead rats never saw active duty; according to the BBC, "The first consignment was seized by the Germans and the secret was blown. The Germans were fascinated by the idea, however, and the rats were exhibited at the top military schools. Indeed, SOE files show that the Germans actually organized searches for these rodent explosives."

• **Project Airport Gerbil.** In the 1970s the MI5 section of the British Security Service tried to use gerbils to detect spies and terrorists as they passed through the country's airports. Gerbils are able to detect increased adrenaline levels in human sweat when people are nervous; the idea was that passengers prepared to board would walk past a fan that would blow air into a hidden gerbil cage. If the gerbils smelled extra adrenaline, they were trained to press a lever that would alert security and also give them a treat. So how many terrorists did the gerbils catch? Not even one: The program was abandoned after researchers discovered "the gerbils could not tell the difference between terrorists and passengers who were scared of flying."

* * *

RANDOM ODDITY

Burlington, Vermont, is home to the World's Tallest Filing Cabinet, made of dozens of individual cabinets welded together. (It's also home to the eight-foot-tall "Shopping Cart Arch.")

The scientific name for stinky armpits: *Tragomaschalia.*

CLOSE ENCOUNTERS OF THE CREDIBLE KIND

Investigations into 99% of UFO sightings have resulted in rational and very Earthly explanations. But then there are those few that simply have no explanation. Here are three cases that still have the experts baffled.

STRANGE BALL

In 1783 a London, England, man named Tiberius Cavallo, Fellow of the Royal Society, witnessed something that was unlike anything he'd ever seen before. "Northeast of the Terrace," he wrote in his memoirs, "in clear sky and warm weather, I saw appear suddenly an oblong cloud nearly parallel to the horizon. Below the cloud was seen a luminous body, brightly lit up and almost stationary." Cavallo described the object as a "strange ball" that was faint blue when he first saw it but then grew brighter and brighter. At one point, it flew high up into the air, then back down, and flew low across the horizon. After a few minutes, "it changed shape to oblong, acquired a tail, and seemed to split up into two bodies of small size." The object then disappeared over the horizon in a flash, and the last thing Cavallo heard from it was a "loud rumble like an explosion." Thinking the object may have crashed, Cavallo and other witnesses searched the area, but couldn't find a craft or an impact crater. One possible explanation: The "explosion" may have been a sonic boom, created when an object goes faster than the speed of sound...but this happened more than 150 years before humans had invented any type of vehicle that could break the sound barrier.

STS 48

While stationed in Earth orbit in September 1991, the Space Shuttle *Columbia*'s aft-mounted TV camera recorded video of several unidentified objects that seemed to be "swimming around." The camera was focused on an experimental tether 44 miles away, and beyond that was the horizon of the Earth. The glowing white objects intermittently entered the frame, and then turned and swam around, like microbes swimming in a petri dish. After a few minutes, a white flash appeared in the bottom left corner of the screen and suddenly, as if on cue, the little white objects all turned in unison and zoomed out of the frame. A few seconds later, a streak of light entered the frame and seemed to pause. Then, inexplicably, the camera rotated down toward the cargo bay, which was completely out of focus, then rotated back up…and the lights were gone.

NASA has dismissed the objects as "normal ice and debris" that sometimes float around ships in orbit. But these weren't floating; they were moving independently of each other and changing direction. And the occasional "debris" NASA referred to is usually found close to the ship. The camera was focused miles away on the long tether, and some of the objects appeared to fly *behind* the tether. So what were these things? No one knows for sure. They are truly unidentified flying objects.

FLAMING ARROW

On the night of June 30, 2002, a UFO was sighted across nearly all of central China. It was first seen over the eastern province of Jiangsu, then moved west, over Henan province, then Xiaxi province, and then Sichuan. "At 10:30 p.m., an object resembling a flaming arrow appeared in the night sky," wrote Henan's *City Morning Post* the next day. "Then the tail of the fiery arrow opened up like a fan, which emitted bright light. The light-emitting section then changed into a crescent. A fireball on top of the crescent glowed brilliantly. Five minutes later, the UFO disappeared."

Dozens of other newspapers reported the event, based on thousands of eyewitness accounts. The government had no explanation, except to say that it was definitely not a Chinese craft. Wang Sichao, a well-respected astronomer at Nanjing's Zijinshan Astronomy Center, studied the reports and photographs, and offered this conclusion: "It is a dimensional flying machine. But whether it is of human origin or extraterrestrial, whether it is controlled inside or remotely, are still unknown. Maybe we will not be able to uncover the truth for many years, but human curiosity will never let us stop searching."

What does author Bram Stoker's Dracula have that movie Draculas do not? A mustache.

THE FINAL DAYS OF KING CHARLES II

Next time you feel yourself coming down with a cold, thank your lucky stars for 21st-century medicine.

MONDAY

On the morning of February 2, 1685, King Charles II of England was preparing to shave when he suddenly cried out in pain, fell to the floor, and started having fits. Six royal physicians rushed in and administered emergency "aid."

• They let (drained) 16 ounces of blood.

• Then they applied heated cups to the skin, which formed large round blisters, in order to "stimulate the system."

• They let eight more ounces of blood.

• They induced vomiting to purify his stomach, gave an enema to purify his bowels, and made him swallow a purgative to clean out his intestines.

• Then they force-fed him syrup of blackthorn and rock salt.

• They shaved his hair and put blistering plasters on his scalp. The king regained consciousness. The treatment seemed to be working, so they kept at it.

• They gave him another enema.

• Then they applied hellebore root to the nostrils, more blistering plasters to the skin, and powdered cowslip flowers to the stomach.

• Special plasters made from pigeon droppings were attached to his feet. After 12 hours of care, they put the ailing king to bed.

TUESDAY

• Charles awoke and seemed much improved. The attending physicians congratulated themselves and continued the treatment.

• They let 10 more ounces of blood.

• They gave him a potion of black cherry, peony, lavender, crushed pearls, and sugar. Charles slept for the rest of the day and through the night.

First movie with outtakes in the credits: *Smokey and the Bandit* (1977).

WEDNESDAY

• He awoke, had another fit, and was bled again.

• They gave him senna pods in spring water, and white wine with nutmeg.

• They force-fed him a drink made from "40 drops of extract of human skull" from a man who had met a violent death.

• They made him eat a gallstone from an East Indian goat.

• Then they proudly announced that King Charles was definitely on the road to recovery.

THURSDAY

• The king was near death.

• He was blistered again, re-bled, repurged, and given another enema.

• He was given Jesuits' powder—a controversial malaria remedy—laced with opium and wine. His doctors were mystified by the king's weakening condition.

FRIDAY

• Showing no improvement, the king was bled almost bloodless.

• They scoured the palace grounds and created a last-ditch antidote containing "extracts of all the herbs and animals of the kingdom."

SATURDAY

The king was dead.

Postmortem: It was rumored at the time that King Charles II had been poisoned, but no proof was ever found. Modern doctors offer three theories as to cause of death:

1. He *was* poisoned—but not by an enemy—by himself. He often played with chemicals in an unventilated palace laboratory, where he contracted acute mercury poisoning.

2. He suffered from kidney failure.

3. He had a brain hemorrhage.

Would the king have survived without treatment? Probably not. But at least his death wouldn't have been so excruciating.

WHAT'S EATIN' YOU?

Do you have a nagging, gnawing feeling that... well, just a nagging, gnawing feeling? You should—odds are you're being slowly devoured by one of these tiny, vicious parasites right this very second.

EATIN' YOU: Fleas
BIO: Fleas are tiny insects that just can't live without blood. They can eat more than 15 times their body weight in blood in a single day. That includes the blood of dogs, cats, rats, rabbits, and any other mammal that's handy, including you. They're also "Super Bugs": Fleas can pull 160,000 times their own weight (the equivalent of a human pulling 24 million pounds) and can jump over 150 times their own size (the equivalent of a human jumping about 1,000 feet).
DANGER! In the right—or wrong—conditions, fleas are disease machines. They can transmit tapeworm to pets or humans, and can carry a number of diseases, including the blood parasite *babesia*, and the dreaded *bubonic* plague. Thankfully, they're not nearly as bad as they were in the days before the vacuum cleaner. (Most eggs hatch in your carpet.)

EATIN' YOU: Bedbugs
BIO: Tiny, painful, smelly, and disgusting, bedbugs are nocturnal, spending the day in walls, furniture, or your bed. At night they crawl out of the mattress and suck your blood. And they can wait up to a year in that mattress between feedings.
DANGER! Their bites are often painful, but, thankfully, bedbugs are not known to transmit any diseases.

EATIN' YOU: Ticks
BIO: Ticks are arachnids—not insects—and are related to spiders. There are no ticks that live solely on humans, but if there are no deer, cattle, birds, or reptiles handy, you'll do. They have three life stages after hatching—larva, pupa and adult—and each stage needs a "blood meal" before morphing into the next stage. Ticks use a hunting technique known as "questing." That means that since

The Mt. Rushmore monument was never finished—Lincoln's head is missing an ear.

they can't hop or fly or run after prey, they wait around on grass or twigs for a host to come to them. How long will they wait? Years, possibly decades. And despite all that sitting they can leap into action the instant they sense a host coming by. One female tick can increase its body weight 200 times in a six-day feeding. Human equivalent: going from 170 pounds to 34,000 pounds in a week.

DANGER! Only mosquitoes transmit more diseases to humans than ticks do.

EATIN' YOU: Chiggers

BIO: Chiggers are the blood-sucking, infant larvae of mites, but before they can grow up, they must eat. They prefer rodents and lizards, but they'll happily dine on you. These ravenous babies digest skin cells by spitting up powerful enzymes. Irritated skin cells react by building a hard mound around the tiny hole created by the enzymes, forming a "straw" (called a *stylostome*) through which the chigger continues to suck your mushed skin.

DANGER! Chigger bites are possibly the most irritating and itchy bites in the world—and the sores can itch for *weeks*—but they're not known to carry any diseases. Old wive's tale: Putting nail polish over the hole will suffocate the submerged parasite. Wrong! Chiggers do not burrow underneath the skin. If you have sores, you probably already scratched the chiggers off.

EATIN' YOU: Face mites

BIO: What's that on your eyelid? It might be one of these microscopic mites. They live in the pores and hair follicles of the face, especially around the nose and eyelashes. They plant themselves head-down in a pore or follicle, and happily live there feeding on sebaceous secretions and dead skin debris.

DANGER! Usually you wouldn't notice them, but bad infestations can cause the face to become polluted by the excrement and corpses of these invisible bugs. That and their eating of hair roots and oil glands may cause hair loss, rashes, and rough skin. They are not known to transmit diseases.

EATIN' YOU: Head lice

BIO: These bloodsuckers live their entire lives on the human scalp and hair. They puncture your skin with special piercing/

Stallions and bulls don't have nipples.

sucking mouthparts and feed two to six times a day. They're particularly prevalent among children, who can spread them easily by sharing hats and combs, and by playing games such as "I'm gonna rub my lice-infested head against your head...because it's fun!" (But personal hygiene is irrelevant—they'll live on anybody.)

DANGER! The bites may itch, but head lice aren't dangerous.

EATIN' YOU: Crab lice

BIO: Also permanent human residents, these larger lice live in the warmer, moister climes of pubic and armpit hair. They're sluggish: If not disturbed, one can live its entire life within a half-inch of where it was born, but, like all lice, can be passed to other people through close contact. Not gross enough? Crab lice can also live in beards, moustaches, eyebrows, and eyelashes.

DANGER! Like head lice, you're only in danger of embarrassment from crab lice.

EATIN' YOU: Human river fluke

BIO: This flatworm is contracted from eating infected fish, and primarily targets humans. They live in your bile ducts and liver tissue, as well as blood, and can grow up to an inch long and can live inside you for 10 years.

DANGER! Symptoms can range from none...to death, for heavy infestations. (There have been cases where one person housed more than 20,000 of the parasites.) They are most prevalent in Asia, where raw and pickled fish are dietary staples.

EATIN' YOU: Mosquitos

BIO: Contrary to popular myth, mosquitos do not live on blood. They survive on nectar and other fluids sucked out of flowers. But females take a "blood meal"—they need the protein to develop their eggs. You can't hide: Mosquitoes home in on their prey using specialized organs that can sense heat, carbon dioxide—which you just exhaled—and other gasses from up to 100 feet away.

DANGER! Mosquitoes traveling between hosts can transmit several diseases to humans, including malaria, sleeping sickness, and elephantiasis. Mosquitoes are the most deadly animal to humans on earth, causing more than 1,000,000 deaths a year.

About 27 people die each year of suffocation from a dry-cleaning bag.

CINEMA ODD

In the 1960s, three Italian filmmakers set out to reinvent the documentary. Did they succeed? Well, film critic Pauline Kael once called them "the most devious and irresponsible filmmakers who have ever lived."

THREE MEN AND A CAMERA

Paolo Cavara, Gualtiero Jacopetti, and Franco Prosperi were three budding documentary filmmakers with a problem: documentaries bored them. They didn't want to paint sedate *National Geographic*-style pictures of foreign cultures. They wanted to show the lurid, shocking, and weird parts of human life that were rarely committed to film. The result: *Mondo Cane* (Italian for "a dog's life"). Released in 1962, the film was a 108-minute travelogue that visits 30 bizarre, violent, and odd places. It's sensational, exploitative, trashy...and really entertaining. Among the scenes recorded by *Mondo Cane* cameras:

- Asian cannibals eating a corpse
- The slaughtering of a bull and a pig
- A Taiwanese tribe eating a dog
- Ritualistic fattening of African women (to increase fertility)
- Sexualized tribal dancing
- A trip to a pet cemetery
- A South Pacific "cargo cult" that worships man-made objects

Critics called the movie "vulgar" and "pornographic," but it was a hit. Surprisingly, the movie's theme song "More" was nominated for Best Song at the 1963 Academy Awards. And, not surprisingly, it inspired several rip-off "Mondo" films including *Mondo Bizarro* and *Mondo Balardo*. Cavara, Jacopetti, and Prosperi themselves had enough leftover footage for three sequels.

- ***Women of the World*** (1963) All of the vignettes were about women, many of whom were naked.
- ***Mondo Cane 2*** (1963) Footage includes flamingo babies dying of sewage poisoning, transvestite cops, a look at torture devices, and a visit to a mortuary school.
- ***Farewell Africa*** (1966) Shocking scenes of Africa, including animal poaching, mercenary tribal slaughter, and executions.

WEIRDMART

It's weir you go to buy weirly weird stuff. Weir going today!

BUY IT NOW! Picking up your dog's or your cat's poop is gross. That's why there's Poop-Freeze. It's an aerosol spray that, according to the Rockville, Maryland, manufacturer, "forms a frosty film on dog poop (or cat poop) to harden the surface for easy pick-up." And it's "perfect for both outside and indoor use." Cost of a four-ounce can: $9.95.

BUY IT NOW! Inventors John Packes and Ramon Peralta have come up with a way to spice up the game of golf: flavored tees. They're made from sanitized, flavored wood, and come in mint, cherry, strawberry, and grape. And you suck on them. "It will knock out the foulest of cigar or beer breath within five seconds," says Packes. Cost: 25¢ each.

BUY IT NOW! Want to save a step in getting the game birds you shoot from the field onto your plate? You soon may be able to with Season Shot: Ammo with Flavor—shotgun shells with pellets that flavor the meat of the animal you just killed. Flavors planned: cajun, lemon pepper, garlic, teriyaki, and honey mustard. The product's inventor, Brett Holm of Chaska, Minnesota, says Season Shot will not only season the birds, but also prevent tooth damage caused by steel shot. "The heat from the stove melts the pellets," he says. He hopes to have the product ready by 2007.

BUY IT NOW! Need a good prank gift? How about "Liquid Ass"? It comes in a small squirt bottle and the makers promise it has a "genuine, foul butt–crack smell." A four-pack costs $17.50. (Available at *liquidass.com.*)

BUY IT NOW! If you go to Powys County in Wales, you can buy Welsh Dragon Sausages. Well, you can't anymore: The Powys County Council made the manufacturers, Black Mountains Smokery, change the name to "Welsh Dragon Pork Sausages"... because they thought some consumers might be confused. "I don't think any of our customers believe that we use dragon meat in our sausages," said company owner Jon Carthew.

BUY IT NOW! Need a set of gallows? British farmer David Lucas has been building them for countries in Africa for years. A single-hanging gallows goes for $22,000, he recently told reporters, and the Multi-Hanging Execution System, mounted on a trailer, goes for $185,000. "The beauty of it," says Lucas, "is you can use it over and over again." When news of of his macabre industry was revealed in May 2006, Lucas defended himself from the storm of criticism that followed. "Business is business," he said.

Update! In June, 2006, Lucas's business partner, Brian Rutterford, came forward and said the entire story was a hoax. "David sells pet food," he told *The Times*. "If he was building gallows for foreign governments, I think I would know about it." The BBC, the *Sydney Morning Herald*, and the *Taipei Times* were just a few of the news agencies around the world that had been duped by the story. (Lucas still denies that the story was a hoax.)

BUY IT NOW! The Isdaan restaurant in Gerona, Philippines, has a unique feature: the "Wall of Fury." For 15 pesos (about 25¢) you can buy a dinner plate, which you then take to the Wall—printed with words like "ex-wife" and "boss"—and smash the plate against the target of your choice. "The top three targets are 'boss/manager,' 'wine, women and gambling,' and 'loan sharks,'" says manager Arnold Viola. For the equivalent of $25 you can also smash a television set. (All this while an Elvis impersonator entertains the guests.)

BUY IT NOW! Got a fish? Gotta go? No problem. AquaOne Technologies, of Westminster, California, released their "Fish-n-Flush" toilet tank in 2006. It's a fully-functioning toilet combined with an aquarium. Half of the two-part see-through tank comes with gravel, plastic plants, a filter system, and lighting, and its operation isn't affected when the toilet is flushed. "We wanted to develop a product that had a dual purpose," said CEO Richard Quintana. "To serve as a proper, fully functional toilet—and also as a source of entertainment and conversation." The Fish-n-Flush is yours for $299.

Live scorpions glow a greenish color when exposed to ultraviolet light.

THEME RESTAURANTS

Dining out can get kind of boring. After all, how many times can you have the same old burger at the same old coffee shop? Fortunately, in the last 20 years, the "theme restaurant" has emerged, offering diners not just a meal...but an experience.

MIM

Location: Barcelona, Spain

Details: Don't speak Spanish? Don't worry, the waiters don't speak it, either. In fact, they don't speak any language at all. That's because MIM is a mime-themed restaurant, housed in an old theater. Staff communicates through body language, and every few minutes, they put on short mime performances, culminating in a flying trapeze act. (Warning: If you suffer from *coulrophobia*—the fear of mimes—avoid this restaurant.)

ADAM & EVE'S

Location: Indiana

Details: No shirt? No shoes? No problem. Adam & Eve's is the world's only naked restaurant. The waiters are nude, the cooks are nude, and the customers are nude. (Better not order anything hot.)

ALCATRAZ BC

Location: Tokyo

Details: If you've ever wondered what life on the brutal, desolate San Francisco island prison was like, go to this Japanese bistro. Uniformed "wardens" (not waiters) cuff patrons at the big steel front door and lead them to "private cells" (not tables). Menu items include chipped beef on toast, pudding cups, and other foods served in a prison cafeteria.

THE NEWS ROOM

Location: Minneapolis

Details: Think reading old newspapers is an exciting way to spend an evening? The News Room celebrates old newspapers and the often-depressing headlines of the 1920s and 1930s. The restaurant is divided into several newspaper "sections," including "The Sports Page" (old sports footage plays on monitors) and "The Financial Page" (a Depression-era stock ticker hangs from the rafters and continually shoots out ticker tape and imaginary stock quotes). In every room, rolled-up giant newspapers hang from the ceiling.

RED SQUARE

Location: Las Vegas

Details: When most Americans think of the Soviet Union they think of a cruel, totalitarian government, breadlines, and impending nuclear war. But Red Square—a family-friendly restaurant located in one of Vegas's grandest hotels, Mandalay Bay—plays up Soviet life as nostalgic and kitschy. The red decor features a headless statue of Lenin, a hammer-and-sickle logo, and propaganda posters that glorify the worker. Naturally, it also has one of Las Vegas's largest assortments of vodka.

HITLER'S CROSS

Location: Mumbai, India

Details: One of the worst restaurant ideas ever. The menu is pizza; the decor is Nazi, featuring lots of swastikas—"Hitler's crosses"—and giant photos of Adolph Hitler. Fewer than 3,000 of India's one billion people are Jewish, but protests led the restaurant's owner, Punit Sabhlok, to consider changing the restaurant's name and theme. "We wanted to be different," he said. "This is one name that will stay in people's minds."

TOILET BOWL

Location: Taipei, Taiwan

Details: Yes, it's a toilet-themed restaurant. Diners sit on toilets and eat out of toilet-shaped bowls and plates. The interior of the restaurant is laid out with brightly colored bathroom tile, and the lights are shaped like urinals. The favorite menu item, says owner Eric Wang, is chocolate ice cream—probably because "it looks like the real thing."

There are 92 known cases of nuclear bombs lost at sea.

SMILE: YOU'RE ON BAIT CAR!

If you're a fan of YouTube but you're tired of sorting through millions of uploaded videos for something fresh, interesting, and (of course) odd, here's a suggestion: Type "bait car" in the search window, press return, and enjoy the ride.

CAR TROUBLE

In the winter of 2001, police in Vancouver, British Columbia, were battling a ring of thieves who were stealing as many as five Japanese sports cars a week from the parking lots of local golf courses, then stripping the cars to sell the parts. Auto theft is a difficult crime to fight: Stolen cars change hands so quickly that even if you catch someone driving one, it's difficult to prove that they know it's stolen, let alone prove they're the one who stole it. You have to catch car thieves in the act, and that's not easy because they tend to break into cars when there are no witnesses around. And because car theft is a property crime, not a violent crime like kidnapping, assault, or murder, there's a limit to how much time and money police agencies can spend fighting it, especially when the odds of winning a conviction are so low. How low? Fewer than 15% of all car thefts end with the thief being jailed.

CANDID CAMERA

The Vancouver police department couldn't spare enough officers to stake out every golf course in the city. If they were going to catch the crooks they'd have to find another way. Phil Ens, a Vancouver police officer assigned to auto-theft detail, had heard about a program in Minneapolis, Minnesota, where police were using "bait cars"—cars wired with hidden audio and video equipment and GPS tracking devices, then left where thieves were likely to steal them. Police could track a car using its GPS signal, then shut off the car's engine by remote control as they moved in to make the arrest. The video evidence was then used to convict the thieves and send them to prison. The approach was effective: Auto thefts were down in Minneapolis, and prosecutors were winning convictions against longtime car thieves, thanks to the video evidence recorded by the bait cars. Even passengers in stolen cars were

It's estimated that about half a ton of Martian material falls to Earth each year.

going to jail as participants in the crimes. Ens approached the Insurance Corporation of British Columbia (ICBC), which sells auto insurance in the province, and Boomerang Tracking Solutions, which makes auto tracking devices, and talked them into helping fund a test of the bait-car concept in British Columbia.

GONE IN 2,700 SECONDS

Boomerang sent Ens an Acura Integra loaded with GPS tracking equipment and the remote-control device that allows police to shut off the engine. Ens added a hidden camera, a microphone, and a VCR. Then the police department placed the car in the parking lot of a local golf course...and made their first bait-car arrest just 45 minutes later.

ICBC was sold on the program—they decided to back it in a big way, donating recovered stolen cars to be wired up as bait cars and spending more than $500,000 a year to make them bait-car-ready. The provincial government of British Columbia agreed to pick up the rest of the tab, with the program to be administered by an interagency task force called the Integrated Municipal Provincial Auto Crime Team (IMPACT).

The program is still going strong today, and IMPACT continues to develop new and creative ways to put this powerful new crime-fighting tool to use. They have studied which cars are likely to be stolen in which parts of town, and plant the bait cars accordingly. They make the cars even more attractive targets by baiting them with a wallet, a purse, a cell phone, or even an open bag of potato chips left in plain view. Because car thieves commonly abandon stolen cars in the neighborhoods where they live (it's easier than walking home), if police can figure out where a particular car thief lives, they'll plant his favorite model of bait car right down the street from his house. Why stop at committed car theives? Sometimes IMPACT even leaves bait cars unlocked with the keys in the ignition and the engine running to tempt opportunists who might not otherwise bother to break into a vehicle.

NOW SHOWING

Most of the time, police agencies keep their crime-fighting method secret to prevent criminals from figuring out ways around them. But IMPACT takes the opposite approach: They hope that

Do you have a gap between your front teeth? It's called a *diasthema*.

by publicizing the bait-car program as much as possible, they can convince criminals (and wannabes) that auto theft is not an easy, low-risk crime—that it's actually a crime in which arrest is almost inevitable, the charges will stick, and the penalty will be months or even years in jail. They want the crooks to believe that bait cars are *everywhere*.

What makes this interesting for the rest of us is that IMPACT has set up a Web site (www.baitcar.com) where they post actual bait-car video clips for you to watch and enjoy. The clips are making their way to other popular sites like Google Video and YouTube, too. They're worth a look: When you watch the grainy hidden-camera footage, it almost feels as like you're there in person to witness the thrill of victory as punks break into cars and speed off on a joyride, followed by the agony of defeat as they are arrested by police a short time later.

CAT AND MOUSE

Vancouver's program is working: Since it was instituted in 2002, car thefts have dropped more than 15%, with 6,000 fewer cars being stolen each year. ICBC is saving nearly $15 million a year through reduced payments to auto-theft victims. The publicity campaign and especially the bait car footage are credited with much of the success: As the bait cars themselves pull incorrigible car thieves off the streets, the footage of them being caught and taken to jail is causing less-committed thieves to lose heart and prompting at-risk, "entry-level" youth to reconsider whether they really want to begin stealing cars in the first place. "Auto theft went down right away because of word-of-mouth among the thieves," Ens told the *Vancouver Province* in 2005. "It created a level of paranoia and the advertising kept it in their conscience."

WATCH, LAUGH...AND LEARN

Are you ready to have a few laughs at the expense of ethically challenged Canadian punks? Here are the titles of some classic bait-car footage to look for. (*Warning!* Bait-car footage contains coarse language and is *not* suitable for children.)

• **I Was Caught By a Bait Car!** A mini-documentary featuring bait-car footage and a later interview with the 22-year-old car thief, who describes what it is like to be caught red-handed stealing a bait car ("I knew it was a #*&$ bait car! They bait-carred my @*&!" he says as the police shut off his engine by remote control), and what it's like for a reformed car thief to view his own bait-car footage for the very first time ("I look like a retard!").

• **The Prayer.** Watch as a 19-year-old car thief and his 21-year-old accomplice steal a car, do donuts in an open field and then, with the driver's hands folded into a steeple on the steering wheel, pray aloud that the car coming up behind them is not a police car. "Please don't be a cop! Pray it's not a cop! Pray, pray, pray, just pray!" (Their prayers went unanswered.)

• **I Hope This Isn't Another %$&* Bait Car, Man!** (a.k.a. The Nose Picker). Who says car thieves have to be men? View footage of British Columbia's first-ever arrest of a *female* car thief. Watch as she and her accomplice pick up a male associate, then tag along as he picks a winner and disposes of the "evidence" in disgusting fashion moments before the police arrive on the scene.

• **If My Mom Calls.** Three punk kids steal a bait car just one day after one of them has been released from custody (perhaps for stealing another car?). Listen as their fear increases with the dawning realization that they are indeed driving a bait car, that arrest is only moments away...and that Mom is going to be really, really mad when she finds out.

• **High-Speed Escape.** Rare footage of crooks stealing *two* bait vehicles at the same time. After the bait *car* program became successful, the Vancouver police department expanded to bait motorcycles, bait ATVs, bait snowmobiles, and even bait Jet Skis. These dopes stole a bait ATV and threw it onto the back of a stolen pickup truck...which turned out to be a bait car, too.

• **So Much for Going Home.** The only thing funnier than watching these four kids count the patrol cars as they close in behind them—"Oh yeah, there's one, two, there's three! Yeah, it's a bait car, dude!"—is listening to them being arrested by a cop with a Scottish accent thicker than *The Simpsons*' Groundskeeper Willie.

* * *

"I'd prefer a smart idiot to a stupid genius any day."

—**Samuel Goldwyn**

FORE!

Next time you're playing golf, watching a match, or even driving past a course, be forewarned—golf balls don't always go where the golfer wants them to go. For example, a ball could hit...

A MOVING VEHICLE

Sean Hutchins regularly drives past San Geronimo Golf Club in California. His advice to other drivers: Beware—"The number of golf balls hitting vehicles seems to be on the rise." His current tally: two have hit his truck; one ball hit his friend's Chevelle; another hit that same friend's mother's pickup; a fifth hit the friend's girlfriend's car; and a sixth smacked a California Highway Patrol car.

A BIRD

Benin, a small nation in Africa, doesn't have a golf course, but that didn't deter Mathieu Boya. He would routinely practice driving balls in a field adjacent to the Benin Air Base—until one day in 1987 when his ball struck a gull, which then fell into the open cockpit of a jet taxiing the runway, which caused the pilot to lose control, which caused the plane to barrel through the other four Mirage fighter jets sitting on the tarmac...which wiped out the entire Benin Air Force.

A FAN'S FOREHEAD

John Yates, 52, realized a dream-come-true when he got to watch the world's most famous golfer, Tiger Woods, in person at the 2003 Buick Open in Grand Blanc, Michigan. But Yates got more than he bargained for. Woods's approach shot on the seventh hole went wild and struck Yates smack-dab on the forehead. After a few dazed minutes on his back, Yates looked up to see Woods leaning over him, apologizing profusely. For his trouble, the fan got three stitches, the errant ball, and an autographed golf glove. Woods got something out of the deal, too. As Yates recalled: "I helped him out because my head knocked the ball back toward the hole. He birdied the hole, I guess. I didn't see it. But it's my most memorable moment in golf."

Saturn's rings are 180,000 miles in diameter...but only about 10 yards thick.

THE BOTTOM OF THE CUP

As the sun was setting on the seventh hole of the Roehampton Golf Club in England in 1964, Bill Carey hit a tee shot that landed near the pin, but because it was getting dark, he couldn't see exactly where it had rolled. So Carey and his opponent, Edgar Winter, went to look for it. After an unsuccessful search of the green and the hill below, Carey finally conceded defeat as darkness settled in. But a few minutes later he found the ball in the one place he never thought to look: at the bottom of the cup.

QUICKSAND

Bayly MacArthur, playing in a 1931 tournament in Australia, hit a ball into what he thought was a sand trap. It wasn't—it was quicksand. And unfortunately, MacArthur found out the hard way when he stepped into the quicksand to play the ball. It took four other golfers to pull him out.

A SPECTATOR'S BRA

At the 1973 Sea Pines Heritage Classic in South Carolina, Hale Irwin's worst shot of the match (and perhaps his career) hit a woman's chest and lodged in her bra. She was relieved when Irwin decided to forgo the shot, taking a two-stroke penalty instead.

THREE SPECTATORS

In 1971 Vice President Spiro Agnew played in the Pro-Am portion of the Bob Hope Desert Classic. After his first two shots injured *three* members of the crowd, Agnew made the wise choice and became a spectator himself.

AN OPPONENT'S ARM

Why hit someone with a golf ball when you've got a golf *club*? In 1980 at the final round of the Boone Golf Club Championship in North Carolina, Margaret McNeil and Earlena Adams were tied for the lead after 18 holes. They had to play one sudden-death hole to decide the match. At the tee, McNeil was practicing her stroke when she accidentally smacked Adams on the arm with her backswing. Result for Adams: Her arm was broken; she couldn't play the hole. Result for McNeil: She was awarded first place.

Mary, the mother of Jesus, is identified by name more times in the Koran than in the Bible.

WEIRD RUSSIA

If you're of a certain age, you probably grew up being extremely afraid of Russia. Nothing to worry about—Russia is just as kooky as America.

NEVER SAY DIE

Since 1984, Russian chess star Viktor Korchnoi has played an ongoing long-distance chess game with Hungarian grand master Geza Maroczy. What's so odd about that? Maroczy died in 1951. Korchnoi and Maroczy "exchange moves" by phone or mail with a Hungarian psychic who claims to be in touch with Maroczy's spirit. Who's winning? Korchnoi. "The match started evenly," he said, "but Maroczy got into trouble after losing a piece."

BOOZE HOUNDS

In 2006, Russian customs officials discovered a secret underground pipeline used to pump bootleg vodka into Latvia. Police in the Russian border town of Buholovo say the tunnel is six feet underground and was used to transport homemade booze with a much higher than normal alcohol content. Why the tunnel was constructed is unclear because homemade alcohol is not illegal in Latvia.

WE'LL GIVE YOU $50 TO READ THIS

To combat the image that Russia has one of the most corrupt governments in the world, the Russian government issued a pamphlet outlining the punishment for giving or receiving a bribe: burning in hell. The weird warning, taken from the Koran, claims that "both the giver and taker of a bribe will burn in the flames of hell." The flyer was sent to every home in Russia.

BUT WHAT IF THEY USE *THAT* MONEY TO GAMBLE?

The Russian government is also trying to curb gambling, so the Moscow city council came up with a surefire plan: They hired actors to stand on street corners outside casinos, pretending to be beggars. The actors are instructed to tell people that they were once rich executives but became destitute and homeless after becoming addicted to gambling. The city council also announced plans to give some of the actors accordions to turn their sad stories into sad songs.

LOVE, MARRIAGE, AND OTHER STRANGE THINGS

Love makes the world go 'round (the bend).

BREAKING (AND ENTERING) HIS HEART

Nickey Davidson of McMinnville, Tennessee, was arrested in 2006 on charges of aggravated burglary. Police said the 25-year-old woman had broken into several houses and stolen item worth tens of thousands of dollars. Her reason: she'd told her new boyfriend that she had a high-paying job (she didn't really)... and now she had to keep up appearances. "When we told her boyfriend about what had happened, he was shocked," Sheriff's Captain Tommy Myers said. "He was even more shocked to find out that she's married."

LOVE, MALAYSIAN-STYLE

Kamaruddin Mohammed of Malaysia got married in 1957. Then he got divorced, and remarried. Then he got divorced, and married again. Then—well, it would take too long to tell the whole story, so we'll just tell you that in 2006 Mohammed, age 72, got married for the 53rd time. All of the first 52 marriages ended in divorce (except one—one wife had passed away), and wife #53 was also wife #1—the same woman who married him in 1957.

THINGS THAT GO BUMP IN THE NIGHT

A Swedish woman filed an official complaint with her local health department in 2006, claiming her neighbors' noisy love-making sessions were making her physically ill. Jon Persson of the Environmental Health Committee said the woman wrote that she was "distressed, angry and tense all over" because her neighbors made so much noise, for hours every night. "You are my last hope. Please help me," she said. Health department officials told the woman that there was nothing they could do about it.

Americans eat nine times more broccoli than they did 20 years ago.

THE FIRST STRAW

In 2006 Ruth Meister of Bonn, Germany, caught her husband Georg having sex with his mistress. She threw him out of the house and filed for divorce. "I showed no mercy," she said. "I just threw him out." The story made news all over the world. Why? Because the Meisters were both in their 80s—and had been married for 60 years.

AGA GOES GAGA

In 2006 a wild donkey in a Croatian national park was shipped off to a deserted island because he was scaring all the females in the herd. According to park officials, Aga the donkey was demanding sex as often as 16 times a day, and the female donkeys were so scared that they hid from him...and couldn't be seen by tourists. "But now that Aga is gone they have come out of hiding," one official said, adding that Aga would be brought back "when he calms down."

HANDKERCHIEF TIME

In 2001 a massive earthquake struck western India's Gujarat state. Several towns were badly hit; more than 16,000 people were killed. The worst hit was Bhachau, a city of 40,000. Rescue crews worked through the night, into the next day, and the next, removing rubble to locate as many survivors as possible. Five days later, a bulldozer was knocking down the walls of an apartment building when somebody heard something. Crews were called in, and Jayesh and Kuntal Thakkar, newlyweds, were rescued from beneath the rubble of the building. How had they managed to survive for so long? They had kept each other alive, they said, by speaking words of love to each other.

* * *

THREE REAL BOOK TITLES

- *Is Your Volkswagen a Sex Symbol?*, by Jean Rosenbaum, M.D.
- *The Yul Brynner Cookbook—Food Fit for the King and You*, by Yul Brynner with Susan Reed
- *Satan Burger*, by Carlton Mellick III

Sea otters tie themselves together with kelp to avoid being separated while they sleep.

FLUBBED HEADLINES

These are 100% real, honest-to-goodness headlines.
Can you figure out what they were trying to say?

Shortage of Brains Slows Medical Research

Hot Lunch Engulfs Man

Well-Stocked Panty Important to Good, Easy Meals

Relief Groups Help Hurt Family

COLLAPSED BRIDGE IN CHINA FAULTY

Sadness is No. 1 Reason Men and Women Cry

BABIES ARE WHAT THE MOTHER EATS

His Humming Rear End Is a Major Distraction

SHUTTLE PASSES TEST; A WORKER IS KILLED

Dishonesty Policy Voted In by Senate

PLENTY DO DO HERE FOR LOCAL "TOURISTS"

More of Us Will Live to Be Centurions

SMOKERS ARE PRODUCTIVE, BUT DEATH CUTS EFFICIENCY

YANKEES TAKE A WALK TO TIE STORE

Coke Head to Speak Here

Brain Bypass Surgery Ineffective

Carbon Man Sets Himself on Fire

Commissioner Davis to Head "Assault on Literacy Month"

Discoveries: Older blacks have edge in longevity

GRANDMOTHER OF EIGHT MAKES HOLE IN ONE

According to manufacturers, the average bra size today is 36C. In 1980, it was 34B.

MORE AMAZING COINCIDENCES

We just can't get enough of these amazing stories. Here are a few more improbable—and real—coincidences.

NEEDS WORK

While eating dinner at Notting Hill Gate restaurant in 1992, a London publisher had her car broken into. One of the things taken from the car was a manuscript she had been reading and found extremely promising. Apparently the thieves weren't interested in literature, though—they threw the manuscript over a fence while driving away. On Monday morning she was desperately trying to come up with a way to explain how she lost the manuscript when the author called. Before she got a chance to apologize, the author asked, "Why did you have my manuscript thrown over my front fence?"

STROKE OF LUCK

During the 1988 Olympic games in Seoul, South Korea, Karen Lord of Australia and Manuella Carosi of Italy swam in different heats of the women's 100-meter backstroke. Both finished with times of exactly one minute, 4.69 seconds, tying them for 16th place. Only one swimmer could hold a lane in the consolation final, so Lord and Carosi were forced to swim again. Amazingly, after the swim-off the officials reported the times were exactly the same: one minute, 5.05 seconds. Officials decided that the two had to swim yet one more time. At the end of the unprecedented third consecutive race Carosi was declared the winner. Her time: one minute, 4.62 seconds. Lord's time: one minute, 4.75 seconds—13 hundredths of a second behind.

LONG SHOT

In 1893 Henry Ziegland of Texas jilted his fiancée, and she killed herself over it. Her brother swore revenge. He took his gun and went after Ziegland, shot him in the face, and then turned the gun on himself. But the bullet only grazed Ziegland and then got lodged in a tree. Twenty years later, Ziegland was removing the tree that had the bullet buried in it, using dynamite to make the job easier. The explosion blasted the bullet out of the tree... striking Ziegland in the head and killing him.

BANK ON IT

In 1977 Vincent Johnson and Frazier Black broke into the Austin, Texas, home of Mr. and Mrs. David Conner and stole two TVs and a checkbook. A few hours later, the two men showed up at a local bank with a check made out to themselves for $200. When they asked the teller to cash it for them, she asked them to wait a minute, and then called security. Why? The bank teller was Mrs. David Conner.

OTHERWISE ENGAGED

Brenda Rawson became engaged to Christopher Firth in 1961. He gave her a diamond ring, but she lost it while they were on vacation in Lancashire, England. In 1979 she was talking to her husband's cousin, John. For some reason the conversation turned to metal detectors and John mentioned that 18 years earlier, one of his kids had discovered a diamond ring near Lancashire. It was her ring.

SPARE ME

In 1971 Mrs. Willard Lovell of Berkeley, California, accidentally locked herself out of the house. She had spent 10 minutes trying to find a way in again when the postman arrived with a letter for her from her brother, who'd been staying with her a few weeks earlier. The letter contained a spare key to the house, which he had borrowed and forgotten to return.

* * *

GO TEAM (WHATEVER YOUR NAME IS)!

In 2005 the Anaheim Angels baseball team changed its name to the Los Angeles Angels of Anaheim. In 2007 the minor league Long Beach Armada spoofed that mouthful of a name by changing its official team name to "The Long Beach Armada of Los Angeles of California of the United States of North America including Barrow, Alaska."

Lions and tigers can't purr. Cougars can.

WORLD NUDES TONIGHT

Mark Twain once wrote, "Clothes make the man. Naked people have little or no influence in society." He was wrong.

PUNCHY

Thirty-year-old Panamanian fighter Celestino Caballero was determined to get a shot at what looked like his last chance at the World Boxing Association's super bantamweight title in October 2006. So when it appeared that he might be over the 122-pound weight limit, which would have disqualified him, he decided to do something drastic: He stripped completely naked so that not even the weight of his boxing trunks and jockstrap would be counted against him during the weigh-in. The move was embarrassing, but it worked—Caballero squeaked in under the weight limit and then clobbered the defending titleholder, Thailand's Somsak Sithchatchawal, in three rounds, sending him to the hospital with a suspected broken nose. Caballero is believed to be the first world title contender to qualify for his bout in the nude.

THE GOOD BOOK

In 2005 a Lutheran church youth group in Nuremberg, Germany, decided to organize a fundraiser to help repaint the youth center. The idea they came up with: a nude calendar depicting 12 different scenes from the Bible—Eve wearing only a strategically placed fig leaf, offering Adam an apple; a topless Delilah cutting Samson's hair, etc. The most amazing thing about the calendar? Bernd Grasser, pastor of the church, *approved* the idea and even let the organizers shoot nude scenes inside the church. At last report the calendar had sold 5,000 copies and raised more than 40,000 euros. "It's just wonderful when teenagers commit themselves with their hair and skin to the Bible," Pastor Grasser says.

COMING CLEAN

In 2001 Michael Lee, a London magistrate, quit his court job and became the head of finance for a furniture company in Manchester, England. It was about that time that he became obsessed with paying a prostitute as much as $500 an hour to clean his house while wearing only rubber gloves. After Lee exhausted his own savings of $49,000, he piled up another $197,000 in credit card debt and stole more than $400,000 from his employer, blowing all of the loot on naked housecleaning. His conscience finally caught up with him in 2006 and he turned himself in to police. Lee pled guilty to theft and at last report was awaiting sentencing. Adding insult to injury: The "maid service" was *terrible*. "If that guy spent $600,000 on a cleaner, he should ask for his money back," says a neighbor. "She obviously didn't have her mind on the cleaning aspect of her work. His place was absolutely filthy."

THE LONG (BARE) ARM OF THE LAW

In October 2006, security guards monitoring video cameras in the Government Services Building in Hamilton, Ohio, spotted a man walking the halls in the wee hours of the morning completely naked. The following night, the naked man was arrested and identified as 35-year-old Scott Blauvelt, a city prosecutor. Blauvelt was charged with two counts of public indecency. He was also fired. So was this Blauvelt's first naked encounter with the law? No—in 2005 he crashed his car while driving nude. Blauvelt's attorney attributes his erratic behavior in both incidents to medication he takes to control seizures. (At last report Blauvelt had pled not guilty by reason of insanity and was awaiting trial.)

LOSING STREAK

Have you ever seen a sporting event where streakers run across the field? It's not that unusual, so when three streakers ran onto the soccer field during a game in Germany in 2003, it didn't attract much media attention...until one of the teams, Hansa Rostock, sued the streakers for 20,000 euros (about $26,000). The team took the step after it was fined 20,000 euros by the German Soccer League for allowing the streakers to gain access to the field; Hansa Rostock paid the fine, then sued the streakers to get the money back. The team won the suit in 2005 and won again in 2006 when the streakers appealed the decision. "Spectators enter an agreement when they arrive in the stadium that forbids them from going onto the playing field," the appellate judge ruled, "thus the defendants must pay the full cost of damages for violating that agreement."

Between death and the onset of rigor mortis, muscle contractions...

MOUNTAIN MAN

More than 2,000 people have climbed Mt. Everest, including many Sherpas, who are native to the region. What makes Lakpa Tharke unique among them is that when he reached the 29,035-foot summit in 2006, he stripped naked and braved the –40°F temperature for three minutes while other climbers took pictures of him. (Twenty-two people made it to the top of Everest on that day alone.) Tharke, believed to be the first person ever to strip completely naked on the world's tallest peak, pulled the stunt hoping it would land him a spot in *Guinness World Records*, but the Nepal Mountaineering Association hopes it lands him in jail. Mt. Everest, known as *Chomolungma* or "Goddess Mother of the World," is a sacred site for both Tibetan and Nepalese Buddhists, and stripping naked at the summit is considered a sacrilege. "I was shocked to hear that a Sherpa stood nude atop the holy mountain for the sake of creating a record," said Ang Tshering Sherpa, head of the association. "The Goddess Mother is holy to us and the deed is tantamount to defiling her."

THE BIRD MAN

One evening in July 2006, two residents of Whaleyville, Virginia, returned home to find 30-year-old Juan Lopez standing naked in their driveway, clutching one of their pet pigeons. As they pulled into the driveway, the naked man began beating their car with the pigeon. A few minutes later the man fled into nearby woods, where he was later arrested and charged with burglary and "larceny of poultry." The couple didn't know Lopez...so why did he attack them? No one knows. "He was obviously having some sort of issues that night," said a police spokesperson.

HOW MUCH IS THAT NUDE GUY IN THE WINDOW?

When Forrest City, Arkansas, police responded to a residential burglary call in October 2006, they found a naked man, 19-year-old Dennis Reed, Jr. wedged between an air conditioner and a window frame. What was he doing there? Reed claims that someone he knows "only by his first name" forced him at gunpoint to break into the apartment. He remained stuck until the fire department was able to enter the apartment and remove the air conditioner. (At last report Reed was sticking to his story.)

IT'S AN ODD WORLD AFTER ALL

We traveled the world to find these.

TOAD IN THE HOLE!

In 2006 the Australian environmental group FrogWatch started selling a new gardening product in order to raise funds. It's called ToadJus—liquid fertilizer made from pulverized toads. Cane toads, which can grow up to 12 inches in length and can weigh up to three pounds, were imported in the 1930s to battle a sugar cane beetle (it didn't work) and are now considered a major pest in Australia. FrogWatch is helping out in efforts to exterminate the toads and the toad juice seemed like a great way to raise cash and awareness on the issue. And the odd product was actually selling well. But there was a problem: ToadJus ferments; bottles of the stuff were exploding in people's garages. FrogWatch issued a news release in September warning people to unscrew the tops of the bottles a half-turn to let the pressure escape. "Otherwise," said FrogWatch employee Graeme Sawyer, "the bottle may explode, or leak, potentially covering the garden shed with an evil-smelling, sticky liquid."

WE MUST. WE MUST...

In 2004 people in the Baltic coastal town of Ustka, Poland, decided that their mermaid needed a boob job. The mermaid is the town's official symbol and appears on its coat of arms. At a public meeting, one of the town's councillors remarked that the mermaid had rather small breasts and was "a bit fat." Everyone agreed. So they hired an artist and their ancient symbol was slimmed down and given "enhanced" breasts.

HOLIER THAN THOU

In 1840 missionaries from the Welsh Presbyterian Church started going to India to convert people to their religion. Missionary activities in the country remained active for more than a hundred years, with several churches being established. But in 2006, the pattern reversed. The Christian Diocese of Mizoram, in northeast India, announced they would be sending Indian Christians to Wales because the Welsh weren't spiritual enough.

HECK'S DEVILS

Police began investigating the Hell's Angels motorcycle chapter in Stockholm, Sweden, in 2005, after more than 70 members were found to be receiving government health benefits for depression, and that they'd all been diagnosed by the same doctor. Investigators confirmed that the Angels were perpetrating a scam, adding that the gang had apparently changed over the years: No longer the wild bunch they used to be, the Angels now make most of their money on non-violent schemes.

HELLO, NURSE

Doctors in the town of Iasi, Romania, wrote to the country's medical officials, demanding that nurses be required to get new uniforms. They were tired of the frumpy outfits the nurses had been wearing for years. "I believe all the women—nurses *and* doctors—should wear mini-skirts," Dr. Iulian Serban, head of the local medical board, said. "It would be more elegant."

DEAD HEAT

In 2005 a student at Sde Boker Academy in Israel's Negev Desert told a radio station host about an odd tradition that had been going on for years among students at the school. He said that teenage Israeli students had been going to the gravesite of Israel's founder, David Ben-Gurion, to lose their virginity. "One friend told me about it," the student said. "He called his girlfriend and asked her to come with him that night to the grave. Two hours later, he came back and told me what they'd done." Academy director Yaakov Aini said he'd never heard about the tradition, but that it was "shameful, distorted, and very serious." But Ben-Gurion's grandson, Dr. Yariv Ben-Eliezer, thought otherwise. "I think it's great," he told Israel's *YNet* news. "I'm happy that years after my grandfather died, he continues to inspire our youth."

WHY DON'T *WE* HAVE A WORD FOR THAT?

Americans excel at inventing colorful expressions and slang, but it turns out other countries are pretty good at it, too.

Kummerspeck (Germany): "Grief bacon"—the weight you gain by overeating when you're worried about something.

Attaccabottoni (Italy): A "buttonholer"—someone who corners casual acquaintances or even complete strangers for the purpose of telling them their miserable life stories.

Modré Pondeli (Czech): "Blue Monday"—When you skip coming in to work to give yourself a three-day weekend.

Razbliuto (Russia): The feeling you have for a person you used to love, but don't anymore.

Shitta (Iran): Leftover dinner that's eaten for breakfast.

Tartle (Scotland): To momentarily forget the name of the person you're talking to. The word helps reduce the social embarrassment of such situations: "I'm sorry, I tartled there for a moment."

Pana po'o (Hawaii): To scratch your head in an attempt to remember something you've forgotten.

Ngaobera (Easter Island): A sore throat caused by too much screaming.

Backpfeifengesicht (Germany): A face that's just begging for somebody to put their fist in it.

Papierkrieg (Germany): "Paper war"—bureaucratic paperwork whose only purpose is to block you from getting the refund, insurance payment, or other benefit that you have coming.

Rujuk (Indonesia): To remarry your ex-wife.

Mokita (New Guinea): The truth that everyone knows, but no one will speak about.

Gorrero (Spain, Central America): Someone who never picks up the check.

Fucha (Poland): Using your employer's time and resources for your own purposes. (Uncle John had never heard of such a thing and wanted to ask around the office if anyone else had, but everyone is still out to lunch.)

In ancient Rome it was considered a sign of leadership to be born with a crooked nose.

ROCK, PAPER, SCISSORS

Uncle John was thinking about saving this chapter for the next book, but Mrs. Uncle John insisted that it should go in this one. They settled the dispute with a good old-fashioned round of Rochambeau. (Uncle John threw scissors, Mrs. Uncle John threw a rock.) It's in.

PAPER TRAIL

No one knows much about the history of Rock, Paper, Scissors, or *Rochambeau,* as it is also known. The game is believed to be more than a century old, and may have originated in Africa, Portugal, Scandanavia, or Japan, where it is known as *Jan Ken Pon.* How it came to be associated with the Comte de Rochambeau, a French general who commanded French troops under George Washington during the Revolutionary War, is anyone's guess.

If you haven't played it since you were a kid, here's a refresher on the rules: A round of Rock, Paper, Scissors is similar to a coin toss. Two players shake or "prime" their fists three times (sometimes calling out "Ro, sham, beau!" as they do), then make a "throw" by forming one of three symbols with their hand: a fist (rock); a flat hand extended straight out (paper); or a V-sign made by extending only the index and middle fingers (scissors). Paper beats rock (the rock is covered by the paper); rock beats scissors (it dulls or smashes the scissors), and scissors beats paper (snip-snip). If you both throw the same symbol, it counts as a tie, and you repeat the process until someone wins.

ALL GROWN UP

If Rock, Paper, Scissors used to be just for kids, it isn't anymore. Today it's practically a professional sport, thanks in large part to two Canadian brothers named Graham and Douglas Walker. One cold winter night in 1995, they were both too lazy to leave their cabin to get more wood for the fire, so they played 15 rounds to decide who would have to get it.

Graham won, but before it was over Doug noticed that he had a habit of throwing whichever symbol would have beaten his previous throw—if he threw a rock, his next throw would be paper, which beats the rock, followed by scissors, which cuts paper. That got the brothers to thinking that there might be a strategic side to the game that they hadn't thought about before.

The brothers also figured that if they still enjoyed playing the game, other adults would, too. They created an organization called the World RPS Society and put up a Web site. By 2002 they were ready to host their first world championship in Toronto. First prize: $800 and an XBox. Today the grand prize has grown to $10,000, and the tournament's success has led to the formation of the rival USA Rock Paper Scissors League, sponsored by Bud Light. It holds its $50,000 annual championship in Las Vegas. Dave McGill, a 30-year-old bartender from Omaha, won the top prize in 2006.

STRATEGIES

The experts differ on the best strategy for winning:

1. Psychology. One school of thought says you should try to read your opponent, guess which symbol they're going to throw, and respond with the symbol that will beat it. Rock is considered the most aggressive symbol, so if you detect signs of aggression, throw paper to beat their rock. Paper is passive, so throw scissors if your opponent appears weak...and hope they aren't just faking you out. If they look neither aggressive nor passive, throw rock to beat their scissors. Playing several rounds? Use your opponent's past throws to predict what their future throws will be, and respond accordingly. If they throw lots of rocks, throw lots of paper, etc.

2. Runs. Another school of thought says that you should ignore psychology entirely by selecting one or more runs or "gambits" of three throws each (paper, scissors, paper, for example; or scissors, scissors, rock) and stick to them no matter what your opponent does. By choosing throws at random, you thwart your opponent's attempts to read your psychology. Some of the most popular runs even have names: Paper Dolls (paper, scissors, scissors); Avalanche (rock, rock, rock); and Bureaucrat (paper, paper, paper).

ROCHAMBEAU IN THE NEWS

In the Art World. In 2005 a wealthy Japanese businessman named Takashi Hashiyama decided to auction off four of his company's most valuable pieces of art: paintings by Pablo Picasso, Paul Cézanne, Vincent van Gogh, and a fourth artist named Alfred Sisley. But when he couldn't decide between the rival Christie's and Sotheby's auction houses, he invited both firms to play a game of Rochambeau to decide the winner. Sotheby's picked paper...and lost to Christie's scissors.

Sotheby's says it didn't have a strategy and just picked a symbol at random. Christie's turned for advice to Flora and Alice Maclean, the twin 11-year-old daughters of Nicholas Maclean, head of the modern art department. They suggested scissors. "Everybody knows you start with scissors," Alice explained to an interviewer. Christie's auctioned the paintings for $17.8 million and pocketed several million dollars in fees from the sales (no word on whether Flora and Alice got a share of the loot).

The Legal World. When two opposing lawyers couldn't agree on the location for a witness's testimony to be taken, Florida judge Gregory Pressnell issued a court order instructing that the lawyers settle the matter by playing a round of Rock, Paper, Scissors. So who won? Nobody—after Judge Pressnell's order made international headlines, the lawyers gave in and settled the dispute themselves.

The Natural World. In 1996 a California biologist named Barry Sinervo published a study claiming that the mating habits of the side-blotched lizard (*Uta stansburiana*) demonstrate a pattern similar to that seen in Rock, Paper, Scissors, according to whether the male lizard has an orange, blue, or yellow throat:

• Orange-throated males are the largest and most aggressive lizards; they easily dominated the blue-throated lizards when competing for mates. (Orange beats blue.)

• Similarly, blue-throated males are larger than the yellow-throated males and had no trouble fending them off. (Blue beats yellow.)

• The yellow-throated males most closely resemble the females of the species. While the aggressive orange-throated males are fighting each other for mates, the yellow-throated males are able to slip in among the females and mate with them without being noticed. (Yellow beats orange.) They are unable to do this with the mates of the blue-throated males, because the blue-throated males form stronger bonds with their mates than the orange-throated males do, and can spot the yellow-throated males among the females.

JUST PLANE WEIRD

Fly the friendly skies—in complete and utter horror after you read this.

ENGINE SCHMENGINE

In 2005 a Los Angeles air traffic controller watched as one engine on a British Airways 747 that was taking off started on fire. "It appears you have flames coming out of your number two engine," the tower radioed, and the pilot responded, "We're shutting it down"—meaning the engine. Then what did he do? He continued flying, reporting his plan to "get as far as we can" toward his destination—London, England, 11 hours away. The plane, which was carrying 351 passengers, started to run out of fuel and made an emergency landing in Manchester. Officials said the pilot acted within Civil Aviation Authority guidelines. (A week later, the same plane lost an engine during a 14-hour flight from Singapore to London. That flight also carried on.)

AMERICAN GASLINES

Passengers aboard an American Airlines flight from Washington, D.C., in 2006 became alarmed when they smelled burning matches in the cabin. They alerted crew members and the plane made a quick emergency landing in Nashville. The plane was searched — and sure enough, burnt matches were found near the seat of a female passenger. When questioned by FBI officers, the woman admitted that she had indeed struck the matches. Why? To cover the smell of her farts. She was eventually released from custody and told that she would never again be allowed on an American Airlines flight.

AND YOUR LITTLE DOG, TOO!

Terry and Susan Smith of Blackburn, England, were about to take off from Manchester Airport to their new home in Lanzarote, Spain. As the plane started down the runway, they looked out the window...and saw their spotted spaniel racing down the runway alongside the plane. "We were in our seats ready for takeoff and looking forward to our new life," said retired truck driver Terry, "when we suddenly saw Poppy on the runway." They screamed for

When a male horse and female donkey mate, the offspring is called a *hinny*.

the plane to stop, and spent the next hour attempting to catch and calm the terrified dog. Poppy had apparently chewed her way out of her travel crate before the hatch closed. The Smiths, including Poppy, took a later flight (at a cost of about $800).

CAN YOU FLY ME NOW?

The 189 passengers seated on a plane at Doncaster Robin Hood Airport in Sheffield, England, in December 2006 were told by the captain that he had dropped his cell phone somewhere in the cockpit. And that they couldn't take off until he found it. Why? Because it was on and, as everyone knows, you have to turn off your cell phone before takeoff. For the next 15 minutes he gave them regular updates, but he still couldn't find the phone. Then he called the ground crew to come in to dismantle the cockpit floor...and they still couldn't find it. After an hour the passengers had to return to the terminal. "We just couldn't believe our ears," one told the *Sun*. "We thought we'd heard every excuse in the book for delays but this one took the biscuit." They finally left—four hours later—on another plane (with another pilot).

GOD WAS HIS CO-PILOT

A pilot for Sriwijaya Air in Indonesia successfully guided a 737 and its 100 passengers to a landing at Jakarta's Sukarno-Hatta International Airport and then, with the plane still taxiing toward the terminal, the pilot died. Captain Sutikno, 54, had suffered a heart attack. The National Committee for Transport Safety launched an inquiry to investigate the incident, though the airline reported that Sutikno had no history of heart disease.

* * *

THE OOPS CHALLENGE

In 2006 writer David Sklansky, an outspoken atheist, made a public challenge: he'd give any practicing Christian who could score higher than him on the SAT test a prize of $50,000. Within a day, someone accepted the challenge: 74-time *Jeopardy* champion (and devout Mormon) Ken Jennings.

You are four times more likely to choke to death on a non-edible object than on food.

KNOW YOUR PHOBIAS

Bibliourophobia: *The fear of not having something to read in the bathroom. (Okay, we made that one up. But the rest of these are real, documented phobias.)*

Peladophobia: Fear of baldness

Alektorophobia: Fear of chickens

Lutraphobia: Fear of otters

Ephebiphobia: Fear of teenagers

Amathophobia: Fear of dust

Zemmiphobia: Fear of mole rats

Arachibutyrophobia: Fear of peanut butter sticking to the roof of the mouth

Asymmetriphobia: Fear of asymmetry

Aulophobia: Fear of flutes

Chromophobia: Fear of colors

Euphobia: Fear of hearing good news

Cibophobia: Fear of food

Automatonophobia: Fear of ventriloquist's dummies

Coprophobia: Fear of poop

Hexakosioihexekontahexaphobia: Fear of the number 666

Consecotaleophobia: Fear of chopsticks

Xylophobia: Fear of wooden objects

Dextrophobia: Fear of things touching the right side of your body

Cherophobia: Fear of happiness

Agyrophobia: Fear of crossing the street

Anthrophobia: Fear of flowers

Melophobia: Fear of music

Chronophobia: Fear of time

Papaphobia: Fear of the Pope

Alliumphobia: Fear of garlic

Walloonphobia: Fear of the Walloons (an ethnic group in Belgium)

Phobophobia: Fear of phobias

Geniophobia: Fear of chins

Logophobia: Fear of words

Hippopotomonstrosesquippedaliophobia: Fear of long words

Shaquille O'Neal wears size-22 shoes.

THE BEST BAD WRITING

A few years ago we discovered the Bulwer-Lytton Fiction Contest. The object: to compose the worst opening sentence to the worst of all possible novels. The competition was created in the early 1980s by a literary professor named Scott Rice. Here are some of our favorite entries from the last few years.

BUT FIRST...

The sentence that started it all, from the 1830 novel *Paul Clifford* by English author Edward George Bulwer-Lytton:

> It was a dark and stormy night; the rain fell in torrents—except at occasional intervals, when it was checked by a violent gust of wind which swept up the streets (for it is in London that our scene lies), rattling along the housetops, and fiercely agitating the scanty flame of the lamps that struggled against the darkness.

Now settle in for some modern-day longwindedness...

• **It was a dark** and stormy night—actually not all that dark, but more dusky or maybe cloudy, and to say "stormy" may be overstating things a bit, although the sidewalks were still wettish and smelled of ozone, and, truth be told, characterizing the time as night is a stretch as it was more in the late, late afternoon because I think Oprah was still on.

—*Gregory Snider, MD, Lexington, KY, 2004 runner-up*

• **Jack planted the magic beans** and in one night a giant beanstalk grew all the way from the earth up to the clouds—which sounds like a lie, but it can be done with genetic engineering, and although a few people are against eating gene-engineered foods like those beans it's a high-paying career to think about for when you grow up.

—*Frances Grimble, San Francisco, CA, 2004 Children's Lit winner*

• **On reflection,** Angela perceived that her relationship with Tom had always been rocky, not quite a roller-coaster ride but more like when the toilet-paper roll gets a little squashed so it hangs crooked and every time you pull some off you can hear the rest going bumpity-bumpity in its holder until you go nuts and push it

Real money: Americans spend $20 billion a year on imitation fats and sugar substitutes.

back into shape, a degree of annoyance that Angela had now almost attained.

—Rephah Berg, Oakland, CA, 2002 winner

AND FINALLY...

A few of our BRI writers decided to try their hand at a horrible sentence.

• **The weary foot soldier** peered out from his squalid foxhole and saw them: a plethora of attacking aliens advancing toward him—or maybe it was a "myriad" of aliens, he thought, pondering the quantitative value of plethoras versus myriads, to and fro, until, sadly, he was instantly vaporized by what his fellow soldiers (who'd barely escaped themselves) would later describe as "a sh*tload of aliens."

—Jay Newman

• **He couldn't sleep** so he did what he always did when he couldn't sleep—he thought about riding a unicorn, like the one he'd dreamt about as a child, the dream which he wasn't totally convinced was a dream, but in actuality was a reality—then he awoke and realized he wasn't really sleeping, but was dreaming about wanting to sleep; he thought it all terribly ironic, until, he noticed, there at the foot of his bed, was the ghost of John Quincy Adams.

—Brian Boone

• **Staring intently across the office** through the bleak October twilight, Matt eyed the empty orange-juice container that he'd "decorated" with a Sharpie to look like a jack-o-lantern face, silently hating the fact that his lame co-workers had actually entered it in the demeaning office pumpkin-decorating contest, but also secretly p*ssed off that they hadn't won and hadn't even gotten honorable mention for "Most Economical."

—G. Javna

• **Though it sickened her** to think that, once again, the old men would ogle her generous hips under the voluminous corduroy skirt, and desire her supple skin, aromatic with Yardley oatmeal soap that you could only find at a Rexall pharmacy, she steeled herself, tightening her moist lips like two tiles in a badly built shower, and pushed through the door of the stamp-collectors' shop.

—Amy Miller

U-WHO?

Here's the story of a shipwreck found 60 miles off the coast of New Jersey in 1991. What's so odd about that? Two things: It wasn't an ordinary ship...and it shouldn't have been there at all.

SECRETS OF THE DEEP

New Jersey may be the known as the Garden State, but sailors have nicknamed its shoreline "The Graveyard of the Atlantic." Why? The coast's treacherous shoals, inlets, and sandbars have been wreaking havoc on ships for centuries. In fact, there are more than 2,000 known wrecks off the New Jersey coast, but one of the most perplexing was a pile of oddly shaped debris that a fishing boat reported finding on the ocean floor there in 1991. After getting the coordinates from the captain who found the wreck, a team of divers led by John Chatterton and Richie Kohler set off from the town of Brielle in September. They knew the waters were treacherous, but they couldn't resist the lure of this "long hunk of metal."

These men are no ordinary hobbyists; they're "deep wreck divers," dedicated adventurers who risk their lives to explore what gets left behind on the bottom of the sea. They usually have some idea of what's waiting for them, but this wreck was different from the start: Since it was lying at a depth of more than 230 feet, a clear description wasn't available. Still, they had their theories: Perhaps it was the *Corvallis*, a ship that was supposedly sunk in the 1930s by a Hollywood film crew making a disaster movie. Or it might be an old subway car, which officials sometimes dumped in the ocean, after which the metal hulks became habitats for marine life. Then again, the wreck might just be an old barge filled with garbage that had been taken out to sea and sunk.

THIS IS NO BARGE

As the dive team's boat approached the coordinates, the mysterious object loomed far below, the dark and murky water obscuring their view. But when they made their first dive down to get a look at it, they saw a familiar—and ominous—shape. "I saw the angled hatch," Chatterton later said. "I went over and I looked into it. I

Out of my way! **City pedestrians walk 10% faster than they did 10 years ago.**

shined my light down, and I could see the unmistakable shape of a torpedo. At that moment, I knew this was a submarine."

But this wasn't just any submarine—the divers soon realized that it was a German U-boat from World War II. Excited by their discovery, they returned to shore to find out the identity of the sub.

A WAYWARD WOLF

Hitler's submarines, called *Unterseeboots* or U-boats, were created to locate and destroy Allied merchant ships during the war. At first, the U-boats were a deadly success. Traveling together in "wolf packs," they inflicted terrible damage as they silently moved along the Atlantic coast of the United States and into the Gulf of Mexico, sinking dozens of Allied ships as they went. British Prime Minister Winston Churchill would later say that the U-boats were "the only thing that really frightened me during the war."

But by 1943 the Allies had developed methods to hunt them down: Sonar, radar, and the eventual cracking of the Axis Enigma code spelled the end of the wolf packs. Allied sub hunters tracked down and destroyed more than 740 German U-boats before the war's end. So that should have explained what the sub was doing so close to U.S. shores. But when Chatterton and Kohler researched the official historical records and pored over maps of known U-boat sinkings, they found that no U-boat had been reported to have sunk within 100 miles of New Jersey's shores. Determined to identify the submarine, they nicknamed it the "U-Who."

A TOUGH SELL

Without any official records, Chatterton and Kohler only had one option: go back down to the submarine and find some kind of identifying markings, or retrieve an artifact from the U-boat that would reveal its name. But it wasn't easy convincing the other divers to go back to the snarled wreckage more than three hours from shore. Kohler had to persuade them: "This is a mystery like you read in a book. A German U-boat comes to our doorstep. It explodes and sinks with maybe 60 guys on board, and no one—no government or navy or historian—has a clue that it's even here." The divers were convinced, and three weeks after the initial discovery, the team went back. "Every single guy, without exception,

The NATO attack on Serbia in 1999 during the Kosovo war killed more animals than people.

that rolled over the side to dive the wreck thought that he was gonna be the guy to solve the mystery," said Chatterton.

DEAD MAN SWIMMING

The very idea of going *inside* the wreckage presented new dangers. Their first obstacle was the depth: While hobbyist divers routinely descend to about 30 feet below the surface, more experienced divers may reach depths of 130 feet. For a wreck that's 230 feet deep, the preferred choice is to take a submersible vehicle. But all these wreck divers had were their skills and their SCUBA gear. At pressure nine times what it is on the surface, the divers only had 25 minutes to explore the sub; they needed extra air in their tanks so they could stop frequently on the way back to the surface and gradually decompress. If they didn't, they risked "the bends," which can cause a diver to become disoriented and pass out.

Making matters worse was the silt: Even the slightest movement churned up enough muck to reduce the visibility to zero. Unable to see, the divers often became snagged in the U-boat's cables and their bulky equipment was slashed by the sharp edges of a massive hole in the sub's hull. Their worst fears were realized when a diver named Steve Feldman was killed while exploring the sub. And it all seemed to be in vain: Except for a few dishes from the galley and the chronometer, the team found nothing that revealed the sub's origins.

Still, they continued to dive down to the wreck over the next three years, during which three more divers (including a father and son) lost their lives. But the team trudged on. Kohler explains why: "When you go inside this U-boat, the viciousness of World War II is really apparent. It's apparent in the grotesque destruction inside the submarine. It's apparent in the fact that there are human remains and skulls, literally at times peeking right at you. And these people, at least to me, wanted me to find out who they were."

DOWN THE RABBIT HOLE

Over the course of their dives, they did make some progress in identifying the sub. In late 1991, Chatterton found a knife engraved with a crewman's name on the handle. They traced his name and found he served on a sub called the *U-869*. But according to official records, that sub had been sunk off of the coast of Gibraltar in

La Paz, Bolivia, is 12,000 feet above sea level. At that elevation...

1945...all the way across the Atlantic. Could the U-Who be the *U-869*? And if so, what was it doing off the coast of New Jersey?

Their next big break came when Chatterton found a piece of metal inscribed with the words "Baurt IXC, Deschimag, Bremen." From that, they found the make and the model of the sub. The *U-869* fit the criteria, and through a painstaking three-year process—on the ground and under the sea—the divers became convinced that this was indeed the *U-869*. But they still needed conclusive evidence. So they went back to the water...and to the books.

In 1994 Kohler's research led to a tip from a contact in Britain, who found that there was little proof that *U-869* actually sank near Gibraltar. And National Archives reports from Allied code breakers, who often had a better idea of where German subs were located than the Germans did, showed that the sub was on its way to the New Jersey coast when it was given new orders to head for Africa instead. But, according to the reports, the *U-869* never received those orders.

In 1997, six years after their initial dive, the team finally found the "smoking gun" in the engine room—the most difficult and dangerous place in the sub to reach. Chatterton had to temporarily remove his gear just to fit inside, but he found a spare part tagged with the ship's identifying number. This, indeed, was the *U-869*.

DAMN THE TORPEDO

Identifying the sub after their long search came at a high price: Four divers had lost their lives, and several others had quit diving entirely after having to swim through the "sunken graveyard." And Chatterton and Kohler had been so wrapped up in the mystery that both of their marriages had ended. Was it worth it? "There were two choices," said Chatterton, "follow it through to its conclusion, or quit. So in many ways, bringing it to a conclusion was difficult. But quitting was just unacceptable."

One unanswered question remains: If the Allies didn't sink the *U-869*, what did? The prevailing theory is that the *U-869* sank itself. Armed with 700-pound "acoustic torpedoes" that followed the sound of enemy propellers, the crew may have launched one... only to have it circle back and destroy the *U-869*.

Postscript: Chatterton and Kohler are now the hosts of *Deep Sea Detectives*, which airs on the History Channel.

ALIENS: WHAT WILL THEY LOOK LIKE?

What will the bug-eyed monsters and little green men of science fiction really *look like when we meet them? According to BRI stalwart Bruce Carlson, you might want to watch where you step.*

WHO'S OUT THERE?

Most scientists believe that there is, in fact, life beyond Earth. But they wonder whether we'll even recognize it if—or when—we first bump into it.

Will alien life be the cute, big-eyed, long-armed aliens in *E.T.: The Extra-Terrestrial*? Or the people-eating, egg-laying monsters in *Alien*? Perhaps they'll be the big, hairy Wookies or overweight, oversexed Jabba the Hutt types from *Star Wars*. Or maybe they're already here—the "grays" who occasionally kidnap people and take them away inside brightly lit UFOs, like the ones in *Close Encounters of the Third Kind* or *The X-Files*.

The list of imaginary aliens goes on and on, but if you ask scientists what a being from another planet might actually look like, they'll tell you that it probably isn't going to look even remotely like anything portrayed in sci-fi movies or anything we've seen before. This raises questions about what life actually is, and how we'll know it if we see it. Anna Lee Strachan of NASA's Astrobiology Institute points out that a being with, say, "a dark matter quantum-like existence, blinking in and out of time and space, without any need for a home planet, water, or energy," would probably be unrecognizable to us as "life."

WHAT TO EXPECT

Extraterrestrials may not have backbones (or any bones at all). They may not have just one brain, or viscera packaged inside skin. They won't necessarily be *bilaterally symmetrical*—having one side the same as the other—as most Earth life is. Most movie aliens have two arms, two legs, two eyes, two ears, one nose, and a mouth that's located in the front of the head. But there's no good reason, other than movie budgets, that this should be the case.

Wearing headphones for an hour can increase the number of bacteria in your ear by 700%.

THE POSSIBILITIES ARE ENDLESS

While many scientists believe quite firmly that life does exist Out There, they say that what it looks like would depend on where it comes from. Life anywhere evolves to prosper in the environment it lives in. For example, astronomer Carl Sagan and Cornell University scientist E. E. Salpeter imagined the possibility of miles-in-diameter hydrogen balloon–type life forms floating high in the atmosphere of a giant gas planet like Jupiter and feeding on organic molecules that fall from the skies, sort of like fish food. They could just float along, controlling their buoyancy so as not to sink too low and get crushed by the gravitational pressure close to the planet's surface.

Life coming from a smaller, rockier planet with higher gravity would be profoundly different. Any creatures there would have to be small and extraordinarily tough, like the life forms science fiction writer Hal Clement created in his stories about a planet he called Mesklin. Unlike Sagan and Salpeter's gossamer floaters, Clement's Mesklinites are insectlike creatures with exoskeletons, built close to the ground, with many legs for support and powerful circulatory systems, well adapted to the strong gravitational pull.

COMMON SENSES

When imagining life elsewhere, scientists have to make some assumptions. They assume, for instance, that any living thing will have senses of some kind to react to its environment—it's just that those senses might not be anything recognizable to humans. Carl Sagan once said, "The number of individually unlikely events in the evolutionary history of Man was so great that nothing like us is ever likely to evolve again anywhere else in the universe." Aliens might "see" via radio waves or "hear" via X-rays. As physicist Philip Morrison points out, they may just be "blue spheres with 12 tentacles."

Life forms from elsewhere may not be carbon-based, as life on Earth is. Many scientists assume they will be, however, because carbon is very good at knitting together chemical chains—acting as a sort of glue for the pieces of life's complex molecules. But still, there are other chemicals that can do that, too. Silicon is often mentioned as a possible base for alien life, because it's a versatile element that combines readily with chemical chains. And depending on the organic groups attached, the result can be solid, fluid, or resinous.

So, too, might be the aliens.

HOWDY, NEIGHBOR

There may even be extraterrestrial life within our own solar system. Most astrobiologists are of the opinion that, if there is, it won't be the monstrous, mechanized Martians of *War of the Worlds*. Instead it will be tiny microbes. And if Jupiter's moon Europa does have oceans of liquid beneath its icy surface, as some scientists believe, then that's one place to look. While some experts hold out hope for something as sophisticated as a worm—there are worms, for example, at the cold, dark bottom of the Pacific Ocean—most put their money on some sort of floating blob of goo. No brains, no arms or legs, no spaceships, no communicators, no phaser guns...just microscopic slime that spends its time eating, excreting, and reproducing.

In December 1984, ALH84001, a Martian meteorite, was discovered in Antarctica. Scientists thought it contained evidence of extraterrestrial life, including organic chemicals and "bacterium-shaped objects." Later studies showed that much of the evidence might well have come from what are called "nonbiological processes," which diminished the excitement a bit. But scientists are still studying it...and who knows what they'll find?

DON'T YOU RECOGNIZE ME?

So the next time you watch a science-fiction movie or TV show, keep in mind that real aliens will most likely look less like ETs and more like...well, like nothing we've ever seen. The best way to consider what extraterrestrials will look like is to do what astrobiologists do: Get your facts straight. Then stretch your imagination.

*   *   *

DOCTOR, DOCTOR

Over the past 20 years, several Brazilians have claimed that their bodies are inhabited by the soul of "Dr. Fritz," a German doctor who served and died in World War I. Today, Dr. Fritz is said to live inside a man named Rubens Faria, Jr. Every day, more than 800 people wait in line for a 30-second healing session with Faria/Fritz.

The world's shortest escalator is at a shopping mall in Japan. It has a vertical height of 2'8".

WEIRD CANADA

We couldn't do a world tour of the odd without a stop up north, eh.

KIM CAMPBELL MEETS SIMON COWELL

In 1995 Canada started a national essay-writing scholarship contest called "As Prime Minister." In 2006, it became a reality TV show called *The Next Great Prime Minister*. For the 2007 installment, the finalists will be judged by a panel of former prime ministers: Brian Mulroney, John Turner, Joe Clark, and Kim Campbell. (Interestingly, the winner doesn't get to be prime minister—they get $44,000 and a government internship.)

WAITING FOR MOMMY

Roxanne Toussaint, a single mother of three, felt unappreciated for the hard work she does cooking, cleaning, and raising her kids. So in 2006, she went on strike. She moved into a tent on her front lawn and spends the day holding up a sign that reads "Mom on Strike." Toussaint's demands: that her kids sign a pledge to clean up their rooms, contribute to the housework, and be quieter.

TAKING A BITE OUT OF CRIME

Aaron Helferty, 31, was drinking in an Edmonton bar when a group of men he didn't know began berating him. He ignored it...until one man approached him, silently stared at him, then suddenly lunged forward and started chewing on his nose. Two bar employees broke up the fight and threw out the attacker, who'd managed to bite off (and swallow) part of Helferty's nose. Helferty plans to get reconstructive surgery; police can't find the attacker.

SOURRY ABOOT THAT, YOUR HONOR

Canadians have a reputation for being extremely polite, saying "I'm sorry" even when they don't really have to. In 2006 the provincial governments of British Columbia and Saskatchewan passed legislation to make saying "I'm sorry" in court not a legal admission of guilt. It allows for defendants to politely acknowledge wrongdoing with a public apology without having to worry about the legal ramifications.

Cockroaches have 6 legs, and at least 18 knees (scientists think they may have more).

LIKE THE ANIMALS DO

Now join host Marlin Perky for another episode of Sexy Kingdom.

NICE LEGS

In 2005 five giant squids washed ashore in a single week in the Bay of Biscay in Spain, giving marine biologists a chance to study the rarely seen creatures. One thing they discovered is that the sex life of giant squids, who make their homes in the deep, dark depths of the world's oceans, can be a violent and haphazard affair. Since it has never actually been observed, biologists can only guess as to the exact mating activity of the animals, based on the study of such washed-up specimens. That has led them to believe that the male of the species "injects" sperm through the skin of the arms of a female, who then saves it until she is ready to lay her eggs. Of the two males found in Spain, one had arms that showed that it had been injected by another male, possibly by one who had mistaken it for a female in the murky depths of the sea. The other one had accidentally injected itself.

YES. OUCH.

As a female porcupine approaches the annual 8–12 hour period during which she is receptive to mating, she stops eating, selects a mate, and starts "moping" around him. The male responds by following her around, "singing" in a whiny voice, engaging in vicious fights with other males, and sniffing wherever the female urinates. (The urine acts as an aphrodisiac.) When mating time finally arrives, the male stands on his back legs, approaches the female, and becomes what experts describe as a "urine cannon." He hoses down the female with a stream of urine that can shoot up to seven feet, covering her from head to toe. The female either emits a high-pitched scream and attacks the male, or she lifts her tail, exposing her unquilled underside, and allows him to gingerly approach—still on his rear legs—and mate with her. When he gets tired out, she makes him do it again…and again…and again. If he won't do it, she finds another male, until the 8–12 hour "receptive" period is over.

In old English gambling dens, one employee's job was to swallow the dice in case of raids.

EEK!

Colonies of the Australian yellow-footed Antechinus—a mouse-sized marsupial—participate in one of the strangest mating events in the animal kingdom. Biologists believe that the increase in daylight hours in the second half of winter induces the males, all of them about eleven months old, to begin a two-week frenetic spree, going from nest to nest in the colony to breed with every female they can, with each mating session taking from six to twelve hours. The physical stress of the mating frenzy, along with having to fight with other males, and the fact that they don't eat *at all* during the period, is too much for them. After the two-week mating marathon, every male in the colony dies. The females have their litters a month later...and eleven months after that, it all starts all over again.

* * *

RESCUED BY DOLPHINS

In November 2004, Ron Howes, 42, his 15-year-old daughter, and two of her friends were swimming about 100 yards offshore near Whangarei on the North Island of New Zealand. During the swim, Howes later told the Canadian Broadcasting Company, a pod of dolphins "came steaming at us" and "pushed all four of us together by doing tight circles around us."

Howes said he tried to leave the circle, but two large dolphins pushed him back—and at that point he saw a great white shark coming toward the group. "I just recoiled," he said. "It was only about two meters away from me." He then realized that the dolphins, which kept slapping the water with their tails, were protecting them. The dolphins kept them in the circle for nearly 40 minutes, until the shark left when a rescue boat showed up. And the dolphins stayed close to the rescued swimmers until they made it all the way back to shore. "I came out of that water and I was stunned," Howe said. "I had no idea how to relay what had happened and how to deal with it." He didn't tell the girls about the shark, which never broke the surface, until the next day.

Construction of Milan's great cathedral, the Duomo, began in 1386 and was finished in 1805.

WHAT A WAY TO GO!

Death awaits us all, but you never know when you're about to breathe your last. Here are some folks who died in bizarre ways.

DANGER! DANGER!

In 2001 Tyron Watson, an employee at a wheel factory in Akron, Ohio, walked into an area that housed an industrial robot in order to repair it. But the robot hadn't been properly turned off, and Watson's presence triggered a motion sensor, which suddenly reactivated the robot. It started moving very fast and smashed Watson into a conveyor belt, killing him instantly.

EIGHT ARMS TO KILL YOU

One of the most popular snacks in South Korea: small octopuses, eaten alive. In 2002 a Seoul man was eating one at home and choked to death on it. Doctors removed the octopus, which was still alive and clinging to the man's throat. Statistics show that as many as six people a year in South Korea die that way.

BY THE BOOK

Early-20th-century Ethiopian emperor Menelik II had an unusual habit: When he felt sick or uneasy, he'd eat a few pages out of a Bible. He was feeling especially sick after suffering a stroke in 1913, so he ate the entire Book of Kings. A few days later he died of an intestinal blockage caused by the paper.

GOOD LUCK, BAD LUCK

Boonchai Lotharakphong, 43, ran a sportswear factory in Thailand. Facing money problems, he bought a flag from a fortuneteller who foretold good luck if Lotharakphong flew it from the roof of his factory. As Lotharakphong was carrying the flag to the roof, he slipped and fell to his death.

CART-ASTROPHE

Eighty-year-old Dennis Wiltshire of Neath, South Wales, liked to race grocery carts in his local supermarket. In August 2005, he

Radio waves from broadcasts of the 1930s have already traveled past 100,000 stars.

hopped on a cart and rode it down a loading ramp, yelling "Wheeeee!" The cart spun out of control and Wiltshire fell off, fracturing his skull on the parking lot pavement. According to reports, he died instantly.

ARTFUL UN-DODGER

Mihaly Gubus, a sculptor from Stuttgart, Germany, was killed in 2006 when he was crushed by his 3,000-pound granite sculpture, *Woman With Four Breasts.*

POLLY WANT A BEAN-O

An unidentified man from Tegelen, the Netherlands, died at home in 2003. He had called an ambulance because he felt sick, but died before paramedics arrived. The man's home was full of dozens of pet parrots. Cause of death: asphyxiation due to overpowering parrot flatulence.

FISHY

In 2003 Lim Vanthan and his family were planting rice near their home in Phnom Penh, Cambodia. Lim went for a swim and caught an eight-inch *kantrob* fish, a prized delicacy in Cambodia. But the fish jumped out of Lim's hands, into his mouth, and down his throat. The fish's sharp, scaly barbs caused it to lodge in Lim's throat, suffocating him.

LIGHTNING NEVER STRIKES TWICE. WAIT...

While climbing a cliff on Steeple Peak in Wyoming in 2003, Ryan Sayers, age 20, was struck by lightning during a storm. Amazingly, he survived relatively unharmed, but decided to wait out the storm. An hour later, Sayers was struck by lightning again. That one killed him.

VIVA LA MARIA!

Maria Antonio Calvo of Spain died in 1994. Well, she didn't really die, but a Barcelona court registered her as dead. After four years of petitioning (Calvo had a child, which was legally declared an orphan), she finally convinced the court that she was living, but since there was no precedent for "resurrection," she remained listed as dead. She was finally recognized as "alive" in 2006.

The average can of cat food has the nutritional equivalent of five mice.

THE STRANGEST DISASTER OF THE 20TH CENTURY, PT. II

If you studied chemistry in high school or college, you may have solved the mystery already. If not, the answer lies just ahead. (Part I of the story is on page 81.)

CONTENTS UNDER PRESSURE

As the scientists took samples from deeper and deeper in Lake Nyos, the already high carbon dioxide (CO_2) levels climbed steadily higher. At the 600 foot depth, the levels suddenly shot off the charts. Beyond that depth, the CO_2 levels were so high that when the scientists tried to pull the samples to the surface, the containers burst from the pressure of all the gas that came out of solution. The scientists had to switch to pressurized containers to collect their samples, and when they did they were stunned to find that the water at the bottom of the lake contained *five gallons* of dissolved CO_2 for every gallon of water.

As the scientists pieced together the evidence, they began to form a theory that centered around the large amount of CO_2 in the lake. The volcano that formed Lake Nyos may have been long extinct, but the magma chamber that fed it was still active deep below the surface of the Earth. And it was still releasing carbon dioxide gas—not just into Lake Nyos, but into the surrounding environment as well. In fact, it's not uncommon in Cameroon to find frogs and other small animals suffocated in CO_2 "puddles" that have formed in low points along the ground. (CO_2 is heavier than air and can pool in low spots until the wind blows it away.)

But what was unusual about Lake Nyos wasn't that there was CO_2 in the lake; that happens in lakes all over the world. What was unusual was that the CO_2 had apparently never *left*—instead of bubbling to the surface and dissipating into the air, the CO_2 was accumulating at the bottom of the lake.

UPS AND DOWNS

In most lakes CO_2 escapes because the water is continually circulating, thanks to a process known as *convection:* Rain, cold weather, or even just wind blowing across the surface of the lake can cause the topmost layer of water to cool, making it denser and therefore heavier than the warmer layers below. The cool water sinks to the bottom of the lake, displacing the warmer, CO_2-rich water and pushing it high enough for the CO_2 to come out of the solution, bubble to the surface, and escape into the air.

STILL WATERS RUN DEEP

That's what *usually* happens, but the water at the bottom of Lake Nyos was so saturated with CO_2 that it was clear that something was interfering with the convection process. As the scientists soon discovered, the waters of Lake Nyos are among the most still in the world: Tall hills surround the lake, blocking the wind and causing the lake to be unusually consistent in temperature from the surface to the bottom. And because Lake Nyos is in a tropical climate that remains hot year round, the water temperature doesn't vary much from season to season, either. Lastly, because the lake is so deep, even when the surface is disturbed, very little of the agitation finds its way to the lake floor. The unusual stillness of the lake is what made it so deadly.

FULL TO BURSTING

There is a physical limit to how much CO_2 water can absorb, even under the tremendous pressures that exist at the bottom of a 690-foot-deep lake. As the bottom layers become saturated, the CO_2 is pushed up to where the water pressure is lower. The CO_2 eventually rises to a level where the pressure is low enough for it to start coming out of solution. At this point any little disturbance—a landslide, stormy weather, or even high winds or just a cold snap—can cause the CO_2 to begin bubbling to the surface. And when the bubbles start rising, they can cause a siphoning or "chimney" effect, triggering a chain reaction that in one giant upheaval can cause the lake to disgorge CO_2 that has been accumulating in the lake for decades.

CO_2 is odorless, colorless, and non-toxic; your body produces it and you exhale some every time you breathe. Even the air you inhale consists of about 0.05% CO_2. What makes it a killer in certain circumstances is the fact that it's heavier than air: If enough

In Natoma, Kansas, it's illegal to throw knives at men wearing striped suits.

escapes into the environment at once, it displaces the air on the ground, making breathing impossible. A mixture of as little as 10% CO_2 in the air can be fatal; even 5% can smother a flame... which explained why the oil lamps went out.

SNUFFED OUT

The scientists figured that if their theory was correct, there might be other instances of similar eruptions in the past. It didn't take very long to find one, and they didn't have to look very far, either: Two years earlier, on August 15, 1984, a loud boom was heard coming from Lake Monoun, a crater lake just 59 miles southeast of Lake Nyos. In the hours that followed, 37 people died mysteriously, including a group of 17 people who died while walking to work when they came to a low point in the road—just the place where CO_2 would have settled after being released from the lake. The incident was small enough that it hadn't attracted much attention from the outside world...until now.

THE BIG BANG

In the months following the disaster at Lake Nyos, the scientists continued to monitor the lake's CO_2 levels. When the levels began to increase again, they concluded that their theory was correct.

In the meantime, they had also come up with an estimate of just how much CO_2 had escaped from the lake on August 22—and were stunned by what they found. Eyewitness accounts from people who were high enough in the hills above the lake to survive the eruption described how the lake began bubbling strangely on August 17, causing a misty cloud to form above the surface of the water. Then without warning, on August 22, the lake suddenly exploded; water and gas shot a couple of hundred feet into the air. The CO_2 had taken up so much space in the lake that when it was finally released, the water level dropped more than three feet. By measuring the change in depth, the scientists estimated that the lake had released 1.2 cubic kilometers of CO_2—enough to fill 10 football stadiums—in as little as 20 seconds. (Are you old enough to remember the huge volume of ash that Mt. Saint Helens released when it erupted in 1980? That eruption released only 1/3 of one cubic kilometer of ash—a quarter of Lake Nyos's emission.)

For the conclusion of the story, turn to page 404.

AMAZING LUCK

It's not always good luck, but these are amazing stories nonetheless.

THIRD TIME'S A...NEVER MIND

On a Sunday morning in March, 2006, Billy McEwen, 25, of L'Anse, Michigan, was driving down a country road when a horse jumped in front of his car. Unable to avoid a collision, he hit the horse, throwing it up into the air, and crushing the roof and windshield of his car. McEwen's two-year-old was in the car, but fortunately, the child was uninjured. Police arrived on the scene and were aiding McEwen when 21-year-old Chris Cavanaugh came by in *his* car...and hit the horse as it lay in the road. The crash caused Cavanaugh's car to roll over, but neither he nor his passenger were injured. McEwen was taken to Baraga County Memorial Hospital, but had to be transferred to nearby Marquette General Hospital. And on the way to Marquette, the ambulance struck and killed a moose. Amazingly, nobody was injured in that accident, either. (Except the moose.)

GOOSEBUMP MATERIAL

In April 2006, Carolyn Holt of St. Charles, Missouri, was driving through the city when she suffered a heart attack. Her car veered across traffic and struck a guardrail before coming to a stop. Other drivers quickly stopped to help. Luckily, two of them were nurses, and after a truck driver used his trailer hitch to smash a window and get Holt out of the car, they immediately started doing CPR. But Holt wasn't responding—her heart had stopped beating. That's when another motorist who had stopped walked up to the scene. He was a defibrillator salesman. And he had one of the devices in his car. The nurses used it to get Holt's heart beating, and, thanks to the improbable circumstances of her rescue, she survived the ordeal. One of the nurses, Mary Blome, said, "It was a true miracle that evening." The salesman, Steve Earle, said it was even more of one than they realized. "It was strange luck," he said, "because when we finish up work for the day, a lot of times we'll get in my wife's car and take it out to eat or to pick my daughter up. For some reason we just happened to get into my car."

Minnesota has 201 Mud Lakes, 154 Long Lakes, and 123 Rice Lakes.

I LEFT THIS HERE FOR YOU

Brandon Day, 28, and Gina Allen, 24, were hiking in the San Jacinto Mountains in Southern California when they left a trail and got lost. They wore only light clothing for what was supposed to be a day trip, and had no food with them. They spent that night in a cave. The next day they followed a creek downstream, hoping it would lead them out of the mountains. The creek led them into a gorge—where they found an abandoned camp site. In the camp was a backpack containing food, warm clothes, and matches. They lit a fire and the next day were rescued by search crews who spotted the smoke. Once rescued, they found out who the backpack belonged to: Papers in it identified the owner as John Donovan. Rescue crews knew who that was. Donovan had disappeared in the mountains almost a year earlier. Neither his remains nor his belongings had ever been found. They contacted his family in West Virginia. Chris Cook, a longtime friend of Donovan's, told reporters, "Even in his death, he was helping people."

* * *

EAT LIKE A KING

Elvis Presley's love of belly-busting fried peanut butter and banana sandwiches is well known—he once ate nothing but them for two months. Here's the recipe for another one of the King's favorite recipes: Ugly Steak.

> Rub a one-pound top sirloin steak with garlic and sprinkle with salt and pepper. Completely cover the steak in flour and fry in a pan filled with oil deep enough to cover the steak. Fry until both sides are brown and the steak is well done. Now, pour out all but about 3 tablespoons of the used cooking oil. Add 3 cups of water and mix thoroughly with all the cooked brown bits and gristle in the bottom of the pan. Boil until you get a thick paste. Add salt and pepper and drizzle over buttered mashed potatoes. Serve with a can of peas simmered in butter. (The King's favorite beverage complement: a quart of buttermilk.)

Cowabunga! A single dairy cow can pass more than 300 pounds of gas per year.

THE DOO-DOO MAN

In our opinion, the ability to take a negative experience and turn it into something positive is a real gift. But what inspired this man could appeal only to bathroom readers.

TRAIL HAZARD

In 1985 Dr. A. Bern Hoff stepped in something unpleasant while hiking in Norway's Jotunheim Mountains. The unpleasant "something" had been deposited right in the middle of the hiking trail and, judging from appearances, only minutes before. Maybe it was his keen eyesight, maybe it was his degree in parasitic pathology, but somehow Dr. Hoff knew right away what he'd stepped in: "people droppings," as he delicately puts it.

It wasn't the first time Hoff had trod on people droppings, either: an avid hiker, he'd had similar experiences atop Africa's Mount Kilimanjaro, Hawaii's Haleakala Crater, and the Grand Canyon in Arizona. He stepped into people's "business" so often that it seemed like every hiking trip was turning into a business trip. As a former official with the Centers for Disease Control, he understood that the problem wasn't just disgusting, it was a serious health hazard. Hoff decided it was time for action.

"I got tired of seeing and smelling this stuff on the trail," he says. "Nobody wanted to deal with it, so I said, 'Hey, I'll do it.' This has got to stop." He formed H.A.D.D.—Hikers Against Doo-Doo.

THE NUMBER TWO PROBLEM

Hoff had stumbled—literally—onto a problem that started growing rapidly in the 1980s and continues today: Record numbers of people are hiking and camping out in the wild. And since most first-timers have never been taught how to properly "do their business" in the backcountry, in many popular outdoor destinations around the country, the results are plain to see, smell...and step in.

To counter this disturbing trend, H.A.D.D. offers a number of different "business plans." It teaches new campers tried-and-true waste-disposal techniques, and serves as an international clearinghouse for new waste-disposal ideas.

THE CAN

H.A.D.D. has also designed a cheap, sturdy, portable privy called "The Can" that can be made from two ordinary 55-gallon drums. At last count, H.A.D.D. members have set up more than 280 Cans in wilderness areas around the world. The organization hopes to one day mount an expedition to bring The Can to the top of Mount Aconcagua, long known as Argentina's "tallest and most defiled peak," and is raising funds to improve the facilities on Russia's Mount Elbrus, which *Outside* magazine dubbed "the world's nastiest outhouse."

When Hoff founded H.A.D.D. in 1990, it consisted of only himself and his soiled hiking boots. Today the organization boasts more than 10,000 members, with chapters all over the world. "We're tongue-in-cheek, of course, but we are serious about trying to clean up the environment," Hoff says.

BUSINESS SCHOOL

Some tips on how to mind your own business in the wild:

• Pack out what you pack in. Bring several square pieces of paper, a paper bag full of kitty litter, and several zipper-type plastic bags or bags with twist-ties. Do your business onto the paper, then put the paper and your business into one of the plastic bags. Pour in some kitty litter, and seal the bag tightly. Dispose of it properly when you get back to civilization.

• If you do have to bury your business, be sure to do it: 1) at least 200 feet away from the nearest water source, trail, or campsite; 2) in organic soil, not sandy soil; and 3) in a "cat hole" dug at least six inches across and six inches deep. (*Hint:* Bring a small shovel.)

• Don't bury your business under a rock: business needs heat and moisture to decompose properly, and the rock will inhibit both.

• Don't bury it in the snow, either: snow melts...but your business doesn't. When spring comes it will reappear.

• Use toilet paper sparingly if at all; if you do use it, *don't* burn it and *don't* bury it with your business. Keep it in a plastic bag and dispose of it properly at the end of your trip.

• Pee at least 200 feet from the nearest water source, and *don't* pee on green plants—otherwise, when your pee dries, animals will be attracted to the salt.

Q: How many bedrooms are there on the board game Clue? A: None.

HE VOODOOED THE PREZ

Maybe there's more to voodoo curses than we think...

CURSES

In November 2006, President George W. Bush made a brief stop in Jakarta for a meeting with Indonesian President Susilo Yudhoyono. At the same exact time, an Indonesian man was slitting the throats of a goat and a snake and stabbing a crow in the chest so he could mix their blood together—with some spices and broccoli—and then drink the concoction. And whatever he couldn't drink, he smeared on his face.

Ki Gendeng Pamungkas, a well-known "Black Magic" practitioner in Jakarta, was performing what he said was a Voodoo ritual to curse the president and his Secret Service contingent. The ritual, he said, would put Secret Service agents into a trance, making them believe they were under attack, which would lead to chaos. As for President Bush: "My curse will make him bloat like broccoli," he said. He added that it was sure to work, because "the devil is with me today."

VOODOO? WHO DO?

While the president never complained (publicly) of any intestinal trouble during his trip, shortly after the curse several strange incidents occurred. Voodoo or coincidence? You be the judge.

- Just hours before arriving in Jakarta, the auto-brake on Air Force One malfunctioned and six tires blew out as the plane was landing in Ho Chi Minh City, Vietnam (nobody was hurt).
- The next day, the presidential contingent traveled to Hawaii, where the president's travel director, Greg Pitts, 25, was mugged and beaten after leaving a nightclub in Waikiki. Newspaper reports said he was "too drunk" to describe the suspects to police.
- And across the globe, presidential daughter Barbara Bush had her purse stolen from her table at a restaurant in Argentina...right under the noses of her Secret Service guards. (The night before, another agent was involved in an altercation after a night out. Secret Service officials said it was a "mugging.")

Marie Antoinette took her bidet to prison with her.

NEW PRODUCTS

Just when you think everything that could possibly be invented has already been invented, along comes something like rejection-letter toilet paper.

TRUTH IN ADVERTISING

Say, what's that suspicious looking device? It's the "Suspicious Looking Device!" A darkly humorous response to the increased fears of terrorism in recent years, the SLD is a red metal box with dotted lights, a small screen, a buzzer, and whirring motor. What does it do? Nothing. It's just supposed to *appear* suspicious.

I WISH...FOR AN FTC INVESTIGATION

A company called Life Technology Research International has created the seemingly impossible: a magical wishing machine. You simply speak into the microphone on the Psychotronic Wishing Machine to tell it what you want...then sit back and wait a few days for your wish to come true. Just make sure the machine is on—LTRI says that the wish is far less likely to ever come true if the machine is turned off while the wish is still being "processed." Nevertheless, results are still *not* guaranteed. How does it work? "Conscious human interaction and energy fields." Cost: $499.

GET YOUR MOTOR RUNNIN'

For the cat owner who has everything: A California man has invented the Purr Detector. It's a small motion detector and light embedded inside a cat collar. Whenever the cat purrs, the collar glows. It's only available by mail order, so if you need to know if your cat is purring before the Purr Detector arrives, you can always use your ears.

TASTE IS NOT A FACTOR

The gross-out game show *Fear Factor* is no longer on the air, but it's still going strong with a line of candy based on its most memorable segment: people eating disgusting animal parts. There are lollipops in the shape of a chicken's foot, pig's snout, and cow's heart (flavored lemon, bubblegum, and cinnamon, respectively)

The opposite of "cross-eyed" is "wall-eyed."

as well as candy sheep eyeballs (mango) and "coagulated blood balls" (mmm...cherry!).

POT STICKERS

Many toddlers resist potty training because they're afraid of the toilet. The white porcelain behemoth is supposed to look a lot less imposing with Toilet Buddies: brightly-colored animal stickers that affix to the toilet, making it look kid-friendly enough for the little ones to use it. They're available in Poo P. Bunny, Puddles Puppy, and Ca Ca Cow.

NO, *YOU'RE* REJECTED!

Most successful writers had a period of frequent rejection letters from publishers (even Uncle John). Now, jilted authors can happily take out their revenge on those who have denied them literary glory with Rejection Letter Toilet Paper. You go to the Web site of a company called Lulu, upload the text of a rejection letter, and the company prints it onto four rolls of toilet paper for you.

ZOMBIE-UTIFUL

A few years ago, friends of Canadian artist Rob Sacchetto asked him to draw pictures of them as zombies to use as decorations for a Halloween party. Now Sacchetto runs a business selling Zombie Portraits. For $80, Sacchetto takes a photograph of you and uses it as the basis for a hand-drawn caricature of you as a zombie, complete with rotting flesh, oozing brains, and sagging eyeballs.

BRUSH YOUR CASTLE

Sarah Witmer had a tradition with her grandchildren: Whenever they lost a tooth, they'd put it under their pillow and the "tooth fairy" (Witmer) took it away. But this tooth fairy was a little different: A couple of days later, the kid would get a small sculpture of a castle made out of sand and the ground-up tooth. Now Witmer makes "Fairy Tooth Castles" professionally. When *your* child loses a tooth, you can send it to Witmer. She'll grind it up, mix it with sand and a hardening agent, sculpt a nine-inch-tall castle out of it, and send it back to you.

How about you? Only 30% of people can flare their nostrils.

MINNESOTISMS

Minnesota: a land of many lakes, and a people of few words. The language they speak there may sound like English, but it's a little different. Here's a short guide to get you speaking like a native.

BASIC CONVERSATION

Term: Ya

Meaning: Yes (direct form)

Used in conversation: "Would you like some coffee?"

"Ya."

Term: If it's not too much trouble

Meaning: Yes (indirect form)

Used in conversation: "Would you like another cup of coffee?"

"If it's not too much trouble."

Term: Then

Meaning: Sentence extender, used to fill the space just before the period

Used in conversation: "I've still got a full pot in the kitchen."

"I'll have another cup then."

Term: It's different

Meaning: I hate it (indirect form)

Used in conversation: "Do you like the coffee? It's flavored with garlic."

"It's different."

Term: That's different

Meaning: That's crazy (indirect form)

Used in conversation: "We bought the coffee from a guy pushing garlic at the State Fair."

"That's different."

Term: Heckuva deal

Meaning: A good opportunity or bargain

Used in conversation: "It was only 5 pounds for $4."

"That's a heckuva deal then."

Term: You bet

Meaning: Yes indeed; absolutely

Used in conversation: "We thought, what the hey, we might as well get some."

"You bet, a heckuva deal."

Term: A guy

Meaning: A generic male

Used in conversation: "It was too good to pass up."

"Ya, I can see why a guy would buy five pounds at those prices."

John Steinbeck's dog ate his first draft of *Of Mice and Men*.

Term: Could be worse
Meaning: Bad (indirect form)
Used in conversation: "So, how's it going with your mother-in-law living with you then?"
"Oh, could be worse."

Term: Uff Da
Meaning: An exclamation, most often used for emphasis at the beginning of a sentence
Used in conversation: "And how about your brother? He still living in your basement?"
"Uff Da! It's cold outside!"

WEATHER

Season: Winter
Sample conversation: "Cold enough for you?"
"Ya, she's a cold one, but it's the windchill that really gets to a guy."

Season: Spring
Sample conversation: "Nice weather for a change."
"Ya, but it won't be long before it's hotter than heck."

Season: Summer
Sample conversation: "Hot enough for you?"
"Ya, she's a hot one, but it's the humidity that really gets to a guy."

Season: Fall
Sample conversation: "Nice weather for a change."
"Ya, but it won't be long before the snow flies."

MISCELLANEOUS FOOD TERMS

Lutefisk: Dried codfish soaked in lye until it's the consistency of Jell-O. Served with melted butter or white sauce.

Lefse: Potato-and-flour flatbread

Jell-O Salad: Any combination of Jell-O with fruits, vegetables, milk products, and/or marshmallows. Example. lime Jell-O, crushed pineapple, and cream.

Fishboil: A communal picnic where fish, potato, and onions are boiled in a large kettle

Bars: A dessert baked in a pan and cut into squares. Usually includes chocolate chips, oatmeal, butter, and eggs.

Dinner: Lunch

Supper: Dinner

A Little Lunch: An afternoon snack, most often including coffee and bars

Montreal finished paying off construction costs for the 1976 Olympics in 2006.

SHANGHAIED!

Here's a look at one of the strangest crime waves in American history—one that terrorized even the toughest characters in town—as city officials, the police, and even the public looked the other way.

OUT TO SEA

One evening in the early 1900s, 19-year-old Max DeVeer and a friend were living it up in a San Francisco honky tonk called the Barbary Coast. There they met a man who asked them if they'd like to meet some girls.

"Well, naturally at that age we were raring to go anywhere—females were few and far between," DeVeer told an interviewer half a century later. On the promise of meeting women, he and his friend went to the man's room, where he served them drinks.

"That was the last that I remember," DeVeer said. "The results of it was we woke up on a three-mast ship going through the Golden Gate....Besides my partner and myself, there were three other guys. One of them was a city fireman, and one was a store clerk and the other one was a wino, I guess."

DeVeer and company had all been "shanghaied"—drugged, kidnapped, and sold for as little as $50 a head to the captain of a sailing ship headed for the high seas. When they might make it back to San Francisco was anyone's guess; people who had been shanghaied might remain at sea, working as little more than slaves, for years at a time.

DeVeer's experience wasn't unique. For more than half a century it had been a common practice in San Francisco, Seattle, Portland, and other West Coast ports for men known as "crimps" to shanghai thousands of men every year. Shanghai, China, was a distant port of call, so when someone of seafaring age disappeared from city streets without a trace, people said they'd been "sent to Shanghai" or "shanghaied."

CANVAS AND GOLD

Two events led to the heyday of shanghaiing in the late 1840s. The first was the invention of the clipper ship, a sleek and very fast sailing ship that got its speed from more than 30 sails that were mounted on three giant masts. Lots of sails required lots of sailors to manage them, which increased the demand for sailors.

The second was the California gold rush of 1849, which caused men to abandon the low-paying, dangerous life of a sailor to seek their fortune as "Forty-Niners." There were always plenty of sailors willing to go *to* San Francisco; the problem was that as soon as a ship dropped anchor in San Francisco Bay, the crew abandoned ship and headed for the gold fields. By the end of 1849 more than 700 abandoned ships lay at anchor in the bay in need of crews to sail them back out again.

For San Francisco's merchants and city fathers, the situation was intolerable. If the city was going to grow, the port had to function normally—San Franciscans had to be able to import the supplies they needed and export the goods they produced, and ship owners had to feel confident that if they sent a ship to San Francisco, they'd eventually get it back again. So when ship captains began offering $50 per head to anyone who could find them sailors to get their ships back out of port, crimps with colorful nicknames like Scab Johnny, Chloroform Kate and the Shanghai Chicken set to work meeting the demand. Business leaders, City Hall, and even the police turned a blind eye.

THE WORST PORT IN THE WORLD

Shanghaiing was a common practice in just about every port city on the West Coast. But San Francisco's reputation paled in comparison to Portland, Oregon, which was known as the "Unheavenly City," the "Forbidden City," and "The Worst Port in the World." If the sophistication of the city's shanghai network was any measure, the nicknames were well deserved.

Portland's waterfront was one of the seediest parts of town. The neighborhood was filled with saloons, pool halls, brothels, and even opium dens that served not only sailors on shore leave, but also any loggers, ranch hands, river workers, and other laborers who might be in town looking for a good time. Even when these establishments weren't owned outright by crimp gangs, they were usually in cahoots with them.

Some business owners trapped their victims just by letting nature take its course—when a customer passed out drunk in a bar or became incapacitated in an opium den, the saloon keeper left

The Uape Indians of Brazil mix the ashes of their dead with their alcohol.

them to the mercy of the crimp gangs. If two drunks got in a bar fight, the crimps waited for it to end and then dragged away the loser. (If the winner got enough of a beating, they'd drag him away, too.)

Other proprietors took a more active approach: They served up punches made of beer mixed with schnapps and laced with laudanum or other drugs, or gave their customers "Shanghai smokes" —cigars laced with opium. Some businesses even had trap doors in the floor that sent unsuspecting victims plunging to the cellar, into the arms of waiting crimps. In Portland alone, 1,500 people were shanghaied in a typical year. In the busiest years the number climbed as high as 3,000—more than eight victims a day.

THE SHANGHAI TUNNELS

Nearly everyone who was shanghaied in Portland ended up in a cellar below street level. In the neighborhoods near the waterfront, all the buildings' cellars were connected to a network of tunnels and alleyways that ran all the way to the water's edge. This elaborate maze of underground passages, infamously known as the "Shanghai Tunnels," are what set Portland apart from other West Coast cities.

In other towns crimp gangs only shanghaied sailors as the need arose. If a ship pulled into port and the captain let it be known that he needed seven men to fill out his crew, the crimp gangs went out and kidnapped seven men. But Portland's crimp gangs outfitted the Shanghai Tunnels with makeshift prison cells, which allowed the gangs to kidnap people, then hold them captive underground for weeks at a time. Then, when a ship needing men sailed into port, the crimp gangs were ready. They slipped drugs into their victims' food and dragged them through the tunnels to the waiting ship. By the time the drugs wore off, the victims were out to sea with no hope of escape. They had only two choices: work or get thrown overboard.

Some captains paid their shanghaied sailors nothing; others paid a nominal wage but then charged the victims for their food and necessities and even deducted the crimp gang's kidnapping fee from their pay. Either way the result was the same: After everything was totaled up, the sailors were essentially working for free.

Wrestler "The Rock" has a degree in criminology.

NOBODY'S PERFECT

Crimp gangs and sea captains weren't the only ones who benefited from the shanghai system; that was why it lasted as long as it did. Kidnapping waterfront riffraff and sending them off to sea lowered the crime rate (excluding kidnapping, of course). If you had lent someone money and they refused to pay it back, you could arrange to have them shanghaied. Likewise, if *you* owed someone money and didn't want to pay it back, you could have the lender shanghaied, too. Not many people concerned themselves with the plight of shanghaied sailors or even noticed when they disappeared—most were transients with few ties to the community.

The crimp gangs protected their interests by being active in the political machines that dominated government in cities like Portland and San Francisco. In California, two crimps named Joseph "Frenchy" Franklin and George Lewis even managed to get themselves elected to the state legislature, where they succeeded in blocking laws that attempted to outlaw shanghaiing.

PULLING INTO PORT

In the end it wasn't a legal or moral crusade that ended the cruel shanghai system, it was steam: Steamships didn't have sails, and could get by with less than half the crew of a sailing ship. By the time Max DeVeer and his friend woke up on their sailing ship as it was headed out of the Golden Gate, steamships were already overtaking sailing ships and the age of shanghaiing was drawing to a close.

* * *

SEEING IS BELIEVING

The age of shanghaiing may be over, but Portland's Shanghai Tunnels are still there, and parts of them are open for public tours. Look them up online or contact the city's tourist bureau for more information. Reservations are required, and it's a good idea to book well in advance—the tours are popular and frequently sell out.

ANIMAL ODDITIES

Strange tales of creatures great, small, and stupid.

TURTLE POWER

A family in Kent, England, accidentally threw out their pet turtle, Murphy, with the trash. Murphy then went through a trash pulverizing machine, was scooped up with a load of garbage by a bulldozer, and processed through a giant, bottle-smashing drum. Somehow, the turtle survived and was discovered alive at the recycling plant.

JIVE ~~TURKEY~~ KITTY

In March 1993, a cat named Cingene (Turkish for "gypsy") appeared on a television news show in Turkey and reportedly spoke seven words in clear Turkish. The words: *ver* (give), *demen* ("I don't say!"), *Nalan* and *Derya* (popular girls' names), *naynay* (a slang term for music), *nine* (a colloquial word for grandmother), and *babaane* (grandmother).

BAD NEWS BEARS

In 2002 dozens of drivers were injured by rockslides on a mountain road between the Russian resort towns of Adler and Krasnaya Polyana. The reason for the rockslides: malicious bears. Locals say Caucasian bears had taken to killing cows for entertainment by rolling rocks down the mountains onto them. They had since moved on from hitting cows to trying to hit people and their cars.

CAT NIPS

Katie Perfitt of England wondered why her one-year-old cat Joey's behavior became erratic at night. Turns out he was sneaking out every night and going to the Teal Arms, the local pub. Patrons routinely fed him rum, beer, and hard cider. "He'd attack the duvet, then jump on my plate while I was eating," Perfitt said. "The next minute he'd be snoring his head off." Joey's bar visits ended when the vet discovered Joey had suffered minor liver damage.

Cisvestitism **is the act of wearing weird clothes.**

THE IRON LADY

In February and March 2003, nearly 50 bulls in Wisconsin suffered severe groin injuries trying to mate with an unreceptive cow. The "cow" was made of cast iron and had been placed in a field by a farmer to scare off crows. "I'm currently being sued by several dairy farmers for vet bills," the farmer with the iron cow said.

DOG CALLS

While playing in a park in Erith, England, 14-year-old Nathan Ferro was suddenly blindsided and knocked to the ground by a Labrador retriever. It didn't bite the boy, but it pinned him down, stuck its snout in his pocket, grabbed his $130 cellular phone, and ran off with it. "It seemed to know exactly what it was looking for," Nathan said. The (tooth-marked) phone was later recovered.

STAMPEDE!

A bus in Voi, Kenya, accidentally ran into and killed a three-month-old elephant calf in January 2006. Immediately seeking revenge, eight full-grown, screaming elephants surrounded the bus and tried to tip it over. A 50-car traffic jam ensued as wildlife wardens tried to get the elephants to disperse.

GOOD AIM

In May 1989, an eight-hour traffic jam was caused on the Isle of Wight when falling seagull droppings hit and jammed the electric eye of a bridge's traffic light control system. In April 1994, Newbridge, England, experienced a blackout when a bird of prey dropped a lamb on an electricity substation. (The same thing happened a month later in Morongo Basin, California, except that bird dropped a rosy boa snake.)

FETCH!

Eight-year-old Olivia Parkinson of West Midlands, England, wondered why her usually springy springer spaniel puppy Barney was moving so slowly. A visit to the vet revealed that Barney had been eating everything he played "fetch" with. In his stomach were six fist-size rocks, five twigs, and whole apples. "I could never understand why when we played fetch, he would return empty-mouthed," Olivia said. "Now I know."

Orville Wright numbered his chickens' eggs so he could eat them in the order they were laid.

APOCALYPSE? NAH.

The Cuban Missile Crisis wasn't the only time the United States and the Soviet Union stood on the brink of nuclear war. Here are a few more times that the world nearly plunged into World War III by accident.

CRISIS BEARLY AVERTED

Late on the night of October 25, 1962, a guard at an Air Force base in Minnesota spotted a dark figure climbing the fence surrounding the base. The guard shot and killed the mysterious figure. The fence was wired to detect intruders, and as the culprit fell, it set off an alarm. But the fence was incorrectly wired, and the alarm set off a second alarm hundreds of miles away at an Air National Guard base in Wisconsin. F-106 fighter jets armed with nuclear missiles immediately prepared to take off toward the Soviet Union in response to the intrusion. But the nuclear strike was quickly called off after an investigation determined the identity of the fence-climbing spy: It was a bear.

INDIAN ~~SUMMER~~ NUCLEAR WINTER

In the 1990s, hostilities between India and Pakistan escalated over mutual claims of ownership of the Kashmir region. Both countries conducted nuclear tests in "sabre-rattling" moves. Then, on June 6, 2002, a 32-foot-wide asteroid entered the Earth's atmosphere, breaking up and exploding in a fiery ball over the Mediterranean Sea between Libya and Greece. Just before the explosion—a blast that registered at 26 kilotons, slightly more powerful than the atomic bomb dropped on Nagasaki during World War II—the asteroid flew directly over India and Pakistan. Scientists estimate that if it had landed in either country, it would have looked—and felt—exactly like an unprovoked first strike, and may have prompted the other country to attack.

THEY WOULDN'T BOMB *US*, WOULD THEY?

Just before 1:00 a.m. on September 26, 1983, Soviet defense computers received a message that American-launched intercontinental ballistic missiles had been detected in the sky, and were on their way to Moscow. Col. Stanislav Petrov was the officer in

Tony Blair's schoolmaster called him "the most difficult boy I ever had to deal with."

charge at the Serpukhov-15 bunker outside of Moscow, where it was his job to monitor the early-warning satellite network. In case of attack, he would notify his superiors, who would immediately launch a nuclear counterattack on the United States. But the computers registered only *one* missile launched from the U.S. Petrov reasoned that the message was a false alarm—if the Americans were attacking, they'd launch many missiles, not just one. He was right. The "missile plumes" observed by radar turned out to be glare from the Sun. (Despite acting correctly, Petrov was demoted.)

ROCKET TO RUSSIA

On January 25, 1995, a team of Norwegian and American scientists launched a research rocket off the northwest coast of Norway. It contained equipment to collect data on the aurora borealis, or northern lights. The rocket was noticed by radar operators at the Olengorsk early-warning station in Russia, who mistakenly identified the small, unarmed rocket as a submarine-launched nuclear Trident missile headed for Moscow. The news was sent to Russian president Boris Yeltsin, who, for a moment, was ready to hit the "launch nukes" button. Fortunately, minutes later, the radar operators noticed that the "missile" was heading away from Russia, and determined that it wasn't really a threat. The rocket collected its data and landed safely on an Arctic island a half hour later. Ironically, the scientists had notified the Russian government of the rocket launch weeks in advance, but the information had not made its way to the early-warning radar operators or Yeltsin.

THIS IS ONLY A TEST

On November 9, 1979, computers at three American military control centers (the Pentagon, the Pentagon's emergency site in Maryland, and the Aerospace Defense Command in Colorado) all displayed the same grim news: Soviet nuclear missiles were on their way. Officers immediately put missile launch sites on alert and ten fighter jets took off to patrol the skies and shoot down anything suspicious. However, before launching a counterstrike, officers at the three bases decided to back up the information they'd received. Satellite data and radar across the country showed no signs of Soviet missiles in the air. It turns out that a training tape of attack scenarios had been placed into the computer running the military's early-warning system.

Pumpkins were once recommended for removing freckles and curing snake bites.

I WAS MARILYN MONROE

Do you believe in reincarnation? According to a recent poll, 25 percent of Americans do. Wouldn't it be fascinating if the spirit of a dead celebrity was inhabiting you?

SOME LIKE IT NOT

Ever since the age of five, Sherrie Lea Laird says she has endured unwanted and troubling memories—memories that she says aren't hers. At first, Laird didn't know who they belonged to, but as the years passed on, they seemed to bear a striking resemblance to those of Marilyn Monroe, who died in 1962—just a few months before Laird was born.

Laird grew up to become the lead singer of a popular Canadian rock band called Pandamonia. But the disturbing memories persisted. She claimed to friends that she could feel the sadness Monroe felt when John F. Kennedy ended their relationship, and even experienced the heart palpitations from the accidental drug overdose that killed Monroe (Laird claims her "memory" debunks all theories of murder or suicide). The memories became so unbearable that in 1998 Laird sought professional help. She was pointed in the direction of a Malibu, California, psychiatrist named Adrian Finkelstein. Perhaps he'd have the answers she was looking for.

YOU ARE GETTING SLEEEEEEPY

For nearly 20 years, Finkelstein has been a leading practitioner of "past-life regression" therapy; he hypnotizes his patients to help them channel the souls that inhabit them. Finkelstein took Laird's case, and over seven years conducted hundreds of hours of hypnosis and interviews. Finkelstein believed Laird, but knew he needed proof before anyone else would, too. So before each session, Finkelstein did exhaustive research about details of Monroe's life, then quizzed the deeply hypnotized Laird about them. She was spot-on every time, he says. Speaking under hypnosis as "Marilyn," Laird answered questions that only the real Marilyn would have known, including details of her relationship with JFK. (According to Laird, he told Monroe state secrets about Cuba, and she first had sex with him in a car.) In addition, Finkelstein showed her photographs of Monroe's relatives, and Laird was able to identify each one and provide more details than even Finkelstein knew.

Laird believes that her own 21-year-old daughter is the reincarnation of Marilyn Monroe's mother, Gladys Baker, who died a few days before Laird's daughter was born. Finkelstein's theory: Monroe and Baker are seeking an opportunity to heal their relationship through Laird and her daughter.

MEET THE NEW MARILYN

Finkelstein released his findings in the May 2005 edition of *Malibu Surfside News*: "I established through research that Sherrie Lea Laird is the reincarnation of Marilyn Monroe." The announcement was big news in both the Hollywood gossip magazines and the spiritual community. Even the *Los Angeles Times* ran a front-page story about it, with the headline, "MARILYN LIVES!"

Skeptics claim that the whole "investigation" is nothing more than a publicity stunt to further the careers of both the psychiatrist and the rock star. If so, it worked. Laird's story has been told in the press and on television; Finkelstein wrote a book about the case, entitled *Marilyn Monroe Returns: The Healing of a Soul.* Both have made the rounds on the talk-show circuit.

The American Psychiatric Association refuses to make an official comment on the merits of past-life regression, and believes that reincarnation is a religious matter. But some in the medical community believe that Laird is a sick woman and that Finkelstein is making matters worse by enabling her. Bethany Marshall, a psychologist who often appears on cable TV news shows, claims Laird suffers from a "delusional disorder." Laird quickly brushes these comments off. "Ask my friends—I'm quite normal. This is not a delusional thing; it's spiritual."

MORE "PROOF"

- One of today's leading "medium channelers," Kevin Ryerson, has announced to the spiritual community that after reviewing Finkelstein's video tapes, and then channeling a 3,000-year-old Egyptian spirit known as Ahtun-Re, that the Egyptian god has confirmed that "Sherrie Lea Laird—and only Laird—is the reincarnation of Marilyn Monroe."

According to poll results, 20% of Americans believe it would be okay to clone extinct species.

• The astrology association Star IQ also conducted an investigation. Michael WolfStar, one of their premier astrologers, released their findings. "Marilyn's Pluto and North Node are conjunct, while Sherrie Lea's Sun and North Node are conjunct, and all four are found together in the middle of Cancer. It's as if Marilyn's death (Pluto) gave rise to Sherrie Lea's personal identity (Sun)." (We're not sure what this means, either.)

CANDLES IN THE WIND

Through all of the hoopla (and her 15 minutes of fame), Laird maintains that the reincarnation is real, and something she never asked for. Feeling Marilyn Monroe's deep sadness all of her life, she says, has taken its toll on her. So why the appearances on talk shows? "It's just a case to bring more attention to reincarnation," she said on the gossip show *Showbiz Tonight*. "The message is so much bigger than Marilyn Monroe. She was just a woman."

* * *

PRIVATE MATTERS

• In 2006, 23-year-old Yarislav Ernst of Glivich, Poland, found out he had a malignant tumor on his tongue. He had a large section of it removed by doctors who then replaced it with tissue from another part of his body. "We removed the tumor and made sure that no malignant cells remained," said Dr. Stanislav Poltorek, the chief oncological surgeon. "Then we collected skin, fat and nerve tissue from his buttocks and put it all together to form a new tongue, which we later sewed into his mouth." The butt-tongue, he said, was working fine.

• In August 2003, Valdemar Lopes de Moraes of Monte Claros, Brazil, walked into a medical clinic to get treated for an earache. A few hours later he walked out—with a vasectomy. What happened? The nurses called *Aldemar* (for a vasectomy), and *Valdemar* thought he'd been called. "The strangest thing," said the clinic manager, "is that he asked no questions when the doctor started preparations in the area which had so little to do with his ear. He later explained that he thought it was an ear inflammation that got down to his testicles."

The 1st time Norma Jean Mortensen signed an autograph as Marilyn Monroe, she spelled it "Marylin."

WEIRD AMERICA

Home of the free, land of the strange.

NO THANKS, I'LL GET IT MYSELF

In 2006, 3-year-old Robert Moore of Antigo, Wisconsin, spotted a Spongebob SquarePants doll in a grocery store's "claw" style vending machine. His grandmother, Fredricka Bierdemann, gave him a dollar to try to get the toy, but he failed. She turned her back to Robert, fishing through her purse for another dollar and when she turned back around, he was gone. Then she spotted him: He was inside the vending machine, surrounded by stuffed animals. He'd reached an arm through the bottom of the machine and then managed to crawl all the way in. The fire department got him out. "He was having a ball in there, hugging all the stuffed animals," Bierdemann said. "But I was shaking like a leaf."

A LOT OF DOUGH

Panera Bread, a sandwich store in the White City Shopping Center in Shrewsbury, Massachusetts, has a clause in its lease that forbids the mall from renting to another sandwich shop. When Qdoba Mexican Grill opened in the mall, Panera tried to stop them, saying that Qdoba's most popular menu item—burritos—are actually sandwiches because they are made of bread (a tortilla) and filling (meat and beans). The dispute went to court. After testimony from a federal agriculture official and a professional chef, Qdoba won, with the judge ruling that a burrito is a burrito, and not a sandwich.

HOLY STAR WARS

John Wilkinson and Charlotte Law, who call themselves "Umada" and "Yunyun," lobbied the United Nations to recognize their faith as an official religion. Their faith: Jedi, based on the *Star Wars* movies. According to Wilkinson and Law, more than half a million people in English-speaking countries identify themselves as Jedi Knights. "Like the U.N., we are peacekeepers and we feel we have the basic right to be recognized by the national and international community." The two also want the U.N. to rename the International Day for Tolerance to Interstellar Day of Tolerance.

When jazz great Louis Armstrong got his first Christmas tree at the age of 40...

DEAR GOD

Bill Lacovara of Ventnor, New Jersey, was fishing with his son near Atlantic City in 2006, when a plastic shopping bag floated by. Lacorva retrieved it. Inside he found several brown-paper wrapped packages containing more than 300 unopened letters to Reverend Grady Cooper, a Jersey City minister who died in 2004. The letters were prayer requests, ranging from the humorous (a man who wanted to win the lottery twice) to the sad (an unwed mother asking God to make her child's father marry her). The letters date as far back as 1973. Who dumped them is a mystery, but Lacorva told reporters that he plans to sell them on eBay.

THANKSGIVING REVENGE

On Thanksgiving in 2006, Sandy and Bill Cobbs were cooking their holiday meal in their Bloomington, Minnesota, home. Suddenly, they heard the sound of smashing glass coming from the dining room. A wild turkey had broken in. It tore around the house, ultimately causing $10,000 in damage to the carpet, windows, and walls. Strangely, the same thing had happened to the Cobbs on Christmas two years earlier. They'd been at their daughter's home across town when a neighbor called to tell them there was a giant hole in their dining room window—a turkey had run through it. "Everybody thinks it's funny," says Sandy Cobbs, "but it's not."

HOW VOODOO YOU PLEAD?

The Miami-Dade County Courthouse has established a Voodoo Squad. Its purpose: to clean up the leftovers from voodoo ceremonies. Florida has a large Caribbean population, many of whom believe voodoo rituals can influence a family member's court case. The Voodoo Squad reports cleaning up sacrificed goats and chickens as well as corn kernels (said to speed up a trial), eggs (which collapse a case), and cakes (which make a judge more lenient).

NOW THAT'S USING YOUR HEAD

In 1995, 37-year-old Peter Jonson of New York was shot in the head by a stray bullet from a gang dispute. He didn't go to a hospital because he didn't have insurance and feared having to pay off a massive medical bill. So he walked home, found a pair of pliers, and removed the bullet himself.

MADE IN JAPAN

On page 21, we told you about the Japanese obsession with strange products known as chindogu. *But those products are designed to be weird; these products are real. And really weird.*

SLIM MOUTH PIECE. This product is designed to "work on flaccid facial muscles" to get "a firm mouth and a slim face line!" You hook a small plastic spring-loaded device into either side of the mouth, and say "oh-oh-oh" and "e-e-e-e" to contract and release the spring. Then, according to the ads, "you can get beautiful and forever facial muscles!"

SMALL FACE IN THE BATH. Called *Ofuro de Kogao* in Japanese, this item is for Japanese people striving for what is called the ideal face: a *chiisai kao*, or "small face." It's a rubber mask that you wear while bathing that will, supposedly, shrink your face.

PERSONAL KARAOKE. It has earphones and a plastic cone that fits over your mouth so you can sing your favorite songs out loud without annoying people nearby.

SAUCE-DISPENSING CHOPSTICKS. These hollow plastic chopsticks dispense your favorite condiment onto the food as you eat. You can fill them with soy sauce or whatever you choose and not have to worry about having to deal with that messy soy sauce bottle. (Except when you fill up the chopsticks.)

WATER SALAD. It's a salad-flavored soft drink made by Coca-Cola. Honest.

THE HEAD BATH CAP. You know how you sometimes you want to take a bath, but not on your whole body—just on your head? Well, you're in luck. Just fasten the Head Bath Cap around your head just above your eyes and give fill it up with warm water and enjoy a nice "head bath." And, according to the ads, the water from the Head Bath Cap actually seeps into the pores in your scalp...stimulating hair growth!

One glass of milk can give a person a .02 blood alcohol concentration on a Breathalyzer test.

WELCOME TO COLLEGE! (NOW GET UNDRESSED), PT. II

Here's the second installment of our story about a very odd college custom that—thankfully—has been gone a long, long time. (*Part I is on page 115.*)

GOING PUBLIC

Photographing naked young *males* was never a problem in the 1940s: In those more innocent days, there was nothing particularly unseemly about a man photographing younger men in the buff. Young men were already used to the idea of stripping down in front of draft boards and athletic coaches; doing it again for William Sheldon wasn't that big a deal. Sheldon was even able to publish hundreds of photos of Harvard freshmen in a book titled *The Atlas of Men,* which explained his theories about an inborn link between behavior and body types.

If you come across a copy of *The Atlas of Men* in a library or used bookstore and flip through it looking for naked photographs of future celebrities and politicians, you might be disappointed: To his credit, Sheldon painted out the faces and the private parts to protect the privacy of his subjects and prevent the *Atlas* from being used for immoral purposes—you'd probably even have trouble recognizing a picture of yourself if one was in there.

GIRL TROUBLE

What ultimately destroyed Sheldon's career were his photographs of young *females*. In September 1950, he traveled to the University of Washington in Seattle to photograph students as part of his current project: amassing tens of thousands of photographs of women that could be used to create an *Atlas of Women*, a complementary volume to his *Atlas of Men*.

Being photographed naked was a completely different experience for the young women than it was for the men. The women had never had to strip down to be examined by draft boards, and since few of them played sports, they had never had to undress in front of a coach, either. The closest many had ever come to disrobing for a stranger was during medical exams. But the family doctor wasn't really a stranger—and he didn't take pictures, either.

One of the Washington coeds was so upset by the experience that she told her parents about it. Could she possibly have been the first young woman ever to complain? Were her parents the first ones to become enraged at Sheldon's photos? Whatever it was, this time it made a difference: The following day the young woman, her parents, and their lawyers descended upon the University of Washington administration and raised such a fuss that school officials shut down Sheldon's operation, seized the pictures he'd already taken, and burned them all.

THE STRANGE DR. WEIRD

Suddenly, something that had been accepted as an uncomfortable but unavoidable fact of college life came to be seen in a very different light. What was this man doing traveling around the country, taking nude pictures of young women fresh out of high school? As word of the brouhaha in Seattle spread, it began to knock sense into parents and colleges all over the country. One by one, schools began shutting their doors to Sheldon. He eventually had to scrap the *Atlas of Women* without finishing it.

Was the controversy surrounding his naked pictures enough to cast his scientific theories into disrepute? Or were his theories so loony that they failed on their own? Either way, Sheldon lived long enough to see his life's work dismissed as nonsense and his professional reputation destroyed. He became an embarrassment to his profession, and spent his final years holed up alone in his home, where he passed the time by reading detective novels, one after another. He died in 1977 at the age of 78.

FILED AND FORGOTTEN

So what happened to all those photographs? When Sheldon died he still had more than 20,000 naked photos from Yale, Princeton, Mount Holyoke College, Vassar, Radcliffe, Smith, Swarthmore, the University of California, Syracuse, the University of Wisconsin, and many other colleges, plus pictures he took at the Oregon Hospital for the Criminally Insane. After his death his assistant, Roland Elderkin, tried to find a college that would take custody of the photographs, but none of them were interested—many had

Drink a lot of coffee? Historians believe author Honoré de Balzac died of caffeine poisoning.

already been shamed into destroying their own collections of posture photos and they weren't about to be saddled with Sheldon's. Finally in 1987, the National Anthropological Archives, part of the Smithsonian Institution's National Museum of Natural History, agreed to accept Sheldon's photos and papers.

BACK IN THE NEWS

The photographs were still sitting, almost completely forgotten, in the Smithsonian's archives in 1992 when Naomi Wolf's letter to the *New York Times* sparked interest in them again. A *Times* reporter named Ron Rosenbaum—who as a Yale freshman in the 1960s had posed for his own posture photo—was assigned to the story. He eventually tracked down Roland Elderkin and learned that the photos were in the Smithsonian.

For five years only Elderkin, a handful of staffers at the Smithsonian, and perhaps a researcher or two who happened to stumble across the photos knew they were there. And even when people did find them it was almost impossible to get permission to see them: The Smithsonian had realized from the start how sensitive the photos were, and had locked them away from prying eyes. Even Rosenbaum, a respected journalist and subject of one of the photos himself, was only allowed to see unlabeled negatives, not the actual images.

NAKED FEAR

But that all changed when Rosenbaum's article, "The Great Ivy League Nude Posture Photo Scandal," was published in the *New York Times*. Suddenly the whole world knew about the pictures and where to find them. They were locked up, but to concerned alumni the pictures seemed to be just one crooked Smithsonian employee away from popping up on the Internet and splashing across the front pages of newspapers all over the world. For decades, thousands of college graduates had wondered about those naked pictures taken so long ago, and now it seemed that their worst fears might soon be realized.

It didn't take long for alumni groups to spring into action. Five days after Rosenbaum's article appeared, the Smithsonian announced that, after talking to representatives from Yale, Mount Holyoke, and other schools, it was cutting off public access to the

A short pass between two mountain ridges is called a *bwlch*.

photographs entirely and launching an investigation to find out how and why they had agreed to take custody of the pictures in the first place. Nine days after that, Smithsonian officials shredded and then burned all of the Yale photographs and negatives in the collection, at the request of the university. In all there were more than *100 pounds* of Yale photographs, and a representative from the school was on hand to make sure that the photos and negatives really were destroyed. The Smithsonian offered to destroy the photographs from other colleges (and the Oregon Hospital for the Criminally Insane) if asked to do so.

Is that the end of the story? Not quite.

A PENNY FOR HIS THOUGHTS

One of William Sheldon's redeeming qualities was that he had a wide range of interests. One of those interests was coin collecting, with particular emphasis on the American penny. So when his reputation as a top psychologist went down in flames, he could at least fall back on the fact that he was also a nationally recognized coin expert, and had written two books on the history of the penny that are considered classics even today.

The *books* are considered classics, but once again Sheldon didn't get off so easy. He did much of his research for the books at the American Numismatic Society in New York, which gave him unfettered access to its enormous collection of early pennies. Sheldon put together an impressive penny collection of his own, and a year before his death he sold it to another collector for $300,000.

How did he amass such a valuable collection?

The American Numismatic Society now believes that he did it by stealing dozens of valuable coins from its collection while he was researching his book, and covering up the theft by replacing them with inferior coins from his own collection. When the society first noticed the irregularities in its collection in the 1980s, it began a search for the missing coins and eventually found 58 of them in Sheldon's collection. In all, Sheldon is believed to have stolen 129 rare and valuable coins from the society's collection; at last report about 40 of the coins were still missing.

It would take five hungry piranhas about seven minutes to completely devour a horse.

RATHERISMS

Anchorman Dan Rather may be known as a serious journalist, but we love him for these odd phrases, ad-libbed during election night coverage.

"This race is hotter than a Times Square Rolex."

"The presidential race is swinging like Count Basie."

"This race is humming along like Ray Charles."

"Bush is sweeping through the South like a big wheel through a cotton field."

"In southern states, Bush beat Kerry like a rented mule."

"You know that old song: It's delightful, it's delicious, it's de-lovely for President Bush in most areas of the country."

"His lead is as thin as turnip soup."

"Keep in mind they are teetotally meetmortally convinced they have Ohio won."

"The re-election of Bill Clinton is as secure as a double-knot tied in wet rawhide."

"We don't know whether to wind a watch or bark at the moon."

"These returns are running like a squirrel in a cage."

"This race is as tight as a too-small bathing suit on a too-hot car ride back from the beach."

"Bush is sweeping through the South like a tornado through a trailer park."

"This race is as tight as the rusted lug nuts on a '55 Ford."

"This race is spandex-tight."

"This race is shakier than cafeteria Jell-O."

"The Michigan Republican primary is tighter than Willie Nelson's headband."

"His lead is as thin as November ice."

"A lot of people in Washington could not be more surprised if Fidel Castro came loping through on the back of a hippopotamus this election night."

"When it comes to a race like this, I'm a long-distance runner and an all-day hunter."

There is an underground church in Poland carved from solid salt.

UNCLE JOHN'S TOP 10 AMAZING COINCIDENCES

We're constantly finding stories about amazing coincidences. Here are some of our very favorites.

10. WHAT GOES AROUND...

"In 1965, at age four, Roger Lausier was saved from drowning off a beach at Salem, Mass., by a woman named Alice Blaise. Nine years later, in 1974, on the same beach, Roger paddled his raft into the water and pulled a drowning man from the water. The man was Alice Blaise's husband."

—***The Book of Lists***

9. NUMBER NINE, NUMBER NINE...

BELOIT, Wisconsin—"Nicholas Stephen Wadle was born at 9:09 a.m. on the ninth day of the ninth month of 1999. But the string of coincidences doesn't end there. He weighed 9 pounds, 9 ounces.

"A spokeswoman for Beloit Memorial Hospitals said the mother 'couldn't believe it,' but 'the most surprised were the professionals involved....As the nines started to stack up, they were going crazy.'

"The baby was due Sept. 15, but complications with the births of Mrs. Wadles's two older children led her doctor to schedule a cesarean section for Thursday, to be safe. The delivery was set for 8:00 a.m. but there was an emergency, which allowed the 9:09 birth."

—**Appleton (Wisconsin) *Post Crescent***

8. ARE YOU MY DADDY?

"Wilf Hewitt, 86, a widower from Southport, England, wanted to look through a list of registered voters in the library, and asked the woman who had the list if she was going to be long. Vivien Fletoridis replied that she was looking for a man named Hewitt. She was his daughter, whom he had not seen for 46 years. Wilf had had a wartime love affair with Vivien's mother, who had died in 1983. Their daughter was adopted in 1941 and went to Australia with her foster parents. In July 1987 she traced her two brothers and sister through an agency, and then set out to find her father."

—***The Fortean Times***

7. REINCARNATED SURVIVOR

"On three separate occasions—in 1664, 1785, and 1860—there were shipwrecks where only one person survived the accident. Each time that one person's name was Hugh Williams."

—***The Book of Useless Information***

6. I DO, I THINK

"A woman in Kissimmee, Florida, should have no trouble remembering her new husband's name. But, following a bizarre chain of coincidences surrounding the couple's wedding, she might have trouble remembering what he looks like.

"Ronald Legendre married his girlfriend, Hope, in August 1995. The best man—who wasn't related to the groom in any way—was also named Ronald Legendre. And the ceremony was performed by someone who wasn't connected to either man: Judge Ronald Legendre."

—***Knuckleheads in the News***

5. SECRET-AGENT KID

"James Bond, 15, a pupil at Argoed High School, North Wales, and a candidate for examinations in 1990, was given the examination number 007 by a computer quirk."

—***The World's Most Incredible Stories***

4. HER NAME IS MY NAME, TOO

"A computer mix-up that gave two American women the same social security number was responsible for highlighting a further series of incredible coincidences. Patricia Kern of Colorado and Patricia di Biasi of Oregon were brought together by the blunder.

"The women discovered they had both been born Patricia Ann Campbell with fathers called Robert. They were born on the same date, too: March 13, 1941. Both Patricias married military men in 1959, within eleven days of one another, and had children aged nineteen and twenty-one. They also shared an interest in painting with oils, had studied cosmetics and worked as bookkeepers."

—One in a Million

3. AND HER NAME IS MY NAME, TOO

"Mother of two, Michelle Samways, was caught up in a spot of trouble—with mother of two Michelle Samways. The two women moved into numbers 5 and 6 Longstone Close, Portland, England, in Oct. 1994 and hardly a day goes by without a mix-up of some kind. They discovered that they share the same name only when they entered a raffle at a toddlers' group. The two Michelles, aged 26 and 27, were both named after the 1965 Beatles song. They are the same height and build, [and have] similar hair color."

—The Fortean Times

2. BABIES KEEP FALLING ON MY HEAD

"Joseph Figlock was passing an apartment block in Detroit in 1975 when he was knocked unconscious. A baby had fallen fourteen stories and landed on him. Both survived. One year later, Figlock was passing the same apartment block—and once again he was hit by a falling child...and survived!"

—One in a Million

And the #1 coincidence is...

1. CIVIL SERVANT

"One of the lesser-known figures of American history is Wilmer McLean, a Virginia farmer who took little interest in politics.

"In 1861, most of the Rebel army marched onto McLean's land. The Union forces attempted to bar their way, and the first full-scale battle of the Civil War (Battle of Bull Run), got underway—right on his farm. Thirteen months later, it happened again. The second battle at Bull Run destroyed McLean's land. McLean had had enough. He packed his wagons and moved two hundred miles away from the war.

"Three years later, in a weird twist of fate, two men confronted each other in Wilmer McLean's parlor. These two men talked and signed a document on McLean's best table; for he had moved to a little village called Appomattox Court House—where Robert E. Lee and Ulysses S. Grant negotiated the end of the Civil War."

—Ripley's Believe It or Not

Coincidence? The Pentagon uses up 666 rolls of toilet paper on an average day.

MYTHICAL CREATURES!

From the depths of some strange, mysterious world they come, sharing our earthly realm—sometimes peacefully, but often not. Are they real? Are we real? Are YOU real? Ahhhhhhhhhh!!!!!!!!!!

CREATURE: El Petizo
SPOTTED IN: Argentina
THE STORY: El Petizo is a "malicious shadow" who attacks lone travelers at night. So far, six people have been wounded by the monster, most recently a teenage boy who was on his way home from a hunting trip. He was knocked off his bike and then rose to his feet to find the dark shadow approaching him. Armed with a gun and a knife, the teen shot and stabbed the shadow, but it had no effect. Before he knew it, he was being dragged across the ground by his hair. A man who was nearby heard the boy's cries and ran to his aid, but by the time he got there, El Petizo was gone.

CREATURE: Horny Horse Man
SPOTTED IN: Nigeria
THE STORY: According to news reports, a menacing half-human/half-horse beast appears at night in the town of Zamfara and chases women into their houses. To local residents, it's no laughing matter. It's so serious, in fact, that many women won't risk being outside between sunset and sunrise. (So far, efforts to capture the horse/man have proven unsuccessful.)

CREATURES: Goblins
SPOTTED IN: Norway
THE STORY: Håkon Robertsen's neighbors want him to tear down his old barn. It's mostly in ruins and could be dangerous to curious children, so local authorities ordered Robertsen to level it. But he refuses. Why? "Underworld creatures have taken up residence in the building." And by "underworld creatures," he means goblins. According to Norwegian folklore, the grotesque little monsters live underground and rarely visit the human world. But Robertsen believes that his barn—built on an ancient Viking

What is *Nessiteras rhombopteryx*? The scientific name for the Loch Ness Monster *and...*

site—must have become some kind of goblin lair...and they do not want it disturbed. "A while back, I removed the top of the building and that is an experience I will not repeat." Robertsen says he got the message that if he disturbed the barn again, his life would be in jeopardy. The town has threatened to fine him 300 kroners ($47.50) every day that the barn remains standing. Robertsen's response: He'll build a fence around it to keep people out—he'll even sue the town to keep the barn undisturbed—but he pledges never to set foot near the barn again.

CREATURES: Fairies
SPOTTED IN: Cumbria, England
THE STORY: Anne Rowe, a historical archivist, unearthed a strange death certificate while searching through the burial register for the parish of Lamplugh. According to the records, between 1656 and 1663 four people were scared to death...by fairies. "I've never come across anything like this," said Rowe, who added that those were "insecure times." Further research of the records mentioned several more fairy encounters...all apparently ending badly.

CREATURE: Yowie
SPOTTED IN: The Megalong Valley in the Australian outback
THE STORY: "It was sniffing the air and turning around to bite me, and I knew something was wrong. At that point I smelt a real foul stench, like salty blood, and I looked—the ground dropped down to the left and it was just standing there...10, 15 meters away, if that. It looked sort of like a monkey, but more human. I pretty much crapped my pants!" What was standing there? A Yowie, also called "Australia's Bigfoot"—approximately four feet tall, very hairy, and very menacing. The sighting was recounted by a woman identified only as Catherine B., 22, who was horseback riding through the area with friends in September 2006. But this was just the most recent sighting. There have been hundreds of reports of these creatures in the Australian wilderness since the country was colonized by the English. And Aboriginal tales of a strange ape man predate those by centuries.

...an anagram for "monster hoax by Sir Peters."

HERE'S A *REALLY* STRANGE IDEA...

Every problem has a solution. Maybe.

WHO: Robert Cole, a 37-year-old Australian
PROBLEM: Incarceration. (Cole was in prison.)
BRIGHT IDEA: Cole decided to escape...by dieting. He consumed copious amounts of laxatives, resulting in the loss of 31 pounds. That took him down to 123 pounds. Why did he want to be so skinny? He planned to squeeze himself through the tiny gap between the bars of his prison cell and a small hole he'd chipped in the adjacent brick wall. Think that's extreme? Well, he made it. Cole was free for three days before he was caught. (He's in a different prison now.)

WHO: Phillip W. Cappella of Boston, Massachusetts
PROBLEM: Cappella was being audited by the IRS. He had won $2.7 million in the Massachusetts Megabucks lottery, which was to be paid to him in annual payments of $135,000 for 20 years. Apparently getting something for nothing wasn't enough for Cappella—he wanted it to be tax-free, too. So he claimed $65,000 in gambling losses the year he got his first payment, saving him more than $20,000 in taxes. The IRS didn't buy it and required him to provide proof.
BRIGHT IDEA: Cappella paid a lottery ticket collector $500 to loan him a pickup truck full of losing tickets—200,000 of them—and then told the IRS that they were all his. The auditors figured out that in order for that to be true, Cappella would have to have scratched 550 tickets every single day of the year (and more tickets if he skipped a day now and then). He was found guilty of tax fraud and sentenced to two years probation.

WHO: Stephen Hawking
PROBLEM: We're all going to die! According to Hawking, the world-famous physicist and author of A *Brief History of Time*, the

The Queen is the only person in Britain who is legally allowed to eat swan.

human race faces extinction from disasters such as asteroid collisions or nuclear war. Hawking said in 2006 that in order for humans to survive into the distant future we must colonize other planets. "Once we spread out into space and establish independent colonies," he said, "our future should be safe." The problem: We would have to find *hospitable* planets—and the closest *possible* one, at speeds that rockets can currently travel—is more than 50,000 years away.

BRIGHT IDEA: No problem, says Hawking. We must simply invent a propulsion system similar to the one used on *Star Trek.* He says that taking advantage of "matter/antimatter annihilation" humans should be able to travel at speeds just below the speed of light. That would allow a ship to make it to the nearest star in six years. "That wouldn't seem so long," he said. (No word on how long it would take to invent such a system, though.)

WHO: The National Crematorium Association of Denmark

PROBLEM: Every year more than 40,000 Danes are cremated in natural-gas ovens at about 1800° Fahrenheit. But all the heat from the process goes directly into the air—so it's wasted.

BRIGHT IDEA: In 2006 the Association sought permission from the Ministry of Ecclesiastical Affairs to pipe the heat from crematoriums into nearby churches. "Instead of just letting the heat out the window, we can use it to warm up church buildings," said Allan Vest, the Association's president. "Maybe we could even sell some of it." The idea, to the surprise of many, was approved. "We do not feel that using the heat defiles the corpses in any way," said Ole Hartling, the head of Denmark's Council of Ethics, "since they are already incinerated."

* * *

"If someone were to harm my family or a friend or somebody I love, I would eat them. I might end up in jail for 500 years, but I would eat them."

—**Johnny Depp**

ODD DISORDERS

These weird conditions aren't humorous, especially to the afflicted. But here's a reality check: They're all real illnesses.

Disorder: Trichotillomania

What is it? People with this condition pull their own hair repeatedly—to the point of pulling it out. That means from the head, the eyebrows, eyelashes, and even pubic hair. It's a painful, debilitating condition, and you might be surprised to learn that experts believe as much as 2–3% of the population has it. It's also embarrassing (many victims don't realize they're pulling their hair out until well after they've done it), and sufferers do their best to hide it. To bring publicity to the disorder, the Trichotillomania Learning Center designated the week of October 1–8, 2006, as National Trichotillomania Awareness Week.

Disorder: Emetophobia

What is it? It's a "persistent, abnormal, irrational fear of vomiting." Millions of people have it. In extreme cases, the fear of encountering something in public that might induce them to vomit keeps victims from leaving their homes for years at a time. Some sufferers become obsessive about what foods they can and can't eat. And perhaps the strangest part is that emetophobics almost never vomit. According to researchers, most sufferers had a traumatic throwing-up experience between the ages of 6 and 10. After that, they do everything they can to avoid it, with many women even going through entire pregnancies without a single throwing-up episode. (*Very* unusual.) Some people who have admitted to suffering from emetophobia: folk singer Joan Baez, actress Denise Richards, and *Today* host Matt Lauer.

Disorder: Nocturnal Sleep-Related Eating Syndrome

What is it? Just what it sounds like. People with this condition get up in the middle of the night, sleepwalk to the refrigerator, and pig out. Some people with NSRED do it often enough to gain a significant amount of weight, yet have no knowledge that they're eating until the next morning when they find the mess in

There's a bar in the building that once housed the National Temperance Society.

the kitchen. Foods eaten tend to be high-fat, high-sugar snacks, and sometimes odd combinations like hot dogs with peanut butter. As many as nine million people in the United States are believed to have it.

Disorder: Two Feet–One Hand Syndrome

What is it? This strange condition is highlighted by dryness and scaling on the soles of both feet, and on the palm of one hand only. It's caused by a fungal infection and can recur several times with or without treatment. But it always affects just one hand. Researchers can't figure out why.

Disorder: Alien Hand Syndrome

What is it? People with this disorder believe that one of their hands has a mind of its own. They can feel the hand and use it normally, but it will sometimes do things seemingly of its own volition and without the person even being aware of it. The "alien" hand can even act *against* the other hand, with one example being someone buttoning their shirt with their right hand while the left hand unbuttons the shirt at the same time. It most frequently occurs in people who have had brain surgery, strokes, or brain infections. You may have seen a comic portrayal of the syndrome if you've seen *Dr. Strangelove or: How I Learned to Stop Worrying and Love the Bomb*, in which Peter Sellers' character's hand acts on its own (like giving an involuntary Nazi salute).

Disorder: Anosgnosia

What is it? This is an unusual reaction some people have to *hemiplegia*—the left- or right-side paralysis that often accompanies strokes. Affected people appear to be unaware of and will deny—vehemently—the paralysis. They can see and speak and retain their normal mental abilities, but they are unable to accept that half their body can't move. Some go so far as demonstrating that they *can* move by waving their arm around…except that it's not really moving. And they aren't trying to deceive anyone; they actually believe they're moving. The weirdest part: Some even deny the disability in *other* anosgnosia sufferers, insisting *they* aren't paralyzed, either.

Why? By law, all Washington, D.C. taxis must carry a broom and a shovel.

Disorder: Body Integrity Identity Disorder

What is it? BIID could be the most bizarre disorder in the medical world. People affected by it feel that one of their limbs, or part of it, does not belong on their body—and actively seek to get rid of it. They often can identify an exact spot where the limb "stops being theirs," and sometimes request needless amputations. But it's nearly impossible to get a doctor to remove one of your limbs simply because you no longer want it, so many victims simulate amputation, binding and hiding the unwanted limb, even to the point of fooling neighbors and employers for years. In the worst cases, people actually try to amputate the limbs themselves, sometimes with guns. In the late 1990s, Dr. Robert Smith of the Falkirk Royal Infirmary in Scotland caused a worldwide controversy when he performed elective amputations on people with BIID. "We have a number of individuals who have deliberately injured themselves," he said, "with train tracks and shotguns and have achieved amputation this way." That, he said, is far worse than his operations. But after public outcry, the hospital announced that Smith would no longer be performing amputations on people with the disorder.

* * *

LOST IN PARIS

In 2006 the British newspaper *The Guardian* reported that every year several Japanese tourists in France get what is called "Paris Syndrome." What's that? A severe psychological reaction to rude French people. "In Japanese shops, the customer is king," explained Bernard Delage, who helps Japanese families settle in France, "whereas here, store clerks hardly look at them." The symptoms can be extreme: In 2006 four people had to be "rescued" by the Japanese embassy in Paris and taken back home, including two women who locked themselves in their hotel room when they thought there was a plot against them. "Fragile travellers can lose their bearings," says psychologist Herve Benhamou. "When the idea they have of the country meets the reality of what they discover, it can provoke an emotional crisis."

Studies show: Cats dislike men with long dark beards.

GHOSTLY GALS OF TEXAS

Some people think Texas is the closest thing to heaven. Here are the stories of three late, lamented ladies who still won't leave...even after death.

Who: Sarah Morgan, a student at Texas Tech University in the city of Lubbock

Background: On December 6, 1967, the body of Sarah Morgan, a custodian at Texas Tech, was found hunched over an aquarium in Room 331 of the biology building. She had been murdered—nearly decapitated with a razor-sharp scalpel—and her key to the building had been stolen. Shortly afterwards, a physiology professor noticed that one of his premed students suddenly began "earning" great grades, where prior to the murder he was in danger of failing the course. The professor alerted the police, and an investigation soon revealed that the student had broken into the building to steal an upcoming test. When he was surprised by Morgan, he panicked and killed her. He was convicted and sent to prison (he was released in 1980).

The Haunting: Today, according to students, the ghost of Sarah Morgan is still walking the third-floor halls of Tech's Chemistry/Geosciences Building, sometimes peeking into the classrooms and shaking her head in disappointment. Room 331 is now used for administration, with carpet covering the linoleum—where bloodstains from the grisly event couldn't be washed away. On the anniversary of the murder and during exams, legend says, the stains grows as wet and dark as the day they were spilled.

Who: "Georgia" (real name unknown)

Background: Texas Wesleyan University is a private liberal arts university with fewer than 4,000 students. In the early 1990s, students in the theater department started seeing something during rehearsals.

The Haunting: The "something" the students saw was a woman —or the seeming ghost of a woman—in the theater. She was dressed in Victorian-era clothes and always kept to herself, staring straight ahead, her face expressionless. The students started calling her "Georgia." Theater director Mason Johnson and his students often saw her, and on occasion they had to pause rehearsals while she moved about or made noise. It was frightening and disruptive at the time, but whenever she appeared, the play they were rehearsing—usually an upbeat production like a musical or a comedy—became a big hit. The actors and staff, normally superstitious anyway before opening night, came to accept her as a good-luck omen. Texas "ghost specialist" and author Docia Schultz Williams speculates that the ghostly guest could be the spirit of Sarah Dobkins, the resident of a cemetery on which the university was built. She was buried in 1896, a year that would be consistent with the descriptions of her clothing.

Who: Josepha "Chipita" Rodriguez

Background: In 1863 Rodriguez owned an inn in the South Texas town of San Patricio, situated on the Arkansas River. In August of that year, the body of a horse trader named John Savage, who had been staying at the inn, was found not far downstream. He had been murdered with an axe and robbed, reportedly, of $600 in gold. Rodriguez, in her 60s, and a younger man by the name of Juan Silvera were accused of the crime. Details of the case are murky, but the best records suggest that there was flimsy evidence against them. Yet they were both convicted. Silvera received a five-year sentence for second-degree murder; Rodriguez, convicted of first-degree murder, was sentenced to hang. On November 13, she became just the second woman to be legally executed in the state of Texas (and the last before Karla Faye Tucker was put to death in 1998). Many people believe that racism had a lot to do with the verdict and the sentence—the victim was white, as were the judge and jury, and Rodriguez and Silvera were Mexican-Americans.

The Haunting: A number of legends have sprung up surrounding Rodriguez, with numerous articles, tales, songs, poems—and even two operas—written about her. Some say that Silvera was Rodriguez's illegitimate son; others that Rodriguez was killed for political reasons related to the ongoing Civil War; yet others believe that the hanging didn't kill her and that she was buried alive. The eeriest story says that Rodriguez's ghost roams the countryside around San Patricio, the noose still dangling from her neck. Others say that she has been seen and heard howling from the bottom of the Arkansas River. She only appears, according to legend, when a woman is wrongfully accused of a crime on Texas soil.

Extra: On June 13, 1985, Texas Governor Mark White put his official pen to a resolution that had just passed the state legislature. With its signing, Josepha "Chipita" Rodriguez was absolved of the charge of murder. (No word on whether her ghost got the news.)

Who: "The Houston Bride"

Background: In 1990 a beautiful socialite from Houston was devastated when her fiancé called their wedding off at the last minute. Bitter, embarrassed, and angry, she decided she needed some time alone, and went to Austin—specifically, to Room 29 on the fourth floor of the luxurious Driskill Hotel—to recover her composure. She spent a week on a shopping spree, using her ex-fiancé's credit cards. Guests reported seeing her arms laden with packages as she walked daily from the elevator to Room 29, until the hotel maids noticed she hadn't appeared for a few days. They checked her room and discovered her dead body in the bathtub; the jilted bride had shot herself with a pistol, using a pillow to muffle the noise.

The Haunting: Years later, two women at the hotel came back from a late night out and were snooping around the fourth floor, which they were told was closed for renovations. The next morning they complained to the front desk clerk that they had seen a pretty young lady carrying an armload of packages emerge from an elevator on the floor and go into Room 29. They had asked her, they told the clerk, if the renovations were bothering her. "No," the woman said. "It's not bothering me." The clerk said it was impossible, and showed them the room: Its walls lined were lined with plastic, it had no bed, and a disconnected sink surrounded by tools and spare parts sat in the middle of the floor. The women had seen the ghost of "The Houston Bride." That's just one of the many reported sightings of the unhappy, and dead, young lady.

***Sesame Street's* Big Bird is part turkey—his costume is made of dyed turkey feathers.**

LAST WISHES

Think it's tough planning ahead now? Try imagining what your dying wish will be. Here are some odd last requests from nine well-known people.

Eleanor Roosevelt: Fearful of being buried alive, the former first lady requested that her major veins be severed to eliminate the possibility of regaining consciousness after burial.

Harry Houdini: The famous escape artist asked to be buried in the "trick" coffin he used in his magic act—with letters from his mother tucked beneath his head.

William Shakespeare: Wanted his oldest daughter, Susanna, to inherit his favorite bed. He left his wife his "second best bed."

President Andrew Johnson: The 17th president asked to be wrapped in an American flag with a copy of the U.S. Constitution placed beneath his head.

J. Paul Getty: Requested a burial on the property of the Getty Museum in Malibu, California. However, his lawyers never applied for burial permits, so his remains had to be refrigerated and stored in a nearby mausoleum for *three years* until the necessary paperwork was completed. (Getty left his son J. Paul, Jr. "the sum of $500, and nothing else.")

W. C. Fields: Wanted a portion of his estate to be used for a "W. C. Fields College for orphan *white* boys and girls." (The request was never honored.)

P. T. Barnum: Wanted to keep the Barnum name from dying with him...so he left his grandson, Clinton Seeley, $25,000—on the condition that he change his middle name to Barnum. Seeley did.

Janis Joplin: Asked friends to have a farewell party for her at her favorite pub, the Lion's Share, in California—and left $2,500 in her will to finance it.

Albert Einstein: No one knows what his last wishes were. On his deathbed, he said something in German to his nurse—but she didn't speak German.

Leonardo da Vinci painted only 17 paintings—and some of them were unfinished.

HOW DO YOU SAY..."MULLET"?

Remember the mullet? That quintessential '80s haircut (think MacGyver, or Billy Ray Cyrus) was short on the top, long in the back...and ridiculed by people all over the world, as you'll see here.

- **France:** *Coupe à la Waddle* (named after a famous 1980s footballer who sported the 'do)
- **French Canadian:** *coupe Longueuil*
- **Sweden:** *hockeyfrilla*
- **Norway:** *hockeysveis*
- **Czech Republic:** *colek* ("newt")
- **Poland:** *Czeski pi karz* ("Czech football player hair")
- **Romania:** *chica*
- **Australia:** *Freddie Firedrill* (as if the haircut was interrupted by a fire alarm)
- **Chile:** *chocopanda* (referring to the typical haircuts of ice cream sellers)
- **Colombia:** *greña paisa*
- **Turkey:** *aslan yelesi* ("lion's mane")
- **Brazil:** *Chitãozinho e Xororó*
- **Croatia:** *fudbalerka* (referring to the soccer-player haircuts of the 1980s)
- **Denmark:** *bundesliga-hår*
- **Finland:** *takatukka* ("rear hair")
- **Germany:** *vokuhila* (short for *vorne kurz, hinten lang* "short in the front, long in the back")
- **Greece:** laspotiras ("mud-flap")
- **Hebrew:** *vilon* ("curtain")
- **Argentina:** *Cubano*
- **Japan:** *urufu hea* ("wolf hair")
- **Puerto Rico:** *playero* ("beachcomber")
- **Serbia:** *Tarzanka* ("Tarzan")
- **Italy:** *capelli alla tedesca* ("German-style hair"), or *alla MacGyver* (hair that resembles Richard Dean Anderson's from the TV show)
- **American terms:** B&T (bridge and tunnel), ape drape, Tennessee top hat, Kentucky waterfall, Missouri compromise

IN SEARCH OF NEW SPECIES

It's pretty amazing that after thousands of years of studying and keeping records of all the creatures with whom we share this planet, we still find new ones all the time. Here are some recent findings.

BACKGROUND

In December 2005, a team of scientists from the United States, Indonesia, and Australia launched an expedition into the Foja mountains in the west of New Guinea. "It's as close to the Garden of Eden as you're going to find on Earth," said co-leader Bruce Beehler. "It's beautiful, untouched, unpopulated forest. There's no evidence of human impact or presence up in these mountains." Not even the native New Guineans were familiar with the area. "The men from the local villages came with us," Beehler said, "and they made it clear that no one they knew had been anywhere near this area—not even their ancestors." The expedition discovered dozens of previously unknown plant and animal species, including 20 new frog species, one of which grows to only about 14 millimeters in length, four new butterfly species, and five new palm species. Some of the animal examples:

THE SMOKY HONEYEATER. Just 10 minutes into the trip Beehler saw a small honeyeater, a common bird in Australia and New Guinea—but this one was different. It had bright orange patches on either side of its face, which at the bottom hung down in flaps, like a chicken's "earlobes." "And then I suddenly woke up and saw that it was a new species," he said. "That's something we've never seen before. So that was pretty darned exciting." Though long known to locals, it was the first new bird species discovered by Western scientists in New Guinea in more than 60 years.

BERLEPSCH'S SIX-WIRED BIRD OF PARADISE. Ornithologists only knew this bird existed from skins kept by the 19th-century German ornithologist Hans von Berlepsch. Several expeditions had been launched to find it, and not one had, so the bird's habitat remained a mystery. But the second day into their trip Beehler and the other scientists watched in amazement as a male performed a mating dance for a female—right in their camp. That was another amazing thing about the trip: The area is so remote that many of the animals had likely never seen humans, and therefore were unafraid of them. The bird was named for Berlepsch, as well as the six wire-like feathers on the head of males which can be raised up for a mating display.

THE GOLDEN FRONTED BOWER BIRD. Famed scientist and author Jared Diamond rediscovered this species—also previously known only through late 19th century records—in 1979. But there were no photographs—until Beehler took one. And the photo showed it doing something odd: It was placing a blueberry on a stick protruding from a "bower" of sticks that it had made. Many other of the protruding sticks already had blueberries attached to them. Scientists concluded that the bird was decorating the bower to attract a mate.

THE GOLDEN-MANTLED TREE KANGAROO. Yes, that says "Tree Kangaroo." Believe it or not there are several species of these jungle-adapted, marsupial relatives of the kangaroo, some of which live in Northeast Australia and the rest in New Guinea. The newest—and rarest—member is the Golden Mantled, which was also found during the joint expedition. They have kangaroo-like faces, reddish-gold fur, and long, striped tails. And they jump from tree to tree…like kangaroos.

LONG BEAKED ECHIDNA. The expedition also found two new species of echidnas, or "spiny anteaters." It was a remarkable find, because echidnas are *monotremes*, a primitive type of mammal that lays eggs—and there are only three other monotremes known on Earth: the platypus, and two other echidna species. Echidnas are small (10 to 15 pounds), have light or dark brown fur, and have sharp spines like porcupines. They also have long, hairless, tubular snouts, with which they dig in the ground to eat earthworms (this species doesn't eat ants). Incredibly, when scientists found the first two specimens, they allowed the scientists to pick them up and carry them back to camp to study them, completely unafraid.

LET'S PLAY STREETWARS!

Adults can do some pretty odd things trying to recapture the carefree fun of a lost childhood.

SHOOT 'EM UP

Did you ever play "Assassin" in high school? That's the game where every player gets a squirt gun and instructions to kill another participant. Your mission: Kill your target before the person who has you as a target finds and kills you. When you kill someone, their intended target becomes your target, and the game continues until only one person—the winner—is still standing.

Assassin used to be limited to school yards, but that was until 2004, when a 29-year-old New York securities lawyer named Franz Aliquo got bored with his daily routine. "I began thinking I had a hell of a lot more fun when I was a kid," Aliquo told an interviewer in 2005. "And I thought, 'What is stopping me from having fun like that now?'" That year he and and a friend from high school, graphic designer Yutai Liao, decided to create a version of Assassin that adults could play on city streets during lunch breaks, after work, and on weekends. They called the game StreetWars and organized their first tournament on the streets of New York City.

BE CAREFUL OUT THERE

Having people run around New York waving (squirt) guns and blasting each other on city streets is a little bit much, especially after the 9/11 attacks. To avoid potential problems, Aliquo and Liao went to the New York police department to get permission to play the game, and also asked for help in drawing up the rules, to reduce the risk of public disturbances or being mistaken for real gun-toting thugs. On the advice of the police, Aliquo and Liao limited the number of participants and required players to use only brightly colored squirt guns and Super Soakers that look nothing like real firearms. (Water balloons are allowed, too.) They also declared subways, buses and bus stops, and other forms of public

A bird known as *Antpitta avis canis Ridgley* makes a "barking" noise that sounds like a dog.

transportation off limits. And to prevent the risk of participants losing their jobs, they also declared the one-block radius around players' workplaces as no-kill zones, too.

Getting the police department to sign off on the game was one thing; winning the approval of New York mayor Michael Bloomberg was another. "Aliquo could probably use some psychiatric help," Bloomberg said when he learned about the game. "If he calls one of the public hospitals, we'll try to arrange that. It is not funny in this day and age." Aliquo and Liao felt exactly the opposite—people needed games like StreetWars as a temporary escape from the bad news they confront in the headlines day after day. They went ahead with the game.

Seventy-five people signed up to play the first StreetWars, and it went off without a hitch. (Aliquo never did ask for psychiatric help.) Since then, Aliquo and Liao have organized tournaments in Vancouver, San Francisco, Los Angeles, London, and Vienna, with future games planned for Paris, Chicago, Rome, Tokyo, Montreal, Amsterdam, and even Reykjavik, Iceland.

KILL...OR BE KILLED

Here's how the game works:

• Each StreetWars tournament lasts for three weeks and is played 24 hours a day, seven days a week. It costs $50 to sign up and is open to anyone over the age of 18. When you sign up, you are required to submit a photograph of yourself as well as your home address, work address, and other contact information.

• Shortly before the game begins, players receive an e-mail telling them where to pick up their "assassination packet," containing the photo, addresses, and contact information of the player who has been designated their assassination target. Each player has a target and is the target for another player.

• As with Assassin, each player's mission is to kill their target and avoid being killed by the person who is targeting them. There are no restrictions on how the target can be hunted down. Stalk them on city streets? Ambush? A fake delivery to their front door? Anything goes. One assassin even staged a fake job interview and "killed" the target when they came to apply for the job.

• Players are allowed to defend themselves from assassins by

In Sweden, cockroaches are called *kackerlacka.*

shooting back and by using an umbrella to block the spray from the assassin's squirt gun. (Raincoats arc not allowed.) If the assassin's spray does not hit the target, the target survives the attack.

• If you succeed in killing your target, your victim hands over their assassination packet and their target becomes your next target. How do you know when you've won? When you kill your target and the packet they give you has *your* picture and contact information inside.

• If a winner is not determined at the end of three weeks, the game moves into a one-week sudden-death tournament where Aliquo, who calls himself "Supreme Commander," becomes the target, and the prize goes to the first person who can kill him as he and his escort of bodyguards move by limousine from one safe house to another.

WITH A TWIST

• Aliquo and Liao have added a few more twists to the game, too: Players are free to form teams and work together to kill their targets. But then they, too, become a single target of sorts—if the team captain is killed, the entire team is out of the game.

• There's also a group within the game called the League of Rogue Assassins. These assassins are free to kill the players in the game, but since they are not players they cannot be killed themselves. Don't feel like taking out your next target? You can hire a member of the League of Rogue Assassins to kill them for you.

• Another departure from Assassin: If you successfully defend yourself against an assassination attempt by shooting your assassin, the attack is thwarted...but the assassin doesn't die. They are free to attack you again at any time in the future.

SEE FOR YOURSELF

That's about all Uncle John has been able to piece together about the game; if you want to know more, you're just going to have to sign up and pay the $50. The official rules to StreetWars are a trade secret and are made available only to people who have signed up to play the game.

A Fla. baby was named Truewilllaughinglifebuckyboomermanifestdestiny (middle name: George).

IRONIC, ISN'T IT?

There's nothing like a good dose of irony to put the problems of day-to-day life into perspective.

NAME YOUR IRONY

In 1978 Giovanna D'Arco of Italy was sitting by her fireplace when a spark jumped out and ignited her clothes. Ironically, her name is Italian for "Joan of Arc." Related irony: In 1979 a Texas man named Stanley Stillsmoking was jailed for trying to steal cigarettes.

BREAKING WIND

Corfe Castle in Dorset, England, is one of the windiest places in Great Britain. In 2003 researchers set out to measure the exact wind speed and what effect it had on the castle. The study had to be postponed because it was too windy to set up the wind-speed recording equipment.

DID THEY YELL "THEATER"?

In 2002 firefighters were called to put out the flames at a factory in Neuruppin, Germany. What did the factory make? Fire extinguishers. But the fire extinguishers were filled with flame retardant at another facility, so at the time of the fire none of them worked.

DON'T FENCE ME OUT

In the late 1990s, Golden State Fence, a California company, was contracted to build a 14-mile fence in San Diego to prevent illegal immigrants from sneaking in. In 2006 Golden State was fined $4.7 million when 10 of the people hired to build the fence were discovered to be illegal immigrants.

LOOK IT UP—WAIT, YOU CAN'T

The legendary library of ancient Alexandria, Egypt, was burned to the ground by the invading Roman army in the 4th century. In 2002 a new $150 million library opened on the exact same site. Five months later, a short-circuit started a fire that destroyed the fourth floor.

CELEBRITY DEATH CONSPIRACIES

Our biggest stars are so much larger than life that it's hard for fans to comprehend their deaths. Maybe that's why people invent bizarre conspiracy theories to explain them.

THEORY: Comedian Andy Kaufman faked his own death.
DETAILS: In addition to playing Latka on the sitcom *Taxi*, Kaufman was known for outlandish stunts, including pretending to be a confused foreigner in his stand-up act, starting a fight with a pro wrestler on *Late Night With David Letterman*, and showing up for performances as an obnoxious lounge singer named Tony Clifton. But Kaufman wanted to pull an even bigger stunt. So, in 1983, he told friends he was going to fake his death and re-emerge 20 years later. In May 1984, he "died" of a rare form of lung cancer. Then what? There are several theories: 1) He moved to a quiet New Mexico town; 2) He changed his name to Steve Rocco and won a seat on the Orange County, California, school board. Rocco, a recluse who rarely leaves home, strongly resembles Kaufman and runs a Web site called andykaufmanlives.com; 3) He underwent plastic surgery and is actually actor Jim Carrey (Carrey played Kaufman in the movie *Man on the Moon*).
TRUTH: Kaufman's friends and fans thought lung cancer was just another joke, especially since he wasn't a smoker. But it wasn't. Kaufman went to a movie premiere in March 1984, painfully thin and nearly bald from radiation treatments. Mourners saw his body at his funeral. But perhaps Kaufman still wanted everyone to think he'd played a trick on them: Tony Clifton showed up at many Kaufman memorials. It wasn't revealed until years later that Clifton was played by Kaufman's friend Bob Zmuda, even while Kaufman was alive.

THEORY: A psychedelic trance-inducing machine drove Nirvana lead singer Kurt Cobain crazy and made him kill himself.
DETAILS: Cobain collaborated with Beat poet William S.

Burroughs on a 1992 album titled *The "Priest" They Called Him*. According to a Seattle-based group called "Friends Understanding Kurt" Burroughs gave Cobain a device called a "Dream Machine," which looks like a space heater outfitted with flashing colored disco lights. Like a powerful drug, the Dream Machine induces mind-altering trances when it's looked at, even through closed eyes. (It was invented in the 1960s by friends of Burroughs.) The Dream Machine made Cobain so crazy that he could only stop the hallucinations by shooting himself. The machine was discovered in the same room as Cobain's dead body in April 1994, but went unreported by both the police and the coroner's office.

TRUTH: A bizarre-looking device going unnoticed next to a body seems unlikely, as does the legitimacy of a group called "Friends Understanding Kurt" (check their initials). Sadly, a weird machine didn't kill Kurt Cobain—years of depression and drug abuse did.

Here are some more rumors of celebrity death conspiracies that have been widely circulated in books and magazines and on the Internet:

• **River Phoenix** didn't die of an accidental drug overdose on a Los Angeles sidewalk. He was poisoned by members of a cult that his parents were involved with.

• **James Dean** didn't crash his car while speeding. He was run off the road by CIA operatives. Reason: Dean was a Communist.

• **Paul McCartney** hired a hit man to kill Yoko Ono. The hit man shot John Lennon by mistake.

• **It wasn't an accident:** Considering her a threat to the throne, Queen Elizabeth II had MI6, the British Secret Service, kill Princess Diana.

• **Tupac Shakur and The Notorious B.I.G.** were not rival rappers at all. They were actually lovers who faked their own deaths to run away and be together.

• **Former Enron CEO Kenneth Lay** reportedly died of a heart attack in his bathroom in 2006. He actually faked his death to escape prison.

• **Marilyn Monroe** didn't die of an overdose. Fidel Castro had her killed and tried to have her former lover, attorney general Robert Kennedy, framed for it.

Experts say it's harder to tell a convincing lie to someone you find sexually attractive.

THE BEAST FROM THE BAD FILM SOCIETY

On page 213 we listed a few of the quirky films that members of the Bad Film Society love to hate. Here are a few more awful gems.

THE BRAIN THAT WOULDN'T DIE (1962)

"A major entry in the absurd trash genre. Love is a many splattered thing when a brilliant surgeon keeps the decapitated head of his fiancée alive after a car crash while he searches for a suitably stacked body onto which to transplant the head. The head talks so much, the Doc tapes her mouth shut!"

MONSTROSITY: THE ATOMIC BRAIN (1964)

A wealthy old crone hires a surgeon to transplant her brain into the body of a beautiful young woman...if one can be found. "Three gorgeous mademoiselles are imported as candidates but the evil doctor and his mutant assistant stray from their mission. There's zombies, and look out when a gal gets a cat's brain! Meow!"

THE UNDERTAKER AND HIS PALS (1966)

"An undertaker befriends a pair of motorcycle-riding, knife-wielding, psycho restaurant owners who kill people for body parts to use in their (gulp!) blue-plate daily specials. Business for the undertaker and cheap meat for the restaurant owners—sounds like a merger made in hell!"

INVISIBLE INVADERS (1959)

Operating from their outpost on the Moon, invisible aliens animate human corpses on Earth and sic them on the living. Meanwhile, a team of researchers hiding inside a cave race to stop the invasion before it's too late. "The big question is, 'Why do these aliens have to use corpses to do things?' In a few scenes, they seem physically capable enough to achieve their goals without the hindrance of rigor mortis, and you'd think invisibility would have more tactical value than looking creepy."

THE DEVIL BAT (1940)

Bela Lugosi plays Dr. Carruthers, a scientist who creates scents for a perfume company. He's also secretly creating a species of giant killer bats that he uses to murder his enemies. "Lugosi makes the bats hate a particular scent, which he then incorporates into an aftershave lotion and gives to his victims as a sample of an upcoming product. 'Rub a little here...on the tender part of your neck.'"

TROG (1970)

Joan Crawford's last—and worst—film. When a mysterious monster kills students in England, researchers trap it and bring it to anthropologist Dr. Brockton (Crawford), who discovers that the monster is actually Trog, the missing link that connects man to his ape ancestors. Rather than kill it as originally planned, Crawford decides to study Trog, but he escapes from the lab and kidnaps a small child. Who will find Trog first—Dr. Brockton or the cops?

ATTACK OF THE 50 FOOT WOMAN (1958)

"Transparent bald aliens in search of diamonds to power their spaceship turn a wealthy, jewelry-loving woman into a giant. Doctors chain her in the house and give her injections out of an elephant syringe. But she breaks out and heads for the bar where her cheating husband is smooching and plotting with Yvette Vickers (*Playboy*'s Miss July 1959). No happy ending here!"

HIDEOUS SUN DEMON (1959)

A scientist with radiation poisoning turns into an ugly homicidal lizard whenever he is exposed to the sun's rays. "Cult B-movie star Robert Clarke wrote, produced, directed, and starred in it the same way Orson Welles did in *Citizen Kane*...only not quite as good."

BEWARE! THE BLOB (1972)

A cheesy remake of the 1958 horror classic (which featured Steve McQueen in his first starring role). In this version, a technician brings back a frozen sample of the original blob (an ever-growing ball of goo from outer space), and when his wife inadvertently thaws it out, it takes off on another rampage. Directed by Larry Hagman of *Dallas* TV fame ("It's the film that J.R. shot!")

A person's sense of hearing becomes less sharp after overeating.

BEHEADING THE GOOSE

And other customs, rituals, and traditions from around the world.

RITUAL: The Beating of the Bounds
LOCATION: Llantrisant, Wales
STORY: Every seven years, the people of Llantrisant walk the seven-mile perimeter of their town and bounce young boys on large boundary stones along the way. In 2003 about 500 people took part in the "Beating of the Bounds," a ritual that dates back to 1346, when the town received its charter from King Edward I. The boundary lines were of the utmost importance, and the children were bounced on the stones so that they'd remember where the line was. The boys are picked up by the shoulders and feet by two men, and their backsides are bounced on a stone. "They used to do it quite hard," Howard Thomas of the Llantrisant Town Trust told the BBC, "because they always said that a bit of pain helped the memory go a long way. But it isn't done as hard as that now." He added, "But I do know some of the old men here who still remember the pain of it now." After the walk and the Bouncing of the Boys, the town has a party. "It is a real high point on the social calendar," said Thomas. "The town has been known to run dry on the Beating of the Bounds day."

RITUAL: Gansabhauet
LOCATION: Sursee, Switzerland
STORY: Believed to have its origin in a medieval religious festival, *Gansabhauet*, or "Beheading the Goose," takes place every year on November 11. Thousands of locals and tourists crowd into the little town's central square where, at 3:00 p.m., the "Gansabhauet guild" leads a procession of townspeople to a small stage. They bring with them a sword, an executioner's costume, and one large dead goose, which is then hung by its neck above the stage. Young men from the town draw lots to be able to put on the costume—a red robe and the golden sun mask—through which they can't see. Then they try to find the goose with the sword. When they do, they get to take one swipe to try to separate its head from

The clowns who portray Ronald McDonald are forbidden to reveal their true identities.

its body. The one who does it wins the (headless) goose, and the crowd continues to party through the evening and night.

RITUAL: Pon

LOCATION: Kemukus Mountain, Java

STORY: Seven times a year, thousands of Indonesians travel to Kemukus to visit the tomb of a revered prince to pray…and make love with strangers. Experts say the event, known as *Pon*, has its roots in the 15th century, but has been practiced in its more modern fashion since the late 19th century. Legend says that Prince Samodra, a famous Javanese ruler, died on the mountain. Pilgrims now make the journey to the mountain for the Friday night Pon, which falls every 35 days, to ask for good fortune. For their wishes to come true they must, according to tradition, come to seven Pons in a row—and have sex with a stranger each time. (It used to be done under trees in the open, but now there are thousands of small rooms for rent.)

CUSTOM: The Batula

LOCATION: Saudi Arabia

STORY: Most people know that Muslim tradition requires women to be covered in public or around men other than their husbands, sons, or brothers. But in some societies it goes much farther than that. Among some Bedouin tribes in Saudi Arabia, the faces of women are never seen by their husbands…*ever*. Or by their sons, or brothers—or in many cases even by their sisters and aunts. "I make sure to wear my veil day and night," a women in her twenties told the Arabic news agency Al-Jazeera, "so that there is no possibility of him seeing my face or how I look." And nearly all the women interviewed said they preferred it that way. "Covering my face is a hundred times better," said one woman, "than mixing with men and painting our faces with makeup."

RITUAL: Tandav

LOCATION: West Bengal, India

STORY: In April 2005, police in a West Bengal village reported that followers of the Hindu sect *Anand Marg* had exhumed freshly buried bodies, decapitated them, and performed a dancing ritual

In Florida, it is illegal to pass gas in a public place after 6:00 p.m. on Thursday.

with the skulls. Group members said they were performing the *Tandav*, or "Anger Dance," in which participants dance with daggers, live snakes, and human body parts in tribute to the Hindu god Shiva. According to Hindu mythology, the angry god danced the Tandav after the death of his wife, Sati. In this case, police arrested members of Anand Marg, which means "Pathway to Bliss," after they had dug up the bodies of an elderly man, a 35-year-old woman, and a 5-year-old boy who had died just hours earlier.

BELIEF: Pontius Pilate was Scottish
LOCATION: Perthshire, Scotland
STORY: In 10 B.C., the Roman Army of Caesar Augustus was camped near the town of Fortingall during one of the first Roman invasions of Scotland. While there, the legend says, a Roman ambassador had a "dalliance" with a local girl, and a son resulted. The child's name: Pontius Pilate. The ambassador took the woman and child to Rome, and the boy eventually grew up to be the governor of Judea—and later ordered the crucifixion of Jesus. Scottish tradition has it that when Pilate died, he was returned "home" to Scotland for burial. Not far from Fortingall is a *cairn*, or ancient burial site, known in Scottish Gaelic as *Uaigh an t-Seanalair*, or "The General's Grave." Locals have a different name for it: "Pontius Pilate's grave."

CUSTOM: The Super Jews
LOCATION: Amsterdam, The Netherlands
STORY: For decades fans of the leading Dutch soccer team Ajax Amsterdam were taunted by rival fans with anti-Semitic slurs because of the city's long Jewish history. In response, many Ajax fans started referring to themselves as "Jews"—though few of them were Jewish. Some went as far as waving Israeli flags at the games. Some went further...having Stars of David tattooed to their foreheads. In 2005 the president of the club issued a statement officially asking the fans to stop referring to themselves as "Jews" because it was actually provoking *more* anti-Semitism from rival teams. One 19-year-old fan, Ilona Korfer, who wears a Star of David necklace to the games, told reporters she wouldn't be stopping. "I don't see the problem—it's part of the game."

In 1984, a Canadian farmer began renting ad space on his cows.

THE TWISTER TEST

The truth about tornadoes can be stranger than fiction. Can you tell the difference?

PATH OF DESTRUCTION

Every year about 1,000 tornadoes whirl across the United States. Most last only a few minutes with winds of less than 112 mph, but some have been clocked at over 200 mph—the fastest winds in nature. Stories abound of the strange things tornadoes have done, and we've assembled a few of them here. But one of them isn't true. Can you spot the phony?

1. A tornado once swept a toddler out of his bed and set him down safely 50 feet away without removing his blankets.

2. A woman walked into her front yard to find a sturdy 40-foot tree gone—even though the lawn furniture around it remained exactly where she had left it.

3. A tornado picked up a tie rack with 10 ties attached and carried it for 40 miles without removing a single tie.

4. While a couple slept, a tornado lifted their cottage, then dropped it into a nearby lake. They remembered only a loud bang before they woke up in deep water.

5. Tornadoes have plucked all the feathers off chickens.

6. After a tornado, you'll sometimes find straw sticking out of telephone poles.

7. A tornado once scooped up five horses that were hitched to a rail, then set the whole arrangement down intact, the horses uninjured, a quarter-mile away.

8. A large rooster that was caught in a tornado got sucked into a small earthenware pitcher with only his head sticking out.

9. After a tornado killed migrating ducks at a bird refuge, it rained dead ducks 40 miles away.

10. In 1987, 12 children walking home from their school in China were sucked up by a tornado and safely deposited 12 miles away in sand dunes.

Answer: #8. (Tornadoes don't suck larger objects into smaller ones.)

STRANDED!

The Adventures of Robinson Crusoe is a wonderful story, but would you really want to be stranded on a raft in the middle of the ocean? Here are four true stories of shipwrecks and castaways.

THE *AURALYN*

Maurice and Maralyn Bailey were aboard their 31-foot sloop *Auralyn* on their way to the Galapagos Islands on March 4, 1973, when their boat was struck by a wounded sperm whale. The *Auralyn* started sinking—an hour later it was gone. They left the ship in a four-foot inflatable life raft tied to a nine-foot inflatable dinghy. They had all their survival supplies with them with one exception—they forgot the fishing gear. Still, they had a 20-day supply of food and water.

Three hundred miles from the Galapagos Islands, the Baileys spent three nights rowing as hard as they could trying to reach land, but it was futile and they gave up, allowing the current to sweep them farther out to sea. On the eighth day, a ship passed nearby but failed to see them, and they wasted three of their six flares. When food ran out, they survived on sea turtles. Then, using turtle scraps as bait and safety pins as hooks, they were able to catch some fish. To pass the time, they played cards and dominoes.

Don't Pass Me By

On the 25th night, another ship went by without seeing either their flare or their flashlight. On the 37th day, another ship passed, and two days later another one. They set off an improvised smoke bomb—kerosene-soaked cloth strips in a turtle shell—but weren't spotted. Another ship went by on the 45th day, but they couldn't get their "smoke bomb" to light. One of the main float tubes of their raft collapsed on the 55th day and couldn't be repaired—after that, they needed to pump it up every 20 minutes. Gradually, their health began to fail.

In June torrential rains came, providing fresh water to drink but the deteriorating canopy above their raft failed to keep them dry. By their 100th day afloat, they had to eat the birds that constantly landed on their raft. They even began catching and eating sharks. On June 30, a Korean ship appeared and saw them waving their jackets. Amazingly, after 118 days at sea, they were able to climb aboard under their own power.

L'HERETIQUE

Alain Bombard was a 27-year-old French doctor who thought it strange that shipwreck survivors on life rafts tend to die quickly. A person can live up to six weeks without food and go up to 10 days without water, so why do so many castaways die within days of being set adrift? The common belief was that they drank salt water, which robs their body's tissues of water. Bombard disagreed. He felt sure that the reason people died was because they waited until their bodies were already dehydrated before drinking the seawater out of desperation.

In 1952 Bombard set out to prove that the ocean will support a castaway indefinitely and that drinking seawater is not detrimental to one's health. He decided to cross the Atlantic Ocean alone in a rubber raft without food or water, taking only emergency supplies in a sealed container to be used as a last resort.

Bombard set out from the Strait of Gibraltar in a 15-foot inflatable sailboat dubbed *L'Hérétique*, French for "The Heretic." He sailed first to Casablanca, which took a week, then to the island of Grand Canary, which took 18 days. From there, he set out to cross the Atlantic, leaving on October 19, 1952.

Recipe for Survival

Bombard caught fish, drank seawater, and even ate a bird that landed on his boat. By straining seawater through fabric, he collected plankton, which provided vitamin C and warded off scurvy. Bad weather resulted in constant bailing, but storms brought fresh rainwater, a welcome change after drinking nothing but saltwater for the first 23 days. He lost weight, began to suffer from saltwater boils, got diarrhea, and became depressed.

On December 6, he wrote out his last will and testament. Then, 53 days after leaving Grand Canary, he encountered the freighter *Arakaka*. But instead of asking to be rescued, Bombard only wanted to know where he was—and his location turned out to be 600 miles away from where he thought he was. It meant he

In 1997, 4,824 British people were treated for injuries caused by opening cans of corned beef.

had at least another 20 days to go. Bombard was miserable, but he refused all assistance except the offer of a hot shower and fresh batteries for his radio. Then he went back to his rubber raft.

Christmas Present

Two weeks later, he made landfall on Barbados. It was the day before Christmas. After surviving on nothing but fish, seawater, rain, and a bird, Bombard had lost 55 pounds—a little less than a pound per day, typical for castaways. He developed a slight case of anemia, he had diarrhea, weak spells, blurry vision, he'd lost of a few toenails, and had a skin rash. But overall he was in fairly good health. And he proved that a person can indeed survive on salt water (most survival experts still insist that it's better to drink nothing at all).

THE *PETRAL*

In August 1985, Gary Mundell set out to sail solo from California to Hawaii aboard his boat *Petral*. Everything went well for the first few days. But then one night, he was jolted awake by a bump. Getting up to investigate, he discovered that the boat had run aground on Caroline Island, one of the most remote pieces of real estate in the Pacific. Mundell had gone to bed thinking the island was at least 15 miles away. Had he miscalculated? It didn't matter now—he was stranded on a deserted island. The island, seven miles long and one mile wide, was completely uninhabited. He couldn't get the boat free and couldn't reach anyone on the radio.

He transferred absolutely everything movable from the boat to the shore using his inflatable raft, and set up camp under a grove of coconut trees. As the days passed, Mundell found plenty of food: coconuts, crabs, and fish. He caught rainwater in his sail and filled the many discarded bottles and jugs that washed up on the beach until he had more than 60 gallons. He never had to ration water—and even filled his raft and had a bath.

Setting Priorities

After the first month passed without spotting a ship or plane, Mundell considered sailing to the nearest inhabited island 460 miles away, but decided to stay put…where at least he had food and water.

On the 50th day, he spotted a ship a few miles away. Taking no

Hot stuff: Oysters can change gender according to the temperature of the water they live in.

chances, he did everything he could to get the crew's attention—flares, smoke signals, and mirror flashes. The ship, the French research vessel *Coriolis*, answered with their searchlight. Rescue! Once aboard the *Coriolis*, he discovered how he had miscalculated his location: he hadn't—Caroline Island was actually 15 miles east of its charted position.

THE *SPIRIT*

In 1974 Ray and Ellen Jackson, experienced sailors, bought a 42-foot yacht called *Spirit* and spent the next year outfitting her with every safety feature money could buy. They left California in 1975 and cruised 8,000 miles all over the Pacific. But after Ray injured his back in Hawaii, they decided to fly home and asked Ellen's brother, Jim Ahola, to sail the boat back to California.

Ahola had considerable experience with the *Spirit* but still decided to hire more experienced help, Bruce Collins to captain and Durel Miller to crew. His girlfriend, Camilla Arthur, and her friend, Nancy Perry, asked to come along, too. On September 12, 1976, the *Spirit* left Hawaii bound for California.

Sinking Spirit

On the morning of September 27, without warning, there was a huge bang and the ship keeled over. Had the boat been hit by whales? Did it strike floating debris? Had a submarine surfaced beneath them? They never found out. Although the *Spirit* righted itself, there was a hole in the bow and it quickly began to sink. Flying debris had smashed the radio—so no SOS could be sent. There were two life rafts on board, but the survival kits had been washed away. Collins, Ahola, and Arthur got into one raft and Miller and Perry took the other. Five minutes later the *Spirit* was gone. They were 750 miles from land.

The castaways tied the two rafts together and distributed the meager supplies. They had no food, no fishing gear, and little water. Eleven hours later, the tether broke and the two rafts drifted apart. The raft carrying Miller and Perry drifted for 22 days. Miller was an experienced seaman but Perry was a complete stranger to the sea and was debilitated by seasickness. By the 12th day, she was incoherent and helpless. By the time they were rescued, she had lost 43 pounds (she only weighed 113 pounds to

The average American woman thinks about politics 12 min. a day. Average man: 6 min.

start with). Miller lost 55 pounds but cared for her constantly, kept a lookout, and flagged down a ship called the *Oriental Financier* on the 22nd day.

Another Survivor

A subsequent search for the second raft covered nearly 200,000 square miles. On the sixth day of the search it was found, but with only one survivor on board, Captain Bruce Collins—Ahola and Arthur were dead. Collins reported that they ran out of fresh water on the 12th day and he had survived by drinking the foul-tasting rainwater he collected from the canopy of the raft. The others had refused to drink it, fearing it was poisonous. Ahola died on the 19th day. His death devastated his girlfriend, and she died two days later.

Camilla's mother sued the Avon life raft company for failing to provide enough survival gear to keep her daughter alive. A court awarded her $70,000, but the company appealed. It was settled out of court.

* * *

ODD (CANADIAN) WORLD RECORDS

• RCMP and youth organizations in Ottawa recently attempted to break the world record for the largest group hug.

• In June 1993, the Hospital Auxiliary of the Kitchener-Waterloo Hospital filled a bowl with a world-record 2,390 kg. of strawberries.

• In Regina, Saskatchewan, Brent Shelton and John Ash performed CPR for 130 hours from October 28 to November 2, 1991, to set the world record in "marathon cardiopulmonary resuscitation."

• Canadian "Fast" Eddie McDonald holds three Guinness records in yo-yo: He performed 35 tricks in one minute on July 22, 1999, to grab the fastest yo-yo trick record; he looped his yo-yo 8,437 times in one hour on July 14, 1990, for the one-hour speed record; and he took the marathon yo-yo looping record on October 14, 1990, by performing 21,663 loops in three hours.

Oops! Herbicide use has created at least 48 "superweeds" that are resistant to chemicals.

WEIRD AUSTRALIA

More strange news, this time from the land down under.
(Where women glow and men chunder.)

HAIR TODAY...

In 2006 Rodney Peterson lost his job as a baggage handler at the Melbourne Airport for stealing things from travelers' luggage. What did he steal? Hair from women's clothing and hairbrushes. Police found over 80 plastic bags in Peterson's home, each containing a few follicles and labeled with the owner's name.

BUSTED

Therese Perry stole a bus from a Sydney depot in 1993. She didn't take it for a joyride—she drove the regular route, picking up and dropping off passengers at scheduled stops on time. Asked why, Perry later explained "Because I thought I was a bus driver." In 2005, a 15-year-old Melbourne boy was arrested after he stole city buses on two occasions and drove their usual routes. He told police it was practice for when he became a bus driver when he grew up.

TASMANIAN DEVIL

In 2006, a 30-year-old-man from Tasmania on vacation in Melbourne visited the city zoo. Just after screaming "I've come to kill a gorilla!" he jumped into the ape enclosure. He repeatedly kicked and punched a 220-pound gorilla before being subdued by zookeepers, who locked the man in a cage.

AUSTRALIAN FOR "STUPID"

In 2005, a 21-year-old man at a bar in Murdoch wanted to find a way to get drunk as quickly as possible without all the trouble of having to drink several pints of beer. He fashioned an electric-drill powered pump, connected it to a beer keg, and connected that to a helmet, which held a hose that led the beer directly down his throat. He turned on the drill, activating the pump; the beer shot down the man's throat with such force that it tore a four-inch hole in his stomach.

World's tallest identical twins: Michael and James Lanier—they're both 7'4" tall.

KEEP OUT: GENIUS AT WORK

Ever wonder what inspires brilliance?
It may not be what you think.

LUDWIG VAN BEETHOVEN poured pitchers of cold water over his head to keep himself focused and awake as he composed from dusk until dawn.

JACK KEROUAC knelt in prayer before writing, then wrote by candlelight.

ALEXANDER GRAHAM BELL insisted on working all night long...and alone. He invented the telephone under the cloak of darkness. Bell said, "To take night from me is to rob me of my life."

COLETTE methodically picked fleas from her cat before she began to write.

CHARLES DICKENS couldn't begin to write until all the furniture in his house was in the proper arrangement. He always wrote in blue ink on blue-gray paper. Every morning he arose at 7:00, bathed in cold water, and wrote two to four pages by lunchtime.

GERTRUDE STEIN and **RAYMOND CARVER** both liked to write in their cars.

FELIX MENDELSSOHN composed entire symphonies completely in his head. When a friend came to visit and was about to excuse himself because Mendelssohn was working, Mendelssohn welcomed him into his room, saying he was only copying out music. "But he was not copying," as the friend told it, "for there was no paper but that on which he was writing. The work whereupon he was busy was the *Overture in* C *Major*. There was no looking forwards or backwards, no comparing, no humming over; the pen kept going steadily on, without pausing, and we never ceased talking. The copying out, therefore, as he called it, meant that the whole composition, to the last note, had been so worked out in his mind, that he beheld it there as though it had been actually lying before him."

THOMAS JEFFERSON and **VIRGINIA WOOLF** both wrote standing up.

ALEX HALEY, the author of *Roots*, booked passage on a freighter at the beginning of each new project. He'd write the entire book at sea, with no distractions.

MARCEL PROUST lined the walls of his writing room with cork to the keep sounds from the outside world…outside.

RAYMOND CHANDLER typed his mystery novels on narrow slips of paper that were the width of a paperback novel turned on its side. This limited him to no more than 10 to 15 lines per page and forced him to put "a bit of magic"—an interesting image, funny quip, or clever bit of dialogue—on every piece of paper.

WALLACE STEVENS, the acclaimed poet, claimed he wrote his best while walking to and from his job as an executive for the Hartford Insurance Company in Connecticut, a position he held for 40 years.

ANTHONY TROLLOPE, a British novelist of the 1800s, wrote for three hours every day, from 5:30 a.m. to 8:30 a.m. He kept a watch in front of him to make sure he wrote 250 words every 15 minutes. (He was so disciplined that if he finished a novel before 8:30, he took out fresh paper and started a new one.)

DAME EDITH SITWELL, the British poet, used to lie in an open coffin before writing.

AGATHA CHRISTIE wrote anywhere and everywhere, and that often included in the bathtub, with a basket of her favorite food—apples—close by.

50,000 people worldwide are killed by snakebites each year, most of them cobras.

BEYOND BIZARRE

News so strange that you can only say, "Huh?"

YOU'RE KILLING ME HERE

In November, 2006, a young woman in the town of Loerrach, Germany, climbed to the roof of the town hall with plans to jump off and commit suicide. A group of homeless people on the sidewalk below started yelling to her, trying to talk her down. Then a group of young people started heckling her—encouraging her to jump. That led to an argument between the two groups, which led to an all out brawl. More than 35 police officers were needed to break up the riot. In the meantime, the woman was talked off the roof by police.

MOOOON WALK

Pop superstar Michael Jackson gave a court deposition in June, 2006, regarding a lawsuit against him by a former business partner. In the course of questioning Jackson—who owns the publishing rights to some of the Beatles' songs—told the ex-partner's lawyer that his manager never gave him any money, and that his only spending money is from the sale of cows on his Neverland ranch. "So all your cash, whenever you need cash to shop or whatever, comes from the cows?" the lawyer asked. "Yes, believe it or not," answered Jackson.

HELL'S SNOW ANGELS

One night in February, 2005, a young couple in a car parked behind an antique store outside of Chicago were doing what young couples sometimes do in parked cars. The 19-year-old Ball State student and her recently-returned Navy boyfriend had just finished their "business" when an Illinois state trooper shined his flashlight into the car and yanked the door open. Trooper Jeremy Dozier, 33, ordered the couple—naked—out of the car. Then he made them lie down in the snow (still naked) and make "snow angels." When the couple later reported the humiliating incident, Dozier admitted not only to this one, but also to an earlier incident when he ordered another couple to strip naked and run to a

World's shortest stage play: Samuel Beckett's *Breath*—35 seconds of screams & heavy breathing.

ditch and urinate (they kept running, and got away). Dozier pleaded guilty to official misconduct, and was sentenced to 30 months probation, $1,000 in fines, and 200 hours of community service. He is no longer a police officer.

WHILE YOU WERE IN

Prisoner Gary Stephen escaped from Castle Huntly prison near Dundee, Scotland, in November, 2006, to see his 35-year-old girlfriend, Tracy Miller, whom he hadn't seen in six months. Upon finding her four months pregnant, a despondent Stephen called the police and asked them to take him back to jail. (They did.)

A VEERRRY STRANGE PERSON

On the night before Thanksgiving, Drew Gagnon of Mahopac, New York, broke into a neighbor's barn, and one by one held down the neighbor's three goats...and spray-painted their genitals bright orange. Then he left porno magazines in the animals' stalls. His bizarre actions were designed to harass the goats' owner, Gail Fiero, with whom he was involved in a feud. Gagnon, 37, was charged with burglary, criminal trespass, and three counts of animal cruelty. The goats, Fiero told police, became ill because they had eaten some of the magazines' pages. (But they were okay.)

THE NOT SO REVEREND

In 2002 Reverend Howard Douglas Porter's truck went off the road in a rural area near Fresno, California, and struck an oak tree. Porter was alright, but his elderly friend, Frank Craig, was crippled in the crash. In 2004 Reverend Porter was driving once again with Craig when the truck flew off the road and landed in an irrigation canal. Porter was okay this time, too—but the 85-year-old Craig was drowned. In 2006 police arrested Reverend Porter for murder, attempted murder, and embezzlement. They say they have evidence that Porter tried to kill Craig in the first crash and *did* kill him in the second. Why? Money. Porter's church was the main beneficiary of Craig's estate and Porter wanted to get access to the man's $4.1 million fortune.

1 in 25 coffins from the 16th century has been found to have scratch marks on the inside.

THE SAGA OF SEALAND

Wouldn't you love to own your own country? Think of it: You'd get to make all the laws, and everyone would have to worship you. Here's the story of one of the strangest "countries" in the world.

E MARE LIBERTAS

On September 2, 1967, a former British Army major by the name of Paddy Roy Bates moved his family six miles off the coast of southwest England—onto a concrete and steel platform on the North Sea—and declared their new home to be "the country of Sealand." He then crowned himself H.R.H. Prince Roy of Sealand, created the country's own postage stamps, passports and currency—the Sealand dollar—and even gave it a national motto, *E Mare Libertas*, or "From the Sea, Freedom."

FOUNDING FATHER

Roy Bates was once the youngest major in the British army, fighting with the Royal Fusiliers in North Africa and Italy during World War II. When he returned home to Essex, England, he made a fortune owning factories, a fishing fleet, and (his own words) "a few other businesses." One of those other businesses: a "pirate" commercial radio station called Radio Essex. At the time (1965), all the radio airwaves in the British Isles were controlled by the state-owned British Broadcasting Corporation, and "pirate" radio was immensely popular. Bates set up his 24-hour radio station on Fort Knock John, a deserted World War II sea fort in the Thames River estuary. But since Fort Knock John was within England's three-mile territorial limit, the British government quickly shut it down and fined Bates for operating a radio station without a license.

Not to be defeated, Bates moved his operation six miles offshore (and outside U.K. territorial waters) to Roughs Tower, an old anti-aircraft platform—abandoned since the end of World War II—that sat on two 60-foot-tall concrete pylons off the southeast coast of England. With the addition of electrical generators, mobile phones, some comfy furniture, and a team of professional security guards, the royal family—Prince Roy, his wife (Princess) Joan, and son (Prince Regent) Michael—declared it their own nation and made themselves at home in the world's smallest principality.

TROUBLE AT SEALAND

Prince Roy soon discovered that once you lay claim to an abandoned outpost and call it a country, you risk opposition from real-life governments, as well as pirates who want to lay claim to your claim. The Royal Navy tried to evict Bates from Sealand—but abandoned the attempt when they were met with warning shots fired from the tower. Following the incident, the British government brought legal action against the Bateses—but the case was dropped in 1968 when the courts ruled that the government had no jurisdiction outside British territorial waters. After that, the British authorities contented themselves with making life for the Bateses miserable during customs inspections whenever they set foot on the British mainland. But the next invasion came from an unexpected quarter.

Every prince needs a cabinet of ministers to help run his country, so Bates appointed one Professor Alexander G. Achenbach, a German national and Sealand resident, as Prime Minister. Then, in August 1978, while Prince Roy and Princess Joan were away, Achenbach staged a palace coup. Joined by a number of Dutch citizens, Achenbach captured the Bateses' son Michael, held him hostage, and declared himself the new Prince of Sealand.

THIS MEANS WAR

Bates wasn't about to take that without a fight. After convincing his former P.M. to release his son several days later, Bates assembled a few associates—his "army"—to retake the platform. In a daring helicopter assault, he and his men stormed the fort and captured Achenbach and his gang—and held them as prisoners of war. Bates released the prisoners when "the conflict" ended (he said it was the right thing to do, according to the Geneva Conventions). But he kept one hostage: a German lawyer named Gernot Pütz. The fact that Pütz held a Sealand passport, Bates said, made him guilty of treason, and he wouldn't be freed until he paid an £18,000 fine. The move actually strengthened Bates's position in the world of nations, because when the German government petitioned the British for Pütz's release, the Brits would have nothing to do with it, citing the 1968 ruling in which Sealand was declared outside of British jurisdiction. The Germans finally sent an envoy to Roughs Tower. After several weeks Bates released Pütz, saying that the visit amounted to a formal recognition of Sealand by Germany. (German officials disagreed.)

ACHENBACH'S REVENGE

Roy of Sealand continued to rule his strange little country for the next 30 years, thwarting several takeover attempts by makeshift "armies" and making the news numerous times in humorous and not-so-humorous ways. The worst came in 1997, through the unlikely route of the murder of fashion icon Gianni Versace and the suicide of his killer, Andrew Cunanan. The two were found on a Miami houseboat, which investigators found was registered to a German businessman...who held a Sealand passport and diplomatic license plates. Bates didn't understand how that was possible; he had given away a few hundred passports to friends over the years, but the German wasn't one of them. (And he'd *never* made any "diplomatic license plates.") As he would soon find out, the culprit was Achenbach.

EXILE ON MAIN STREET

Bates's old nemesis had returned to Germany in 1978, and had then set up a Sealand "government in exile," declaring himself "Chairman of the Privy Council." He had retired from the organization in 1989, but it continued without him, and the Versace investigation revealed that by 1997 Achenbach's organization had sold an estimated 150,000 fake Sealand passports at $1,000 each. Then the passports had been used by drug smugglers, identity-fraud criminals—and worse. One group from Spain had issued Sealand Army uniforms and attempted to buy 50 tanks and 10 fighter jets, in order to resell them to Sudan for $50 million. The Bateses were found to have no link to the crooks, and they expressed their dismay at finding that their "country" had been so misused. "They're stealing our name, and they're stealing from other people," Joan Bates said. "How disgusting can you get?"

Electrifying statistic: Lightning strikes men about seven times more often than it does women.

ROY SAILS ON

In 1999 Bates passed the rule of Sealand to his son Michael. In 2000 they made international news again, this time with the announcement that the site would become a "datahaven"—basically a pirate internet business. With Roy's blessing, Prince Regent Michael and a few associates created HavenCo, a secure computer power and internet data storage space (eerily reminiscent of the fictional haven created by novelist Neal Stephenson in his bestseller *Cryptonomicon*). The company got publicity all over the world and even attracted some high-profile customers (the Dalai Lama's Tibetan government-in-exile Web site was hosted by HavenCo). But, although it still exists, the company never really took off.

Today Prince Roy and Princess Joan live in England; Prince Regent Michael, who now runs Sealand, also lives on land. In June 2006, Sealand suffered a disastrous fire; the one person aboard the platform at the time was rescued by a Royal Air Force helicopter. But the Royal family didn't let this latest obstacle stop them. With a projected cost of fire repairs and renovations expected to top $1 million, the Web site Sealandgov.org gives regular and cheerful updates about the rebuilding progress. And a special bonus that might help the Bateses' financial fortunes: film director Mike Newell (*Four Weddings and a Funeral* and *Harry Potter and the Goblet of Fire*), is slated to direct a film, due out in 2008, about Roy and Joan Bates—entitled *Sealand.*

* * *

SOLID FUEL

Lauri Venøy, a Norwegian businessman, believes he has found the renewable energy source of the future: human fat. His idea is to use the fatty by-products left over from liposuction operations and convert them into biodiesel fuel. Where does Venøy intend to farm the fat from? The United States, where approximately 60% of the populace is overweight. He's made a deal with Jackson Memorial Hospital in Miami, Florida, to obtain all of its extracted fat, estimated at 3,000 gallons per week. "Maybe we should urge people to eat more so we can create more raw material for fuel," Venøy said.

YOU WANT A PIECE OF ME?

Organ transplants are a miracle of science and an incredible act of human kinship: A part of one person can help another person live or live better. But it's not just hearts and livers anymore—it seems like doctors can transplant nearly anything *these days.*

BODY PART: Face
RECIPIENT: Isabelle Dinoire
STORY: In May 2005, 38-year-old Dinoire of Valenciennes, France, was depressed and took a large dose of sleeping pills. Her dog tried to wake her up, but couldn't, and became more and more alarmed. In its zeal to rouse Dinoire, the dog inadvertently mauled her, destroying her nose, lips, and chin. Dinoire recovered, but she could barely eat and couldn't speak at all. Two surgeons from Amiens, France, took an interest in the case and proposed a triangular skin graft. The tissues, muscles, arteries, and veins would be taken from the face of a brain-dead donor and transplanted onto Dinoire. The skin had to come from a living donor because live tissue ensured proper blood flow. Skin from somewhere else on Dinoire's body would be too different in color and texture. The five-hour procedure took place in November 2005, and it worked. Dinoire's appearance isn't exactly what it used to be—it's more of a hybrid between her old face and the donor's face. (Her nose is narrower and her mouth is fuller.) She still can't move her lips very well, but she's able to speak, eat, and even smoke again. (After all, she's French.)

BODY PART: Head
RECIPIENT: Some monkeys
STORY: On March 4, 1970, a team of scientists at Case Western Reserve University in Ohio, led by Dr. Robert J. White, successfully attached the head of one rhesus monkey to the body of another rhesus monkey. First, White cooled the brain to the point where all neural activity stopped. It would still be chemically "alive" if the volume of blood was kept at a normal level. This was

Paul McCartney wrote the Beatles song "Martha My Dear" about his sheepdog, Martha.

achieved by carefully cauterizing all the arteries and veins in the head. Then the old head—brain and skull intact—was grafted onto the new body...and it was still alive. After the monkey recovered from the anesthesia, it tried to bite one of the researchers, but it could eat, hear, smell, and follow things with its eyes, meaning all nerves were intact with the brain. It lived for about four hours. Thirty-one years later, White tried the experiment again and this time was able to get the new body breathing on its own, controlled by the transplanted brain, allowing the monkey to live for eight days. Neither the 1970 nor 2001 experiment resulted in the attachment of the spinal cord, so neither monkey could voluntarily control the action of their new bodies. White is now retired, but has a standing offer to perform the procedure on a human being. (So far, no takers.)

BODY PART: Hand
RECIPIENT: Matthew Scott
STORY: In 1985, 24-year-old Scott, a paramedic from New Jersey, severely damaged his left hand from a blast by an M80 firecracker. It had to be amputated and Scott was fitted with a prosthetic hand. In 1998, Scott decided he wanted a real hand. Hand transplants weren't unheard of—the procedure had been attempted before—but it had never been successful in the long term. That's because it's one of the most complicated surgeries conceivable: the hand contains 27 bones, 28 muscles, three nerves, two arteries, tendons, veins, soft tissue, and skin. To get the new hand to perform normally would be more akin to performing several dozen micro-surgeries. The surgery was performed in 1999 at the Jewish Hospital in Louisville, Kentucky, by University of Louisville surgeons Warren Breidenbach and Tsu-Min Tsai. Using a hand from a 58-year-old male cadaver, it took a surgical team of 17 people nearly 15 hours to attach the new hand (heart transplants take about seven). After the surgery, Dr. Breidenbach told the media "it could be at least a year if we know if it's a good functioning hand. We hope for a good grip and some sensation of hot and cold." Amazingly, Scott could move his new fingers just a week later. In April 2000, he threw out the first pitch at a Philadelphia Phillies game. And amazingly, after just one year Scott could sense temperature, pressure, and pain...and could use his new hand to write, turn pages, and tie his shoelaces.

September 22 is *Happy Days* actor Scott Baio's birthday *and* Elephant Appreciation Day.

VIDEO GAMES

Basically, all video games are pretty weird. After all, who would have thought a multibillion-dollar industry could be built on the backs of an Italian plumber and a yellow circle that eats white pills? These get our award for weirdest of the weird.

• **Wild Woody** (1995) A magic totem pole brings to life a pencil that belongs to an treasure-hunting archaeologist. In order to save the world, the pencil must recover artifacts from around the globe.

• **Pesterminator: The Western Exterminator** (1990) The object of the game is to kill termites. The player assumes the identity of Kernel Kleanup, the exterminator mascot of a tiny, real-life pest control company called Western Exterminators.

• **Captain Novolin** (1992) Captain Novolin is a diabetic superhero (named after a brand of insulin). Object of the game: Novolin must defeat alien invaders who have turned themselves into dangerous sugary snacks. Bonus: Extra points are awarded for correctly answering trivia questions about diabetes.

• **Baby Boomer** (1989) To prevent a baby from crawling near perilous pitfalls such as bottomless pits or hungry falcons, the player must shoot and kill things before they can harm the infant.

• **Elf Bowling** (2005) In this Christmas-themed bowling game, the player knocks over Santa's elves instead of pins.

• **Shaq Fu** (1994) NBA star Shaquille O'Neal travels to another dimension and uses martial arts to rescue a kidnapped boy.

• **Journey Escape** (1982) The player guides the rock band Journey as they try to escape mobs of lusty groupies. The game was the first to feature photo-realistic images, with the faces of the band members plastered onto tiny, pixilated bodies.

• **Bible Adventures** (1991) Three Old Testament-themed games in one package: *Noah's Ark* (knock out animals and put them on the boat), *Baby Moses* (help Moses avoid the Pharaoh's decree to kill all male babies), and *David and Goliath* (slingshot warfare).

Well-named: Mockingbirds can imitate nearly any sound, from a squeaky door to a cat's meow.

KOOKY CROOKS

We love to write about criminals in Uncle John's Bathroom Reader. *Over the years, we've covered dumb crooks, nice crooks, and even clever crooks. But sometimes criminals do things that make no sense whatsoever.*

WHEN ART REALLY BOMBS

In 2002, Luke Helder, a University of Wisconsin art student, was arrested for planting 18 pipe bombs in mailboxes in half a dozen states. It was all part of a bizarre "art" project: When plotted on a map, the bomb sites formed a "smiley face," with the "eyes" in Nebraska and Iowa and the left side of the "mouth" in Colorado and Texas. The right side remained unfinished because police caught Helder after his father turned him in. (Nobody died.)

SLEEPY CRIME

Two women approached a man in a park in Sibu, Romania, and struck up a friendly conversation with him. In the course of conversation they asked him to let them hypnotize him. The man agreed, thinking it might be fun. A half hour later the man woke up from his trance. The women were gone, and so was his wallet.

STRESSLING

Simon Andrews of Osbaldwick, England, was sentenced to six months house arrest in 2003. The crime: Andrews had attacked four random men on the street, wrestling them to the ground and taking off—but not stealing—their shoes and socks. Why'd he do it? Andrews, an accountant, says he was "stressed out."

LIFE ON MARS

Dusco Stuppar, 32, of France was able to con an old childhood friend, known only as "Christophe H." into giving him 650,000 francs (about $62,000) to help fund the construction of a city to be built under a secret river on the planet Mars. Stuppar told Christophe that he was part of a secret society of ultra-intelligent people who had the technology possible to make the underwater space city possible. Even more bizarre: Stuppar claimed his evil clone (also part of the Mars project) had injected him with explosives. If Christophe didn't hand over the money, he said, the clone would blow up Stuppar. Christophe later told the story to a psychiatrist, leading to Stuppar's arrest and an 18-month jail term.

HE JUST WANTED TO WATCH TV

A couple living in Dorset, England, called the police in 2001 when they realized their home had been broken into while they were out. An investigation revealed that the thief hadn't actually stolen anything, but had left behind a new television and an unopened bottle of Zima.

CRIME PLAGUE

A biological terror alert went out in January 2003 when Dr. Thomas Butler, an infectious disease researcher at Texas Tech University, informed police that 30 vials of bubonic plague were missing from his lab. Police feared the vials were stolen by terrorists who could convert the samples into a chemical weapon. Even President Bush was briefed about the incident. A day later, Dr. Butler was arrested when it was discovered he'd accidentally destroyed the plague vials himself, and had lied to cover up the error.

IT'S ELECTRIC

In fall 2005, a strange crime wave hit Baltimore: Over the course of six weeks, 130 light poles were stolen. Each pole measured 30 feet tall, weighed 250 pounds, and cost $1,200. There were no witnesses and police were baffled. More baffling is why the thieves were so neat—when they stole the poles, they left all the high voltage wiring cleanly wrapped in black electric tape.

OH, *THAT'S* WHERE I LEFT THEM

In 2003, a 23-year-old woman from Tyrol, Austria, went to a police station to report that her expensive pair of ski pants had been stolen. Officers quickly solved the case—they pointed out to the woman that she was *wearing* the pants. "I was so nervous that I forgot to take them off," she said.

...the opera is performed in Canada. (The building sits on the U.S./Canadian border).

AMAZING TALES OF SURVIVAL

These people cheated death. Not with brains, not with brawn—but with pure, dumb luck.

BATHROOM BREAK

After an evening of heavy drinking, a 47-year-old man was stumbling through the streets of Fischbachtal, Germany, in a heavy downpour. While looking for a dry place to take refuge, he found a dumpster in an alley, climbed inside, and passed out.

An hour or so later, a garbage truck entered the alley, scooped up the dumpster with its metal claws, and dropped the contents into the truck. The driver then pressed a button that activated the hydraulic mechanism designed to crush the contents of the container into a tiny cube. Normally, the driver would have remained in the truck until the crushing was completed, but on this particular occasion, he had to pee. So he got out and walked behind the truck to do his business. That's when he heard the muffled screams and swear words coming from his container. He immediately cut the power, then ran back and opened the back of the truck. There he found a very upset man (who had probably sobered up pretty quickly), and helped him get out. Thanks to the driver's pee break, the drunk man suffered only minor injuries.

THE TANKER AND THE BEEMER

On the outside lane of a roundabout in Lancaster, England, a man was driving a BMW. On the inside lane was a 44-ton tanker truck...which tipped over and fell right on top of the BMW. To make matters worse, powder started pouring out of a hole in the tanker and filling up what little room was left in the crushed car. Rescuers furiously tried to get to the car so that they could free the driver, but they couldn't budge the truck. A crane was called in, and after several long minutes it finally lifted the truck off the car. Expecting the worst, the rescuers and onlookers couldn't believe their eyes: The man was crouched into the only uncrushed and unpowdered section of his little car. The door was removed,

It's against the law in Jefferson City, Missouri, to tie a boat to the railroad tracks.

and the dazed driver got out and walked over to the ambulance where he was treated for minor scratches. The tanker driver wasn't quite as lucky—he broke his arm.

JUST HANG IN THERE

While gazing at a beautiful vista in the French Alps, a 45-year-old woman fell from a precipice that jutted out hundreds of feet above a canyon floor. Her fall came to an abrupt halt, however, when her foot got caught in a tree root sticking out from a cliff. There she dangled for more than two hours while waiting for a rescue team to free her. They did, and she walked away unhurt.

YOU SPIN ME RIGHT ROUND, BABY, RIGHT ROUND

A man got caught in the spinning blades of a plane's propeller... and lived. It happened in the small town of Kleefield, near Winnipeg, Manitoba, Canada. The owner of a small Cessna aircraft had to move it from a local church parking lot to a hangar on his property, and decided to get it there by taxiing it down a town road. He had a friend walk alongside the plane to help redirect traffic along the way. When the plane approached an intersection, the 50-year-old friend ran around to the front of the plane to check for oncoming cars. That's when he ran right into the path of the spinning propeller and suffered major lacerations along his right side, then was thrown into the air, and then landed hard on the pavement, dislocating his shoulder. After a lengthy stay in the hospital, the man is expected to fully recover. "This gentleman is extremely fortunate," an RCMP spokesman told reporters. "The chances of surviving impact with a propeller on any aircraft is remote."

* * *

FLY THE FREAKY SKIES

In July 2006, former Israeli army colonel Reuven Zelinkovsky suggested a new way to protect the country from long-range missiles: Station a battalion of "yogic flyers" around the country to create a "shield of invincibility." Yogic flyers are adherents of Transcendental Meditation who are allegedly able to fly while sitting cross-legged.

WHY A RABBIT'S FOOT?

When we were kids, they sold rabbits' feet at the local variety store for "luck." We always wondered how a rabbit's foot could be lucky, since it obviously didn't do the rabbit any good. Anyway, one day someone wondered aloud where the idea came from, and we went to our BRI library to look it up. To our surprise, no two books gave the same answer. After a while, we were just looking to see how many "reasons" we could find. Here are some favorites.

***ORIGINS AND FIRSTS*, by Jacob M. Braude**

"The rabbit's foot originated as a good luck symbol in show business, where it was used as a powder puff in makeup, and when lost or misplaced, it might delay a performance...bad luck. Hence the reverse when it wasn't."

***SUPERSTITIOUS!* by Willard Heap**

"The rabbit is a prolific animal, producing large numbers of offspring. For that reason, it was thought to possess a creative power superior to other animals, and thus became associated with prosperity and success. If a person carries a rabbit's foot, preferably the left hind foot, good luck is sure to follow. True believers stroke their hands or faces with it, so they will have success in a new venture."

***SUPERSTITIOUS? HERE'S WHY*, by Julie Forsyth Batchelor and Claudia De Lys**

"The first fears and superstitions developed about the European hare....Since most of the habits of these two are alike, superstitions about the hare also apply to the bunny.

"The ancients noticed many things about these timid creatures that they couldn't explain, so they considered them both good and evil. They saw how rabbits came out at night to feed, and how they gathered in bands on clear moonlit nights to play as if influenced by the moon. Another astonishing fact was that northern hares were brown in summer and white in winter.

"But one thing especially impressed primitive man, and that was how the rabbit used his hind legs. There are only two other animals, the greyhound and cheetah, whose rear feet hit the ground in front of the forefeet when running swiftly. Also, rabbits thump the ground with their hind legs as if 'speaking' with them. So their hind feet came to be looked upon as a powerful charm against evil forces."

***SUPERSTITIONS*, by Peter Lorie**

"The idea of a hare's foot as a lucky charm...arose out of the primitive medical belief that the bone of a hare's foot cured gout and cramp, though the bone had to be one with a joint in it intact, to be effective. Carrying a hare's foot bone, with joint, would keep away all forms of rheumatism."

***ENCYCLOPEDIA OF SUPERSTITIONS*, by Edwin and Mona Radford**

"The origin of the superstitions concerning the luck of the rabbit's foot lies in the belief that young rabbits are born with their eyes open, and thus have the power of the Evil Eye, and can shoo away the Evil One."

***EXTRAORDINARY ORIGINS OF EVERYDAY THINGS*, by Charles Panati**

"The rabbit's habit of burrowing lent it an aura of mystery. The Celts, for instance, believed that the animal spent so much time underground because it was in secret communication with the netherworld of numinia. Thus, a rabbit was privy to information humans were denied. And the fact that most animals, including humans, are born with their eyes closed, while rabbits enter the world with eyes open, imbued them with an image of wisdom for the Celts; rabbits witnessed the mysteries of prenatal life. (Actually, the hare is born with open eyes; the rabbit is born blind. And it is the rabbit that burrows; hares live aboveground. Confusion abounded.)"

* * *

"A room without a book is like a body without a soul." **—Cicero**

World leaders: The U.S. is #1 in gun ownership per capita; Finland is #2.

LOVE IS STRANGE

Love is all you need...to do really strange things.

BACKGROUND: In 2002 Jian Feng, of Hegang, China, got married. Two years later his wife had a baby.

LOVE IS STRANGE: Jian accused his wife of having an affair—because she was so beautiful and the baby was "so ugly." His wife finally confessed: She hadn't had an affair—she'd had plastic surgery before they met. She showed him a pre-surgery photograph of herself to prove it. Jian immediately filed for divorce and sued for deceit.

OUTCOME: He won the divorce case, and got $99,700 for his wife's ugly past.

BACKGROUND: Romanian Nicolae Popa said he couldn't take his wife Maria's nagging when he got home from work. "My business is going well but it takes all my energy," he said. "So when I get home in the evening I am so tired I just want to go to bed."

LOVE IS STRANGE: Popa made a deal with his wife: He paid her to be quiet. "I pay her $500 a month as long as she doesn't nag me," he said.

OUTCOME: Maria agreed to the deal, and the couple are even planning to have a child. But Mrs. Popa said that her husband will have to double her salary to keep the child quiet.

BACKGROUND: In 2003 German singer Werner Boehm, 62, made a music video which happened to feature a female baboon.

LOVE IS STRANGE: Boehm brought the animal home and, "It was love at first sight," he said. "We're on the same wavelength." Boehm's wife Susanne, 31, wasn't amused. In 2004 she left the singer, telling reporters, "I gave him the choice: the monkey or me. He chose the monkey."

OUTCOME: After complaints from animal-rights groups, police removed the baboon from Boehm's home and put it in a zoo. Then he asked his wife to come back. "I didn't want to," said Susanne, "but Werner assured me I feel much nicer in bed than the monkey did."

The scum found on top of aged wine is called *beeswing*.

THE FLAMING *MORRO*

On the morning of September 8, 1934, crowds gathered on the boardwalk in Asbury Park, New Jersey, to gape at the smoldering remains of a luxurious cruise ship that had been burning throughout the night. Was it merely an accident...or was there something more sinister at work?

CRUISING TO CATASTROPHE

The *Morro Castle*, named for the 16th-century fortress on Cuba's Havana Bay, was a four-year-old, 11,520-ton steamship liner operated by the Ward Line. On what was to be its final voyage, it set out in early September 1934 from Havana, Cuba, carrying 316 passengers and 230 officers and crew. Their destination: New York City. But only a day into the trip, gail-force winds began to pelt the *Morro* with rain. By that evening, the ship was cruising at top speed into a full-fledged Northeaster. And while the storm raged above decks, a storm of a different kind had been raging below decks for quite some time.

TEMPEST IN A TEAPOT

It was the height of the Great Depression, when a precious few people got richer while everyone else got poorer. The *Morro*'s wealthy passengers were primarily on board to get drunk (Prohibition had been repealed only a year earlier). As the party raged on, they were unaware of the mounting frustration of the underpaid, overworked crewmen below. Most of the men lacked proper training, and rumors abounded that many of their papers had been forged. One sailor reported that while the officers and passengers dined on gourmet meals, the crew was fed "awful slop."

The object of the crew's scorn was Captain Robert Wilmott. He never seemed to take their side in anything, especially after some of the crew tried to make extra money by smuggling narcotics and rum from Cuba. Captain Wilmott seemed more intent on punishing the bad crewmen than rewarding the honest ones.

Perhaps something snapped that evening. As the *Morro* was getting tossed around in the growing storm and the passengers were partying at the farewell gala, Captain Wilmott complained of an upset stomach and retired to his cabin. An hour later, he was

Last U.S. president who wasn't a Democrat or a Republican: Millard Fillmore (1850–53).

found dead in his bed. The ship's doctor suspected a heart attack, but no conclusive evidence was ever found.

First Officer William Warms took over the helm and made the decision to keep going full speed ahead into the storm instead of finding a safe harbor. Warms figured (correctly) that the *Morro*, at more than 500 feet long, could handle the rough waters. Below decks, news of the captain's death was spreading. Many crewmembers were overjoyed and decided to celebrate with a party of their own. Then, at 2:15 a.m., a passenger smelled smoke coming from a locker room. And then all hell broke loose.

UTTER CHAOS BELOW

Many of the crewmen abandoned their posts, while others tried haphazardly to fight the fire as it quickly spread throughout the *Morro*. They tried spraying it with water from the ship's 42 hydrants, but because only six were designed to be used at once, none of the hoses had enough pressure. Several crewmen broke windows to escape from the thick smoke, allowing the high winds from the storm to rush into the ship's interior, spreading the flames further. The electrical cables on the *Morro* began to melt and shorted out the lighting system, leaving both passengers and crew to fight for their lives in the dark. Acting Captain Warms tried to steer the *Morro* toward the shore, but couldn't control the ship's direction because the hydraulic lines in the wheelhouse had burned. And, for reasons still unknown, Warms never gave the order to send out an SOS. The flames spread. Chief Engineer Eban Abbot ordered his crew to stay at their posts below decks—while he jumped into a lifeboat. In fact, most of the crewmembers left their posts and took the few accessible lifeboats for themselves, leaving many passenger stranded. At around 3:20 a.m., radioman George Rogers decided not to wait for the SOS order and battled through the smoke to get into the radio room and send one out himself. He only had a few minutes to transmit before the fire shorted out communications. It would be hours before first rescue ship arrived. By this point, flames had engulfed more than half of the *Morro*.

UTTER CHAOS ABOVE

The passengers, meanwhile, were cold, frightened, tired, and still somewhat drunk. Because no official order was given by Captain

Warms to abandon ship, many passengers stayed aboard, believing the fire was under control and rescue freighters would soon arrive. Further complicating matters was the fact that fire drills, usually conducted at the beginning of every civilian ocean voyage, had never taken place on this trip. So though the passengers had access to life preservers, they hadn't been told how to properly put on the bulky contraptions. As a result, many passengers who dove overboard wearing the clumsy preservers were knocked unconscious when they hit the water. And those who managed to jump safely found themselves at the mercy of the high swells and driving rain. Of the first 98 survivors to reach the New Jersey shore, only six were passengers.

Back on the ship, the flames raged on for the rest of the night. The first rescue boats didn't arrive until just before dawn. When the sun rose, the *Morro* was a complete loss. Of the 134 people who lost their lives, more than 100 were passengers.

PLACING THE BLAME

In the wake of the disaster, people wanted answers. How could such a modern luxury liner be left to burn when it was only a few miles off shore? Where were the rescue ships? And why didn't the *Morro's* fire doors keep the flames contained? Official investigations revealed a long list of problems, from poor training of the crew to the inexperience of First Officer Warms to the negligence of Chief Engineer Abbot. Both men were convicted and sentenced to prison, but their sentences were overturned and neither served any time.

The fire was determined to have been started by highly flammable blankets stored inside a locker. The blankets rested against a wall facing a smokestack, which could have overheated and started the fire. The fire doors didn't do their job because large gaps between the floors allowed the fire to spread. The failure of the rescue boats to come in a timely manner was blamed on many things: the storm, the delay in calling for help, and the lack of communication between the Coast Guard and other vessels in the area.

The only name to come out of the tragedy in a positive light was George Rogers, the radioman who heroically took it upon himself to fight through the flames and call for help.

But what if the disaster was caused by Rogers himself?

FROM HERO TO ZERO

After the *Morro* fire, Rogers was a golden boy. The Veteran Wireless Operators Association named him the maritime hero of the year. He soon opened a radio repair shop...which later burned down in a mysterious fire, leaving Rogers with a hefty sum of insurance money. In 1936 Rogers served on the Bayonne, New Jersey, police force until he was arrested for attempting to murder his supervisor with a bomb. After emerging from prison in the 1950s, Rogers was sent back for life for murdering his two elderly neighbors. These horrific deeds made people wonder about the "hero" who called for help from the burning *Morro*. Officials dug up Rogers's juvenile records and discovered that he had a history of arson. Then one of Rogers's former crew members told of a smuggling ring that the radioman had been running—one that Captain Wilmott found out about. Earlier on that fateful day in 1934, the captain confronted Rogers and threatened to turn him over to the authorities when the *Morro* reached New York.

The picture was becoming clearer: Rogers had the motive and the means to poison his captain and then start the fire to cover his tracks. It also makes sense that he was one of the first men on the scene, and his call to save the ship may have simply stemmed from a desire to save his own skin. Thomas Gallagher, author of the book *Fire at Sea*, visited Rogers in prison to ask the convict if he had started the *Morro* fire. Rogers refused to answer. More than 70 years after the tragedy, no version of what happened that night can prove that murder or arson occurred.

NOT IN VAIN

After the shipwreck, the United States government pledged more federal involvement in maritime training. Congressional hearings led to the Merchant Marine Act of 1936, which provided tougher safety regulations including mandatory lifeboat drills for passengers. The *Morro Castle* disaster also led to the creation of the U.S. Merchant Marine Academy, where seafaring men and women could be professionally educated and trained.

The *Morro Castle* was one of the saddest moments in maritime history, but it ensured that future seafarers might have a better chance of surviving a fire...even it they happened to be traveling with a lone crewman who had an axe to grind.

I'VE GOT A SECRET(ION)

Strange things abound in the world around us. Most of them we never even see. Here are a few examples, which give new meaning to the term "bug Juice."

THE ANT, THE WASP, AND THE BUTTERFLY

The dark blue, female *Maculinea* butterfly lays her eggs on plants; the newly-hatched larvae feed on the plant for about two weeks. Then they fall to the ground, where they are found by foraging *Myrmica* ants. Do they get eaten? No. The young caterpillars secrete chemicals that have a biological "mothering" effect on the ants. They are carried back to the nest, where they are given their own chambers. The ants treat them like royalty—even feeding them their own eggs. After about 10 months the caterpillars leave the ant colony, form their cocoons, become butterflies, and fly off...if they're lucky.

If the *Ichneumon eumerus* wasp happens by the ant hill and detects a caterpillar inside, it has another trick to fool the already-fooled ants. It secretes a concoction of six different pheromones that first attracts the ants, then drives them into a fighting frenzy. The wasp can then safely make its way deep into the nest to the caterpillar's chamber, where it lays its eggs inside the caterpillar while the ants are busy killing each other. The wasp then exits, leaving the eggs to develop, and eat the caterpillar from the inside out. When they finally emerge, the young wasps find themselves surrounded by hungry ants. Do they get eaten? No. The wasps release the magic potion that sends the ants into their civil war, and make their way out of the nest.

Scientists are studying the chemicals produced by the wasps—four of which were previously unknown—in hopes of producing a poison free ant repellent. The chemicals are so strong that the ants can still be fighting 50 days later.

THE ARACHNID KID

Spiders make their silk by secreting a liquid protein through movable nozzles called *spinnerets*. The liquid hardens on contact with air and the spider manipulates it with its legs to create a super-strong elastic thread. How strong? Engineers have determined that if you had a cord of spider's silk as thick as a pencil—it could stop a jet airliner in flight! It's also waterproof, and can stay flexible at temperatures as low as -40° C. There are seven different silk-spinning glands for making seven different types of silk, but no spider has all seven. There's non-sticky silk for web frames and support lines, special silk for wrapping prey, another for wrapping eggs, and a fluffy, slightly sticky one for catching hairy-legged flying insects.

Only about one-third of spiders spin webs to catch their prey. The rest use other methods. Some create webs they hold in their forelegs and cast over passing insects. *Spitting Spiders* spray glue-venom through their fangs to immobilize their prey. One, the *African Bola Spider*, adds another secretion to the mix.

The Bola sits on the end of a twig, covered in sticky web to disguise itself as bird droppings. It hangs a single thread from its legs, weighted with a drop of a glue-like excretion at the end. The thread is scented with chemical secretions that mimic a female moth's pheromones, which—no surprise—attracts male moths. When one gets close enough, the spider whirls the thread and releases it—capturing the moth in mid-flight with the drop of glue, then hauls it in for dinner. And the bola spider can change the chemicals it secretes to attract different types of moths as they enter their different breeding seasons.

MILLIPEDES—THE CAMPER'S FRIEND

When scientists observed *Capuchin* monkeys in Venezuela digging around termite mounds, looking for a specific bug—the *Orthoporus dorsovittatus* millipede—and then rubbing the bug all over their bodies, they couldn't figure it out. And once a monkey was done, it would pass the millipede on to another monkey, who would do the same thing. After a while one of the monkeys would pop the bug into its mouth for a few seconds, spit it back out—and continue the rubbing-of-the-millipede ritual.

The puzzled scientists studied the bugs' secretions: They were full of chemicals known as *benzoquinones*, which are toxic and would be very painful inside the monkeys' mouths (one scientist proved this by doing it himself). So why the ritual? Because benzoquinones are powerful insect repellents, stronger than those used by the U.S. Army. The monkeys had somehow figured out that

World record for the cat with most toes: Jake, who has 28 (seven on each paw).

rubbing them on their bodies would help ward off the annual onslaught of mosquitoes and the painful sores of the bot fly. And putting them in their mouths? The monkeys' saliva induces the bug to secrete more of the chemical, and ward off more of the bugs.

AM I BUGGING YOU?

The *Bombardier Beetle* is less than an inch long and is not a great flier (some species can't fly at all), but it has a defense system that can make much larger prey run for cover. Near the end of their abdomen, bombardiers have a special, two-chambered gland: The larger chamber produces irritating chemicals called *hydroquinones* mixed with hydrogen peroxide; the smaller one produces two enzymes, *catalase* and *peroxidase*. The chemicals are harmless when separate, but when a Bombardier beetle feels threatened, it secretes all these chemicals into an insulated "explosion chamber," where they react violently with each other. The bug then "shoots" bursts of audibly exploding, boiling, corrosive liquid and steam from an opening at the end of its abdomen. (The spray can reach temperatures of 212° F.) The beetle can rotate that abdominal tip 270 degrees, so it can shoot a predator with great accuracy wherever it's attacking from—from the left side, the right side, from underneath, and even from over its own back. The spray can shoot as far as four times the beetle's length and a single beetle can make as many as 20 shots from its built-in farting-flame-thrower before it runs out of fuel.

* * *

WHITE HOUSE TOILETRIES

Got a presidential case of dry skin? Try Secret Service hand lotion, the official lotion of the Commander in Chief's "handlers." It's called "1600 for Men" (after the White House's address) and even has the official U.S. Presidential Seal on the label. There's also Secret Service antibacterial hand wash, glycerin soap, aftershave, and other toiletries, all available in the White House gift shop and on eBay. All proceeds go to the U.S. Secret Service Uniformed Division Benefit Fund and other charities.

The Dead Sea Scrolls were found in a cave in 1947 by herdsmen searching for their lost goat.

WHAT'S FOR THORRABLOT?

Uncle John's theory about whether or not to eat weird food: If some culture eats it—and has eaten it for decades—it's probably okay...but then there's Thorrablot.

BACKGROUND

Iceland is located in the far north Atlantic Ocean. Because of its northern location, for several weeks during the winter it is almost constantly dark. In order to cheer people up during this dark, cold time of the year, beginning late each January, Iceland holds a month-long festival known as *Thorrablot*. Thorrablot translates to "the blessing of Thorri," an ancient Icelandic mythological spirit of winter. Traditional activities include dances, concerts, and plenty of drinking.

The festival isn't all fun. Thorrablot also serves to remind residents that, despite the harsh conditions, their forefathers had it a lot worse. Iceland was first settled more than 1,000 years ago, when the only methods for preserving and cooking foods were salting, smoking, pickling, and fermenting. On top of that, there were few food options in Iceland. So today, with a strong sense of cultural pride—and stronger stomachs—modern Icelanders prepare and eat foods the way their ancestors did hundreds of years ago. Do you think you could handle...

HÁKARL: Shark has always been the most plentiful food source in the ocean around Iceland. But before shark meat can be eaten, it has to be thoroughly treated—sharks secrete urine through their skin, which has to be purged before cooking. First, a side of shark meat is washed, gutted, and placed in a hole in the ground filled with gravel...for *two months*. Then it's hung outside (Icelanders sometimes use a small wooden shed, or drying shack) for *another* two months. Then the urine is expunged, forming a thick, brown, rotten crust around the shark meat. The crust is peeled off, and though the meat inside looks putrid and smells of ammonia, it is finally safe to cook and eat.

Rule of thumb: Your thumb is approximately the same length as your nose.

BRENNIVÍN: The national drink of Iceland, this is a schnapps traditionally served with hákarl. Made of potatoes and carroway, it's extremely bitter and very potent. Nickname: "Black Death."

SVIÓ: Sheep have survived in Iceland for hundreds of years—their wool coats protect them from the harsh elements. They're also a food source. This dish is a lamb's head chopped in half, charred in fire (to singe off the hair), then boiled. It's then served as is, or pickled, or mashed up and mixed with whey into a paste.

LUNDABAGGAR: A sheep's liver, colon, and other organs are ground, then mixed with animal fat and rye meal. The mixture is then stuffed back into the sheep stomach where it's then boiled, pickled, and sliced.

SVIOASULTA: The meat from a cooked sheep's head is pressed into a mold and cools. As the meat cools, it softens and congeals into a gelatinous, meaty goo.

HRÚTSPUNGUR: After being pickled in whey, ram's testicles are formed into small cakes.

LUTEFISK: Cod live in cold waters, so this dried, pickled dish is common in nearby Scandinavian countries such as Sweden and Norway, but it's done a bit differently in Iceland. First, long pieces of cod are hung outdoors so that the wind dries them. Next, lye and wood ashes are added to a bowl of river water, and the cod soaks in the mixture for 24 hours. It's drained, then re-soaked in water and ash for another 24 hours. Next, the lye is washed off and the fish boils for an hour. It's salted, then covered with butter and mustard.

RÚGBRAU: What goes best with this blackened, bitter rye bread that's traditionally served as hard as a rock? Iceland's favorite condiment: pickled herring.

HVALSPIK: This is boiled whale blubber. Stringy, tough, and chewy after boiling, it's pickled to make it softer to eat (and easier to digest). If whale blubber is unavailable, Icelanders eat *selshreifar* —seal flippers—instead. Happy Thorrablot!

During WWII, the Pittsburgh Steelers & Philadelphia Eagles combined as "the Steagles."

LOVE ME TENDER

Elvis Presley always had a way with women.

ELVIS AND THE WOMEN'S-LIB MOVEMENT

In 1996 Professor Joel Williamson of the University of North Carolina spoke at the Second Annual International Conference on Elvis Presley, where he presented an interesting (and odd) theory: The Elvis craze of the 1950s—featuring thousands of women screaming at his concerts—actually laid the groundwork for the Women's Liberation movement. Williamson's unusual explanation: "Elvis's performance provided a venue in which young women could publicly and all together claim ownership of their bodies, declare themselves loudly, clearly, and explicitly to be sexual as well as spiritual characters."

ELVIS AND THE BLONDE BOMBSHELL

According to Byron Raphael, Presley's one-time agent, it didn't take long for the sparks to fly when the King met Marilyn Monroe in 1956. Fifty years later, Raphael divulged the details of the tryst. Raphael picked up Monroe and brought her to Presley's hotel suite. "When Elvis saw her," said Raphael, "they came together and, without saying a word, started kissing. I was in shock. Marilyn, who was 10 years older, said, 'You're pretty good for a guitar player.' Then they went into the bedroom. I didn't know if I was supposed to leave, or stay and wait, so I just dozed off. The next thing I knew I was startled awake by the door opening and I dove behind the bar. And they both walked out stark naked."

ELVIS IN THE HEREAFTER

When a teacher and his sixth-grade class visited Graceland in 2005, they reported hearing music coming from the chapel—an eerie rendition of Marilyn Monroe's *Diamonds Are a Girl's Best Friend*. They peered into the room and saw the ghosts of Presley and Monroe getting married. The teacher said that Monroe looked great, but that Presley "didn't look so good. He was sweating an awful lot." A clerk who worked at Graceland's Heartbreak Hotel was there as well. He turned on the lights to get a better look...and the heavenly couple "whisked away into thin air."

The call of a humpback whale is louder than a Concord jet and can be heard 500 miles away.

ODD OFF THE PRESSES!

Some news stories are so weird that they need their own special category.

JUST ANOTHER NIGHT IN ANN ARBOR

"A marriage-minded man ran naked through his neighborhood, trying to show his hesitant girlfriend that taking risks is important. He got more than he bargained for when he ended up being chased and shot at. The couple were discussing marriage when the woman said she wasn't sure if she was ready, and the man sprang into action to prove he was. After running naked across the street, the man ducked into some bushes when he spotted a couple walking. A 28-year-old man spotted the bushes rustling and bare feet underneath, and drew a .40-caliber handgun, and ordered the naked man to come out, according to police. The naked suitor ran away, but the armed man gave chase and eventually fired a shot. The naked man fell to the ground, suffering minor injuries. Police arrested the gunman on charges of aggravated assault. The naked man was not arrested."

—Associated Press

GOOD GRIEF

"Liu Chun-lin, 22, brushes her eyelashes, fastens her flowing raven hair and then sets off for another day of crying her heart out for someone else's dead relatives. Liu and her five-member Filial Daughters' Band are part of a thriving mourning business in Taiwan. They're professional entertainers paid by grieving families to wail, scream and create the anguished sorrow befitting a proper funeral. The performances are as much a status symbol for the living as a show of respect for the dead. Weary relatives hire groups like the Filial Daughters' Band for $600 for a half day's work."

—*Taipei Times*, 2005

COMRADES OF THE APES

"The Soviet dictator Josef Stalin ordered the creation of Planet of the Apes-style warriors by crossing humans with apes, according to recently uncovered secret documents. Moscow archives show that in the mid-1920s Russia's top animal-breeding scientist, Ilya

Ivanov, was ordered to turn his skills from horse and animal work to the quest for a super-warrior. According to Moscow newspapers, Stalin told the scientist: 'I want a new invincible human being, insensitive to pain, resistant and indifferent about the quality of food they eat.' Mr Ivanov was highly regarded. He had established his reputation under the Tsar when in 1901 he established the world's first centre for the artificial insemination of racehorses. In 1926 he was dispatched to West Africa with $200,000 to conduct his first experiment in impregnating chimpanzees. Meanwhile, a centre for the experiments was set up in Georgia—Stalin's birthplace—for the apes to be raised. Mr Ivanov's experiments, unsurprisingly from what we now know, were a total failure."

—*The Scotsman*

CASTAWAY

"Ernest G. Johnson, 42, was arrested in Shreveport, La., in May after he, posing as an insurance company employee, roamed the corridors at LSU Hospital seeking to photograph women wearing casts. Said a police detective, 'It's like all he wants is to be in the presence of a woman with a cast on and have her attention.'"

—News of the Weird

NUMBSKULL

"Hundreds of people are thronging a hospital in the eastern Indian city of Kolkata to see a patient holding a piece of his own skull that fell off. Doctors say a large, dead section of 25-year-old electrician Sambhu Roy's skull came away Sunday after severe burns starved it of blood. 'When he came to us late last year, his scalp was completely burned. Within months it came off exposing the skull,' Ratan Lal Bandyopadhyay, the surgeon who treated Roy told Reuters. 'Later, we noticed that part of his skull was loosening due to lack of blood supply to the area, which can happen in such cases.' The piece came off Sunday and hundreds of people and dozens of doctors now crowd around his bed, where he lies holding the bone. 'Doctors say a new skull covering has replaced the old one, but I am not letting go of this one,' Roy said. He intends to keep his prized possession for life and not hand it over to the hospital when he leaves: 'My skull has made me famous,' he says."

—Yahoo! News

Other ways to become a vampire, according to myth: be born with red hair, or be promiscuous.

THE PRINCE OF WHALES

This just wouldn't be an "odd" book without some crazy royals, a class of people who seem to specialize in weird behavior. Here's the story of a royal couple whose scandalous fights fed the gossip columns and outraged the public…200 years ago. Some things never change.

BIG SPENDER

When George, England's Prince of Wales, turned 21 in 1783, the British government gave him a birthday present of £60,000 (about $6.2 million in today's dollars). And his father, King George III, set him up with an annual allowance of £50,000 ($5.2 million). Most people could get by on that, but young Prince George couldn't. He blew every penny—and much more—on expensive dining, furniture, tailors, racehorses, home renovations, and anything else his heart desired. By his mid-30s, George was broke—and in addition, he owed a staggering £660,000 ($70 million) in debts.

Normally, lending money to a future king was a good idea: After he was crowned, such "investors" could call in their loans and expect a handsome repayment. But George was so deep in debt that his funding completely dried up. Nobody would lend him money until his father, the king, intervened…with two conditions: He wanted George to marry a princess and produce an heir. If the prince would do these two things, the king promised, he'd raise his allowance and help pay down his debts.

There was one small problem: George was *already* married—and worse, to a Catholic woman. As the future head of the Anglican Church, George was forbidden by law to marry a Catholic. But he had, in a secret ceremony a few years earlier, and the marriage had soured since then. Now, badly in need of cash, George reached an agreement with his father: George would pretend he wasn't married, and his father would pretend to believe him. The search for a princess was on.

PICTURE PERFECT

George considered a number of potential brides before settling on his first cousin, Princess Caroline of Brunswick, Germany. He did so sight unseen—the two had never met. They "introduced" themselves by sending each other small portraits: Each liked what they saw, so they agreed to marry. But painted portraits can be deceiving. Unlike his picture, George was grossly overweight and widely considered unattractive; he was once described as looking "like a woman in men's clothes."

And if George was already on his way to earning his nickname "Prince of Whales," the future "Princess of Whales" was close behind. Caroline was also pudgy, and was missing most of her teeth; those few she had left were rotten. But even worse than the sight of Caroline was her smell: Like many people of the 18th century, she rarely changed her clothes or bathed.

To make matters worse, Princess Caroline had a well-known reputation for loose morals and indiscretion—very unfitting for a future queen of England. "All amusements have been forbidden her because of her indecent conduct," the prince's brother wrote home after meeting Caroline and hearing stories of her lewd conversations—and worse—with men. "There, dear brother, is a woman I do not recommend at all." But George ignored his brother. He had decided on Caroline, whom he still had not met, and that was that.

ON SECOND THOUGHT

George's determination lasted until the moment he met Caroline in person, three days before their wedding. His desire then vanished, never to return. Was it her gap-toothed grin? Or the stench? Whatever it was, when chubby Prince George finally laid eyes on his unattractive bride, he backed away, exclaiming to a friend, "I am not very well. Pray get me a glass of brandy." Then he ran from the room.

Princess Caroline was equally unimpressed. "Does the prince always act like this?" she said as he ran off. "I think he's very fat and nothing like his portrait."

THE ROYAL PAIN OF MARRIAGE

At the wedding three days later, George showed up so drunk that he couldn't stand without assistance, and so agitated that he looked like he was about to cry. But somehow the wedding went off without a hitch, and nine months later—to the day—Caroline gave

A cat can rotate each of its ears independently 180°.

birth to a baby girl named Charlotte. His commitment to produce an heir having been fulfilled, George separated from Caroline.

That could have been the end of it. George and Caroline might have been able to lead completely separate lives, appearing together only on public occasions when duty called. They *might* have been able to, were it not for the fact that Caroline, for all her faults, became an extremely popular princess, adored by the public—and that drove George crazy. So George shut her up in one of his houses, refused to let anyone visit her without his approval, and even installed his own mistress as her lady in waiting. Word of George's cruel treatment leaked out, and, added to rumors of his own drunkenness, debauchery, and reckless spending, made him the most despised man in England. Meanwhile, Caroline became more popular than ever.

Caroline put up with the abuse until the end of 1799, when she told George that she no longer considered herself bound by his rules and moved to a small house outside of London. But as soon as she was out from under her husband's thumb, the princess's loose morals and lack of discretion began to reassert themselves. She threw wild dinner parties during which she danced topless, flirted shamelessly with male guests, and, after selecting one of them as her favorite, disappeared downstairs for "indecent interludes."

THE "DELICATE INVESTIGATION"

Prince George reveled in the stories told by Caroline's dinner guests, and hoped they would damage her reputation and provide him with the proof he needed to sue for divorce on grounds of adultery.

He got his chance in 1805, when a story began to circulate that a four-year-old boy whom Caroline had adopted was actually her natural son. What better evidence for adultery than an illegitimate son? George pushed the prime minister into launching what became known as the "Delicate Investigation." But the commission eventually concluded that there was no solid evidence to prove adultery. It turned out that the boy really was adopted after all.

The seamy investigation made George even less popular and generated even more sympathy for Caroline, whom the public saw as an "injured and unprotected female." Every sin George committed stuck to him like glue, but Caroline got away with everything.

In some parts of the Italian Riviera, soups traditionally contain one stone from the sea.

When she went out in public, people applauded; when he went out, they threw things at him. All George could do was wait and hope for an opportunity to rid himself of the woman he called the "vilest wretch this world was ever cursed with."

THWARTED AGAIN...

In 1817, George and Caroline's only daughter, by now 21 and married to a Belgian prince, died after giving birth to a stillborn son. Now living in Europe, Caroline felt that her daughter's death had severed her last ties to George. So she sent word to him that she would agree to a "divorce by consent," in which neither party had to admit to adultery. George agreed, but the British government refused: For the divorce to be legal, they said, Caroline had to admit to being an adulteress. And she wasn't about to do that.

That meant Prince George would have to file suit and try to prove her guilty of adultery in open court...but again, the government wouldn't let him. Caroline was still well loved by the British public, and George's advisers knew that battling her in a nasty lawsuit might spark a rebellion. Keeping in mind the revolution that had toppled the French monarchy only 30 years earlier, they knew they couldn't risk it. So George was right back where he started—married to a woman he couldn't stand, and powerless to do anything about it.

The matter came to a head in January 1820, when George's father, King George III, died. Prince George became King George IV...and Caroline was now the Queen of England. The thought of it was more than George could bear, but now that he was king, he figured he was in a position to rid himself of his queen. So he pushed the House of Lords into introducing the "Pains and Penalties Bill," a bit of legislation with the sole purpose of annulling his marriage and stripping Caroline of her title of queen.

...AND AGAIN

On June 5, 1820, Caroline returned to England to defend her honor in person. And judging from the size of the crowd that turned out to greet her, she was more popular than ever.

For three long, lurid months, the House of Lords debated the Pains and Penalties Bill. Each of Caroline's alleged indiscretions was recounted in vivid, painstaking detail, mostly provided by spies

According to studies, the average American is in a bad mood 110 days out of the year.

George had hired. Gavel-to-gavel press coverage inflated the story into a massive public spectacle, and restless crowds began to gather outside Parliament. After weeks of debate, it became clear that even if Caroline wasn't guilty of *all* the allegations made against her, she was probably guilty of plenty of them. But the Lords, all too aware of that mob outside their chambers, quietly quashed the bill and made sure it never became law. The spectacle was over.

FINAL INSULT

The queen was still the queen—George had lost again, this time for good. But he had one last insult to dish out: His coronation—the formal crowning ceremony—had been delayed until the queen's status was resolved. Now that the matter was closed, George had his legal advisers find out whether a queen was entitled to be crowned in her own right, or whether she could only be crowned at the pleasure of the king. This time the king's advisers sided with him—Caroline had no independent right to participate in the coronation. George immediately barred her from the ceremony. Queen Caroline showed up at Westminster Abbey anyway, but when she tried to enter the building, the guards slammed the door in her face.

But the day had greater repercussions than George had planned: Caroline, upset by the snub, fell ill that night. Three weeks later, she died. Her body was returned to Germany and buried in a tomb marked CAROLINE, THE INJURED QUEEN OF ENGLAND.

THE LONELY KING

King George was finally free of his wife, but it didn't bring him happiness. By now 57, morbidly obese, alcoholic, and addicted to medicinal opium, he spent his time in seclusion at Windsor Castle, where he died in 1830 at the age of 67. He never did win the love of his subjects, as his wife had; he was as despised in death as he was in life. Even his own brother, the new King William IV, left George's funeral early, before the coffin had been lowered into the ground.

"There never was an individual less regretted by his fellow-creatures than this deceased King," the London *Times* wrote after his death. "What eye has wept for him? If he ever had a friend, a devoted friend in any rank of life, we protest that the name of him or her never reached us."

Research has shown that dogs can locate the source of a sound in 6/100ths of a second.

LAND MINES AND CROCODILES

Think auto racing or mountain climbing are the most dangerous sports? Try golfing these courses.

COURSE: The Hans Merensky Golf Course, South Africa
DANGER! This course is in the town of Phalaborwa, and borders one of Africa's largest game preserves. There's a fence, but it won't stop the antelope, giraffes, impalas, and monkeys from sharing the course with you. Don't worry, though; they're not really a danger—it's the warthogs, hyenas, water buffalo, cheetahs, leopards, crocodiles, and lions you have to watch out for. And the elephants. In 1988 a visitor was trampled to death when she frightened an elephant with her camera.

COURSE: Singapore Island Country Club, Singapore
DANGER! The course has unusual hazards: poisonous snakes. During the 1982 Singapore Open, golfer Jim Stewart encountered a 10-foot cobra on the course. (He killed it with his club.)

COURSE: Lost City Golf Course, Sun City, South Africa
DANGER! The par-3 13th at this beautiful course is one of the most dangerous in the world. There are nine bunkers and water hazards around the hole—and 38 Nile crocodiles live in the water, some up to 15 feet long.

COURSE: The Scott Base Golf Course
DANGER! What's so dangerous about this course? Geography: it's in Antarctica, where the average summer temperature is –20°F and there's no dirt, just snow and ice. And you have to use pink golf balls (because you can't see the white ones in the snow, of course).

COURSE: Henderson Golf Club, Savannah, Georgia
DANGER! In 2003 Roy Williamson was playing at this club when he hit his ball into the deep rough. "I saw my ball pretty

Pro golfer Ky Laffoon once punished his putters by dragging them behind his car.

much in plain view," he said. "Unfortunately, it was being tended to by a rattlesnake that I *didn't* see." When he went to pick the ball up (naughty, naughty), the six-foot-long snake bit him on the right temple. Williamson, severely poisoned, woke up in the hospital three days later. He said he would be golfing again soon, but added, "If I go out now and hit a ball off of the fairway in any fashion or form, I will not go after it."

COURSE: Camp Bonifas Country Club, the DMZ

DANGER! The DMZ is the demilitarized zone between North Korea and South Korea. American soldiers stationed there at Camp Bonifas wanted to play golf, so they built themselves a one-hole, 192-yard, par-3 course. But they have to play very carefully. A sign on the course reads: "Danger! Do Not Retrieve Balls From The Rough. Live Mine Fields!"

COURSE: Elephant Hills Country Club, Zimbabwe

DANGER! This course was designed by South African PGA legend Gary Player. It boasts the largest water hazard in the world—Victoria Falls, which is right next to the course. Another feature is the wildlife, of which you must remain constantly aware. One of the club's many unique rules: "Players may take a free drop with any ball that lands in a hippopotamus print."

COURSE: Pelham Bay Golf Course and Split Rock Golf Course, Bronx, New York

DANGER! These two courses are among New York's finest—but they also have a creepy reputation...as dumping grounds for dead bodies. Thirteen corpses have been found on the two courses in the last 20 years.

COURSE: Scholl Canyon Golf Course, Glendale, California

DANGER! The course was built on an unused section of the massive Scholl Canyon Landfill in Los Angeles County—atop three million tons of garbage. And if that seems a little ripe for your golfing pleasure, consider this: other sections of the landfill are still in use. So golf away, but you may want to wear a gas mask. According to some reports, methane gas occasionally escapes from divots.

Most dinosaurs were vegetarians, but they didn't eat grass...there wasn't any at that time.

OBSOLETE WORD QUIZ

We found a bunch of old words that nobody uses much anymore. See if you can guess their definitions.

1. Thutter
2. Hierophant
3. Pettifogger
4. Cark
5. Sequacity
6. Elflocks
7. Abecedarian
8. Compossible
9. Gruntle
10. Desuetude
11. Epicene
12. Demulcent
13. Fichu
14. Carriwitchet
15. Wopsy
16. Dormition
17. Volitate

A. Compatible
B. To burden someone
C. A priest
D. Hair matted from sleep
E. A triangular scarf
F. Of indeterminate gender
G. A dull, repetitive sound
H. A tendency to be servile
I. A beginner
J. Relating to a dead custom
K. A riddle or word puzzle
L. To soothe
M. A lozenge
N. An unscrupulous lawyer
O. Painless death
P. Tangled
Q. To fly aimlessly

Answers: 1–G, 2–C, 3–N, 4–B, 5–H, 6–D, 7–I, 8–A, 9–L, 10–J, 11–F, 12–M, 13–E, 14–K, 15–P, 16–O, 17–Q

WEIRD GERMANY

First it was a bunch of kingdoms, then one large country, then two countries, now one big country again...united in weirdness.

WHAT'S THAT JELLY-LIKE SUBSTANCE?

On a road outside Leipzig in 2006, hikers spotted something weird: a "flabby red, orange, and green" jelly. They called authorities, who shut down traffic and brought in scientists in anti-contamination suits to investigate the goo, fearing it might be toxic waste. However, the mystery was solved before the jelly could be tested. A policeman learned that a wedding reception had taken place in the area a few days earlier. The party had gotten out of control and ended in a jelly fight. So what was the jelly-like substance? Jelly.

DISREGARD THE PREVIOUS LETTER

In 1990, a German terrorist group called the Red Army Faction sent a letter to the federal prosecutor's office to claim responsibility for the assassination of agriculture minister Ignaz Kiechle at his 60th birthday party. One problem: Kiechle's party wasn't scheduled until March 3, and the letter arrived on March 2. Realizing their mistake, the Red Army Faction immediately sent another letter, saying that the assassination attempt was cancelled due to a "mistake in coordination."

GOOD (BAD) HUSBAND

Men refusing to help with housework has probably contributed to many divorces around the world. But in 1982, a woman from Luebben split from her husband because he did *too much* housework. She testified in court that for the first few years of their marriage her husband was "a dream" because he did all the cooking, cleaning, and shopping. He even washed the windows and took care of their baby perfectly. But the woman suddenly became despondent when she realized that she had nothing to do, which made her feel inferior. Apparently it was enough to convince the judge, who granted the divorce.

FORBIDDEN LOVE

On the Aasee Lake in Muenster, a black swan has fallen in love with a black plastic paddleboat shaped like a swan. Biologists say the (real) swan is displaying all the signs of the desire to mate: circling the boat, staring at it, and cooing at it. Tourists and locals alike have become reluctant to use the paddleboat. "When I sail too close to it, the black bird puffs up its feathers and hoots at me," said one resident.

*   *   *

MORE STRANGE (BUT REAL) CLASSIFIED ADS

Wanted: Hair-cutter. Excellent growth potential.

Bill's Septic Cleaning. "We haul American made products."

Do Plants Think? Test yours with new bio-meter portable lie detector. Works on people, too!

Bar-sliced bologna regular or tasty save 30¢ on 2.

Now is your chance to have your ears pierced and get an extra pair to take home, too.

Get rid of aunts: Zap does the job in 24 hours.

Ground beast: 99¢/lb.

Vacation Special: Have your home exterminated.

Toaster: A gift that every member of the family appreciates. Automatically burns toast.

No matter what your topcoat is made of, this miracle spray will make it really repellent.

Auto Repair Service. Free pick-up and delivery. Try us once, you'll never go anywhere again.

This is the model home for your future. It was panned by Better Homes and Gardens.

Christmas tag-sale. Handmade gifts for the hard-to-find person.

And now, the Superstore—unequaled in size, unmatched in variety, unrivaled inconvenience.

When dropped in water, a fresh egg will sink; a stale one won't.

I'M NOT DEAD YET!

We don't know about you, but the idea of being mistaken for dead is about the scariest thing we can think of. Fortunately for these folks, someone discovered the horrifying goof before funeral arrangements were made.

DECEASED: An 83-year-old resident of a senior care facility in British Columbia, Canada

STORY: Funeral home drivers arrived at the Shirley Dean Pavilion, in Surrey, British Columbia, in 2005 to pick up a woman who had died there. They took her body to the Surrey hospital, where they left it on a gurney in a hallway for attendants to take to the morgue.

RESURRECTION: Some time later a porter at the hospital noticed the corpse's leg move. The drivers had inadvertently picked up the dead woman's roommate—who was sleeping, not dead. She was immediately taken back to the facility, and the truly-deceased woman was then taken to the morgue. The not-deceased 91-year-old woman's son-in-law, Paul Boyle, was infuriated. "The number-one thing is to get her out of there...and then legal action," he said. "There's a difference between a dead person and a live person." The facility promised an investigation.

DECEASED: Bogdan Georgescu, a 16-year-old boy from Fagaras, Romania

STORY: Georgescu collapsed after being punched by a friend. Rescue crews arrived and could find no signs of life, so he was pronounced dead and taken to the local morgue.

RESURRECTION: A few hours after arriving at the morgue, an attendant thought he saw the boy's body move, so he bent over the body to get a closer look—and the boy punched him in the face. "I woke up and had no idea where I was," he said later. "I looked to the left and right and saw dead women on either side. Then I saw a man in a white coat. I panicked. I thought he was going to kill me." The boy was taken to a neurological hospital for tests, and the doctor he punched was treated for shock—and given some time off to recover from the "corpse" attack.

DECEASED: Subash Bag, an 8-year-old boy from a small village in West Bengal, India

STORY: Subash was bitten by a poisonous snake near his home in Sonapalasi village and died a short time later. His grieving family performed the traditional funeral, putting his body on a raft and sending him down the nearby Damodar River.

RESURRECTION: The boy's body was found some time later down river near the village of Chandipur…and he wasn't dead. The snake bite had not been fatal, but it was close. He was nursed back to health by villagers, but could remember nothing of his past. He stayed and was raised in the village of Chandipur. Eleven years later, in 2004, now 19 years old, married, and with a daughter, the young man was seen in a nearby town and recognized by one of his relatives. The relative informed Subash's father and the elated family was reunited. Subash soon returned to live in his home village with his wife and daughter.

* * *

ON-THE-JOB NEWS

• **Cushy Job:** Mike Pixley of Monroe, Michigan, is a recliner tester for La-Z-Boy. He sits in and rocks about 2,800 easy chairs every day.

• **Put On a Happy Face—Or Else:** Nutzwerk LTD, an IT firm in Leipzig, Germany, has banned its employees from whining and complaining. A manager explained, "We made the ban official after one female employee refused to subscribe to the company's philosophy of always smiling." Workers are advised to keep their opinions to themselves; any griping could lead to immediate dismissal.

• **This Bites:** Ellie Jenkins is a counter for the Savannah, Georgia, Mosquito Control Commission. What does she count? Mosquitos. Jenkins drives to 38 different locations and stands still at each one with her arms and legs exposed. If she receives five bites in a minute, she calls pest-control services.

At any point in time, 0.7% of the world's population is drunk.

MITCH HEDBERG

Sadly, stand-up comedian Mitch Hedberg died of a drug overdose in 2005 at age 37. But, thankfully, he left us with a treasure trove of witty observations about the mundane things in life. He didn't make them interesting, just funny.

"My fake plants died because I did not pretend to water them."

"Rice is great if you're really hungry and want to eat two thousand of something."

"I would imagine the inside of a bottle of cleaning fluid is really clean. I would imagine a vodka bottle is really drunk."

"I like refried beans. That's why I wanna try *fried* beans, because maybe they're just as good and we're just wasting time. You don't have to fry them again after all."

"I have an underwater camera, just in case I crash my car into a river, and at the last minute I have a chance to take a picture of a fish that I've never seen."

"My sister wanted to be an actress. She got halfway: She does live in a trailer, but she never gets called to the set."

"I can whistle with my fingers, especially if I have a whistle."

"I bought a seven-dollar pen because I always lose pens, and I got sick of not caring."

"I bought myself a parrot. The parrot talked. But it did not say, 'I'm hungry'...so it died."

"I'd like to get four people who do cartwheels very good, and make a cart."

"An escalator can never break; it can only become stairs."

"If I had nine of my fingers missing, I wouldn't type any slower."

"I like to hold the microphone cord like this: I pinch it together, then I let it go, then you hear a whole bunch of jokes at once."

"I remixed a remix; it went back to normal."

"I used to be a hot-tar roofer. Yeah, I remember that day."

Q: What's the only place where a flag always flies, and is never raised or lowered? A: The Moon.

(BAT) BOMBS AWAY!

Here's a batty bit of World War II history you may not have heard before.

BAT MAN

In the days and weeks following the bombing of Pearl Harbor on December 7, 1941, a lot of people wrote letters to President Roosevelt. Some wrote to express their sympathy with the victims or their outrage at the attack; others made suggestions about how to fight back against Japan.

One man, a dentist from Irwin, Pennsylvania, wanted to talk about bats. His name was Lytle S. Adams, and he had recently been to the Carlsbad Caverns in New Mexico, home to one of the largest bat colonies in North America. When Adams learned of the attack on Pearl Harbor, his thoughts returned to the bats he'd seen—could they be useful to the war effort? He was convinced they could.

COM-BAT

In his letter to the president, Adams explained that bats are capable of carrying more than their own weight in flight. In many species, for example, the mother bat carries two or even three of her young as she searches for food. If bats could carry their children, Adams reasoned, why couldn't they carry tiny bombs?

The dentist's plan went further: Bats hate sunlight, so if bats carrying time-delayed incendiary devices could be released over a Japanese city shortly before dawn, as the sun rose, the bats would seek refuge from the light. Many would roost in the eaves and attics of buildings—a great number of which were made of flammable materials like wood, bamboo, and paper soaked in fish oil. When the firebombs detonated, thousands of tiny fires would start in buildings all over the city.

Not only that, bats typically hide out of sight in hard-to-reach places, and that would make the fires difficult to detect. By the time they were discovered, the fires would be well established but still small enough at first (each bat would weigh less than half an ounce, so the bombs would have to be small, too) that people would have a fighting chance to escape. Casualties would be lower than with conventional firebombs, which weighed hundreds of pounds and engulfed entire buildings on impact, giving occupants no warning and no chance to escape. For all their destructive power, Adams believed that "bat bombs" could be a more humane weapon of war than regular firebombs.

How many fires could be started with bats? "Approximately 200,000 bats could be transported in one airplane," Adams wrote, "and still allow one-half the payload capacity to permit free air circulation and increased gasoline load. Ten such planes would carry two million fire starters."

ASSAULT AND BAT-TERY

Perhaps the most impressive feature of bat bombs was not their destructive power, but the psychological impact they could have on the Japanese. The bats would be dropped by planes before dawn, and by the time the bombs went off, the planes would be long gone. Entire cities would ignite spontaneously and burn to the ground...with no warning and no explanation.

"The effect of the destruction from such a mysterious source would be a shock to the morale of the Japanese people as no amount of ordinary bombing could accomplish," Adams wrote to Roosevelt. "It would render the Japanese people homeless and their industries useless, yet the innocent could escape with their lives."

How flammable were Japanese cities? When a woman living in Osaka, Japan, knocked over her hibachi-type cookstove in 1911, 11,000 homes burned to the ground. And it was *raining*.

TO THE BAT CAVE!

President Roosevelt forwarded Adams's letter to Colonel William J. Donovan, who would soon head the Office of Strategic Services, forerunner of the CIA. "It sounds like a perfectly wild idea but is worth looking into," FDR wrote. "This man is *not* a nut."

Dr. Adams got the go-ahead to assemble a 20-person staff and begin working out the details on how such a weapon might be built. What species of bats would be best? What kind of firebomb would be used? How would the device be attached to the bat? How would the bats be dropped over cities? There was a lot to figure out. Here's what they came up with:

High life: 74% of New York City residents live at least one flight of stairs above ground.

The Bats

The researchers decided early on that they would use a species called the Mexican free-tailed bat. They weighed about half an ounce but were capable of carrying a load of as much as three-quarters of an ounce. Tens of millions of them made their summer homes in caves in Texas and other southwestern states. Just as important, these bats hibernated in the winter. That meant they could be put into artificial hibernation so that the bombs could be attached, then kept in cold storage until they were ready to be released over Japan.

The Incendiary Bombs

One of the researchers assigned to the project was an incendiary bomb specialist—a chemist named Louis Fieser. He devised a tiny bomb that weighed a little over half an ounce and consisted of a timer and a thin plastic capsule measuring three-quarters of an inch in diameter by two inches long, filled with a jellied gasoline he'd invented, napalm.

Initially the designers planned to attach a bomb to each bat's chest with a piece of string and a surgical clip that mimicked the way baby bats latched onto their mother's fur with their claws. But that turned out to be too complicated, so they switched to a simple adhesive and just glued the bombs to the bats.

The "Bombshell"

If you just threw a bunch of hibernating bats out of an airplane, their fragile wings would break the moment they hit the airstream at 150 mph or else they would fall all the way to the ground—and die on impact—before they could emerge from hibernation. So the researchers designed a protective bomb-shaped canister to put the bats into. The "bombshell" was cigar-shaped and had fins, just like a regular bomb—except that it was filled with bats and was poked full of holes so they could breathe.

Inside the canister, the hibernating bats were packed into cardboard trays similar to eggshell cartons, and these cartons were stacked one on top of the other. Each bombshell held 26 cardboard trays, each of which held 40 bats. That meant each bomb would contain 1,040 bats.

Look before you leap: All bullfrogs close their eyes when they jump.

HOW IT WORKED

• The bombshell was designed so that when it was dropped from a plane, it would free-fall to an altitude of 4,000 feet, at which point a parachute would deploy, slowing its descent.

• When the parachute opened, the bomb's outer shell would pop off and fall away. The stacked cardboard trays, which were tied to one another with short lengths of string, would then drop down and hang from the parachute about three inches apart, like rungs on a rope ladder.

• As the cardboard trays dropped into position, a tiny wire would be pulled from the incendiary device attached to each bat. Just like pulling a pin from a hand grenade, when the string was pulled, the firebombs would be armed and set to go off in 30 minutes, 60 minutes, or whatever interval the bombers chose.

• The bats, now exposed to the warm air and floating slowly to earth, would have enough time to warm up, emerge from their hibernating state, climb out of their individual egg-carton compartments, and fly away to seek shelter.

• When time ran out, the incendiary device glued to their chest would explode into flames, incinerating them instantly and setting fire to whatever structure they had taken refuge in.

BAT-TLE GROUND

A bombshell filled with bats and tiny firebombs sounded clever, but would it really work? Dr. Adams's team built a prototype, loaded it with 1,040 bats fitted with dummy bombs, and dropped it from a plane in a remote region outside Carlsbad Air Force Base in New Mexico. The test went off nearly without a hitch: the parachute deployed, the trays dropped open, and the bats awakened from hibernation and flew off in search of shelter from the sun.

The only snafu was that the researchers misjudged how far winds would carry the bat trays. Instead of landing in the middle of nowhere (the project was top secret, after all), the bats ended up flying to a ranch and roosting in the barn and ranch house. The researchers caught up with the creatures half an hour later and collected them as the mystified rancher looked on (he never did learn what the bats were carrying or what they were for).

BAT REVENGE

But the real proof of the power of bat bombs came later that day when Louis Fieser, the incendiary specialist, wanted some film footage of a bat armed with a live incendiary bomb actually exploding into flames. He took six hibernating bats out of cold storage and set their bombs to detonate in 15 minutes, figuring that in such a short time, the bats would still be hibernating and wouldn't fly away.

What Fieser failed to take into consideration was that on a hot New Mexico afternoon, the bats would come out of hibernation quickly. All six bats woke up within 10 minutes, escaped, and roosted in the rafters of various buildings of the airfield where the test was being conducted. Five minutes later the bombs went off, and every building on the airfield—the control tower, barracks, offices, and hangars—burned to the ground.

BAT TO THE DRAWING BOARD

Believe it or not, bat bombs were found to be *more* effective than conventional firebombs. One study concluded that a planeload of conventional firebombs would start between 167 and 400 fires, whereas a planeload of bat bombs would start between 3,625 and 4,748 fires.

So how many bats died in combat during World War II? Not even one. After spending 27 months and $2 million looking into the feasibility of bat bombs, the Pentagon canceled the program in March 1944. The military claimed that the bats were too unpredictable to be useful, but Jack Couffer, a research scientist who worked on the project, has a different theory. Couffer speculates in his memoirs that the government knew the Manhattan Project was making steady progress toward the world's first atomic bomb, and the military decided to focus on that instead.

Which explanation is true? Only the U.S. government knows for sure. Sixty years later, the reasons for the cancellation of the program, like the blueprints to the incendiary device itself, are still classified.

* * *

A weapon is an enemy even to its owner. —**Turkish proverb**

Mel Gibson turned down the role of James Bond.

UNCLE JOHN'S STALL OF FAME

More recipients of the BRI's highest honor.

Honoree: Lt. Col. Mike Presnell, who participated in the U.S. overthrow of Saddam Hussein in the spring of 2003

Notable Achievement: Making a historical pit stop.

True Story: In April 2003, Gloria Presnell was at home in Grand Island, Nebraska, when she received a satellite phone call from her son Mike in Baghdad. "I'm always worried when the phone rings," Mrs. Presnell said, but this time it was good news: her son's unit had just occupied one of Saddam's palaces, and he was calling from the dictator's personal "throne room" just to say hello. "Mike told me he was going to wash his hair and brush his teeth in Saddam's private bathroom," Mrs. Presnell told reporters. "The only thing I could say to him was, 'Use your own toothbrush.'"

Honoree: IKEA, the giant Swedish furniture company

Notable Achievement: Filling job positions by going where people…go.

True Story: In 2000 IKEA needed to fill some positions at its office in Malmö, Sweden. Rather than take out newspaper ads, the company hired people to go to trendy restaurants and scribble job notices onto restroom walls by hand. Result: "After only four days we had received 60 applications," says company spokesman Jimmy Ostholm. "That's four times more than what we would get from a newspaper ad," at about a tenth of the cost. Why was the campaign so successful? "In the toilet, people are more relaxed and receptive to our message," Ostholm explains.

Honoree: Coolidge Winesett, a retired janitor

Notable Achievement: Finding fame in an outhouse.

True Story: For years Winesett, 75, was a popular banjo and fiddle player in local bluegrass bands, but he longed for wider fame. One afternoon in August 2000, Winesett went out behind his house to

The secret code for unlocking U.S. nuclear missiles during the Cold War was 00000000.

use the outhouse—he didn't have indoor plumbing—and when he sat down to do his business, the floor gave way. The floorboards protected Winesett from splashing into the "bad stuff," as he put it, but he was stuck in the hole and couldn't get out. And because he lived out in the country, nobody heard his cries for help.

Three days later, postal carrier Jimmy Jackson noticed that the old man's mail was starting to pile up, so he decided to investigate. He found Winesett—still stuck in the outhouse—and called the volunteer fire department to help get him out. The story made the local newspaper, then got picked up by the wire services and spread around the world. Winesett was famous at last. "I wish there was some other way I could get popular," he groused to reporters. "This is an insult to my ego."

Honoree: Rella Morris, mayor of Granite Falls, Washington
Notable Achievement: Being the first U.S. elected official to preside at an official function...dressed in toilet paper.
True Story: Long known as the gateway to Washington's Cascade Mountains, Granite Falls became better known as "the town without a toilet" years ago when vandals blew up the town's only portable public restroom. The town went without *any* public facilities until the late 1990s, when Mayor Morris and the city council decided it was time for a change. They raised the $91,000 needed to build a public restroom complete with four stalls, two urinals, and sinks with infrared sensors to turn the faucets on and off.

When the restrooms were finally constructed (which took more than a year), the town celebrated with its first-ever Toilet Festival. They had an exhibition of toilet-themed art, a toilet-paper-tearing ceremony (instead of a ribbon-cutting), and a raffle to determine which lucky citizen would get to flush the first flush. Mayor Morris didn't exactly dress to the nines for the occasion, but she did dress to the two-plies, wearing a robe made of toilet paper and carrying a toilet plunger for a scepter. "This town," she told the crowd, "really knows how to potty!"

* * *

"March is a month that helps to use up some of the bad weather that February just couldn't fit in."

—Doug Larson

THE COW WHISPERER

The way you think about the meat you eat depends on a lot of things, including your philosophy and your upbringing. Here's one man who makes it his business.

BOVINE INSPIRATION

Guy Glosson has a unique job: He trains farmers to reduce the stress in beef cows. That translates to a happier, better life for the cows and an easier job for ranchers. Glosson is a member of the New Ranch Network, a 21st-century farming organization that combines the efforts of ranchers, scientists, and conservationists to find better ways to farm in this ever-changing world. For Glosson's part, he travels from his native Texas to farms all across the country and teaches ranchers how to commune with their cattle.

At one such workshop in Michigan, 60 farmers came from two states to watch Glosson work his magic. Grazing in a nearby field were 40 cows and a 2,000-pound bull. Glosson walked up and spoke calmly to a few cows, who then stopped grazing and formed a line. Then, without another word from Glosson, the rest of the cows joined the formation, followed by the bull. Finally, the Cow Whisperer and the herd started marching in unison. They walked past the crowd of awestruck onlookers and then back to the field. A task such as that would usually take at least two ranchers and a dog much longer to perform—and it still would have been tough. Cows love to roam, and herding them together is a difficult and time-consuming task. So how does Guy Glosson do it? "If you approach the first handful correctly, they seem to tell the rest of them: 'He's not going to eat us today!'"

Glosson doesn't expect all of the farmers who attend his workshops to pick up his cow-municating skills, admitting that they're mostly instinctive. But he can at least teach them methods to keep their cattle happy—and a happy cow is less dangerous, less prone to illness, has a better appetite, and makes for better-tasting beef. (Stressed-out carcass meat is usually tougher and darker, and ends up in the discount bin at the supermarket.)

So if you have unhappy cows, you know who to call.

THE STRANGEST DISASTER OF THE 20TH CENTURY, PT. III

Natural disasters aren't uncommon. Unfortunately, we often read about devastation caused by floods, hurricanes, and earthquakes. But how often do you hear about death and destruction caused by a giant burp? *(Part II of the story is on page 287.)*

CLOUD OF DOOM

Cattle herders graze their animals on the hills above Lake Nyos, and after the lake disgorged as much as 80% of its massive store of CO_2 in one big burst, dead cattle were found as high as 300 feet above the lake, indicating that the suffocating cloud shot at least that high before settling back onto the surface. Then the gas poured over the crater's edge into the valleys below, traveling at an estimated 45 miles per hour.

For people living in the villages closest to the lake, death was almost inevitable. A few people on hillsides had the presence of mind to climb to higher ground; one man who saw his neighbors drop like flies jumped on his motorcycle and managed to keep ahead of the gas as he sped to safety. These were the lucky few. Most people didn't realize the danger until they were being overcome by the gas. Even if they had, it would have been impossible to outrun such a fast-moving cloud.

CURIOSITY KILLED THE CAT

In villages farther away from the lake, people had a better chance of survival, especially if they ignored the noise the lake made as it disgorged its CO_2. Some survivors said it sounded like a gunshot or an explosion; others described it as a rumble. But people who stepped outside their homes to see where the noise had come from, or to see what had caused the rotten egg smell (a common smell "hallucination" associated with CO_2 poisoning) quickly collapsed and died right on their own doorsteps. The sight of these first victims passing out often brought other members of the household to the door, where they, too, were overcome...and killed.

Each hair on your head grows approximately 0.3 mm (1/100th of an inch) per day.

People who were inside with their windows and doors shut had a better chance of surviving. There were even cases where enough CO_2 seeped into homes to smother people who were lying down asleep, but not enough to kill the people who were standing up and had their heads above the gas. Some of these survivors did not even realize anything unusual had happened until they checked on their sleeping loved ones and discovered they were already dead.

AN OUNCE OF PREVENTION

The disaster at Lake Nyos was only the second such incident in recorded history—the 1984 incident at Lake Monoun was the first. To date, scientists believe that only three lakes in the entire world, Nyos, Monoun, and a third lake called Lake Kivu on the border of Congo and Rwanda, accumulate deadly amounts of dissolved CO_2 at great depths.

It had taken about a year to figure out what had happenend at Nyos. Then, when it became clear that the lake was filling with CO_2 again, the government of Cameroon evacuated all the villages within 18 miles of the lake and razed them to prevent their inhabitants from coming back until the lake could be made safe.

Scientists spent the next decade trying to figure out a way to safely release the gas before disaster struck again. They eventually settled on a plan to sink a 5½-inch diameter tube down more than 600 feet, to just above the floor of the lake. Then, when some of the water from the bottom was pumped up to the top of the tube, it would rise high enough in the tube for the CO_2 to come out of solution and form bubbles, which would cause it to shoot out the top of the tube, blasting water and gas more than 150 feet into the sky. Once it got started, the siphon effect would cause the reaction to continue indefinitely, or at least until the CO_2 ran out. A prototype was installed and tested in 1995, and after it proved to be safe, a permanent tube was installed in 2001.

RACE AGAINST TIME

As of the fall of 2006 the tube was still in place and releasing more than 700 million cubic feet of CO_2 into the air each year. That's a little bit more than enters the lake in the same amount of

In Arizona, any misdemeanor committed while wearing a red mask is considered a felony.

time. Between 2001 and 2006, the CO_2 levels in Lake Nyos dropped 13%.

But the scientists who study the lake are concerned that 13% is too small an amount. The lake still contains more CO_2 than was released in the 1986 disaster, and as if that's not bad enough, a natural dam on the north side of the lake is eroding and could fail in as little as five years. If the dam collapses, the disaster of 1986 may prove to be just a small taste of things to come: In the event of a dam failure, 50 million cubic meters of water could pour out of the lake, drowning as many as 10,000 people as it washes through the valleys below. That's only the beginning—releasing that much water from the lake would cause the level of the lake to drop as much as 130 feet, removing the water pressure that keeps the CO_2 at the bottom of the lake and causing a release of gas even more catastrophic than the devastation of 1986.

SOLUTION

Scientists and engineers have devised a plan for shoring up the natural dam with concrete, and it's believed that the installation of as few as four more siphon tubes could reduce the CO_2 in the lake to safe levels in as little as four years. The scientists are hard at work trying to find the funding to do it, and there's no time to waste: "We could have a gas burst tomorrow that is bigger than either [the Lake Monoun or the Lake Nyos] disaster," says Dr. George Kling, a University of Michigan ecologist who has been studying the lake for 20 years. "Every day we wait is just an accumulation of the probability that something bad is going to happen."

* * *

THIRSTY?

Pete Conklin worked as a lemonade vendor for the Mabie Circus in the 1850s. One hot day, business was so brisk he had to make a batch in a hurry and used a bucket of water from a nearby tent. When he poured his first glass, he noticed the lemonade was pink. Conklin immediately began selling his mistake as "strawberry lemonade." So what made it pink? A circus performer's red tights had been soaking in the bucket of water Conklin had used.

Cats lose almost as much fluid through grooming as they do through urination.

JESUS IN SHINGO

An unusual legend, and a fascinating place to visit.

THE ROYAL TOMB

If you're visiting the tiny village of Shingo in the far north of Honshu island in Japan, you can take a path up into the woods until you come to a dirt burial mound. Rising above it is a large wooden cross. This, says local legend, is the last resting place of Jesus Christ.

The legend claims that Jesus' brother took his place on the cross, allowing Jesus to escape from Israel. He made his way across Siberia, then traveled into what is now Alaska, and finally ended up in Japan. There, the legend continues, he married a Japanese woman named Miyuko, had three daughters, and lived to the ripe old age of 106. Many people in Shingo believe the legend is true—and the "Christ Museum" next to the tomb claims it has the proof.

The story seems to have started somewhere around 1935, when a priest in the area discovered what he claimed were ancient scrolls. The 1,900-year-old documents were Christ's last will and testament, he said, indicating that Shingo is the location of Jesus' grave. According to a local museum, the original scrolls were destroyed in World War II and all that exist now are copies. But other evidence supposedly supports the claim:

- Although the tomb was never opened, rods thrust into the dirt around it confirm it is lined by stones, an honor only bestowed on people of great importance.
- For hundreds of years it has been a local tradition to draw charcoal crosses onto babies' foreheads, a practice found nowhere else in Japan.
- Many ancient kimonos from Shingo have been found decorated with what appears to be a Star of David.

No serious historian believes the legend, but more than 40,000 people make the trip to the "Tomb of Christ" every year, and many visit with the garlic farmer who owns the land on which the tomb sits—a man who is reputed to be a direct descendant of Jesus. He, like a surprising number of other people in the area, has blue eyes.

In 2003 Andy Martell of Canada created the world's largest ball of plastic wrap: 54 inches across.

MUMMY'S THE WORD

Mummies are as much a part of American pop culture as they are a part of ancient Egyptian culture. But how much do you know about them?

RAG TIME

As long as there have been people in Egypt, there have been mummies—not necessarily *man-made* mummies, but mummies nonetheless. The extreme conditions of the desert environment guaranteed that any corpse exposed to the elements for more than a day or two dried out completely, a process that halted decomposition in its tracks.

The ancient Egyptian culture that arose on the banks of the Nile River believed very strongly in preserving human bodies, which they believed were as necessary a part of the afterlife as they were a part of daily life. The formula was simple: no body, no afterlife—you couldn't have one without the other. The only problem: As Egyptian civilization advanced and burial tombs became increasingly elaborate, bodies also became more insulated from the very elements—high temperatures and dry air—that made natural preservation possible in the first place.

The result was that a new science emerged: artificial mummification. From 3100 B.C. to 649 A.D., the ancient Egyptians deliberately mummified the bodies of their dead, using methods that became more sophisticated and successful over time.

MUMMY SECRETS

Scientists have yet to unlock all of the secrets of Egyptian mummification, but they have a pretty good idea of how the process worked:

• When a king or other high official died, the embalmers slit open the body and removed nearly all the organs, which they preserved separately in special ceremonial jars. A few of the important organs, like the heart and kidneys, were left in place. The Egyptians apparently thought the brain was useless and in most cases they shredded it with small hooks inserted through the nostrils, pulled it out of the nose using tiny spoons, and then threw it away.

Some Egyptian mummies wore dentures.

• Next, the embalmers packed the body in oil of cedar (similar to turpentine) and natron, a special mineral with a high salt content. The chemicals slowly dried the body out, a process that took from 40 to 70 days.

• The body was now completely dried out and "preserved," but the process invariably left it shrunken and wrinkled like a prune, so the next step was to stuff the mouth, nose, chest cavities, etc., with sawdust, pottery, cloth, and other items to fill it out and make it look more human. In many cases the eyes were removed and artificial ones put in their place.

• Then the embalmers doused the body with a waterproofing substance similar to tar, which protected the dried body from moisture. In fact, the word mummy comes from the Persian word *mumiai*, which means "pitch" or "asphalt," and was originally used to describe the preservatives themselves, not the corpse that had been preserved.

• Finally, the body was carefully wrapped in narrow strips of linen and a funerary mask resembling the deceased was placed on the head. Afterwards it was placed in a large coffin that was also carved and painted to look like the deceased, and the coffin was placed in a tomb outfitted with the everyday items that the deceased would need in the afterlife.

THE MUMMY GLUT

Pharaohs weren't the only ancient Egyptians who were mummified—nearly anyone in Egyptian society who could afford it had it done. The result: By the end of the Late Period of Ancient Egypt in the seventh century A.D., the country contained an estimated 500 million mummies, far more than anyone knew what to do with. They were too numerous to count, too disconnected from modern Egyptian life to have any sacred spiritual value, and in most cases were thought to be too insignificant to be worthy of study. Egyptians from the 1100s onward thought of them as more of a natural resource than as the bodies of distant relatives, and treated them as such.

Well into the 19th century, mummies were used as a major fuel source for locomotives of the Egyptian railroad, which bought them by the ton (or by the graveyard). They were cheaper than wood and burned very well.

For more than 400 years, mummies were one of Egypt's largest export industries, and the supply was so plentiful that by 1600 you could buy a pound of mummy powder in Scotland for about eight shillings. As early as 1100 A.D., Arabs and Christians ground them up for use as medicine, which was often rubbed into wounds, mixed into food, or stirred into tea.

By the 1600s, the medicinal use of mummies began to decline, as many doctors began to question the practice. "Not only does this wretched drug do no good to the sick," the French surgeon Ambrose Paré wrote in his medical journal, "but it causes them great pain in their stomach, gives them evil smelling breath, and brings on serious vomiting which is more likely to stir up the blood and worsen hemorrhaging than to stop it." He recommended using mummies as fish bait.

By the 1800s, mummies were imported only as curiosities, where it was fashionable to unwrap them during dinner parties.

Mummies were also one of the first sources of recycled paper: During one 19th-century rag shortage (in the days when paper was made from *cloth* fibers, not wood fibers), one Canadian paper manufacturer imported Egyptian mummies as a source of raw materials: he unwrapped the cloth and made it into sturdy brown paper, which he sold to butchers and grocers for use as a food wrap. The scheme died out after only a few months, when employees in charge of unwrapping them began coming down with cholera.

Note: What happened when the supply of mummies became scarce? A grisly "instant mummy" industry sprang up in which fresh corpses of criminals and beggars were hastily embalmed and sold as real mummies.

MUMMY FACTS

• Scientists in South America have discovered mummies from the ancient civilization of Chinchorros that are more than 7,800 years old—nearly twice as old as the oldest Egyptian mummy. And, just as in Egypt, the mummies are plentiful there. "Every time we dug in the garden or dug to add a section to our house, we found bodies," one elderly South American woman told *Discover* magazine. "But I got used to it. We'd throw their bones out on a hill, and the dogs would take them away."

Among many other things, Thomas Jefferson is the inventor of the calendar clock.

• The average Egyptian mummy contains more than 20 layers of cloth that, laid end-to-end, would be more than four football fields long.

• In 1977, an Egyptian scientist discovered that the mummy of Pharaoh Ramses II, more than 3,000 years old, was infested with beetles. So they sent it to France for treatment, complete with an Egyptian passport describing his occupation as "King, deceased."

• What's the quickest way to tell if an Egyptian mummy still has its brains? Shake the skull—if it rattles, the brain is still in there.

• The Egyptians were also fond of mummifying animals. To date, scientists have discovered the preserved remains of bulls, cats, baboons, birds, crocodiles, fish, scorpions, insects…even wild dogs. One tomb contained the remains of more than one *million* mummified birds.

• Some mummies have been discovered in coffins containing chicken bones. Some scientists believe the bones have special religious meaning, but (no kidding) other experts theorize that the bones are actually leftover garbage from the embalmer's lunch.

* * *

CELEBRITY MUMMIES

Jeremy Bentham and his "Auto Icon." Bentham was a famous 19th-century English philosopher. When he died in 1832, he left instructions with a surgeon friend that his body be decapitated, mummified, dressed in his everyday clothes, and propped up in a chair, and that a wax head be placed on his neck to give the corpse a more realistic appearance. He further instructed that his real head also be mummified and placed at his feet, and that the whole arrangement be put on public display. The corpse and its head(s) can still be seen at University College in London, where they sit in a glass case specially built for that purpose.

Vladimir Lenin. When the Soviet leader died on January 21, 1924, the Communist Party assembled a team of top embalmers to preserve his corpse for all eternity. Unlike the embalming processes of the ancient Egyptians, which prevented decomposition by removing body fluids, the Soviets *replaced* cell fluids with liquids that inhibited deterioration.

A column of air one inch square and 600 miles high weighs about 15 lbs.

THE CURSE OF *MACBETH*

Actors won't even call it by its name—they refer to it as "the Scottish play." Why? Because they say it's cursed. And after reading this, you may think so too. Here's one of our favorite "classic" Bathroom Reader articles.

OUT, OUT DAMN SPOT

In a scene from Shakespeare's *Macbeth*, three witches stand around a bubbling cauldron, brewing up a stew which includes ingredients such as eye of newt and toe of frog, wool of bat, and tongue of dog—"double, double, toil and trouble, fire burn and cauldron bubble"—we all know the scene. But there's a story behind that scene…and a curse on the play.

In 1606 King James I commissioned Shakespeare to write a play in honor of the visit of his brother-in-law, King Christian of Denmark. The play Shakespeare wrote was *Macbeth*.

POOR KING

James was no stranger to tragedy. He was taken from his mother shortly after birth and never knew her. His father was murdered soon after that. His mother was forced from the throne of Scotland, imprisoned for 19 years in England, and beheaded by her cousin, Queen Elizabeth I. James began his rule of Scotland at age 19, married Anne of Denmark, had nine children, and survived a number of assassination attempts. When Queen Elizabeth died, he ascended the throne.

Moving to England from Scotland was like turning on a light in a dark room for James. He was particularly taken with Shakespeare's plays. He gave Shakespeare and his company royal protection in a time when actors were considered scoundrels. Shakespeare now had the security, popularity, respect, and money that he needed. He produced six new plays in the next five years.

HERE COMES TROUBLE

King James was fascinated by witchcraft and obsessed by death and

The Finnish language has about 4,000 irregular verbs (English has less than 500).

demons. He wrote a book about demonology and was considered the foremost authority on the subject. With this in mind, Shakespeare sat down to write a play that looked seriously at the king's favorite subject, and he did his homework. The plot was a thinly disguised account of the death of James's father; the witchcraft scene was crafted with care and filled with authentic details.

CURSES!

Some say the play's witchcraft spells and incantations were so faithfully reproduced that they created a curse, and that the curse is renewed every time the words are uttered. Others claim that local witches were so incensed at having their secrets revealed that they placed a perpetual curse upon the play. Whatever the case, for 400 years, *Macbeth* has been uncannily surrounded by death and disaster. So malevolent is the spell that it is said that bad luck will befall any actor who merely quotes from the play.

The curse manifested itself immediately. The young actor scheduled to play Lady Macbeth for King James came down with a fever right before the performance. Some accounts say he died. King James, who had a phobia about knives and gore, was horrified by the death scenes, which were realistically portrayed with guts and blood secured from a butcher. He immediately banned performances of *Macbeth* for five years.

After the ban ended, the play was performed at Shakespeare's Globe Theater. A few days later, the theater burned to the ground and with it all of the company's scenery, props, costumes, and manuscripts.

DISASTER STRIKES

Skeptical? Here is just a sampling of the disasters that have surrounded *Macbeth* in the 20th century:

• In the early 1900s, the Moscow Arts Company was doing a dress rehearsal when actor Constantin Stanislavski forgot his lines in the middle of the murder scene. He whispered for a prompt but the prompter was silent. He *yelled* for a prompt, but the prompter remained silent. Investigating, he found the prompter slumped over the script, dead. The show never opened.

• During a 1937 production at the Old Vic Theatre in England, the theater's founder, Lilian Baylis, suddenly died of a heart attack just before the play opened. Laurence Olivier, who was starring in the lead role, missed death by seconds when a sandbag accidentally fell from the rafters.

• In 1948, during a production in Stratford, Connecticut, Diana Wynyard as Lady Macbeth loudly announced she thought the curse was ridiculous. She also decided it was silly to play her sleepwalking scene with her eyes open, and tried it with her eyes closed. She walked off the edge of the stage during the next performance and fell 15 feet down.

• A version of the play directed by John Gielgud in 1942 was plagued by death. First, Beatrice Fielden-Kaye, in the role of one of the witches, died of a heart attack. Next, Marcus Barron, in the role of Duncan, died of angina. Another of the witches, Annie Esmond, died on stage one night while she was vigorously dancing around the cauldron. Finally, set designer John Minton committed suicide in his studio, surrounded by his designs for the *Macbeth* sets and costumes. The repainted sets were later sent on tour with matinee idol Owen Nares, who died during the tour.

• A Russian film version of the play was canceled when nine members of the crew died of food poisoning.

• During a 1971 production at the Mercer O'Casey Theatre, no less than seven burglaries and one fire marred the three-month run.

A CURE

To avoid the curse, veteran actors give this advice: Walk out of the dressing room, turn around three times, spit or swear, knock on the door three times, and then humbly ask for readmittance. If that doesn't work, try quoting this line from one of Shakespeare's "lucky" plays, *The Merchant of Venice:* "Fair thoughts and happy hours attend you."

Final note: Abraham Lincoln was quoting passages from *Macbeth* to his friends the evening before he was assassinated.

*   *   *

Random Fact: The Cairo Opera House was destroyed by fire in 1970. The Cairo fire station was located in the same building.

INCIDENT AT HAVERING

A sheepish tale of political intrigue from the United Kingdom.

BAAACKGROUND

In September 2005, a zoning meeting took place in the town hall of the east London borough of Havering. The meeting concerned a proposal to convert an exotic horse and sheep farm into a mobile home park. To do so would require a zoning change and the council would have to approve it. Such zoning changes are commonplace throughout the world, but this one was different. Councilman Jeff Tucker, who represented the area where the proposed mobile home park would be built, got up to speak in favor of the idea. And that's when the trouble started.

Somebody in the room apparently did not agree with Tucker. The anonymous adversary began making loud, sheep-like "baa" noises whenever Tucker tried to talk, drowning him out. Despite the fact that there were only a handful of people in the room—including just five city council members—nobody could figure out who made the noises...and nobody would own up to it.

BAAAD FORM

Councilman Tucker was enraged (and the proposal failed). He lodged a complaint with the Standards Board for England, an oversight agency for governmental disputes. The board didn't think it worthy of their time to determine who made the sheep noises and why, so they referred it back to the Havering council. The Havering Standards Hearings Sub-Committee began an investigation. They narrowed down the source of the "baa"-ing to four culprits, all of them city councilors. One of the suspects, councilor Denis O'Flynn, called the process "an extremely expensive example of the worst kind of bureaucracy" and "the height of stupidity."

Fourteen months later the Havering city council issued a 300-page report, the result of an investigation that cost £10,000 (about $20,000). What did they find? The source of the sheep noises was Denis O'Flynn. The punishment: nothing. By the time the investigation was completed, O'Flynn was no longer a city council member...and no longer subject to any disciplinary action.

Georgia resident Gary Duda (pronounced "doo-dah") legally changed his first name to Zippidy.

RANDOM ACTS OF ODDNESS

Proof that truth really is stranger than fiction.

TOP CAT

"A 43-year-old man was hospitalized in Richmond, Virginia, after being blown off the top of a van moving at about 50 miles per hour. Police said the man was trying to hold down some wooden fencing that he and another man were trying to move without the benefit of rope, when a gust of wind carried him off."

—***Funny Times***

BUT HE HAD A BEARD!

"A Frenchman was convicted for trying to run over a pedestrian he mistook for Osama bin Laden. The 35-year-old, identified as a struggling artist named Pierre, was sentenced to a three-month suspended prison term and ordered to pay 500 euros (about $615) to the victim. Pierre's lawyer said his client was traumatized by recent terror attacks in Madrid and was temporarily the 'victim of a hallucination.' The victim was unharmed. He was able to run from the oncoming car, which crashed along the side of a street."

—Associated Press

PULL MY FINGER

"Rose Woodland of Winnipeg, Manitoba, is suing Dr. Andrew Robertson after he tried to fix her middle finger, which would 'occasionally lock up.' Instead, he made the finger extend permanently. She claims the stress of constantly giving people 'the finger' has led to a heart condition and she now needs surgery."

—***Winnipeg Sun***

I LIKE BIKE

"It was simply a case of notifying the next of kin, but when police arrived at the dead man's house they found the three-bedroom Geelong, Australia, home virtually packed to the brim with bicycles—more than 1,000 of them. 'In every room including the bathroom and kitchen there are bikes, bike helmets, chains, seats, and tires. It's something else,' said Sergeant Adrian Benny. 'There are also bikes down the side of the house and there are two sheds full.' He added that it was 'ironic' the man, who was aged in his 60s, died in the process of stealing a bike in Melbourne last week. 'He must have had a bike fetish,' he said."

—Free Republic

DIDN'T SEE THAT COMING

"A Chinese pensioner who exercises by walking backwards around a lake had to be rescued after he lost concentration and fell in. *China Daily*, quoting the *Beijing Times*, says Yan, 72, believes his daily routine of walking backwards around Bayi Lake is good for his health. But he was apparently counting his steps instead of checking his surroundings, miscalculated, and fell backwards. Three other fitness enthusiasts saved him and took him to hospital, where he received three stitches on his head."

***—Daily Times* (Pakistan)**

THAT'S A LAUGH

"Members of a 'laughter club' in Patna, India, described the decision to ban laughing at their local zoo as 'autocratic.' Chuckling was outlawed after Laloo Prasad Yadav, the president of Bihar state's ruling party, was angered by the group 'merrily laughing in chorus' when he walked past them in the Sanjay Gandhi Botanical Garden and Zoo. 'You are disturbing the peace of the flora and fauna of the zoo,' Laloo reportedly told the group, before issuing instructions to zoo officials to enforce an immediate ban. Laughter clubs—groups of people who gather to laugh loudly in public to relieve stress—are a phenomenon in parts of India."

—The Economic Times

* * *

BOLD PREDICTION

"We stand on the threshold of rocket mail."

—Postmaster general Arthur Summerfield, 1959

The fastest-moving muscle in the human body is the one that opens and closes the eyelid.

UNCLE JOHN'S BATHROOM *READER* CLASSIC SERIES

Find these and other great titles from the *Uncle John's Bathroom Reader* Classic Series online at **www.bathroomreader.com.** Or contact us at:

Bathroom Readers' Institute
P.O. Box 1117
Ashland, OR 97520
(888) 488-4642

Also available from *Uncle John's Bathroom Reader*!

THE LAST PAGE

FELLOW BATHROOM READERS:
The fight for good bathroom reading should never be taken loosely—we must do our duty and sit firmly for what we believe in, even while the rest of the world is taking pot shots at us.

We'll be brief. Now that we've proven we're not simply a flush-in-the-pan, we invite you to take the plunge: Sit Down and Be Counted! Become a member of the Bathroom Readers' Institute. Log on to *www.bathroomreader.com*, or send a self-addressed, stamped, business-sized envelope to: BRI, PO Box 1117, Ashland, Oregon 97520. You'll receive your free membership card, get discounts when ordering directly through the BRI, and earn a permanent spot on the BRI honor roll!

If you like reading our books...

VISIT THE BRI'S WEB SITE!

www.bathroomreader.com

- Visit "The Throne Room"—a great place to read!
- Receive our irregular newsletters via e-mail
- Order additional *Bathroom Readers*
- Become a BRI member

Go *with the Flow...*

Well, we're out of space, and when you've gotta go, you've gotta go. Tanks for all your support. Hope to hear from you soon. Meanwhile, remember...

Keep on flushin'!